Sustaining
New Orleans

Sustaining New Orleans

Literature, Local Memory, and the Fate of a City

Barbara Eckstein

Routledge
Taylor & Francis Group
New York   London

Published in 2006 by
Routledge
Taylor & Francis Group
270 Madison Avenue
New York, NY 10016

Published in Great Britain by
Routledge
Taylor & Francis Group
2 Park Square
Milton Park, Abingdon
Oxon OX14 4RN

Printed in the United States of America on acid-free paper
10 9 8 7 6 5 4 3 2 1

International Standard Book Number-10: 0-415-94782-0 (Hardcover) 0-415-94783-9 (Softcover)
International Standard Book Number-13: 978-0-415-94782-4 (Hardcover) 978-0-415-94783-1 (Softcover)
Library of Congress Card Number 2005012589

Library of Congress Cataloging-in-Publication Data

Eckstein, Barbara J.
    Sustaining New Orleans : literature, local memory, and the fate of a city / Barbara Eckstein.
        p. cm.
    Includes bibliographical references and index.
    ISBN 0-415-94782-0 (alk. paper) -- ISBN 0-415-94783-9 (pbk. : alk. paper)
    1. American literature--Louisiana--New Orleans--History and criticism. 2. New Orleans (La.)--Intellectual life. 3. New Orleans (La.)--In literature. 4. New Orleans (La.)--Civilization. I. Title.

PS267.N49E27 2005
810.9'9763--dc22   2005012589

Taylor & Francis Group
is the Academic Division of T&F Informa plc.

Visit the Taylor & Francis Web site at
http://www.taylorandfrancis.com

and the Routledge Web site at
http://www.routledge-ny.com

For Robert Udick, 1957–1999, and Jim Knudsen, 1950–2004,
friends of New Orleans and friends of mine.

Contents

List of Illustrations

Preface

When, in the mid-1950s, Harvard social scientist David Riesman suggested that New Orleans and its residents be federally subsidized as were Yellowstone and its denizens so that they might serve as a living history and culture lesson for Americans, he was not being facetious. He was trying to imagine an object of rampant post–World War II consumer desire worth the purchase price. The further commodification of New Orleans did not seem to trouble Riesman as it later did architecture scholar Christine Boyer. When he asked himself "Abundance for What?" in an article by the same name, sustaining New Orleans was one answer he proffered.

This book pursues two meanings of "sustaining New Orleans." One is the perpetuation of the images and ideas and tales of New Orleans sustained in public memory—local and not—through a range of activities and media, widely read literature notable among them. The other references the concept of sustainability, understood here to mean the struggle to balance the competing demands of social justice, environmental health, and economic viability. This book argues that these two definitions of sustaining New Orleans are mutually constitutive, or, more precisely, that they are two features of an ongoing dialectic. It further argues that widely read literature set in the city, through its engagement with urban folkways that shape and reshape public memory, has participated, for good and ill, in the framing of the city's problems, the proposed solutions to those problems, and the perceived effectiveness of those solutions.

I employ Southern regionalist Howard Odum's 1930s vision of local folkways and national (or transnational) technicways working together to root and revise a region. It is the dialectic of platial folkways, spatially circulating technicways, and the evolving region that I think of as the pulse of the place-tone, drawing on this conjunction created by Amiria Baraka in his review of David Henderson's poetry.[1] If I inevitably work Odum's tripartite concept with post-structural humanist hindsight rather than the commitment to collecting and cataloguing that typified his social science method, I also look beneath my feet for foundational principles necessary for sustaining the local place and its inhabitants.

The post-War literary texts in question are Tennessee Williams's *A Streetcar Named Desire*, Nelson Algren's *A Walk on the Wild Side*, Walker Percy's *The Moviegoer*, Ishmael Reed's *Mumbo Jumbo*, Anne Rice's *Interview with the Vampire*, and Helen Prejean's *Dead Man Walking*. The first chapter, "The Claims for New Orleans's Exceptionalism," explicates the conventional land use in the greater New Orleans metropolitan area alongside telling examples from the extensive body of oral and informal histories that claim, through their folkways, New Orleans's exceptionalism. Pursuing the claims for exceptionalism also through the distinctive features of the greater New Orleans bioregion, this initial chapter links these geographical conditions to the tales about the city that have been repeated and refashioned over time to meet the social or political, economic, or emotional demands of their tellers and their critical moments.

These folkways circumscribe all material decisions, I argue; they are, like the encroaching waters of the Gulf of Mexico and the Mississippi River's will to change, always with New Orleans.

Central to these dynamic folkways is a lingering and racially evolving nineteenth-century image of the city as feminine. I pursue this line of thought from New Orleans frontier streets to the rage for simulacra at the close of the twentieth century. I then specifically focus my lens on the evolving permutations of ambiguous voodoo queen Marie Laveau, arguing that her racial, class, and religious indeterminacy alongside the claims for her abiding power and even status are foundational to any analysis of the city.

The next three chapters take up key issues in the sustainability of New Orleans: mass transit, preservation, and prostitution in and around the French Quarter; African American demands for equality; and the growth of the petrochemical corridor. Specifically, the second chapter examines the reciprocal relations of New Orleans's post-War transit decision concerning the streetcar named Desire and Tennessee Williams's simultaneous overnight success. The third chapter investigates the uneasy relationship of sex and historic preservation in the French Quarter at mid-century, paying particular attention to the transformations between the mid-1930s when Algren first saw and wrote about the Quarter's wild side, and the mid-1950s when his

revised narrative was published under the title *A Walk on the Wild Side*.
The fourth chapter takes the lid off of the late 1950s New Orleans that
Percy's moviegoer suppresses through passive spectatorship and Kierkegaardian despair and that the city contained within the riverfront
barriers of railroad tracks, levees, warehouses, and wharves. Inside that
boiling pot are desegregation, anti-Communist xenophobia, local and
global environmental hazards on an unprecedented scale, and New
Orleans Carnival traditions designed to render multivalent chaos as
hierarchical parade. Percy's protagonist faces choices among competing
claims for social justice, public health, and economic viability that do
not disappear, but are only differently mediated when he retreats into
movie theaters. I pay particular attention to the protagonist's response
to Elia Kazan's *Panic in the Streets,* a film that penetrated New Orleans
waterfront even before a visual corridor through its riverfront barriers
was reopened to the public. But Kazan's plot finds a foreign threat to
national public health at the nation's backdoor rather than the toxins
coming down river.

The book's final three chapters explore three texts that use Laveau
folkways to address the city's problems. For Reed, Laveau's voodoo
legacy—what he calls the Neo-HooDoo Aesthetic—offers a spiritual,
culturally diverse, carnivalized alternative to the racial and class hierarchies that characterize the US inner city battles of the late 1960s and
early 1970s. As I pursue the implications of Reed's vision of New
Orleans, I note its own inner city battles, focusing particularly on
confrontations between police and an inchoate chapter of the Black
Panthers at the Desire Housing Development in 1970. Anne Rice draws
on the tales of Laveau's exoticism and her celebrated genius for
publicity to build her own vampire nation in New Orleans. As with this
construction of Laveau, Rice's power depends as much on her performance of herself as on any creation apart from her person. The haunted
city's folkways serve Rice and she them because many of her fans,
unconventional and conventional, have flocked to the city to visit her
residence and museums and to attend her seasonal rituals. Her investment in New Orleans's historic preservation and in the city's Francophilia, two staples of its self-definition and tourist industry, are topics of
particular concern in Chapter 6. I attend especially to the late 1970s
when Rice first came to prominence and, ironically, when New Orleans
was rediscovering its emplacement, not in the French Empire but rather
in the New World, on the Gulf, or "Third," Coast. In the final chapter,
Laveau reappears as the historical woman leader ministering to
prisoners awaiting execution. In this guise, she provides the folkways
necessary to interpret the work of Sister Helen Prejean who must transform herself from a middle-class, white Catholic into a creolized servant
of the poor to aid not only Angola's death row inmates, but also the

inner city survivors of crime in the St. Thomas Housing Development where she lives. I argue that she understands geography as a constitutive part of negotiating local moral decisions of this magnitude. To resist execution, she maps a spirit region in south Louisiana in defiance of the execution zone set by the geopolitical boundaries of the state. The transforming parameters of this spirit region are determined by the competing needs to broadcast the abolition message nationally, even globally, and to come face-to-face, locally, with condemned men, survivors, and executioners. Spiritual well-being, I further argue, is a necessary fourth leg in the definition of sustainability. The St. Thomas Residents Council and their struggle to participate with HUD (the Department of Housing and Urban Development), HANO (the Housing Authority of New Orleans), and local developers in deciding the future of their HOPE-VI-razed-and-renovated home act as a necessary antidote to romanticizing the singular efforts of Prejean. They map a spirit region of their own on a different scale as they struggle to retain a voice in decisions about the land on which their homes sat.

In the epilogue, I examine two New Orleans advertisements for itself that appeared on the heels of the 9/11 tragedy: one in the Sunday *New York Times*; the other in The *Des Moines Register*. These major travel pieces permit me to revisit the complexities of sustaining New Orleans in the current political climate. How is the city's reputation for being an exceptional place within the United States used by boosters to console an embattled New York City and an aggrieved nation? Do the present offers made by the New Orleans tourist industry and by travel editors push the living city closer to a gated "International-land" for a wary national audience or to a historical national reserve such as the one Riesman imagined?

In the same era that Riesman made his modest proposal for New Orleans, the Vieux Carré Commission and other opponents of the Vieux Carré riverfront expressway—proposed first by Harland Bartholomew in 1927 and later by Robert Moses in 1946—were embroiled in the so-called second Battle of New Orleans. This was only the most nationally notorious of ongoing battles fought to preserve, building by building, the *tout ensemble* of the French Quarter. The French Quarter is only one neighborhood and this is only one of the questions that permeate this book's chapters. But I end this preface with some volleys from that battle as a means to display the kinds of specific action, provocative discourse, and nagging questions that, over decades, set the stage for the literary and urban analysis of this project. In this case, a central question is preserve for whom and for what?

In the minds of freeway opponents, their task was to protect the river vista of Jackson Square, recently reclaimed by demolishing an eroding warehouse on the wharf. The obstacle to the opponents' desire was a proposed interstate overpass, supported by the Chamber of Commerce, city and state transportation planners, *The Times-Picayune*, and most politicians most of the time. Local architectural historian Samuel Wilson Jr. claimed the historic Quarter served not only its residents' sense of history in place but also the need of American citizens to stand in Jackson Square on the site where the Louisiana Purchase was signed in 1803 and face the Mississippi River unencumbered by a looming expressway (albeit by a levee).[2] In 1965, another expressway opponent wrote to *The Washington Post* on behalf of "the civilized citizens of New Orleans, who happen to know something of classic urban traditions elsewhere." They are, wrote Walter B. Lowrey, "focusing their attention with great interest . . . upon the Nation's Capital, where the President, the First Lady and the Secretary of the Interior have recently made eloquent declarations of concern about a physical environment worthy of something called a Great Society."[3] The freeway battle did not end until 1969 when Richard Nixon's Transportation Secretary John Volpe canceled the proposed Vieux Carré Expressway and removed it from the Interstate Highway System. The river (levee) view at Jackson Square had outlasted not only the Interstate Highway System, but also the rhetoric of the Great Society. The question of whether it, or other New Orleans neighborhoods, were a physical environment worthy of the social justice goals of the Great Society remains an open question, however. It is one of the persistent questions that announce the stakes for sustaining New Orleans.

Through the last half-century, some notable residents have had their eye on a sustainable city while dwelling in the regional folkways that, for good and ill, sustain New Orleans images in public memory and shape the city's participation in nationally defined urban imperatives. Among them are the Gentilly residents, who, in 1948, provided solid reasons for retaining the streetcar that served them. They also include the community leaders of the Desire Housing Development, who, in 1970, stood between the children of Desire and the violence of a state afraid for its security. Tulane architecture students and faculty had their eye on a sustainable city as well when, in the 1970s, they imagined a renewed relationship at the city's edge between the city and the river it shares with the continent. Also in the 1970s, the Vieux Carré Commission leadership, spurred by the National Endowment for the Arts, ventured, however briefly, beyond the boundaries of the French Quarter and the demands of the tourist industry to the provocative place of New Orleans in the Latin Roots of its hemisphere. More recently, the St. Thomas Residents Council and the collection of health, legal, and spiritual advisors who have fostered their struggle to negotiate as equals with developers of valuable St. Thomas Housing Development property have played a role in promoting a sustainable New Orleans.

The stony-faced jurors unmoved by the stories Governor Edwin Edwards told in defiance of the facts at his most recent trial have had an ear and eye on a sustainable city, too. The creators of the city's Urban Conservancy Web site and listserv who engage the city and the world in discussion of its battles, site by site, serve New Orleans by honing the meaning of the complex production of space called sustainability. I thank them all for their instruction in what matters. And I maintain a special appreciation for certain New Orleans activist nuns who first offered a (col)lapsed Catholic lessons in what it means to commit oneself to social and economic justice.

I also thank all those others in New Orleans who have shared their urban expertise and facilitated a scholar's work: Wayne Everard and the staff at the city archives in the New Orleans Public Library; Pamela Arceneaux, Sally Stassi, and the staff at the Historic New Orleans Collection; and Robert Udick, Jim Knudsen, Jeanne Cunningham, and Celeste Knudsen, hosts of a high order. Travel and research funds from the University of Iowa's Arts and Humanities Initiative, the College of Liberal Arts and Sciences, and the Department of English have sustained this project. And so have audiences and readers from the fields of planning, American studies, English, and interdisciplinary venues such as Iowa's Project on the Rhetoric of Inquiry and Program on Place Studies. Questions and suggestions from colleagues, conference goers, and students shape the arguments at every turn. I am especially grateful for the help of research assistants over the years—most notably Jessica DeSpain and Brian Whitehead—and for the reading lists, encouragement, and editorial guidance provided by Jim Throgmorton, Carlo Rotella, Alex Reichl, Virginia Dominguez, and Dave McBride.

1

The Claims for New Orleans's Exceptionalism

One of New Orleans's many informal historians begins her 1973 outsider's guide with a description of signage "mercilessly bludgeoning" the tourist entering the city. Visible there is what she calls clashing legends: an elegant Latin culture doing battle with corruption and turpitude. Both are for sale.[1] "A dreadful whimsy assaults the stranger's intelligence, threatens everything of beauty in the city, peers out between the pages of the countless 'stories of new Orleans.'"[2] Determined not to write a booster's book, she introduces New Orleans's merciless advertisements for itself before she has a sazerac in hand, shrimp remoulade in her mouth, and the scent of urine-soaked pavement and sweet olive in her head. She will not succumb to these charms. The corruption and violence that are as endemic as the poverty contribute to a frontier atmosphere, whose other aspects—an untarnished landscape, a simplicity, a friendliness—an outsider finds hard to resist; he is even hypnotized by it all, as if the heavy scent of the flowers, the rank acridity of the Delta, the heat and haze and humidity had lulled him like a lotus-eater to forget the harsher realities.[3] No lotus-eater, she purports to correct the work of other writers who do not separate fact from fiction about the city.

If, like most visitors to New Orleans of the last decades, she entered the metropolitan area at the airport, then she approached the city from the west on Interstate 10, which floats above the swamp and above the physical barriers on the ground that separate more affluent suburban Metairie from lower-income central city Gerttown. Traveling I-10, she would have run parallel to a suburban stretch along Veterans Memorial Boulevard that has, for a number of decades, been cultivating the Los Angeles look. Where New Orleans could most easily extend, it has developed US outposts as typical as Home Depot. Although Lake Pontchartrain to the north; the Mississippi River to the south; swamp-land south, west, and east; and the threat of major hurricanes and floods to the whole metropolitan area create some obstacles to sprawl, even these have been largely overcome (or ignored) in the pursuit of medium-density housing subdivisions and commercial strips, health facilities, and shopping malls. New Orleans is a twentieth-century city in the US automotive grain. Yet, even as the US attachment to standard-ization is visible in the greater New Orleans metropolitan area, a unique place "arising from the sediment of history" and geography continues to assert and to advertise itself.[4]

Given the typical US land use in the greater New Orleans area, abun-dant and persistent claims for the city's exceptionalism are noteworthy. Take our informal historian, Sarah Searight. Having entered New Orleans via the billboards, she then seeks words for New Orleans's difference. She finds a foundational answer not in facts about housing density or private space, not even in environmental conditions or polit-ical practices. The distinction lies in New Orleans being impervious to criticism, more than sensual in pursuit of pleasure, more than usually tolerant of human frailties, she proffers.[5] City fact and fiction, or fact and feeling, as Carlo Rotella has observed, cannot be kept apart after all.[6] New Orleans is a place that elicits in its human inhabitants and even in visitors a distinctive somatic and affective response to the place, a relation that Yi-Fu Tuan has labeled *topophilia*.[7]

Folkways and Technicways

The city's affect arises from a network of folkways linked to the rivers and bayous that flow toward and away from the Gulf, into and out of the swamps. In negotiation with this fluid and fragile bioregion and its powerful regional folkways, the city maintains its existence. The inter-action of geography and histories, formal and informal, is visible in the decisions made about the city's transportation, social practices, land use, and governance and in the stories and other public discourse about the city—including literature. In reading widely circulated literature about New Orleans in dialectical relation to some decisions made about the city and the public discourse around those decisions, I position literature within the flow of the city's folkways.

I borrow this term from the 1930s southern social scientist and public intellectual Howard Odum. Arguing in the 1930s for a regionalism that was the product of local folk practices enacted in a particular geographical setting, Odum had some success in persuading Franklin Roosevelt's federal government to take a regionally sensitive, which is to say also folkways-sensitive, approach to national planning. The Odum of the 1930s believed technicways—the machine-driven, standardizing industrialism and media of modern (national) society, most often manifest in urban locations—should be encouraged and analyzed always as coexistent with regional folkways.[8] It is true that, despite his collecting African American folkways as well as white, he shared a short-sightedness common to his time and place about the multiplex folk defining the region. He was not eager to see, for example, the synergism between African American and southern white folkways.[9] And he practiced—even initiated—a social scientific method mostly about collection and taxonomy. His vision of an interrelation among expanding national technologies, regional geography, and local folkways serves, nonetheless, as a significant guide for analyzing history and geography, folkways and technicways together.

As I pursue that vision in New Orleans and its environs, the importance of multiplex folk quickly emerges as a necessary complication of Odum's categories. In fact, the interracialism and other boundary violations that emerge in the mongrel tales and informal histories that claim exceptional status for New Orleans are arguably *the* defining characteristic of the city's folkways. Pursuing the meaning of New Orleans's so-called creolization, historians Joseph Logsdon and Arnold Hirsch conclude that "[New Orleans] is an intellectual hinge connecting the two interracial systems [of the French and Spanish empires and of the US empire] that appeared in the Western Hemisphere."[10]

I focus here on a dynamic site of production not of the book artifact per se, but of the literary art that represents and inscribes the relationship between the dynamics of place and the circulation of that dynamism across space and time. That circulation occurs through the distribution of a literary text as idea or as book, but also through the distribution of rumor, reputation, film, advertisement, or any reference to a place wherever and however it occurs. That dynamism of place and space over time and in relation to economic, environmental, social, and cultural forces that impinge on a place is one way of describing what I am calling the pulse of the place-tone. I say pulse, because this dynamism produces a variable rhythm, not a constant hum; place-tone, because it is an ongoing dialectic of materiality and representation.

The pulse of the place-tone is not then only a cultural force; it is as much a social one. But, in either case, it is not normative.

In the post–World War II years of the mid-twentieth century, while David Riesman asked "Abundance for What?", Odum feared that abundance produced by national and international technicways was overwhelming regional folkways and so, sadly, turned toward the Agrarians, hunkered down in a pastoral golden age.[11] But if we keep our eyes on his earlier vision of folkways and technicways acting together, on the regional place-tone audible through the sounds of modernization and urbanization, then three-quarters of a century later, we have a good model for platial analysis generally. Applied to New Orleans in particular, his model is especially appealing if we also expand his definition of folk to recognize not only diverse but also evolving mongrel urban folkways drawing from the city's emplacement within greater transAmerican, Third Coast, and transAtlantic territories.[12]

Beyond the end of the twentieth century, this foundational, regional dialectic of capital and culture has survived, even in predominantly economic analysis in which it has emerged as a telling paradox: extraordinary innovations in transportation and communication have produced a smaller globe on which all points could be in close contact, and yet many social and economic transactions are problematical and fail when executed across great distance. The globalizing, netocratizing trends have not, argues Allen Scott, simply undermined "the region as the basis of dense and many-sided human interactions (though they have greatly affected many of the qualitative attributes of those interactions), but in many respects have actually reinforced it."[13] One effect of these geographic circumstances has been, Scott continues,

> alternative approaches to practical governance which spring out of civil society as spontaneous responses to the search for collective order, or as cultural accretions that in one way or another come to function (well or badly) as regulatory institutions of the economy. In any case, they help sustain capitalism as a functioning social system.[14]

Capitalism, he adds, would implode if it depended upon profitability and price signals for its "social reproduction." Although sustaining capitalism, understood as economic expansion that leaves uneven development in its wake, is pointedly not my mission, Scott's observation about regionalist economic folkways does usefully temper a neoconservative (and neo-Marxist) view that sees only globalization and sees it, whether with anticipation or alarm, only as a monolithic opportunity for hyperprivatization and anticollective choice in economic matters.[15] Those who develop a good ear for the pulse of the place-tone stand to influence whether it is uneven development or a sustainable alternative that will shape the future of a place.

Regional folkways and technicways, and conceptions and expressions of them, are transforming over time and space and society, because neither history nor territory nor people are inert. The two terms of Odum's binary are no more neatly oppositional than other distinctions whose differences matter. This said, in this binary is a means to begin understanding, from our present globalist presumptions, the stories of a city's exceptionalism, the ways literary texts have taken up these circulating claims, and the place of both in the evolving material conditions of the city in the latter half of the twentieth century and the beginnings of the twenty-first. How, specifically, have the folk claims for New Orleans's exceptionalism and the technicways that have produced, by some measures, a typically US metropolitan area coexisted? What has been the place of well-known literature in the reproduction of that platial exceptionalism and typicality? This book analyzes together the work literature does amid a local discursive context and some of the nondiscursive realities of a city's survival.

Sustainability

A city's survival, in today's urban parlance, inevitably evokes the term sustainability. Leaving for others the extensive debate about the term's ubiquitous use and abuse, I take as its central tenet the goal of balancing competing claims for environmental health, social justice, and economic viability. Often functioning to repel one another, these three values are too important to be left to fly apart, particularly if the presumption of economic growth is mindfully reconsidered.[16] In many places our human *need* is not for economic growth but a "need to redirect our economic engine into paths that are restorative rather than exploitative."[17] This said, juxtaposing the three competing values as an interactive triangle, as planning scholar Scott Campbell does, has considerable value. He acutely observes,

> sustainability . . . can become a powerful and useful organizing principle for planning . . . if, instead of merely evoking a misty-eyed vision of a peaceful ecotopia, it acts as a lightening rod to focus conflicting economic, environmental, and social interests. The more it stirs up conflict and sharpens the debate, the more effective the idea of sustainability will be in the long run.[18]

The critical and elusive goal of integrating these claims—these ideals and practices called sustainability—gives one set of meanings to

sustaining New Orleans and provides one set of questions to guide the
interpretive work of this book. In short, how has widely circulated literature set in the city participated in public discourse and actions in and
about the city? How has literature even participated in decisions that
impinge on the city's sustainability? How, in turn, have those decisions
emphasized New Orleans's places in historical time, those chronotopes
that give meaning to the literature's narratives for its national and international audiences?[19]

Sustaining New Orleans also refers to the function of literature in the
development of public memory, which percolates the circulating
discourse, beliefs, institutions, rituals, social relations, and power structures shaping the past and envisioning the future. What images and
ideas of the city, for good and ill, does well-known literature help to
sustain in public memory within and beyond the city? How does this
public memory contribute to the setting of problems addressed within
the city, such that it also affects the solutions that are possible? Michael
Kammen's comprehensive *Mystic Chords of Memory* draws conclusions
not unique to the scale of the US nation. He could be writing specifically
about the city of New Orleans when he repeatedly warns that the details
of commemorative practices are in excess of any general conclusions.
When studying memory and commemoration, the best deduction
possible puts the binary of tradition and progress in an ambivalent and
not always dialectic relation.[20] Public or collective memory is, like
sustainability, bound to be an elusive object of study. Yet it is the
geological foundation, however shifting, on which environmental
health, social justice, and economic viability interact.

With clear-eyed skepticism, Campbell notes the tendency to locate
sustainable development in preindustrial and non-Western cultures.
This so-called undeveloped world is not the desiderata some scholars
would have it be, he insists.

> The international division of labor and trade, the movement of most
> people away from agriculture into cities, and exponential population
> growth lead us irrevocably down a unidirectional, not a circular path:
> the transformation of pre-industrial, indigenous settlements into mass
> urban society is irreversible. Our modern path to sustainability lies
> forward, not behind us.[21]

Although I do not doubt that transformations of the kind and of
the scope Campbell describes are and have been afoot for some time,
I question that the result of those transformations is and will be world-
wide, monolithic mass urban society, the triumph of modernizing
technicways that Odum feared. One of the dimensions of human place-
connectedness Lawrence Buell delineates, in his twenty-first century

extension of Yi-Fu Tuan's concept of topophilia, is the accumulation of platial experience by a mobile individual or diasporic population that inflects their lives and perception in each new location.[22] And this is only one manifestation of place-connectedness. Folkways, changing in place and mobile across space, are repeated and reformulated in the crucible of urban geographies with their diverse and protean populations. If some set of cross-national urban practices called cosmopolitanism offers hope for peaceful coexistence, it is because they reflect the place-tone of history modulated by the folkways of new diasporic populations, not because the elite of urban Asia, America, Europe, Africa, and Australia share the same technology.

Cities and city-regions, of which New Orleans and its metropolitan area are a provocative example, teem with folkways that re-create the past in the present, thus transforming the future—for good and ill. Literature, which is often asked to serve the analysis of sustainability only in its fantasies of the future, has more to offer as a compelling expression of the historically produced place-tone in a critical present. As a conduit of evolving local folkways, literature conveys its version of the stories to a national and international audience. This is not to say that in being compelling literature necessarily offers a utopic, edifying, or progressive representation of the critical present of a place—although it frequently offers a complex and provocative one. It is to say that its aesthetic qualities, the stuff of epigraphs and memories, pulse with the power of the place-tone, and this, for good and ill, plays a role in platial sustainability.

The project here is to understand how folkways, together with the literary arts read in situ, help shape the affective bonds to and collective memories of place, participate in setting the public problems for which solutions will be sought, inform the solutions proposed for those problems, and influence the effectiveness of solutions pursued. Having fingers in so many pies, the project may not always be tidy. But only in pursuing multidisciplinary perspectives can it work across key questions toward a significant degree of what cartographers call ground truth, a measure of a map's representational accuracy relative to facts on the ground. The facts of sustainability—economic facts, environmental facts, facts of social justice—and the urban stories sustained in public memory are dialectically constitutive.[23]

Exceptionalism

Rather than perceiving New Orleans as exceptional, architecture scholar Christine Boyer pronounces New Orleans the model for the US city of collective memory. "One American city, above all others, holds a

central place in the invention of American traditions and in the
development of cultural tourism that the nostalgic art of historic preservation has spurred. This is the city of New Orleans. . . . The Vieux
Carré turned inward upon itself, blatantly ignoring the forces of
modernization."[24] It is true. As early as 1925, citizens of the French
Quarter organized to preserve its crumbling eighteenth- and nineteenth-
century buildings. The federal Historic Sites Act of 1935, a 1936 change
to the Louisiana Constitution naming the Vieux Carré as a unique
historic area deserving of unique legal protections; the 1937 federal
designation of the Quarter as the first Historic District; and the creation
of the Vieux Carré Commission (VCC) to discover and punish architectural infractions all established New Orleans as the US expert in
preserving historic areas.[25] New Orleans's early reputation as a unique
haven of preservation prompted the extraordinary suggestion of David
Riesman "that New Orleans ... be made a national park, with its homes
inhabited by subsidized families (much as bear or deer are 'subsidized'
to live in Yellowstone)" so that Americans could develop a "culture of
desire" for "the textures (and aesthetic values generally) which have
been built over generations into whole regions and cities." In 1957, he
emphasized that this idea was taken but not intended as a joke.[26]

If, at the end of the century, New Orleans was the most commodified
of US cities, as Boyer claims, then it would seem the cultivation of desire
for textures built over generations has been taken very seriously, at least
in the sense that tourists pay to see it. The inhabitants are not, however,
federally subsidized to be simulacra of themselves, and the display
of sexual license and cultural diversity remains as central to the city's
economic base and culture of desire as historic preservation. The living
folkways of New Orleans inhabitants, even in the tourist-trammeled
Quarter, foil the inclination of some to make the eighteenth- and
nineteenth-century city a gated model of colonial community like
Williamsburg or a purely fabricated settlement like Disneyland.[27] Desire
by definition cannot contain its object. And it is this excess as much as
any desire for safe diversion that attracts so many tourists to New
Orleans.

The sprawling city has been built in greater New Orleans as it has
across the nation. The technology of A. Baldwin Wood's 1914 pumps
and subsequent drainage systems have permitted the city to venture off
the ridge along the river and stretch north, in the 1920s, into new
(white) suburbs approaching Lake Pontchartrain. After World War II,
the city extended along the new I-10 and across the Mississippi River
Bridge as mud dredged from the river turned wetlands into building
sites.[28]

Still, throughout the twentieth century, the river continued to lap at
the ankles of the city and region, threatening to poison it, inundate it, or

desert it altogether. If historic preservation has made New Orleans a model for the commodified US city and suburban expansion has made it a typically sprawling US city, location in the delta of the Mississippi River has rendered New Orleans a palpably vulnerable city on a shifting terrain. One such instability concerns the dangers of the water's quality. Scholars and other storytellers of the Mississippi often quote the 1839 diary of Captain Frederick Marryat, who wrote that the grand river was in fact a great "common sewer."[29] The development of the petrochemical river corridor, beginning early in the twentieth century with Standard Oil in Baton Rouge and expanding after World War II below that city, has intensified that nom de guerre to "cancer alley."[30] The further instability caused by flooding, real or potential, has periodically shaken the solidity of the levees and spillways, as structures, as ideas, and as mechanisms of political power. On one notable occasion when the city's coherence was threatened by the 1927 flood, the city's leaders—bankers, more than politicians—used their influence to blast a crevass into the levee of neighboring Plaquemines Parish rather than risk the newly expanding city.[31]

Although the river is sometimes too much for New Orleans—never mind the Gulf and lake in hurricane season—it threatens always not to be there at all. North of Baton Rouge, in the back yard of Louisiana State Penitentiary at Angola, the Corps of Engineers force the river to flow east toward New Orleans and away from Old River that heads due south to the Atachafalaya Basin. (In *Mississippi Floods*, Anuradha Mathur and Dilip da Cunha describe this engineering feat as stopping time because it inhibits the geological shift at work in the Mississippi Delta for centuries.[32]) That the city should have become and remain a major ocean port some ninety miles upriver from the Gulf of Mexico is a geoeconomic irony of its place. The scale of international ships and petrochemical plants along the New Orleans river corridor suggest a grand enterprise such as those launched from the Thames in earlier centuries. They dwarf the old, low-rise city. Yet the fluid terrain endangers as much as it is endangered by the objects and enterprises of such proportions. On any day, one can visit the site at Old River where the Corps turned the river; every day the salt water of the Gulf inches up the shores of south Louisiana. This bioregion, the territory from Angola south to the Gulf, is New Orleans's exceptional home. In New Orleans, a distinctive wilderness of conflicted landscape and demanding climate are the uncommon urban nature that permeates the refinements of historic preservation and the licentiousness of sexual display.[33]

Traveling along the skeins of memory that uniquely link site to site, person to place, public life to private life, are the platial folkways, prominent among them the stories people tell and name history.[34] The various claims for New Orleans's exceptionalism are such folkways. In reviewing the case for New Orleans's exceptionalism, Robert Dupont recently pronounced that "the accumulated evidence [of place, people, and public imagination] in favor of the unique character of New Orleans is strong," and so it is.[35] But as with all claims for exceptionalism —of the unique US democracy, of the uniquely racist South—claims for New Orleans's exceptionalism are best measured by what truths are purported and whose interests are served. Oral history—often recorded in "informal histories"—are often "lies," as Zora Neale Hurston's folk call their tales, and in being "lies," they offer insights into truths about the city, true as much in the patterns of their repeated factual errors as in their accuracy as corroborated in other documents.[36] This sort of truth influences how residents and homeless occupants, tourists and conventioneers, business investors and government agencies make decisions about a city and how readers interpret literature about a city. The claims for New Orleans's exceptionalism, often determinedly irreverent, insert some surprises into such familiar US urban narratives as African American in-migration; inner-city degradation, renewal and rerenewal; tainted water, land, and air; suburban sprawl; not-in-my-backyard self-protection; and privatized segregation. If in surprise lies the possibility of transformation, as Michel de Certeau claims, then we might rejoice in the agency of "lies," but not before we ask, transformation from what to what?[37] For whom?

The Stories People Tell

The stories people tell about New Orleans are alive—orally, musically, visually, textually. Here I offer an evolution of some of those verbal tales, told mostly by residents and recorded, usually by a second party, in print. This evolution is, like the delta, so many-fingered that I present it not in strict chronology but with something of the reversal, repetition, and reimagining that gives longevity to ever-emerging folkways in a shifting landscape where water does not necessarily run to the sea. I have not tried, like the Corps of Engineers, to send the flow of narrative in a single direction I choose. This strategy would fail the tests of narrative truth and sustainable urban imperatives. I have instead teased from these narratives thematic threads that I see otherwise deployed in problem-setting and decision-making about the city: race, gender, sex, violence, carnival and slavery, lawlessness and new beginnings, Francophilia and US heritage, emplacement in the Middle Passage, and emplacement along the Third Coast of the Gulf. Most important for defining New Orleans, none of these social and geographic forces maintains a distinctive character separable from the others.

In the end—my end, not the folkways'—the nineteenth-century voodoo queen Marie Laveau emerges as a paradigmatic, enigmatic figure whose mixed race, ambiguous class, unusual gender practices, syncretic spirituality, Franco African roots, and undeniable social and even political power bring complex coherence to my understanding of New Orleans folkways.[38] My last three chapters, especially, demonstrate the significance of her legacy in understanding the sustainability of the city in the twentieth century and beyond. With this end in mind, I pick a moment to begin these stories.

A New England Congressman who, in 1811, wanted to make an exception of Louisiana, objected to the admission of the territory as a state into the United States on the grounds that its corruption and vice would violently rupture the Union.[39] A verse set in the year 1829 is representative of many tales from the eighteenth and nineteenth centuries that can offer insight into the congressman's attitude about Louisiana and its major city, New Orleans. Written by Colonel James R. Creecy in the Antebellum Period, the poem, "The Duel in New Orleans, in 1829," was published by his widow in *Scenes in the South and Other Miscellaneous Pieces* through subscription sales to the likes of US senators and cabinet members in the auspicious year 1860. Creecy, North Carolina–born, had worked for the US government as a land clerk and had been hired from Louisiana.[40] Essays in Creecy's mixed-genre collection provide impressions of the city and its people from the point of view of one who had come to the racially and culturally unfamiliar Delta South, as had Faulkner's Thomas Sutpen, to capitalize on the rich lands of the Mississippi Delta frontier. *Scenes in the South*, wrote Mrs. Creecy in 1860, provided the national public true pictures of the South.[41]

The duel referenced in the poem's title arises between a ravenous Kentuck, gorging himself on meats in a New Orleans restaurant, and a genteel Frenchman in awe of these American consuming habits and daring to question them. This story of the newly American city where Creoles regarded Americans with wonder, if not disgust, is told by a narrator, like many before and after him, who has seen the city first hand but is, it seems, not of it. He begins,

> Have you ever been in New Orleans? If not you'd better go,
> It's a nation of a queer place; day and night a show!
> Frenchmen, Spaniards, with Indians, Creoles, Mustees,[42]
> Yankees, Kentuckians, Tennesseans, lawyers, and trustees,
> Clergymen, priests, friars, nuns, women of all stains;
> Negroes in purple and fine linen, and slaves in rags and chains.
> Ships, arks, steamboats, robbers, pirates, alligators,
> Assassins, gamblers, drunkards, and cotton speculators;

> Sailors, soldiers, pretty girls, and ugly fortune-tellers;
> Pimps, imps, shrimps, and all sort of dirty fellows;
> White men with black wives, et *vice-versa* too.
> A progeny of all colors—an infernal motley crew![43]

The verse, the rhymes of which leave no doubt about its tone, begs
the question why the outsider should go to New Orleans: to see the
"nation" whose street life every day is an infernal pre-Lenten carnival.
Mustees—that is, people of mixed race—jostle trustees; people of the
cloth accompany women of all stains; Negroes in linen travel with
slaves in chains; assassins and gamblers cavort with cotton speculators;
pretty girls join hands with ugly fortune tellers, implying together that
each and all may be a costume, a performance, a dangerous opportunity
for cross-dressing and fluid identity. Friars' robes may cover the body of
a prostitute; Negroes' linen or slaves' chains, the body of a white cotton
speculator. To some in the nineteenth-century audience accustomed to
ribald minstrelsy, the lines about slaves' chains, loose women, and interracial marriage might not have elicited shock and censorship as they did
for the Work Projects Administration (WPA) writers who deleted those
references in their reprinting of the verse for the 1938 WPA *City Guide*.
But we are still left to ask, for whom would this invitation be tempting
or pointedly alienating? From what position is it issued? To whom is it
addressed? The senators and cabinet members who supported the
publishing venture of the widow Creecy on the brink of the Civil War?

Although local scholar Patricia Brady argues from Creecy's poem
that New Orleans is a city haunted by its past, this verse invites a
different conclusion. Rhymes such as "Mustees" with "trustees" and
"alligators" with "cotton speculators" offer a satire of the city's vices.
Creecy's New Orleans is a city without remorse despite mortal sins
against nineteenth-century US mores: miscegenation; corruption of
Church, business, law, and the whole territory of the Middle South by
proximity to gambling and prostitution; and failure to clearly define the
place of Negroes in its society. Whether as a booster Creecy promotes
New Orleans as the titillating, steamy place fellow Americans love to
disdain, or as a North Carolinian he is offering New Orleans's urban
mob as a scapegoat that will contain the South's sins and leave the rest
of the region untainted, or as a federal employee he is controlling
Northerners' anxieties by providing them familiar ridicule of this
powerful southern city in a fractured nation, his verse implies that life in
New Orleans is an exceptional urban spectacle of "infernal," mixed-
race "progeny" that needs to be visited to be believed. In the narration
of the duel, following the roll call above, the big, hot-tempered American kills the Frenchman, then is beset by regret for having so easily
destroyed what he did not understand. Although Creecy's narration

stipulates a date of 1829, his published poem ironically invites his readers on the eve of the Civil War to know more about the city and its sins against US values by immersing themselves in the carnival of everyday New Orleans life. In doing so, he contributes to the city's already established reputation, which circumscribes subsequent internal and external interpretation of New Orleans's problems, solutions, and the effectiveness of those solutions.[44]

Lyle Saxon, who presided over the 1938 WPA *City Guide* that bowdlerized Creecy's poem, also offers spectacle as New Orleans's identifying mark in his well-known 1928 book, *Fabulous New Orleans*. An unmistakable booster, he introduces the city by claiming that "'New Orleans' brings to mind a Mardi Gras pageant moving through the streets at night."[45] Flambeaux—hand-held, kerosene-lit chandeliers—casting as much shadow as light on the passing parades, do create romantic night performance, secret and seductive, and not the infernal heat of the motley crowd of the street in the earlier verse. Even the gyrations of the African American flambeaux carriers could not—cannot—fully disrupt the ordered pageantry of these staged Mardi Gras parades as distinct from street costuming and status shifting by individual revelers. Saxon's image climbs aboard a metonymy already set in motion during Reconstruction by boosters such as the Krewe of Rex; this night image makes New Orleans "fabulous," a place of enticing fables, but fables written and staged at the direction of carnival clubs or krewes, the oldest and most influential of which were and are white businessmen, bankers, and other moneyed professionals.[46]

Also interested in fabula, Herbert Asbury nonetheless leaves the prestigious citizens of carnival krewes and returns to the attractions of sin that fortify Creecy's invitation. In his 1936 book, *The French Quarter: Informal History of the New Orleans Underworld*, his subtitle characterizes the territory specified by his title. Informality leaves Asbury, like many other self-styled historians of the city, free to indulge fully in the stories that circulate in and about New Orleans's locales. For him, these stories add up to a developed reputation as a city of "sin and gayety," beginning in the eighteenth century and extending through the heyday of Storyville, New Orleans's much cited red light district. Asbury's catalog of sin and gayety runs from gambling to voodoo and prostitution to the 1891 lynching of acquitted Sicilians by a distinguished mob. He ends with a lament for the 1917 closing of Storyville by the US Navy, arguing that the segregated sex district had not only served its employees and their clients, but also had protected respectable property owners from brothels that spring up next door.[47] Although, in *The Awakening*, Kate Chopin imagined Edna Pontellier traveling the streets of the late nineteenth-century Creole French Quarter unaccompanied, seeing little but the interior domestic courtyards and drawing rooms of her compatriots, Asbury implies a French Quarter utterly defined by its underworld, of which the spiritual/medicinal/spectacular practice of voodoo is part. Asbury's Depression-era interest in gothic stories supercedes any gallantry about protecting New Orleans's reputation on the eve of its push for historic preservation.

Historic preservationist and advocate of riverviews, Harnett Kane, in a tamer popular history—*Queen New Orleans: City by the River*—introduces the city to outsiders in the post–World War II period as more southern European than American.[48] The many veterans of the recent war in Europe had joined an elite class of Americans who held in their memories images of that continent; thus, they swelled the ranks of those who could especially appreciate this common claim about the city. In New Orleans, Kane implies in his 1949 book, veterans could return to the scenes of their European foray without confronting the ruins of war or leaving the United States, an invitation that has continued to serve New Orleans, the tourist city.[49]

Liberal journalist Hodding Carter, in a 1968 volume celebrating the 250th anniversary of the French founding of the city, configures its racial indeterminacy, its spectacle, its "sin and gayety," and its southern European architecture, as uniquely American. In Carter's "Introduction, With Love," the city has four claims to national fame: "our nation's first melting pot," "spiritually and culturally the greatest Catholic city in the United States," "America's good-time town," and "the voodoo heartland of Africa in America."[50] Carter's love, as love will, pulls him in opposing directions at once. Although he claims heartland status for the city in the swamp, that claim is based on its balancing west Africa's heartland on the edge of the North American continent. The extraordinary phrase "voodoo heartland" encourages one to imagine voodoo practitioners as hardy and bold in the sunlight as Midwestern wheat farmers, but at the same time elicits the sensationalist stories of voodoo animal and even human sacrifice as well as the more usual gothic stories of voodoo's effect on believers' affairs of the heart. Although Carter presents New Orleans as serving the nation in its capacity as multiracial, spiritual (not sinning), gay, and voodoo-endowed, his opening gambit announces that "the town Bienville founded ... in 1718 became an amoral queen among American cities."[51] But whether in grace or sin, New Orleans's exceptionalism needed definition always within the union, at least for Carter, writing in 1968. Images of the racial-ravished South and divided nation of the 1960s lie silently behind Carter's reaffirmation of the union through the eccentricities of its amoral southern city.

Thirty years later, scholar David C. Estes also posits New Orleans as serving the US nation by offering an alternative founding narrative but one less equivocal about the African presence in this story. In his reading of the HooDoo section of Zora Neale Hurston's *Mules and Men* as an important revision of her earlier piece on New Orleans voodoo for *The Journal of American Folklore,* Estes argues that Hurston moves the focal geography of voodoo from the Caribbean to the margin of mainland North America. In so doing, she "discovers" New Orleans as

> an alternative site of America's national inception, a shrine counterpoised to Jamestown and Plymouth Rock. . . . The Crescent City becomes a New World center of the ancient mysteries of creative, spiritual power. Thus it is the urban mother of all African American culture, a sacred place where myth becomes a potent force in history.[52]

Among subsequent in-migrants, fabulous New Orleans has found new informal historians. Transylvanian immigrant, Dadaist poet, and National Public Radio essayist Andrei Codrescu is one of these. In two collections of essays published in the 1990s, this new resident claims New Orleans's exceptional status within the US nation. In the eponymous essay of his collection, *The Muse Is Always Half-dressed in New Orleans*, European Codrescu writes of New Orleans, first of all, as an old city. As did Riesman before him, Codrescu sees in New Orleans the development of textures over generations.

> Old cities soothe and ease the pain of living because wherever you are someone else was there before, had troubles worse than yours, and passed on. I don't see how people can live in spanking new suburbs without succumbing to terminal anxiety. We need the dead to make us feel alive. In New Orleans they're at it full time.[53]

Codrescu claims that the only public clocks in New Orleans are on funeral parlors. These sites of transition from life to death are the appropriate keepers of New Orleans time because they are locales that mark the passing on of stories across generations. Storytelling and listening determine the experience of time in Codrescu's New Orleans. In New Orleans, he says, no one wears a watch.

In *Hail Babylon! In Search of the American City at the End of the Millennium*, Codrescu returns to the significance of time and timelessness, placing New Orleans at the beginning of his journey in pursuit of the US city, thus inflecting his vision of urban America through New Orleans Southland. New Orleans, Codrescu claims, is the most timeless city of the United States. That is, the city and its region contain the most time in "reservoirs." Thus he begins his quest there. New York City,

New Orleans's other, is the least timeless US city and thus ends his journey. If New York City "patented the idea of history as a form of instant irony" and thus "revealed every distortion and falsity in things once held timeless and true"; if this New York, being the base for the development of media, was, therefore, the foundation for US common language and character as well, then the vehicles of modernization—nationhood, capitalism, ideology—that Odum understood as technicways came to define the New York region.[54] Codrescu's judgment about New York's assault on timelessness (and New Orleans's suspension in it), at the end of the twentieth century, interpolates these reputations in place.

> The timelessness of New Orleans, enforced by the cotton softness of the dream-imbued and nightmare-rattled region of the South, is deeply haunted by the urgency of time in the guise of economic development and tourism over a background of corrupt politics and crime. New York, on the other hand, chopped to pieces as it is by the guillotine hands of global-economy time, hides pockets of timelessness yet, possible precisely because so much stays behind while the race speeds on.[55]

The acknowledged internal struggles between time and timelessness in each city do not temper his claim that the distance between the two cities is "1500 miles of frontline in America's meanest war: that between time and timelessness."[56]

Seeing New Orleans through the platial experience of his Transylvanian youth, Codrescu has taken root in New Orleans. A New Orleans topophiliac, but not a booster, he is a conduit of the folkways—whether of gaiety or vice—that shape the New Orleans region, timeless stories evolving in time and place along the big river. That the city is geologically timeless because of the technicways of the Corps of Engineers is not a feature of the time and timeless binary that he unravels. But the interdependence of nature and civilization do preoccupy his portrait of the city.

His epigraphs, from New Yorkers, in fact, lay the foundations of his urban beliefs. One from Lewis Mumford declares the purpose of cities is "to put the gods in their place," to unite scattered fragments of dismembered bureaucrats and experts, repairing the damage done them by vocational separation, overcultivation, tribalisms, and nationalisms and making them complete human beings again through "organic partnerships and ideal purposes." Another from Jane Jacobs insists that cities are not passive victims or the "malignant opposite of nature." Codrescu begins *Hail, Babylon!* by stating:

My nature is the city. Not any city: only those cities, like New Orleans, which have become nature. Here, there are doors older than most American trees, street corners dense with the psychic substance of past events, manhole covers that can be read just like a natural formation. This kind of city accrues a nature to itself over time: doors *are* trees, street corners are hot springs, manhole covers are arroyos. Forms become organic through use: who can deny that jazz can have the force of wind, or that cafe au lait at Kaldi's on a rainy day is possessed of duration?[57]

In Codrescu's old New Orleans, nature and civilization are not that paradigmatic US binary "with its residues of guilt and recrimination."[58] In following Jacobs, he even comes close to William Cronon's call for an urban environmental consciousness or closer still to Raymond Williams's nuanced environmental thinking that seeks to avoid a crude contrast between nature and production.[59] But Codrescu's New Orleans is more an environment of unconsciousness than its opposite. It is dreamy, lazy, tolerant, and indolent "against the very grain of American civilization as we know it. We lie incongruously in the way of the thrifty, Puritan America whose concerns, including environmental ones, are driven by the logic of economies and planning." Neither historic preservationists nor scientific searchers for sustainability will find in Codrescu's vision of timelessness a formula serving their goals. He does not want New Orleans's endangered nature defended by their logic. Instead, he suggests, New Orleans's nature becomes natural by evolving from folkways told in storytime.[60] This process that Codrescu describes can be seen as a feature of New Orleans's livelihood, the term of compromise Williams imagines between evolving nature and goal-driven production.[61]

Yet among New Orleans stories are those boosters never tell. Codrescu turns from his cafe au lait to tell violent tales of murder and police corruption in some of New Orleans's worst crime years, 1993–1994. In "America's meanest war between time and timelessness" is this violence. And in this violence is an implicit story about regionally uneven development. Codrescu's prose links a New Orleanian—if not *the South's*—lost economic cause to the local practices of crime and corruption and the gothic tales they produce. He thus shows that the crime, the tales, and the lost cause are in a positive feedback loop that is its own kind of dialectic. His more explicit assertion is that this violence, in many years, distinguishes New Orleans from other US cities. (After this essay's original publication in *Playboy*, boosters of the usual kind accused Codrescu of doing damage to his adopted home.[62])

The Feminine Image in the Stories People Tell

In Codrescu's essay, what links New Orleans's exceptional timeless nature—the first part of his essay—to its exceptional incidences of murder and police corruption in 1993 and 1994—the second part of his essay—is a metaphor identifying the city with a female figure, a rhetorical move of especial pertinence in *Playboy.* "New Orleans *is* Blanche Dubois, and that mix of knowledge, denial, hunger, and experience is precisely what makes her so attractive to outsiders."[63] That mix of knowledge, denial, hunger, experience *and*—the succeeding gruesome crime stories imply—the excesses of horror and corruption. In fact, Codrescu's first story of violence and police misconduct is about Antoinette Frank, a mixed race, fresh-faced young policewoman who is condemned to death after she robs and murders those she was hired to protect, then enacts a response to the 911 call at the scene of her own crime.[64]

In 1895, Creole writer Grace King acknowledges in her often-reprinted *New Orleans: The Place and the People* that the custom is to personify *all* cities as women, although many cities and some women are not well suited to the comparison.[65] Indeed, Boyer observes, "in their attempt to heal the ills of the city, [nascent planners of the nineteenth century] disavowed its physical form, treating the space of the city like the body of a woman, who also in the nineteenth century was envisioned as a site of excess, of hysterias, of illnesses and exclusions."[66] For Codrescu, twentieth-century New Orleans is still such a woman of excess whose ills are not easily excised from her charms. But a century earlier, for King, New Orleans was defensible against the racial charges of fellow New Orleanian George Washington Cable and was desirable because "among cities, [it is] the most feminine of women, always using the old standard of feminine distinction."[67] For so-called local color writer King, this "old standard" needs no definition. But because for King some women are not suitable objects of comparison for a city, we can surmise that the "old standard" must not include what Creecy called "women of all stains." King's New Orleans is, she declares, the transplanted Parisian woman whose feminine need for pleasure justifies slavery and whose implied need for defense, in a Reconstruction and post-Reconstruction United States, justifies exclusive white male enfranchisement. By this logic the Mechanics Institute Riot of 1866 or the White League battle in 1874 or the white mob rule in 1900 becomes a necessary assertion of white power.[68] Blanche Dubois and Antoinette Frank are the residue of these folkways.

One hundred years after King's pronouncement, Violet Bryan laments the penchant for defining New Orleans through female figures. Whether the female in question is King's belle, Faulkner's Storyville courtesan, a quadroon, or a voodoo queen, she resists these characterizations of the city that associate it principally with romanticized class and race dominance, prostitution, sentimentalized multiracialism, and exoticized superstition. Serious mixed-race writers such as Alice Dunbar-Nelson, Bryan argues, disappear in a haze of perfume and humidity.[69] The real spaces of the city disappear as well, Boyer adds. But reasonable assertions that these feminine associations lack veracity or moral worthiness or inclusivity cannot erase their preponderance in the service of defining New Orleans's distinctive urban character. The evolution of these feminine folkways calls for a platial reading across time. As these feminine images continue throughout the twentieth century, they are one form of significant historic preservation situating New Orleans within colonial or antebellum metaphors, whether the history they preserve is accurate or not. King, for example, imagines her Parisian woman that is New Orleans basking in the glow of the long-eclipsed Sun King. Her error is consistent with local New Orleans tradition. In the 1870s, Mardi Gras' Krewe of Rex was created by rooting its power as a social institution in the image of the Sun King. That New Orleans was built as a European colonial site during the reign of and named for the regent Philip of Orleans is useful information to contrast to King's claims and to those of the Krewe of Rex. That the regent moved the French seat of power from the exclusive court of Versailles to the public sphere of Paris provides an even more telling contrast to the foundational myths of New Orleans's elite institutions and their chroniclers.[70] In short, feminine metaphors, as with other significant metaphors, appear in the stories of many different kinds of tellers. This is reason alone to inhale enough of the perfume to sample and analyze this scent of the place-tone.

Progressive southerner Hodding Carter, who repeatedly positions a city of the Deep South within the 1960s US national context, is a storyteller who also relies on New Orleans's feminine associations. He imagines the early men of New Orleans dreaming of Indian and dark Caribbean women who became mistresses with lighter children. While dreaming of these mistresses, European men married the "right sort" (imported by the French for this purpose), claims Carter. Nevertheless, he cautions,

> these gaudy visions and real presences made too many forget, then and now, the good women, the faithful women, the gentle women who were the cement of city and colony. New Orleans would be a sensual town if only because the girls of the Indian tribes and the branded women of the Salpêtriére made it so at the beginning and a passionate one, more tolerant than gentle, but with a history not often written in blood except when men fought over women.[71]

Although Carter claims that New Orleans was "our nation's first melting pot," he explains that the city first had to emerge from the dreamland of white men with African, American Indian, and Caribbean women or French prostitutes on their minds before it could become part of America's heartland. In the French colony and in the US nation, Carter repeats from a distance of 250 years, these women in the city were a distracting sexual presence keeping desiring men from commerce and appropriate marriage contracts that "cement city and colony." Yet Carter equivocates on whether New Orleans ever did emerge from this dreamland and on whether a city and colony of merit can be held together by mongrel female material such as was present in the early colonial city. Carter implies that if New Orleans is, in 1968, more sensual, passionate, and tolerant but less "gentle" or aggressive than other (riot-torn) US cities—as was New Orleans's reputation in 1968 and as it was in 1860—it is because the bodies of Indian women and French prostitutes—not to mention African women—provide the mortar. Yet the "old standard of feminine distinction" of which Grace King wrote haunts the fable of early New Orleans that Carter tells.[72]

During the Moon Landrieu mayoralty of the 1970s, Clay Shaw, founder of the International Trade Mart, controversial defendant in Jim Garrison's notorious case for a conspiracy murder of President Kennedy, and historic preservationist, applied what he calls "a process of self-analysis" and "the best psychoanalytic theory" to explicate the feminine and masculine images of the city for the purpose of promoting it to tourists. "Self-analysis" and "the best psychoanalytic theory" in Shaw's case may imply a tongue-in-cheek reference to his own homosexuality, notorious after his 1967 indictment on a charge of participating in a sexual thrills conspiracy to assassinate President Kennedy. Despite his acquittal in an hour, this notoriety denied him the privacy of gay salon culture that Lyle Saxon and his coterie, Robert Tallant, for example, had enjoyed earlier in the Quarter.[73] Among the sixteen feminine images Clay Shaw generated in his private memo to the VCC are

1. The French Quarter
2. Creole culture and Creole history
3. Blacks, mulattos, octoroons, cafe-au-lait, slavery
4. St. Louis Cathedral and French Catholic church (note that the Irish Catholic church jars on this image) . . .
13. Latin-type girls, octoroons, pretty women of all sorts . . .
14. The confederacy and remnants of the Civil War; the image of the Confederacy fascinates Southerners and Northerners alike. . . .
16. The Mississippi and all the river mystique

Among the eleven masculine images are

1. Trade and commerce
2. Spanish names and remnants of Spanish culture . . .
3. Hard-drinking bars . . .
4. Jazz, spirituals, marching music, etc. . . .
8. Anything that suggests Anglo-Saxon, German, or Scandinavian antecedents of city
9. Anything that suggests Huey Long–type politicians, red-necked racism, segregation, lower middle-class stupidity
10. Prostitution, women who are easy lays
11. New Orleans cops, state troopers, National Guard, etc.

He concludes that "it is the Creole feminine image of the city that underlies all the tourist interest," seeming to corroborate the presumption of Grace King eighty years earlier.[74] But, as with Carter, Shaw implies that the New Orleans Creole is French, black, mulatto, octoroon, Latin-type, a slave even—or at least the descendent of slaves—a remnant of the Civil War.

The definition of Creole, explicated in full by Virginia Dominguez in *White by Definition*, here slides, as it often has in New Orleans, between New World–born of French or Spanish stock, to French only, to French and African mixed-race of varying dimensions.[75] In Shaw's definition, he includes Latin types (Latin Americans? Italians? American Indians?) if they are female and pretty and occupying places such as French restaurants and coffee shops and French Catholic churches. He may also imply slippage in the word "women." "Pretty women of all sorts" may include transgender individuals or beautiful male cross-dressers whom outsiders—Jim Garrison included—could not distinguish from other Creole women. However Shaw and his VCC associates understood "women," his proposal privileges his deployment of creole feminine images over the images of Bourbon Street and explicit prostitution, part of the enticing dreamland of Carter's metaphor. Clay sides, it seems, with his historic preservationist cohort against those who explicitly promote sex amidst the historic architecture in the city's self-sale.[76]

A generation later, David Estes does not retreat from the conclusion that the city itself is both African American and female. Following the lead of Zora Neale Hurston's urban study of HooDoo New Orleans and her sketch of the spiritualist leader Mother Catherine, he heightens his rhetoric to assert, "For [Hurston], New Orleans is the holy, the eternal, and the female, and the wellspring of its identity is the perpetual ritual enactment by its African American citizens of their religious folk culture." Similarly, he concludes that voodoo queen Marie Laveau's "life in legend is intertwined with the history and geography of the city. . . . This New Orleans is essentially female as well as essentially black."[77] The ubiquitous presence of the Laveau legend that frustrates Bryan (and dwells, unnamed, in the psyches of Hodding Carter and Clay Shaw) provides Estes the occasion to celebrate Hurston's urban acumen and the city's central Africanist "religious folk culture."[78]

There is reason for frustration with the black feminization of New Orleans when we remember that nineteenth-century race science associated blackness with feminization and with sexual deviance and thus erased the black male and waylaid his citizenship—not to mention the citizenship of African American women.[79] What is her route to equal citizenship? The legends of Marie Laveau and the folkways that derive from this figure go a long way toward answering that question and toward defining what distinctively constitutes *civitas* in the city of New Orleans.

The Legend of Laveau in the Stories People Tell

When, in 1885, Lafcadio Hearn wrote his essay about "The last of the Voudoos," he was referring not to Marie Laveau but to Jean Montanet, more popularly known as Dr. John. Born in Africa—Senegal, most say—Dr. John is occasionally presented as the mentor of Laveau. But for many storytellers she is *sui generis* in a city of numerous contending practitioners of voodoo.[80] As with all legends, Laveau's does different work for each person who tells it. The perpetuation of her legend, in its many guises, is not a quixotic cultural process of "Americans, black and white, discovering their African-American heritage of folk and popular art."[81] The battle in New Orleans over the meaning of creolization, and the role of Laveau in that struggle, is a battle to control public memory, public image, and public projects.

In *Fabulous New Orleans,* Lyle Saxon quotes an oft-cited *Times-Picayune* 1881 obituary of the elder Marie Laveau, by G. William Nott, which declares her the last of the voodoo queens. Despite these claims for the truncated career of voodoo, Saxon himself repeats the legend, reiterated many times since, that in antebellum New Orleans voodoo extended through *all* slaves and free Negroes too.[82] And he informs his readers of his own frequent attempts to participate in a voodoo ritual in the early twentieth century. In "Voodoo," an article written for the *New Republic* and reprinted in *Fabulous New Orleans*, Saxon writes of the successful culmination of his search. He poses as a distraught lover who wants to eliminate his rival, a pose that grants him entry. What he finds, he claims, is an orgy of ragged, drunken, wild, ignorant, sensual Negroes. Saxon's Negroes in blackface, men and women, intoxicate and frighten the novice white man in this comic tale. When the voodoo queen and her court are lost to the sensual power of their dance and drink, Saxon slips away. Saxon's story assured the jazz age readers of *The New Republic* that something called voodoo was still to be found in New Orleans, but it also assured national readers that if voodoo ever had the power of sober gossip, religious belief, or rebellious slave culture under the leadership of Laveau in the antebellum city, or a more direct agency in the Reconstruction city, it was now, in the Jim Crow South, nothing more than the drunken sex of uneducated Negroes and the entertainment of white fools like himself. Voodoo had been minstrelized. By implication, the rising stars of the Harlem Renaissance were brought down as well.

Saxon's protégé, Robert Tallant, perpetuated the identification of New Orleans with voodoo and with Marie Laveau specifically, while also producing a voodoo discourse such as Saxon's that works to disempower the very preoccupation it feeds. Author of numerous informal histories and fiction about New Orleans, Tallant's urbane comedic work consistently found a national audience in the 1940s and 1950s. He eventually took up residence in a more national location, New York City, from which he continued to write about New Orleans. Tallant's 1946, WPA-researched *Voodoo in New Orleans*, so riled Zora Neal Hurston that in her review for the *Journal of American Folklore* she describes the book as a "nuisance." Hoodoo is never defined or sources documented. No attempt is made to establish the relation of voodoo in New Orleans to African religions and similar practices in Santo Domingo (Haiti). The author relies too much on newspaper and police reports of HooDoo practices without noticing those practitioners who did not attract press or police. Too much time is spent on establishing Marie Laveau as a procurer and gambler and on the "spurious Marie Laveau II" and too little time on the methods of current HooDoo doctors. These complaints by the devotee of African American folklore point to obvious shortcomings in Tallant's book as an anthropological or a folkloric study.[83] But in fact it is neither, Tallant's friend Saxon's claims for its authenticity notwithstanding. It is a compilation of oral legends, interviews, and gossip structured by the subject position and the literary skill of a white man from New Orleans cultivating New York publishers and a national audience.

Chapter one, "Evolution" begins, "Sometimes a white man in New Orleans takes a walk along South Rampart Street, one of the famous Negro thoroughfares of America. . . . He finds himself in a new world," the world of Negroes, jazz, and, most of all, voodoo, "with its own particular sights and sounds and smells."[84] Although Tallant places himself in New Orleans, a city where Negroes, whites, and people of various colors have lived and worked (albeit unequally) in close proximity through Colonial, Antebellum, and even Jim Crow years, his introduction ironically describes a wholly Negro urban ghetto in an American city. Such a segregated locale would have been familiar and probably frightening to white readers in every recently overcrowded Northern, Midwestern, or Western US city in the war and post-War years. For these cities were, in 1946, home to many more Southern Negro migrants than ever before, and Negroes were confined, on arrival, to segregated, overcrowded urban ghettos. As the resident of a southern city long accustomed to the coexistence of whites and Negroes, Tallant is an "expert" in racial coexistence. He is willing to venture such a walk to demonstrate that, after all, Negroes still step aside on the sidewalk to let a white man pass. He also presents himself as a white outsider taking a daring stroll into the most exotic Negro territory of his city, to offer an on-the-scene description that both titillates his readers and, in the end, mocks the idea that any real danger resides there. Negro exoticism and separateness are reinforced; the status of the white flâneur is unscathed. Tallant's rhetorical moves not only empower his readers, they also ambivalently empower and disempower his subjects in a familiar way. He grants them some spiritual and cultural integrity but isolates them, rhetorically and geographically, from political and economic efficacy. Folkways and technicways are kept distinct.

Tallant's is an urban walk usefully contrasted to Lewis Mumford's and Jane Jacobs's in New York. For, despite the unforgettable pungent smells of 1940s Rampart Street, Tallant's perambulations uncover more past legend than present built space or social subjects. In fact, his walk begins Part I, which is entitled "The Way It Was."

Part II, entitled simply "Marie Laveau," places that voodoo queen and her daughter—also, in Tallant's text, called Marie Laveau—at the center of voodoo in New Orleans and at the center of the Negro thoroughfare. As with Saxon, Tallant asserts that *every* Negro was in Laveau's power from the 1830s through the 1870s. He further asserts that the gossip that fueled her power was extorted from blacks on pain of voodoo spells. This assertion begs the question of how Laveau acquired the power to make threats that could stick.

Laveau was, in the stories Tallant relates, a tall, erect, strikingly beautiful mixed-race woman whose stride parted crowds and whose stunning eyes mesmerized those who looked on her. Sometimes described as part American Indian and African, Laveau married a light man from Santo Domingo named Paris in 1819 and, after his death in 1820, entered into a relationship with another light, or white, man from Santo Domingo named Glapion. With Glapion, or perhaps with the two men, she had, most stories tell, fifteen children. One, Tallant claims, was a daughter born in 1827, who was also named Marie and who worked to sustain the Laveau power and legend. Although one of Tallant's sources claims all of Laveau's daughters were named Marie with distinctive second names, Tallant asserts the authenticity of this second Marie Laveau. Tallant further surmises from his sources that another daughter, Madame Legendre, who married a white man and who took over management of her mother's St. Ann cottage and legend, turned her mother, the voodoo queen, into a pious Catholic. Madame Legendre also bore white children who, it was said, moved effortlessly into a white world. Tallant's version of the Laveau legend ends with the Glapion sisters struggling over the definition of their mother's legacy and the disposition of her property on St. Ann and at Lake Pontchartrain.

The St. Ann house in the Quarter was said to be the site of the serious and secret voodoo work of healing and advising. The latter site, where the Lake and Bayou St. John meet, was frequently described by the press and oral historians as the place of more public voodoo rituals—mixed-race dances and other provocative acts. Tallant's informants also claim Laveau had a house of prostitution—or at least of procured female entertainment for men—called Maison Blanche. He writes that although Marie Laveau II controlled Maison Blanche and the Lake site, the Catholic sister took over the important French Quarter house where their mother died after six years in confinement. Madame Legendre banned her voodoo sister. Tallant deduces about Marie Laveau II that she kept a following only among the "uneducated class of Negroes" and "lost herself completely in the Negro world."[85] Shakespeare could not ask for better material on which to build the dramatic history of a place than these stories of the beautiful quadroon Marie Laveau and the warring daughters who come to occupy two separate racial and religious cultures. The evocation, then suppression, of the titillating mixed-race heritage and the final neat separation of white and Negro worlds—even in notorious New Orleans—served the desires of the post–World War II national audience Tallant addressed.

Although there is widespread acceptance of the Laveau presence in nineteenth-century New Orleans, African Americans have interpreted her history and influence differently from Tallant or Saxon. In Hurston's review of Tallant's book, she dismisses the second Marie Laveau and emphasizes instead the impact of the first Marie's legend. Every HooDoo doctor she encountered in the 1920s claimed a Laveau link, she declares. African American poet Marcus Christian, who was an important unacknowledged black poet in the New Orleans WPA project and who did much of the research for Tallant's book, emphasized instead the sociopolitical features of Laveau's power.[86] He discounted the claims of Laveau's supernatural power and dwelled instead on her gossip network among black slaves and servants and among the wealthy white women whose hair she dressed. He emphasized as well her role as herbal healer and as spiritual advisor to prisoners awaiting execution in the Parish Prison only blocks from her St. Ann home.

In Caryn Cosse Bell's project to explicate an Afro-Creole protest tradition in Louisiana between 1718 and 1868, she restricts New Orleans voodoo and thus Marie Laveau even more, confining them to a brief footnote.[87] Bell focuses instead on what she sees as the neglected literate Creoles of color who drew on French political philosophy for their inspiration. It is from this class that Juan Victor Sejour Marcou et Ferrand arose. The author of "The Mulatto," the first known work of African American fiction, published his story in France two years after the 1835 appearance not only of Alexis de Tocqueville's *De la Democratie en Amerique*, but also of his traveling companion Gustave de Beaumont's *Marie, ou l'Esclavage aus Etats-Unis, Tableau de Moeurs Americaines*. Beaumont, as with Sejour soon after, took up the subject of mixed race as a means to explicate the horrors and ironies of New World slavery. Nearly a century later, Charles Chesnutt rewrote the story of New Orleans's wealthy, French-educated Creoles of color, but in the 1920s, his tragic romance met with rejection—whereas Saxon's book went into multiple printings.[88] Not everyone, then, repeats the trope that Marie Laveau was the "boss" of nineteenth-century New Orleans, that all residents of and tourists to New Orleans at least once made a pilgrimage to her St. Ann home or Lake Pontchartrain rituals.[89] And yet the proliferation of stories about her, the repeated tropes of those stories, and the hyperbolic claims for her legendary power that have expanded since her death argue for her position at the center of New Orleans distinctive folkways.

The tales of the Laveau-Glapion family are the unfolding stories of New Orleans's racial configuration, often feminized and exoticized—— turned to minstrelsy—to contain the power of an African-descended population dispersed throughout the history, the bloodlines, and the territory of the city. Awe marks the repeated descriptions of Marie Laveau—sometimes also of Marie Laveau II: tall, beautiful, irresistible to men, yet not vulnerable to them. It is a description Hurston borrows for her Janie in the novel *Their Eyes Were Watching God*, when her protagonist returns, in the opening frame tale, to walk down main street in front of town gossips. The mixed-race complexion, proudly displayed, does not shrink from the heritage of slavery or of the abused and sexually exploited female body. As the body of a Storyville prostitute or courted quadroon trained to please white men, it defies characterization. Men and women, black and white, pursue her beauty and her power. The swinging rope of Indian hair further corroborates both women's claims to a rightful place in the US city. Marie and Janie are even property holders. But, of course, Hurston's novel celebrates Janie's strength, echoing her own refusal to accept any status as victim; Tallant's text has other purposes.[90]

Tallant's and later informal historian Mel Leavitt's repeated claim that "that woman [Laveau] was the real boss of New Orleans," or Saxon and Tallant's insistence that every Negro, slave or free—no, correction, every *person* in and through New Orleans—went to Laveau as to a shrine are tropes that seem to concede to Laveau and the reality of racial mixing a genuine social, aesthetic, and political influence.[91] But Saxon and Tallant offer this presentation of power in the 1920s or 1940s to demonstrate how modern New Orleans has changed. For Saxon, writing in the Jazz Age, voodoo has become primitivist entertainment. For Tallant, the modern, post–World War II New Orleans segregates Creecy's "infernal crew," separating Negroes from whites geographically, culturally, and spiritually in ways recognizable to other residents of US cities. What remains of Laveau and HooDoo are exotic and harmless rituals still titillating to tourists, but contained in a nineteenth-century realm separate from the rational economic and social hierarchy of good women and men cementing the modern city and the nation. The syncretic power of HooDoo, which mixes African, European, and American Indian social and somatic traits and incorporating Catholicism, evangelical protestantism, spiritualism, and African voodoo, is neatly divided and apportioned.

For booster Leavitt, writing in the post–oil boom, depression-era 1980s, Laveau stands with a cast of eccentric New Orleanians, such as wealthy white Frenchmen Bernard de Marigny, equal in their ability to provide sensational stories. But if their public behavior offers fascination, opines Leavitt, their real fortunes were won or lost in "intrigue."[92] As it happens, the late twentieth-century versions of the Marigny and Laveau legends, as with those told by Leavitt, have broadcast stories of that nineteenth-century intrigue amid the continued corporate and financial secrecy that has characterized posh private clubs and Mardi Gras krewes, such as the Boston Club and the Pickwick Club, through the twentieth century. At the same time, the folkways of "boss" Laveau's power, fortune, and intrigue—always ambiguously flamboyant in their performance yet secret in their power—also provide a fanciful context for contemporary stories about the more public intrigue of financial leaders (and the governor) winning and losing fortunes in the city at the end of the twentieth century. As soon as they are told, the latter can easily become folkways themselves, received as timeless traditions that evoke bemusement even when the city's immediate well being is at stake.

The elder Laveau is said by all storytellers to have left New Orleans public life and retreated into her St. Ann cottage in 1875, living there until her death in 1881. Illness and old age are the proffered credible explanation. But the year 1875 provokes another explanation as well. The revolt of the White League against the mixed-race government of Reconstruction Louisiana, staged in New Orleans in 1874, and the subsequent demise of radical Reconstruction in the South generally in 1876–1877 left little room for a city boss such as Laveau. And so the Laveau influence of fact or legend achieved closure concomitant to the events of the 1870s. Laveau's voodoo daughter is said either to have died with her mother in 1881—no causes are given—or to have disappeared into the Negro world, forgetting her English and muttering "scorching French." The lightest Glapions, in Tallant's compilation of the stories, easily take on the mantle of whiteness, the trust of *Times-Picayune* reporters, and the orthodox practices of Roman Catholicism.

It is the Laveau legacy with its dual implications of evil criminality and spiritual generosity that lies at the center of claims for New Orleans exceptionalism. Although some storytellers imagine that Laveau owned most of the French Quarter, they also concede that she was a wicked woman. Others who claim she accrued no wealth also assert her generosity and virtue. For some, she is the madam who procured quadroon beauties for wealthy white men, but, to others, she is the beauty who rejected or controlled all men who pursued her. For some, she was the abortionist who killed unwanted babies and kept their skeletons in her house; for others, she was an herbal healer who nursed the sick in deadly yellow fever epidemics.[93] Some said she walked on Lake Pontchartrain; others said that she nearly drowned in it. In either case, many concluded that she rose to voodoo power from among the competition because of her genius for publicity. The popular rituals on the Lake were elaborate spectacles that drew large crowds. Yet, spectacle notwithstanding, for many, she genuinely had the power to control the police and politicians. Hurston describes her spinning the police in circles and rendering them unconscious on her front steps. Others tell less supernatural tales of her spiritual advice to Parish prisoners awaiting execution.[94] She helped them build altars and provided them coffins.[95] Whether stories of her virtue or vice, her racial and religious indeterminacy pervades them all. So great was her fame and, especially after 1876, the threat of her bold racial mix, that when the New Orleans newspapers wanted to discredit George Washington Cable, the Confederate veteran New Orleanian who later embraced the freedmen's case for equity, they claimed he had danced with Marie Laveau.[96]

If New Orleans is possessed of a dreadful whimsy, an overendowed sensuality that averts its eyes from problems of unequal development, street lawlessness, internal corruption, and environmental degradation, those problems cannot be understood outside the context of the stories people tell on the streets, in the newspapers, in letters and meetings, in the spectacles of parades and musical performances, and in literary texts. One need not wait, with Codrescu, for urban nature to run its course, to accept, with him, that storytelling and the folkways that ride on its currents are fundamental to the time and place of New Orleans, past, present, and future—historic preservation and urban sprawl notwithstanding. It is not adjudication of the case for New Orleans exceptionalism that is necessary for the city's well being. Rather, the claims for New Orleans's exceptionalism need interpretation. They are active participants in the production of space in critical moments throughout the city's history. They punctuate the rhythm of the place-tone.

2

"Indiscourageable Progress"

The Decline of the New Orleans Streetcar and the Rise of *A Streetcar Named Desire*

People lined New Orleans's Magazine Street in the July heat of 1948 to see a parade introducing the electric trolley coaches (electric buses on rubber tires) that were replacing the Magazine streetcars. Sponsored by New Orleans Public Service, Inc. (NOPSI), and the Magazine Street Businessmen's Association, the parade offered four familiar Mardi Gras krewes running off season, the young Mayor Morrison, and a transportation history of the city. From mule-drawn streetcars ferrying belles in hoop skirts, to the first and then a later version of the electric streetcar, to the new electric trolley coach, the parade presented its audience a linear narrative of progress set within a familiar power structure embodied in antebellum costumes, Mardi Gras krewes, and a young mayor for whom reform did not mean desegregation. While Navy planes overhead reminded parade-goers of the power of American progress, absent from this urban parade were the streetcar histories of Negro New Orleanians and of the Amalgamated Association of Street Railway Employees and any reference to the fifty-four motor buses that were also replacing electric streetcars on the Magazine Street line.

Earlier that same year, in May 1948, Tennessee Williams had won the Pulitzer Prize for his play, *A Streetcar Named Desire*, and NOPSI, the utility and public transit company of the city, ran the last streetcar on the Desire line.[1] Shortly after *Streetcar*'s successful debut on Broadway in December 1947, the play—or rather, the fact of the

Figure 2.1 Streetcars and automobiles sharing space on Canal Street after World War II. (Historic New Orleans Collection, #1988.36147 NOPSI)

play—entered New Orleans public discourse about the scheduled 1948 closing of the Desire streetcar line. Its title provided a timely symbol for the concurrent changes in public transportation undertaken by NOPSI with the support of the much-touted reform administration of Mayor DeLessups S. Morrison. The intersection of Williams's success and the Desire line's demise affords a pointed opportunity to read the literature of the city in dialectical relation to the city streets. Interpreting the urban scale inflected by the scales of region and nation, I argue that Williams's play enacts a national crisis of post–World War II capitalist obsolescence through a southern regional heritage about the Lost Cause and uneven development and a feminized New Orleans heritage about waywardness and corruption. As this distinctive southern city and the capitalist nation call on one another's ideology to define themselves, they rely on Williams's symbol of the streetcar named Desire and beg the question about what is desired and by whom. By reinserting this popular symbol—and memorable title—into its geohistorical urban reality, we stand a better chance of understanding how the symbol has entered public memories in the city, the nation, and wherever the play has been produced throughout the world. We can also understand how the symbol has participated in real-life transportation changes on the local level. The route to this understanding is inevitably a dialectic of representation, social practices, and conceived spatial arrangements that keeps passing the same stops but finds them always changed.

As with the intricate tracks at a switching station, the intersection of *Streetcar*'s success and the streetcar's demise warrants knowledge of the multidirectional details. In the complexity of these details is a "displacement of the angle of vision" through which Walter Benjamin reframed the negative component of obsolescence, which conventionally stands as necessary context for the other economic story of positive progress. Through this "modest methodological proposal," Benjamin imagined that "a positive element emerges anew in [the negative obsolescent component] too—something different from that previously signified. And so on, ad infinitum, until the entire past is brought into the present in a historical apocatastasis."[2] I am not prepared to set a goal of messianic realignment of the planets or even to declare culture prevails over capital. However, a methodology that displaces the "determinate points of view" of obsolescence and progress, folkways and technicways, is definitely in order.

I set the fact and the content of Williams's play in relation to the material restructuring of New Orleans's post–World War II streets and official attempts to fashion the public's responses to those changes.[3] In staging this interaction, I understand the rhetoric of the play and various official attempts to structure public sentiment—the 1948 parade, for example—as commemorative gestures, that is, gestures constructed to set public memory. But in fact they were engaged not just in imagining and using the past (history), but also in imagining and using the future (planning). And they did both to affect political decisions in the present of the post-War 1940s.

"I live," Williams wrote in the autumn of 1946, "near the main street of the Quarter. Down this street, running on the same tracks, are two streetcars, one named 'Desire' and the other named 'Cemeteries.' Their indiscourageable progress up and down Royal Street struck me as having some symbolic bearing of a broad nature on the life in the Vieux Carré—and everywhere else, for that matter."[4] The repetitive route yet indefatigable progress Williams describes here differs from the purportedly linear progress promoted by General Motors (GM) in New Orleans at their Parade of Progress in 1937 and again in 1955.[5] From the 1930s through the early 1960s, NOPSI, New Orleans's white newspapers, and most of those citizens whose letters the editors published repeated the refrain of the automobile manufacturers: streetcars are archaic; automobiles and motor buses are modern. It is understood that cars—and motor buses, when mentioning them cannot be avoided—participate in improvement, beautification, and progress, but streetcars cannot. In the post-War years, only a few train spotters such as Edwin Quinby and urban analysts such as Lewis Mumford worried publicly about what the loss of electric railways and the hegemony of the internal combustion engine would do to US cities.[6] On the face of it, Williams was mistaken, it seems, about the "indiscourageable progress" of the Perley Thomas 800 or 900 series cars rumbling by his apartment on Royal, but the immediate and continued success of his play suggests that he was somehow also exactly right.

The story of the declining streetcar line and the inclusion of Williams's Broadway production in that narrative is told here primarily on an urban scale, but it is a story embedded in a national tale of systematically, even conspiratorially, discontinued urban electric rail systems. Although familiar to transportation analysts and US urban planners and historians, this national story has not stuck in the broader public's imagination. Yet, given the effect of de-electrifying public transport on the nation's urban populations and spaces and the streetcar's abiding symbolism as doomed and quaint other, this narrative deserves brief recitation.

In 1935, the Public Holding Company Act required that urban utility companies divest themselves of their electric rail systems, thereby separating the streetcar from its source of power. Whether this law was primarily driven by a reaction against monopolies or by the highway lobby is a matter of some debate. In any case, by 1935, National City Lines, a GM-backed bus company, was already buying, then expeditiously dismantling, urban electric rail systems in cities coast to coast. Their crowning achievement, by some accounts, was the destruction of the Los Angeles area streetcar system. During World War II, the federal government prohibited transforming streetcar lines that served city centers, but conversion activity resumed with vigor at the War's close. Rail enthusiast Edwin Quinby's post-War broadside warned of a corporate conspiracy to deny the public its remaining electric rail service and thus also to pollute its cities through the overuse of fossil fuels. For his trouble, he was labeled by a transportation publication as a member of the lunatic fringe.[7]

In 1947, another such lunatic, Attorney General Francis Biddle, indicted National City Lines, American City Lines, Pacific City Lines, Standard Oil, Federal Engineering Corporation, Phillips Petroleum Co., GM, Firestone Tire and Rubber Co., and Mack Manufacturing Corporation on just such charges as related to forty-six local electric rail systems. Eventually, the government scored a victory in this case, but only a Pyrrhic one: by 1952, supplier-defendants had already disposed of all investments in City Lines and their subsidiaries.[8]

Economist David St. Clair asks the pertinent question about the City Lines consortium and the decline of urban electric rail systems. If the conspiracy occurred, is it significant that it occurred? That is: (1) if the US public had been hell-bent on owning automobiles since before the 1920s and did so in increasing numbers through the decades and (2) if motor buses were cheaper and more profitable to run than electric streetcars or trolley coaches (electric-run buses with rubber tires), then wasn't electric mass transit doomed no matter what trust violations City Lines, GM, and Standard Oil might have engaged in? St. Clair does corroborate, with ample evidence, the government's conspiracy case, but he also concedes the public's substantial, albeit far-from-simple, devotion to the automobile.[9] That devotion was already much in evidence in 1903 when Henry Ford's company was formed, and, by 1933, the President's Research Committee on Recent Social Trends could observe, "It is probable that no invention of such far reaching importance was ever diffused with such rapidity or so quickly exerted influences that ramified through the national culture, transforming even habits of thought and language."[10] Given the expanse of the American continent and US national ideology about privately owned space, Americans' love of the car, in retrospect, seems inevitable.

Indeed, Mark Rose begins his analysis of the interstate highway system convinced that just as country dwellers of the early twentieth century were weary of impassable roads, city dwellers were exasperated by streetcars crowded with thugs and drunks.[11] Mid-century highway engineers, in Rose's analysis, "may have embedded class and racial judgments in the calculus of highway benefits," but they were acting on "commonplace assumptions of American acculturation." In doing so, Rose insists, they largely delivered on their promises that highways would offer economic growth, renewed cities, and fast-flowing traffic. Rose ends with a eulogy for road engineers replaced in the 1980s by politicians who "blocked highway construction and then stripped state road engineers of the authority to determine the location of urban highways."[12] Similarly, Scott Bottles sees no tragedy in the demise of the Los Angeles streetcars, which had exhausted the patience of the region's residents eager for a car culture.[13] But as we concede the depths of this desire, we might also recall Lewis Mumford's essay "The Highway and the City," in which he grants the attractions of the car on the open road but distinguishes this from its inefficiency within urban spaces. Mumford argues that the highway lobby largely removed Americans' opportunity to choose among different modes of transportation—be it feet, bicycles, streetcars, trains, buses, planes, or automobiles—based on their suitability for different spaces.[14]

Granting Americans' devotion to the car, St. Clair turns his attention to the economic assumption that motor buses were less expensive than streetcars. What he finds, considering size of vehicles, size of cities where they were used, labor costs, maintenance and replacement costs, operating costs, and profit, is that the most profitable urban public transport vehicles were trolley coaches. Of the three, the second most profitable were electric streetcars—these larger vehicles being most effective in large urban areas and at peak commuter hours. Because many cities—including New Orleans—had two-man ordinances governing the operation of streetcars, this extra labor cost cut into profits, but even accounting for this factor, streetcars proved more profitable, in St. Clair's analysis, than motor buses.

To be sure, many urban transit systems were not in sound financial condition when the nine corporations named in the government's conspiracy case began to convert them. George Smerk, a 1960s transportation analyst, provides historical perspective:

> Since the days when fast-talking promoters had pushed the building of the first horsecar lines, the street railways had been burdened by over-capitalization—that is, the capital represented by shares of stock and bonded indebtedness was far in excess of the assets, and hence the earning power of the firm.[15]

In his study of the street railroads in Syracuse, New York, Robert Carson confirms this opinion, but concludes that

> the non-profitability of the trolley was not an inevitable event at all. Instead, it reflected the very considerable bad management of operations and finances by the owners and managers and external economic and social pressures. . . . The contraction and degeneration of service and the lack of management vitality supported a psychology of obsolescence *that the public soon fastened to the streetcar.*[16]

Obvious here is both an economic, material reality about urban streetcars and a discourse of streetcar obsolescence and decline. Robert Beauregard concludes from his study of US post-War urban discourse that "urban decline discursively *precedes* the city's deteriorating conditions and its bleak future." He claims that it was the nation's "deepening contradictions," displaced onto the scale of the city, not racial ghettos or fiscal weakness, that generated a discourse of urban decline.[17] At the very least, we have in the streetcar and the discourse announcing its obsolescence a chicken and egg conundrum.

The streetcar emerges from this conundrum not just as the victim of a GM conspiracy and a hefty advertising budget, the aging companion jilted by Americans in love with the automobile. It had also become a synecdoche for decline in US post-War urban discourse. New Orleans streetcar history, Mayor Morrison's plans for progress, and Williams's play all enter this discursive field, this "collection of unstable and contentious interpretations."[18] Indeed, New Orleans was the perfect urban theater for this drama of decline.

New Orleans Streetcar History

Despite New Orleans's frequently cited, often cultivated, exceptionalism in the US scene, the Crescent City's streetcar history follows the pattern of other US cities in several ways. The various New Orleans–area rail companies that had been formed in the nineteenth century on the basis of steam or mule power converted to electric power at the end of the century. Four separately owned companies were then consolidated into one enterprise in 1922: New Orleans Public Service. A stockholder-owned utility company, it "was chartered to buy existing railway, electric and gas lines, and to build new street railways and bus lines."[19] At the height of the electric rail system, streetcar lines ran from Faubourg Marigny (home of the Kowalskis and the street named Desire adjacent to the French Quarter), upriver to neighboring Carrollton, and from the Mississippi River north to the West End pier extending into Lake Pontchartrain. Before World War II, however, twenty-three lines had already been converted to buses or abandoned, and after the war, twelve of the remaining thirteen were converted.[20] Removal of tracks, such as those on Dryades Street linking the principal Negro shopping area to the Central Business District, was a familiar sight both before and after the war. The 1996 documentary *Taken for a Ride* claims that when the federal government filed suit against the City Lines consortium in 1947, New Orleans was listed in the trial transcripts as among the eighty-three cities whose transit systems were affected by the National City Lines conspiracy.[21]

New Orleans's public transit history thus follows the national pattern, but it was unlike systems in other US cities in at least two ways: the first is that both utility and transit operations continued to be run by New Orleans Public Service Inc. decades beyond the 1935 Public Holding Company Act required separation of these two activities. As a subsidiary of Middle South Utilities, a company owned by Electric Power and Light Corporation (of New York City) until a reorganization separately incorporated Middle South in 1949, NOPSI was investigated by the Securities and Exchange Commission from 1941 to 1953 and threatened again with a Securities and Exchange Commission investigation in 1962 for failure to separate its power-generating activities from its transportation activities.[22] Although Middle South was, in 1953, ordered to divest itself of various operations, NOPSI managed to evade

Figure 2.2 1929 removal of streetcar tracks on Dryades Street. (Historic New Orleans Collection, #1979.325.5208)

a direct order to relinquish its transit operations. By 1962, with a mass transportation crisis looming throughout the country, Congress was willing to pass a law introduced by New Orleans Representatives Hale Boggs and Edward Hebert exempting NOPSI from the dictates of the 1935 act. NOPSI and the New Orleans representatives argued that transit fares in New Orleans were among the lowest in the nation because NOPSI subsidized transit operations with utilities profits and yet managed to keep utilities costs low as well.[23] Indeed, it looks as though NOPSI's maintenance of a populist-defined monopoly in defiance of federal law was part of the renegade legacy of Huey Long.

New Orleans was also unlike most other cities in that streetcar tracks were placed in the neutral grounds (medians, to non–New Orleanians) of major thoroughfares and did not compete with carriages, or later, automobiles, for space. The wide neutral grounds of Esplanade and Claiborne, for example, were not only rights of way for streetcars, but also important shady green spaces in the middle of steamy city streets. Even such a notoriously autocratic city planner as Robert Moses decried the removal of New Orleans's streetcars when he was hired by the Louisiana Department of Transportation as an outside engineering

Figure 2.3 The Esplanade neutral ground in the 1920s. (Historic New Orleans Collection, #1979.325.5250)

consultant to devise an arterial plan for the city. His committee's report, filed June 24, 1946, concluded, the following:

It seems to have been urged from time to time that the trolley track in the so-called neutral ground . . . be eliminated to produce additional vehicular pavement. This could be done by substituting buses. We see no advantage in this scheme. In fact those who have wrestled with the free, mobile franchise bus on city streets envy New Orleans a separate right-of-way which completely segregates street cars and at the same time serves as a safety zone. Franchise buses where no separate lanes are provided for them have a tendency to confuse traffic by weaving, stopping and doubling, and to preempt the curbs of ordinary streets. It is the vogue, no doubt stimulated by shrewd advertising and lobbying, to scrap all trolleys in favor of buses. New Orleans with its separate neutral ground right-of-way would gain nothing by shifting from street cars to buses and giving up a unique and on the whole very successful local rapid transit trolley system. . . . We have heard of proposals to remove street cars on some lines and substitute buses. As a general rule, this change is not recommended and replacement of old equipment should be accomplished by purchase of modern [street]cars.[24]

This 1946 arterial plan notwithstanding, NOPSI converted one streetcar line to buses in 1946, another in 1947, and three in 1948: Magazine, Gentilly, and Desire. The "vogue . . . to scrap all trolleys" emanated not only from "shrewd advertising and lobbying" on the part of car and tire manufacturers and petroleum producers, but also from the new mayor's public relations campaigns to woo voters with the promise of street repairs and from local news reporting and editorials, both of which rendered "modern [street]cars" an oxymoron. The New Orleans that veteran Stanley Kowalski reentered was one where very visible desire and obsolescence were subject to predictable management strategies.

The Mayor of a Modern New Orleans

When, in 1946, Colonel DeLessups (Chep) Morrison agreed to run against incumbent mayor Robert Maestri, a New Orleans Democratic Regular and Huey Long associate, he launched a self-proclaimed reform campaign reliant on women, veterans, and his military experience reconstructing the German port city of Bremen. Comparing New Orleans's decrepit streets with those in war-torn Bremen and also emphasizing poor garbage collection and insoluble traffic, Morrison defeated Maestri. Having pledged not to raise taxes, the new mayor found financial support for street repair in NOPSI, which contributed $3 million of the $15 million street program by agreeing to repave (for buses and automobiles) all streets from which they were removing streetcar tracks.[25] Implicit in the mayor's street program is the modernist conception of a panoramic city providing long vistas down boulevards unobstructed by streetcars in their neutral grounds.[26]

The July 1948 parade celebrating the transformation of the Magazine line from streetcars to trolley coaches well illustrates the role of the Morrison public relations mayoralty in the post-War present of the New Orleans streetcar. The genius of this particular public relations effort lay in its narration of a New Orleans history malleable to the mayor's plans for an economically progressive and socially reactionary future. People fanning themselves on Magazine Street that July saw an event that called on both the city's tradition of parading—principally Carnival parading—and the national passion for historical pageants commemorating important "firsts" for a region.[27]

The "first" celebrated in the July 1948 parade was interestingly the trolley coach (the electric bus) as distinct from the motor bus (the fossil fuel vehicle). The unromantic motor bus had been buried in the back pages of a February 1948 issue of *The New Orleans States*, a daily newspaper. Placed between a quaint advertisement for a red-blood cell tonic and an overpowering advertisement for a Buick pointed into the future, the small article announced that fifty-four motor buses replaced thirty-one streetcars that day on the Magazine line.[28] The page's layout obviated any opposition to the assumption that the Buick was a "fashion plate." Its dominant image promised a private comfort and quiet that the motor buses could not deliver.

New Orleans's consumers had, of course, long since bought into the idea of car ownership. Blaine Brownell reports that in 1920 there were 20,000 cars in New Orleans, but by 1930 there were 70,000. Already in the 1920s the issue was not whether to indulge in cars but how to cope with car traffic and safety hazards. Brownell quotes William Faulkner's 1927 novel *Mosquitoes* in which he laments New Orleans traffic inching along and cites as well a 1926 city commission report about what was perceived as the appalling traffic death rate.[29] By 1948, New Orleanians were well accustomed to diverting their eyes from the small print and toward the image of the large Buick. Car-proud Stanley Kowalski was no exception.

In contrast to the *States*'s obscure announcement about motor buses, "the advent of modern electric trolley coaches" was heralded by two days of parades in July.[30] On the first page of the "Society: Woman's Page" of the July 10, 1948, issue, the *Times-Picayune* asserted, "Magazine Buses Are Welcomed: Gala 52-Block Parade Evokes Memories."[31] As with the GM Parades of Progress, this parade carefully distinguished obsolescence as the other of modernity while also explicating a simple, comprehensible history from one to the other: a mule-drawn car, an early and a later electric streetcar, and finally the new electric trolley coach. Yet, fragmented memories were also evoked through disparate, implicitly defunct modes of transportation: bicycles, a Model T, and the mule-drawn streetcar occupied by young women in antebellum costumes, avatars of that southern femininity from which Blanche DuBois had fallen. Riding with the southern belles were an elderly mule-car driver, oral historian for the relics; thirty-six-year-old Mayor Morrison; and orphans from four homes, the first customers on the Magazine trolley coaches and then guests at a party thrown by the Magazine Street Businessmen's Association. Often pictured with children, the mayor was making a name for himself by devoting city funds to the New Orleans Recreation Department's (separate) facilities for Negro and white children.[32] The *States* article on July 10, 1948, "Magazine Parade is Progress Review," captured the strategy of the parade: "Ancient vehicles were used to accentuate the progress made in city transportation over the years."[33] Indeed, the parade's exhibits, old and new, retold the necessity of obsolescence for the assertion of modernity despite the rhetoric of progress from one to the other. In this parade, the apotheosis of that progress seemed to be the (short-lived) trolley coach, an innovative, and, as we know from St. Clair's economic analysis, cost-efficient public vehicle that made use of the power source already at hand. But this anomaly, the "modern streetcar," was inevitably short-lived because it used the wrong source of locomotion—electricity—and because it provided insufficient contrast of obsolescence and modernity in a burgeoning car culture. The motor bus, touted vehicle of the National City Lines/GM conspiracy, remained off-stage, at least at this event, hiding behind the Buick in the back pages.

In this 1948 parade, when the trolley coach was in favor, it was shown to have roots in the Old South, when women wore hoops and men, not motorettes, drove streetcars.[34] As the women in hoop skirts elicited the regional myth of the Lost Cause, the additional presence of four Mardi Gras krewes parading on Magazine Street in Carnival's off-season reasserted the mythologized white New Orleanian past that they first created before the Civil War. Out of the white panic of Reconstruction, Carnival was re-created as both a racial class narrative and business—principally tourist business—venture. Although organized Carnival parades were initially the brainchild of the Americans in New Orleans, augmented Carnival activities in the nineteenth century also provided the disempowered French- and Spanish-descended New Orleanians an opportunity to construct a racially pure, culturally refined, Catholic, Creole heritage as consolation for their dual defeats in the Civil War and in their intraurban competition with the Anglo Americans.[35] On this summer occasion in 1948, these regional and urban mythologies were linked to an ostensibly depoliticized transition from streetcar to trolley coach and to a young post–World War II mayor whose organization knew how to stage reform for the public's edification. In early July, the season of national commemoration, this urban parade of progress provided a narrative about the city's future in the American Century tied securely to a mythologized, white New Orleanian past. This is the world that Williams's characters enter.

Absent—predictably absent—from the parade's narrative are the relevant histories of New Orleans Negroes and labor unions. The mayor's announcement in November 1947 of a Negro Advancement Week notwithstanding,[36] there is no commemoration here of the resistance to segregating the streetcars led by black Creoles even after the defeat of Plessy[37] or any acknowledgement of the post-War ill treatment of Negro veterans on public transportation[38] or the national efforts to desegregate interstate public transportation. NOPSI's transferal of the segregating color screens streetcars motor buses and trolley coaches received no comment in the coverage of the ostensibly depoliticized July pageant featuring the young segregationist mayor. When the courts did finally order desegregation of city streetcars and buses in 1958, only two streetcar lines remained—St. Charles, which has run continuously since it first began, and Canal, which was removed in 1964 and was reinstated in 1998.[39] To quell the debate arising over removal of the Canal Street line in the 1960s, NOPSI argued that residents of Lakeview (an all-white suburb) could, on completion of conversion, take an express air-conditioned bus from Lakeview to downtown without transferring at the cemeteries to a streetcar, thus without stopping in central

Figure 2.4 The color screen moved from streetcar to bus. (Historic New Orleans Collection, #s 1979.325.6210 and 6234)

city neighborhoods—that is, predominantly Negro neighborhoods.[40] Transferring at the cemeteries, as Blanche DuBois is advised to do, came to bear a symbolic weight of social death that precedes physical death. In other words, the kindness of Negro strangers to Blanche in Williams's French Quarter was not a social interaction NOPSI and the white newspapers encouraged Lakeview residents to pursue. (When the motor buses replaced streetcars on modernized Canal Street in 1964, the tidy square buses were, this time, presented to the public in the formation of an unequivocally victorious army, for by then the trolley coaches too were waning.)[41]

Rolling, as it did, in early July 1948, the streetcar parade might have commemorated the dramatic 1929 strike waged by the Amalgamated Association of Street Railway Employees, which began on July 1 of that year. Instead, the 1948 parade's oral historian and motorman recalls the distant days of mule-drawn cars. In 1929, the union's demands for a closed shop and "stronger curbs on the company's power to discharge men" and their subsequent strike were met with combined forces of mounted police and US marshals. NOPSI used strikebreakers and management personnel to try and keep the cars running. On July 4, 400 strikebreakers arrived via train and met at the station angry strikers, one of whom was hit by a police bullet and killed. The marshals deputized the Northern strikebreakers, who functioned more as highly paid mercenaries ($50/day) than as streetcar drivers and conductors. What fares they collected they kept, participants on either side of the strike later remembered. The union and the public, which boycotted the street-cars in solidarity with their familiar local streetcarmen, retaliated with picketing, parades, and violence of their own. They surrounded car barns, and 10,000 gathered at the foot of Canal Street to overturn a streetcar and the truck that came to rescue it. Local historian "Pie" Dufour claims that the company, with governmental support, was determined as much to break the cross-class public support as it was to break the union.[42]

On July 5, after much bad feeling and destruction, NOPSI began negotiating with the American Federation of Labor and the Street Railway Employees. According to Louis Hennick and Harper Charlton, who are, as I am, indebted to NOPSI's records and photographs, the company lost $2 million in 1929 because of the strike and was forced to cease rail operations on five lines on July 2, 1929, the first full day of the strike.[43] Hennick and Charlton claim strikes and the two-man-per streetcar ordinance compelled the company to increase fares and abandon or convert lines.[44] NOPSI had, however, also abandoned or converted four lines in 1925 when there was no strike.[45] The stories emanating from the parade and from Hennick and Charlton's

Figure 2.5 Burning of a streetcar and truck during the 1929 carmen's strike. (Historic New Orleans Collection, #1988.31.241)

commemorative book are both insufficient and excessive in their explanation of the streetcar's fate, caught as they are in the contradictions of obsolescence and progress. The angle of vision Dufour focuses on the public, New Orleans's own Communard, provides, in the 1990s, a positive component for the negative assumptions of streetcar obsolescence and economically destructive Union demands. But the parade of 1948 recalled neither this nor any other perspective on the strike that some say New Orleans never forgot.

Morrison was unlikely to participate in any commemoration of the 1929 streetcar strike. Initially no friend to labor, the reform mayor endorsed the firing of 300 sanitation workers on October 25, 1946, when they struck over uneven collection routes, antiquated equipment, and the lack of extra pay for extra work. On October 27, dressed in his army fatigues, he organized young businessmen, Tulane students, and military personnel to act as volunteers—some said scabs—to collect and incinerate the city's garbage and created a photo opportunity for himself.[46] Morrison's modern city required a very particular positivist streetcar heritage that, by all accounts, excluded Negroes and labor. It also omitted any reference to the elegaic title *Streetcar Named Desire*.

Williams's *Streetcar* on the Rise and the Desire Car in Decline

Although the July 1948 parade of progress ignored Williams's play, the New Orleans newspapers had not. Even as early as February 1948, the *New Orleans Item* had juxtaposed nostalgia for the streetcar, framed in terms of Williams's very recent success on Broadway, to facts about hard money in their report on the Desire line.

> Death knell for New Orleans' celebrated "Streetcar Called Desire" [*sic*] sounded yesterday. The trolley so romantically named which has received national attention through the Broadway production of "The Streetcar Called Desire," will roll on its last trip sometime this year. . . . These tradition-stirring events cast their coming shadow today when Commission Council approved a NOPSI budget of $5,466,365 for new work in the months ahead.[47]

Imbricating the play's success of less than two months' standing with the tradition of the "trolley so romantically named," the article created a metonym for loss that stretched into some fading past of sufficient length to cast a shadow across the future expenditure of $5.5 million to remove streetcars. Told that the death knell for the streetcar named Desire had already sounded, *Item* readers of February 1948 were asked to lament the demise of tradition even though the Desire cars were still running and NOPSI did not actually pull up the tracks until May.

Speaking, in *Mystic Chords of Memory*, of the "antipodal possibilities of tradition and progress," and the "crucial ambivalence between the two," Michael Kammen concludes,

> that peculiar concatenation of tradition and progress had been a prominent feature of American culture during the mid-nineteenth century; it reappeared forcefully in most of the great expositions (including 1939); and then emerged in diverse modes after World War II, when old myths would turn up in new bottles.[48]

In the February 1948 *New Orleans Item* article, the tradition of the Desire trolley turned up in the Broadway success of *Streetcar* as it reentered public discourse in New Orleans.[49] The ambivalence of tradition and progress here manifested itself in this New Orleans journalist's use of the play's notoriety to confirm the association of streetcars and obsolescence. The play's success was established proof of the streetcar's demise—or so the article implied. In doing so, its author aided a capitalist management of obsolescence by nostalgically presenting the removal of the Desire line as an already accomplished, undebatable fact. Bridging an imagined past and an imagined future, the article evacuated the material present when and where democratic political dialogue about the streetcar might have taken place. New Orleans citizens and residents were invited to be spectators of tragedy or nothing at all.

Two months after the *Item* article, the newspapers reported that there had been no opposition to removal of the Desire line even though 900 residents of the newer working class suburb Gentilly had signed a petition opposing conversion of their neighborhood line, citing safety, comfort, and cost as the streetcar's advantages. NOPSI responded that conversion was cheaper than replacement, and that new rails would be unavailable from the steel industry for another two years.[50] Three weeks later, the French Quarter Residents Association did finally pass a resolution opposing removal of the Desire line because the city would lose the publicity generated by Williams' play. By contrast, they simultaneously voted to cooperate with Mayor Morrison's friends, the Young Men's Business Club (YMBC), in "its work to preserve and clean up the French Quarter."[51] From this phrase, we might infer the French Quarter Association's ultimate cooperation with the Desire line conversion in that the YMBC were perennial supporters of NOPSI plans always referred to as "improvement projects." And yet the Vieux Carré's protectors—the residents' association, the Vieux Carré

Commission—defined improvement as historic preservation whereas Mayor Morrison, like NOPSI, defined it as modernization tied to certain technology (for example, the internal combustion engine) but not others (such as electric rail).[52] The association's argument for keeping the Desire line, however half-hearted, was the first incidence of the ongoing reasoning that some remnant of the Desire line must remain to represent the reality of Williams's successful play.[53]

On the op-ed page of April 12, 1948, the *Times-Picayune* editors made this inversion of the material streetcar and the symbolic *Streetcar* more explicit. The editors compared the Desire line to Basin Street, immortalized in song but lost in substance for twenty years until New Orleans officials woke up to the fact that the "street had become so real to so many people everywhere" and so changed a few street name-plates.[54]

> Few will assert with confidence that "A Streetcar Named Desire," which has just received the coveted New York Drama Critics' Circle Award, will become a similar institution, provoke a similar nostalgia, cause a similar search for something that isn't here.

Having proffered this back-handed prescience, the editors were, however, at a loss. They were "helpless" to explain why "'Bus Named Desire' won't fill the sentimental or symbolic bill" or who, "like our present 'antiquarians' of jazz music, will be there to make things right again." Knowing it was inadequate, they could only suggest laying a single piece of track near the "milling crowds" on which could sit a single streetcar with a plaque.[55]

Quite possibly, Edwin Quinby and Lewis Mumford could have explained to the *Times-Picayune* editors why Bus Named Desire would not fill the symbolic bill: obsolescence had been affixed to the *streetcar*.[56] The plot of Williams's play aside—none of these early 1948 news pieces refers to the plot—the mere fact of a successful play bearing this title and set in New Orleans calls on a long-established discourse of streetcar obsolescence and inevitable doom and a New Orleans reputation of feminized decrepitude and missed opportunity.[57] Together they elicit an elegiac response. The title's juxtaposition of the words "streetcar" and "desire," widely disseminated because of the play's immediate and phenomenal success, promoted this complicated assumption of mourning.

In an intensifying post–World War II commodity culture, the streetcar is no match for the automobile, that perfect marriage of image and useful object on offer to individuals. By contrast, the purchase and sustenance of a streetcar required a collective subject ready to act on its

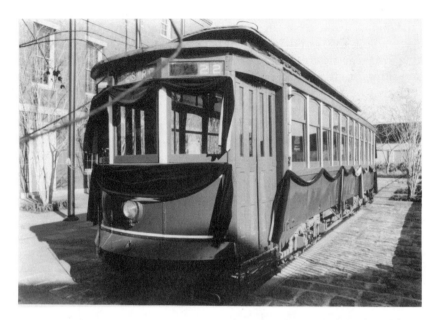

Figure 2.6 The Desire streetcar on a single piece of track beside the Old Mint museum, draped in crepe mourning the 1983 death of Tennessee Williams. (Historic New Orleans Collection, #1983.56.2, photo by Jan White Brantley)

behalf as public citizens and users. Although the late twentieth-century documentary *Streetcar Stories* contains interviews with various nostalgic New Orleanians and retrospectively defines them as this collective subject, the social divisions and ideological strategies of the 1940s present produced no such collective subject united by a shared desire. The assemblage of streetcar society and culture narrated in *Streetcar Stories* retrospectively places the streetcar at the center of desire. But social machinery of the 1940s had constructed a different familial assemblage that fostered consumption of the automobile.[58] In between the fight for streetcar transportation and its parochial social sphere that had motivated mass public support of the carmen in 1929 and the nostalgic reminiscence about streetcar culture in the 1990s is a desire sustained by loss and by a single streetcar line—St. Charles—that functioned as monument even before it was named one. The stories— Tennessee Williams's play among them—became the docents for that monument, keeping alive the past and its loss, and thus arguably serving the Buick advertisers more than the proponents of any innovative rail technology.

The streetcar called Desire derived its name from the street called Desire.[59] The urban pedestrian walks on "named ground," observed

Walter Benjamin, with every step encountering in street names the city as a "linguistic universe" igniting the imagination to "build a whole quarter about the sound."[60] When that street name is affixed to a circulating streetcar where it is seen by riders, pedestrians, motorists, and porchsitters, that linguistic universe of the city is orature in motion. When that name is Desire—and especially when Desire intersects with Cemeteries, as it does in the beginning of Williams's play—the fire ignited by imagination is a funeral pyre such as the ones built to incinerate the hundreds of streetcars discarded in the middle twentieth century.[61] But, of course, such literal fires were all offstage. What was coursing through post-War urban streets was an unrequited desire less precisely articulated.

Within New Orleans public discourse about the streetcar, that grieving was put to a very particular use. This effect was later heightened and imprinted after the public—in New Orleans and throughout the nation and the world—actually confronted the play's representation of US capitalist contradictions through the successful Broadway production and then the 1951 film version. There they met the character Blanche DuBois, played in the film by an aging Scarlet O'Hara, and saw and heard the arresting performance of Marlon Brando. But even as early as 1948, in New Orleans, the mourning assumed in Williams's title entered the city's public discourse about its streetcars as though it were referencing a lost tradition that had always already been there, a lost cause of *the* Lost Cause, aged uselessness amidst decaying gentility and sensuality.

Who "will be there to make things right again"? The *Times-Picayune* editors' nostalgia for the heritage that was right was, indeed, the national order of the day in the post-War period. Kammen has amassed the evidence: the phenomenal success of *American Heritage* magazine, first published in 1947, the increasing popularity of a reconstructed Colonial Williamsburg, and the 1947 government-initiated, privately funded and advertised Freedom Train that toured 322 US cities displaying the nation's founding documents are just three of the events pointing to a post-War heritage craze that was, as Kammen notes, if not unique to the that era, certainly prominent in it.[62] The words of the *Times-Picayune* editors underwrite the New Orleans that sought to model its Vieux Carré reclamation and marketing on the Williamsburg success and thus make it right. For they foster the city's role as both preserver of an historical site for the benefit of the nation's citizens and as entrepreneur satisfying future tourists with simulacra of authenticity. The Desire car parked on a fragment of track would commemorate Williams's play, the success of which was proof that the New Orleans it represented had value of an unspecified nature in an unspecified past. In April 1948, however, the Desire streetcar, although imagined as a monument, was, in fact, still a working vehicle of public transportation.

To make things economically right for the city and politically right for himself, Mayor Morrison and his public relations man appealed to the national press. They sought to sell the young mayor's image as a reformer cleaning up an old city and creating a new city with a revitalized port and important new links to Central and South America.[63] Engaged by the energetic mayor and his miraculous 1946 victory over Huey Long's Old Regulars, the national press cooperated—to the point of mistakenly awarding the mayor a Rhodes Scholarship. Even so, they kept distinct the new mayor and the old city. New Orleans itself remained a wayward woman, an aging prostitute, performing sensuality, exoticism, and hedonistic license for northern consumption: "New Orleans Has Its Face Lifted" announces *The New Republic* in June 1947[64]; "Old Girl's New Boy" declares *Time* in November 1947, describing the image of Morrison on its cover.[65] In its apparent commitment to offer consumers post-War modernity and progress, this national discourse exploited Old New Orleans, the traditional locale of the rattletrap streetcar named Desire. The way was cleared for Williams's explication of the streetcar and its "indiscourageable progress."

The Plot and Performance of the Streetcar

While the fact of Williams's play was entering New Orleans public discourse ahead of its plot, the power of the first production brought the conflicts and contradictions of Williams's American characters of New Orleans into an ever-widening public domain. When the curtain went up in the Barrymore Theatre on December 3, 1947, the New Orleans that the Broadway audience saw was the one created by scene designer Jo Mielziner.[66] Ronald Hayman reported that the audience applauded the set even before the action began.[67] Seasoned theatergoers would have recognized Mielziner's innovative hybrid of realism and expressionism, described by Brenda Murphy as creating an "illusion of a definite milieu, but also providing a scenic image of the environmental and psychological forces at its center."[68] For this particular play, Mielziner used opaque and transparent scrims so that, with manipulation of the lighting, the audience could see the interior of the apartment or also the street and a (freight) railroad bridge in the far background. Murphy avers that "the real artistry of the design scheme lay in the juxtaposition of this impressionistic background with detailed realism in props and costumes, achieving precisely the contrast [Elia] Kazan was

Figure 2.7 Mayor Morrison with his sleeves rolled up. (Historic New Orleans Collection, #1996.65.1)

looking for in his 'Don Quixote characters' and their stark social reality."[69]

The props Mielziner could collect for *Streetcar* did, however, differ from those he had collected earlier for Williams's *Glass Menagerie* in one central way: the title object was not part of the visual environment. Whereas the glass menagerie's symbolism worked through its presence, the streetcar's worked through its absence. In 1947, the streetcar's significant absence on stage would have been filled in the audience's imagination by those still in use on US urban streets—including New York's—and also by their tracks being pried from the pavement, by their being argued over in the courts, by their being reported about in the news media, and by their ideological association with obsolescence. To assign the resonance of "desire" to this set of quotidian practices, street scars, and discursive battles was, Williams recognized in 1946, already a drama in itself.[70] Just as "public space frequently is arranged as if for a theatrical performance," writes Boyer, "theater is often a foil for the representations of public life."[71]

The title of a 1947 *New York Times* review suggests that when the curtain rose on Mielziner's set design, the audience was applauding not just Mielziner's artistry, but a version of New Orleans they recognized as real. Specifically, Brooks Atkinson's review is entitled "Streetcar Tragedy: Mr. Williams' Report on Life in New Orleans."[72] Outside the play, Williams reported many different things about New Orleans. During World War II, while in New York, he wrote nostalgic poems about New Orleans.[73] In December 1945, having returned to New Orleans from New York, he wrote to Donald Windham that "New York and Broadway were dangerous for the ego—the way the Hotel Shelton was coming dangerously close to being his bordello."[74] But New Orleans was his home, if he could be said to have one, for, he wrote, "'New Orleans . . . provided me with more material than any other part of the country.'"[75] In *Streetcar* and in other New Orleans plays, Williams exploited the nation's and his own preoccupation with Old South ideologies and with the city's semblance of decadence and decrepitude that both attracts tourists (and Williams's audiences) and is maintained for them, a set of visual properties and cultural practices exceptional enough to throw in relief some seemingly more typical US identity.

In a *Fortune* magazine survey of the 1940s, more than 90 percent of the respondents described themselves as middle class regardless of their income, but Williams's, Kazan's, and Mielziner's French Quarter remains at odds with this compulsory, national middle class.[76] Murphy reads Kazan's addition of a shabby "bag lady" and a sailor, for example, as "local color in the poor and somewhat seamy neighborhood of the French Quarter."[77] Philip Kolin tells us that Mielziner collected battered, mismatched, and chipped objects to serve as props in "Stanley's squalid world."[78] Can Stanley and Stella claim solidarity with the aspiring 90 percent in this place understood as shabby? Just as the collaboration of Williams, Kazan, and Mielziner produced plays torn between naturalism and theatricality, the New Orleans of *Streetcar* was both a place and the performance of a place, both geography and mythography.[79] Although tired, overused housing in crowded urban spaces was the order of the day throughout the Midwest, Northeast, and West in the post-War period, the *Streetcar* production made it easy for audiences to displace those familiar conditions onto the Old Girl's infamous decrepitude. As with the ambivalent response of love and theft that Eric Lott attributes to white audiences of minstrel shows, attraction and difference characterize the appeal of the Old New Orleans Williams, Kazan, and Mielziner presented so skillfully.[80] Mayor Morrison notwithstanding, New Orleans remained the useful exception to a United States defined by a 90 percent middle-class citizenry.

The Williams, Kazan, and Mielziner collaboration asked its audience to imagine a French Quarter like the one they had already heard of, a place incapable of modernization and middle-class values, a place of the Old South and yet always the promiscuous undoing of claims to social superiority and plantation gentility.[81] In part, this perception derives from what Williams's first stage directions for the play describe as "relatively warm and easy" "intermingling of races in the old part of town." Critic Lionel Kelly even compares the comfortably sensual Negro woman in the first scene with what he calls the tense "white goddess" Blanche.[82] In one earlier 1947 version of the written play, the Negro woman in the first scene has a larger part but one that overemphasizes her lasciviousness (and thus her stereotypicality). Williams's final, more tempered use, of this character to introduce the Quarter and his use of the blues piano that permeates his Quarter still follow a well-established pattern of representing sensuality and unreasoning tradition—forces opposing both Old South gentility *and* new national modernity—with African-descended people and culture.

Cutting against the grain of presumptions about Blanche as a "white goddess," Kazan wrote in his notebook that the play's music is "an extension of the loneliness and rejection, the exclusion and isolation of the Negro and their longing for love and connection. Blanche, too is 'looking for a home,' abandoned and friendless."[83] Even though New Orleans Negro jazz artists were experiencing a 1940s national revival and in 1949 Morrison gave Louis Armstrong a key to the city, jazz innovations and racial intermingling, integral to the idea of New Orleans, continued to provide Williams and his audiences an aberrant exception to the Old South and to the renewed nation.[84] On a national scale, the presence of many new Negro residents in non-Southern cities created a crisis for those cities' enforcement of segregated and unequal neighborhoods—a crisis in a reciprocal relationship with a discourse of central city decline. Even on a New Orleans scale, the idea of a racially diverse Quarter remained aberrant because—Recreation Department improvements notwithstanding—Negroes played no substantive role in Morrison's economic or political reform in fact or in *Time*. Yet precisely because the old Quarter of the living city did not reach the preservation perfectibility of deracialized and deracinated Colonial Williamsburg and because it entered the mayor's national reform image largely as the "Before" to his "After," its streetcar named Desire and Williams's could rival (and, with the substantial help of the 1951 *Streetcar* film, in the end, outlast) the national Freedom Train as a vehicle for interpreting the nation's unstable post-War relationship to its heritage and its identity.

Kazan located what he called the spine of Blanche's social character in the Old South.[85] Prohibiting the audience's idealization of the southern belle, Blanche is, more precisely, the carrier and the victim of the Old South's promiscuity and prejudices. No longer the excuse for white male rape of slave women and lynching of black men, the southern belle becomes the recipient of that violence. Also, arriving by and being identified with the streetcar of desire, Blanche—the woman alone—is, in the first scene, already understood to be obsolete. Promiscuity and its convoluted relation to Old South ideologies and New Orleans traditions leave Blanche vulnerable to Stanley's cruelty and Mitch's rejection. In (and with) New Orleans, Blanche is the Old Girl. But her frail, alcoholic body decked in fake jewels and furs is neither a monument to the Old South nor a desirable link from its stable white identity to the newest post-War Reconstruction being managed by such interests as GM, National City Lines, and NOPSI and displayed in Parades of Progress. In the post-War world, Blanche is the sexualized, single, now-jobless woman for whom there is no room in the mandatory post-War, nuclear family planned for the future of the United States.

Kazan seemed to locate the spine of Stanley's character in the national present, which he understood as a place and time of hedonism. "This is symbolic. True of our *National State of Cynicism. No values.* There is *nothing to command his loyalty.* . . . Every bar in the nation is full of Stanleys ready to explode."[86] This is not the New South, the modern American man that NOPSI, the YMBC, and Mayor Morrison were counting on. It is, however, the portrait of veterans in Arthur Miller's *All My Sons*, which Kazan had directed the previous season, and in the 1946 Academy Award–winning film, *Best Years of Our Lives*. In his discussion of that movie, David Gerber describes the extensive advice literature of the time that instructs women how to cope—for it was their responsibility to cope—with the angry, injured, alienated, as-yet-unemployed veterans, and how to extricate them from male camaraderie and reinsert them in the nuclear family.[87] Although Kazan does not name it, in fact Stanley, like Blanche, does have a past—the war. And, unlike Blanche, he does have a place in a national plan for the future—reasserted domestic capitalism. The play painfully enacts the consequences of the advice that *at all costs* a place be made in the home and in the workplace for the untamed warrior. Stella no longer

earns her own living in New Orleans as she once did; she asks Stanley
for money. Her job, as Blanche points out, is to sleep with Stanley,
leaving no job for the likes of Blanche. Although Stanley strikes his wife
and rapes her sister, in the original theater production Stella remains
with him and her desire for him remains intact. In Stella's post-War role
as homebound wife, life can go on only if a place is cleared for Stanley
in the nuclear family and in the corporate structure and if depression
(economic and psychological) is averted.[88]

Williams remained ambivalent, however, about the proper role for
Stella in the final scene. Perhaps like the character Stella herself,
he could not decide whether the greater threat was to ignore the plight
of Blanche or to ignore the plight of Stanley.[89] As gendered characters,
their adversarial relationship is very real, but they are also mirrors of
one another.[90] Blanche's deviant and damaged sensuality renders her
irrecoverable as the symbol and the excuse of the Old South and unmar-
riageable in post-War social structures. The Old Girl's fate is sealed.
When the curtain closes, with or without Stella's support, Stanley's
fate in the New South of the American Century remains, however,
uncertain. Will his red-pajamaed sensuality, a desire even more untamed
than Blanche's, render him unfit as the style and the excuse for the new
era of big business?

While the nation dominated the international stage, its citizens in the
audience at home could not be sure that the blustering Stanley would
not soon become the lost voice in the big machine, the Willy Loman
Arthur Miller claims he first heard in Stanley.[91] In a 1946 study of GM,
Peter Drucker outlines what he asserts is the US political philosophy
guiding the expectation of workers at all levels. He proposes an appropriate position for the corporation as a *social* institution defined by that
philosophy. "American political philosophy stands on the Christian
basis of the uniqueness of the individual. From this follows (a) the
promise of justice . . . [i.e.], equal opportunity . . . [and] (b) the promise
of individual fulfillment, of the 'good life,' or, . . . the promise of status
and function as an individual." "[The corporation's] social function as a
community," Drucker insists, "is as important as its economic function
as an efficient producer"; the individual must attain social status and
satisfaction from being an employee, not just economic reward.[92]
Stanley, Stella tells us, is the one in his crowd who will get ahead.
Through bullying, he does rule his bowling team and even the poker
games. But will the Alfred P. Sloan of his company (Sloan was president
of GM through its years of explosive growth) give this kind of crude
leadership a place in management rather than just traveling salesman's
space on the road? Stanley and Stella may well think so. The uniqueness
of the individual is understood as a middle-class right, and nearly
everyone is middle class. In Drucker's analysis this means specifically

that US society is classless in the sense of equality of justice rather than in equality of rewards.[93]

Even Drucker admits, however, that this concept of equal justice manifests itself in such traits as deep resentment of anyone who "throws his weight around." Stanley, of course, resents Blanche and Stella too when they throw their class weight around. Stanley does not have their sort of formal education, the sort already being expected for corporate advancement.[94] Yet it is his literal weight, Brando's bulk relative to Jessica Tandy's and then Vivien Leigh's (Blanche's) small frame, that proves most overwhelming in the meantime.[95] In its assumption of class-less individuality, Drucker's theory does not address the insufficiency of space and place for everyone, woman and man, Negro and white—let alone Mexicans, Chinese, or new immigrant groups. The visual environment of the play, in contrast, announces the inadequacy of post-War space from the first humid scene to the last. Whose trinkets, whose costumes, whose sound, whose scent will dominate the small apartment? With the aid of Mielziner's set, which enabled *Streetcar's* audiences to see interior and exterior simultaneously, theatergoers could understand that this interior battle for space and place mirrored the post-War exterior battle in the factories between labor and management; in the neighbor-hoods, streetcars, and buses between Negroes and whites; and on the streets between fossil fuel vehicles and electric vehicles.[96] As the GM-National City Lines consortium demonstrated, the corporation's "social function as a community" did not include responsible public planning to help sustain all the individuals in these crowded social spaces.

After the play's first violent battle for space, the poker night when Stanley extricates his wife from her sister, he takes the car to get it greased. The car, offstage as is the streetcar, takes on pointed significance in this scene. When Stanley returns, "he stands unseen by the women. . . . He wears an undershirt and grease-stained seersucker pants." Although in the conversation he overhears Blanche trying to convince Stella that he is an animal, at the scene's end Stella "fiercely" embraces her grease-stained husband.[97] The women never ride in Stanley's car; Stanley does not offer to drive Blanche back to Laurel and thus get her out of his hair. The car here is neither a public nor a domestic space. Instead his individual success in his job, at least for now, rides on the fitness of his car that he believes he knows better than "them darn mechanics at Fritz's." Stanley's grease-covered pants tell us that he is not an animal; rather, he is "common," as he puts it, one of the blackened figures of history and literature who stoke the fires and oil the machinery. In defiance of the DuBois class status, he boldly demonstrates closer affinity to those unruly members of the Amalga-mated Association of Street Railway Employees than to the members of the growing, postindustrial, middle class that *Fortune* described or to the bare-armed Mayor Morrison. Yet this time the machine—the well-greased car—is his and with it the promise of status and of function as an individual within the social community of the corporation which employs him as a salesman, not as an industrial worker.

Although Blanche arrives in New Orleans via interstate and urban rail, Stanley proposes to get rid of her by buying her a bus ticket, a gesture Stella is sure will insult her sister: "In the first place, Blanche wouldn't go on a bus" (scene seven). As a willful display of power, Stanley presents the bus ticket to Blanche at her disastrous birthday party that the would-be suitor Mitch does not attend. Teasing her with the offer of a birthday gift, Stanley finally reveals what it is: "Ticket! Back to Laurel! On the Greyhound! Tuesday!" (scene eight). Blanche is devastated.[98] Until the boycotters and freedom-riders taught the nation that the bus was a raced battleground and the hippies made it magic, it lacked symbolic bearing. Without the century-long history of interurban and intraurban rail systems, without the individual private mobility that the car promised, and without an advertising and media discourse fueling consumer desire, the bus was only a negation—not archaic streetcars. It was the transportation of last resort.

Only Blanche speaks of the streetcar, even though the Perley 800/900s of the real French Quarter would have been as audible as the street vendors and the freight locomotive. She calls it the "rattle-trap street-car" (scene four) that "grinds along the tracks" (scene six), acknowledging its dilapidated post-War state. It is as worn as she fears herself to be, but the Desire car continues to "bang through the Quarter," even as a late owl car, just as Blanche's own desires have not stopped. She compares its "indiscourageable progress" to Stanley and Stella's sexuality, not her own, but it is she, not they, who is understood to be unmodern and therefore an inappropriate rider of desire. When Mitch confronts her about her sexual past, she asks him to grasp that her desire was an opposition to all of the old people's deaths at the family's crumbling plantation, Belle Reve (scene nine). She and the streetcars are not yet dead, but both have prematurely been declared obsolete. Although both Blanche and the streetcar lose their place in the Quarter, in their absence, the desire for some traditional domain that the streetcar represents and the desire for the streetcar itself continue to circulate. Neither Blanche nor the streetcar is utterly dead, but both are prematurely mourned so that Stanley and the car will seem the only possible ways forward and therefore the only problem requiring Stella's and the nation's energies. Williams does not throw Blanche under the freight train like Anna Karenina; the waste of her ongoing life and the remote possibility of her recovery are better left to haunt Stella and the perpetual present of the play's production. Even Stanley's displacement of Blanche, his temporary victory, has no meaning if Stella does not give it one. She and the audience must collude in his selfishness for him to go on, and even so there are odds against his success. He participates in the sense of corporate entitlement that spurred National City Lines/GM conspirators to change the face of US cities, but he cannot for long be comfortable inside the corporate system. Salesmen, too, are commodities, as theatergoers soon discovered when they met Arthur Miller's Willy Loman.

Remembering the Streetcar/Sustaining the Desire

In a recent *Blondie* cartoon, the child Elmo tells Dagwood that his Uncle Clyde has moved in with them until he gets a job. "What's his occupation?" Dagwood asks. When Elmo replies, "He sells used streetcars," Dagwood gives us a startled, knowing look.[99] Streetcars are the avatar of lost causes. This is the knowledge that the US public shares with Dagwood. If David Lowenthal is right when he asserts that cultural identity better coheres around suffering and loss than around success, then we have one explanation for the post-War triumph of Williams's play and the discursive power of its title.[100] When, in the 1980s, Jonathan Kwitny wanted forcefully to remind *Harper*'s readers of the damage done the nation by the 1947 City Lines/GM conspiracy, he played on their memories of the measure and meaning of Williams's title. To wrest the streetcar from that unrequited desire and name its conquerors, Kwitny called his article "The Great Transportation Conspiracy: A Juggernaut Named Desire."[101] Economist Don H. Pickrell inverted the title, calling his 1992 article "A Desire Named Streetcar" to direct criticism at cities' exploitation of federal funds for expensive, new intraurban rail lines and at the inadequate federal policy governing that funding.[102] But he imagines no object of desire except money. Although Pickrell and Kwitny finger very different culprits, the desire each sees is unambiguous greed. Yet even Pickrell's clean numerical argument does not fully restrain and contain the ambiguous desire named streetcar that his title elicits. Cities' ambitious plans for urban rail transportation cannot be explained simply by the availability of federal funds. (Nor can these plans' link to the traditional streetcar be easily explained.) His clever title exceeds his careful explanation.

It is not only Williams's title that has resonated through the decades. The stage and screen body of Brando has provided an indelible expression of post-War lost causes and rampant desires. Paul Connerton argues in *How Societies Remember* that "images of the past and recollected knowledge of the past . . . are conveyed and sustained by (more or less ritual) performances" by which, Connerton explains, he means decidedly embodied performances.[103] If we include within ritual performances, as Connerton does not, a dramatic performance on stage and screen as popular and powerful and repeated as Brando's Stanley, then one answer to our question, how did the elegiac streetcar of desire get into public memory, is through Brando's performance and Brando's body.[104] In the spirit of the American Century and the Truman Doctrine, Camille Paglia proclaims that, through Stanley, Brando's "bolts of barbaric energy . . . brought American nature to American acting . . . and American personality to the world."[105] With greater subtlety, Marianne Conroy maintains that as one of the first big successes of Method Acting, the scandal of Brando's Stanley, and its power,

> lay not in the style itself, but rather in its assertion that actors might formulate a public sphere of performance in which national cultural identity no longer assumed stable or homogeneous contours. In that sense, the significance of Method acting lies in its implicit argument that actors might intervene actively in the representation of a national culture confronted by the heterogeneity of its own identity and values.[106]

The barbaric yawp of Williams's, Kazan's, and Brando's Stanley is not Whitman's; his American identity promises no inclusiveness. Neither is it sustainable or immune to the management and ideology of obsolescence that doomed the streetcar and Blanche. Stanley is not the well-born young Mayor Morrison with his sleeves rolled up, however much each may be attempting to emulate the image of the other for their own ends. Stanley's loud insistent voice enacts the post-War contradictions of national growth and urban decline, of capitalist creation and destruction. Through his anger, he displays more vulnerability to the lost heritage of the DuBois' plantation Belle Reve than does Blanche, who was in Mississippi to watch the old people die and the columns crumble. Blanche's narrow, perfumed shoulders carry the unspoken guilt of the past—even though Williams has obscured the burden of slavery behind Blanche's obsession with her role in the suicide of her homosexual husband. Stanley bears the weight of a rationalist, capitalist plan for the indefinite future.

Pursuing an understanding of the United States's continued negotiations with the Lost Cause through its arguments over public monuments, Sanford Levinson forthrightly states that to commemorate is to take a stand.[107] When, in 1978, the Tourist Development Commission took the 1948 advice of the *Times-Picayune* editors and transferred ownership of the streetcar named Desire from their Commission to the Louisiana State Museum so they might position a restored, stationary streetcar beside the Old Mint when it reopened in 1983, the Commission

Figure 2.8 Brando's body selling A Streetcar Named Desire (Kobal)

knew that the streetcar had "an intimate association, both technological and literary, with the city of N.O."[108] The museum director agreed, emphasizing the Desire car's "provenance as a part of the New Orleans streetcar system which is now on the National Register and . . . its literary association."[109] But those intimate and ambivalent technological and literary associations—the streetcar's symbolic bearing so tied to New Orleans's urban ambiguity about modernism, to the region and nation's nostalgia for a Lost Cause to mourn, and to national fears of the progress of managed obsolescence—remained largely unarticulated, however powerfully implied.[110]

When, in 1987, the Riverfront Transit Coalition proposed to buy the stationary car from the strapped state museum so that "it would be completely refurbished and become an active, working streetcar reflecting the history of streetcar service in New Orleans," they saw a way to unite economic growth (through tourism) and historic preservation.[111] In this plan, the refurbished streetcar would represent its own comprehensible, albeit arrested, vehicular past and not the mournful irresolution of Williams's play. If a stand was being taken by the Coalition, it was a rational stand for a well-maintained history disassociated from guilt and from fears of uncertainty, decrepitude, obsolescence, and doom, a history as straight as the refurbished riverside tracks. In 2002, New Orleans Mayor Marc Morial went a step further, declaring, "We're returning to the future," as he described the city's plans to use $115 million from a hotel tax to construct a streetcar line called the Desire Corridor. The projected completion date was said to be 2007 or 2008. Claiming "this project works for history, [and] we'll get some cars off the street, get some emissions out of the air," Morial insisted it would not be a tourist attraction but rather sensible transportation for working people and visitors.[112] Postmodern reformist Morial asserted that even a simulacrum can be functional. History works for this project.

Yet memory is not history. "It bursts upon the scene in an unexpected manner . . . connecting disparate events . . . [through] surprise, ruptures, and overturnings. . . . Memory is above all an antimuseum" claims Boyer.[113] Williams's title continues to sound a death knell, yet Williams's play on film and in countless national and international productions ritually reenacts and evocatively remembers the contradictions and quotidian losses of that post-War present—among them, the streetcar named Desire. In the process, it destabilizes the context of obsolescence for the narrative of progress. Long after the interurban Freedom Train, "'re-selling Americanism to Americans,'"[114] pulled back into the station from which it came, audiences, American and not, have been riding round and round Old New Orleans on the *Streetcar Named Desire.*

Figure 2.9 The streetcar named Desire running through the Quarter and through public memory. (Historic New Orleans Collection, #1979.89.7500)

3

Sex and the Historic City

A Walking Tour on the Wild Side

In 1959, a business consultant named James C. Downs Jr. advised the New Orleans Chamber of Commerce to retain both history and honkytonks in its promotion of the Vieux Carré, but he warned them that this valuable economic asset could be "killed" by the excesses of either "history buffs" or the "entrepreneurs of sex and sin." Instead, it is the balance of the two, he said, that makes the Vieux Carré what it is: "the single largest day-in, day-out concentration of out-of-town visitors that exists anywhere in the United States," "a major factor in New Orleans reputation as one of the four most 'popular' convention cities in the nation," and an influence on decisions to locate regional and national offices in the city. The responses of a Vieux Carré Commission (VCC) spokesperson and of a Bourbon Street bar owner give credence to Downs's warning. The first claimed "we could clear out Bourbon St. from one end to the other and . . . [not] affect the French Quarter one-half of one per cent." The other retorted, "People don't come to New Orleans to see the buildings and antique shops; . . . they come to New Orleans to let their hair down."[1] By 1959, the French Quarter's reputation for the uneasy coexistence of historic preservation and vice—legal or illegal—had been decades, even centuries, in the making. At stake in that coexistence and its reputation are issues of land use complicated by competing stories about economic growth and social justice.

Many of those stories—informal, historical, nostalgic, or literary— are about prostitution. About the same time American novelist Nelson

Algren was first preoccupied with New Orleans prostitutes in 1931–1932, Walter Benjamin was following nineteenth-century French poet Charles Baudelaire in a similar preoccupation in Paris. In fact, Benjamin surmised out of Baudelaire that changes in the face of prostitution bear a central but ambivalent relation to the growth of the modern city, where "the rise of the masses has been . . . simultaneous with that of mass-production." Prostitutes, modern figures of thanatos rather than eros, his story goes, had become commodities subject en masse to wage labor, and yet "prostitution opens up the possibility of a mythical communion with the masses." As such, prostitution colorfully frames the labyrinthine character of the growing city even as the prostitute's body acts as a "hieroglyph" onto which the lost past has been unconsciously mapped. "The labyrinth, whose image had passed into flesh and blood in [that privileged, languorous male wanderer] the *flâneur*, is the correct route for those who always arrive at their goal early enough anyway. This goal is the market." However, prostitution, as I read Benjamin, not only frames the labyrinth, but also disposes of the conventional labyrinthine myth of the city in that the market goal of the labyrinth, the minotaur, is not just a force at the core that "should bring death to the individual." This individual death "is not crucial. What is really crucial is the image of the [broader] death-dealing forces which he embodies" and that prostitutes embody throughout the city geographically and socially.[2]

If Benjamin and Baudelaire can be asked thus to comment from the superstructure on Downs's advice about the base, the question is then posed: What occurs when sex and sin—specifically if indirectly acknowledged prostitution—together with historic preservation are expected to serve a New World city's economic well being? Does historic preservation act in opposition to the forces that convert a city such as Baudelaire's nineteenth-century Paris from a home into a modern showplace, a commodity character of things that only finds a human face on the whore? Political scientist Alexander Reichl argues that in the particular case of New Orleans, historic preservation was, indeed, one major force instrumental in delaying the formation of a local progrowth coalition until the 1980s, but the city's reputation for and sale of sex does not figure in his equation.[3]

This chapter explores the interaction of practices and representations of historic preservation and prostitution in New Orleans, understanding that the personal and social need for economic viability and the pressure for economic growth shape these two entities. The foundational questions given previously are part of the problem that underlies this analysis. These questions, provoked by Baudelaire and Benjamin, who see the prostitute as a recurring urban character, an image, a metonymy, are joined here by a social question provoked by a feminist scholar of prostitution, Barbara Meil Hobson, who sees the prostitute as a woman. If "to study prostitution is to confront a society's definition of social justice, its aims for equality between men and women," what becomes of this social justice in the struggle between historic preservation and the modern city?[4]

To cut these crucial but epic questions down to manageable size, this chapter brings together practices and representations of the Vieux Carré's historic preservation and vice, specifically prostitution, especially in the period from the 1930s through the 1950s. It was during this time that historic preservation of the Vieux Carré was given official sanction, and it was in this period that Chicagoan Algren—more self-styled hobo than flâneur—wrote two novels that provocatively represent prostitution and the underworld in the French Quarter. The first, *Somebody in Boots* (1935) is a little-remembered social realist project of a young author university-trained yet very close to the poverty, rail-riding, prison life he describes. It deserves a closer look.[5] The second, *A Walk on the Wild Side* (1956), rewrites *Somebody in Boots* as a farce and in the process hands New Orleans tourist industry a slogan some of its enterprises still used at the end of the century to perpetuate the city's reputation as a place for the virtuous to rub elbows, if not other body parts, with vice. Tracing the transformations of the Quarter and of Algren's fictional depictions of it, we see the dialectical relationship of the two activities. Both are acts of city making in a changing political climate. Both define the city out of its relationship to sexual vices. What gives credence to these broad claims is recognition that in literature as in life, the destination is, ironically, the ongoing process of negotiating the details of the labyrinth, as Benjamin describes the city. This is true even if the minotaur at the center of the labyrinth is, in fact, capitalism's market.

Preserving the Quarter, Prostituting Storyville

When Algren first entered New Orleans in late 1931 or early 1932, historic preservation and prostitution were both established traditions of the French Quarter. Already, in 1840, President Jackson's laying of the cornerstone for the monument in his honor was memorializing Place d'Armes as Jackson Square (although it also remained the site of a pillory for Negroes until 1847).[6] It did take the Creoles of the City's First Municipal District more than a decade to complete the statue. Nevertheless, the idea of the square as an exalted memorialized locale had been established by a portion of the local elite. At century's end, the Creoles' fortunes were receding and the physical environment of the Vieux Carré declining, reaching a particularly sorry state between the

1890s and the 1920s. But even in this period of decline, tourists were beginning to walk the Quarter's streets in pursuit of the places described in George Washington Cable and Lafcadio Hearn's stories. Contiguous Basin Street became another attraction in the new century.[7]

Recognizing the historic character of the *tout ensemble* that was the Quarter, Harland Bartholomew, in 1927, recommended to the city and its new Planning and Zoning Commission that they retain the narrow Quarter streets and send the (automobile) traffic around it.[8] Although the Vieux Carré was designed on a grid too geometrical to be described as a maze, the scale of the buildings with their courtyards and streets with their alleys created the kind of complex intimacy among strangers that Baudelaire (and Benjamin after him) recognized in the old neighborhoods of pre-Haussmannian Paris. By 1925, a Vieux Carré Association created by the city and devoted to promoting material progress and historical landmarks was already in place to encourage conclusions like Bartholomew's that, in this instance, ran against the grain of the suburbanizing US city. Such associations of history and progress flourished in the 1930s, culminating in a 1936 amendment to the Louisiana Constitution designating the Quarter as a historic district with special privileges and appointing the Vieux Carré Commission as a special body to enforce the exercise of those privileges.[9] Thrilled by this degree of public government control over private property, James J. A. Fortier, President of the Louisiana State Museum, exalted, "We have created a new power in America, something tremendous." All Europe has it, he declared, and in a generation or two it will be the law of the land in the United States.[10]

The VCC was quick to exercise its power over the built structures of the Quarter, requiring permits for all building-related activity and encouraging property owners who could not afford to keep their properties "safe" to sell out to those who could. But, their ordinances announced, they had no jurisdiction over the neighborhood's people.[11] In response to a question in March 1937, the VCC explained that the constitutional amendment gave it no legal power, for example, over beggars in the Quarter.[12] Nevertheless, there were ample ordinances, some of them from the nineteenth century, to control the behavior of Quarter denizens: the kind and placement of vendors, the sale of alcohol, the volume of live music and jukeboxes, and the painting of portraits—no caricatures of the tourists, please.[13] Beyond this, the VCC leadership sometimes privately admitted to explicit surveillance of the people through its assiduous monitoring of the area. In the early 1950s, for example, the VCC leaders asked the mayor and the chief of police to intervene in the "indecent" mixing of "colored and white" at an establishment on St. Philip and to protect the public from the "unnatural" behavior of young men at a barroom on Burgundy.[14]

Whether or not the city—especially the Quarter and its edges—was "open" or "closed" to the practice of prostitution depended not on the VCC per se but principally on the inclinations of the governor, the mayor, and the chief of police. This said, the politician's name most remembered in conjunction with New Orleans prostitution is Alderman Sidney Story. In 1897, at his instigation, the New Orleans city government enacted another in a series of prostitution laws and established more constricted boundaries for a legal prostitution district.[15] In the process, ironically, they created what became one of the most famous segregated sex districts in the world, Storyville. This subsequently prosperous district, contiguous to the Quarter, was famously closed in 1917 by the Secretary of the Navy above the protests of the city and its mayor. What is less well known is the look of Basin Street before and after Tom Anderson was its unofficial mayor and the *Blue Book* was its directory of residents selling sexual favors. Similarly, the folkways of Storyville—often linked, however controversially, to the foundations of jazz—overshadow the significant and evolving sex business in the Quarter, just down the street. These practices and representations that are always producing and reproducing the space of the Quarter both identify and complicate what New Orleans was selling through the Vieux Carré in 1959 that so impressed Downs. By studying them together, we can begin to understand the role the prostitute plays in imagining this evolving city of preserved neighborhoods.

Narrating Prostitution

Two informal histories, Herbert Asbury's *The French Quarter: An Informal History of The New Orleans Underworld* (1936) and Christine Wiltz's *The Last Madam: A Life in the New Orleans Underworld* (2000) broaden the geographic and historical frame of the Storyville saga. Asbury describes two periods of prostitution, one following on the heels of the other. Not concerned with the notorious immigrant prostitutes from the French colonial period, Asbury stipulates that the first period of prostitution was from US acquisition of the city in 1803 until 1833 and was a low-class trade catering to the flatboat men. The second began in the 1840s, when, Asbury declares, all New Orleans government was corrupt. Prostitution was entrenched in city government in New Orleans as it was in other cities.[16] It developed above Canal Street but was pushed into the Vieux Carré as the American Sector (above Canal) grew in size and strength. Asbury repeats the refrain, "The authorities made no attempt to halt the march of the harlots into the fine residential areas [in the Creole district below Canal], despite the ruinous effect upon real estate and the complaints of hundreds of property-owners who were forced by the proximity of boisterous brothels to abandon their homes."[17] Brothels, Benjamin observes, were never part of Baudelaire's literal or allegorical vision of prostitution. Prostitutes define his labyrinthine city only from the street.[18] They do not compete with the bourgeoisie for landed property as Asbury's New Orleans madams do. Prostitution within the city, feared by New Orleanians, in Asbury's telling, is not a mythical or allegorical or even a marginal activity.

Beginning at least as early as 1817, Asbury records, a series of New Orleans laws was enacted; they were designed principally to control the behavior of streetwalkers but also prostitutes housed in neighborhoods. Now, a harlot was subject to punishment if she occasioned scandals or disturbed the neighborhood, and a landlord could be fined for renting to such a girl. In 1837, a petition with the signatures of three "respectable" citizens could solicit the mayor to evict a prostitute from any premises. The Vieux Carré, in 1839, prohibited prostitutes from occupying the ground floor of a building. An 1845 law prohibited prostitutes drinking in any coffeehouse or cabaret. These vagrancy and nuisance laws were used primarily to bring in recurring revenues by fining madams ($25) and girls ($10). So to curtail this exploitation as well as prostitution itself, an 1857 ordinance tried to legalize sex for sale in four specific geographic districts—if it was housed above the street level. However, this law was declared unconstitutional two years later.[19]

Ignoring his own evidence about city government corruption throughout the nineteenth century, Asbury concludes that it was permissiveness during Reconstruction that brought the city to the verge of ruin. By 1870, he declares, New Orleans had a population of 190,000 and a $10 bordello or 15¢ Negro crib on virtually every block, "except in the outlying parts of the city." A letter to the *New Orleans Times* of September 22, 1870, from a Basin Street homeowner who signed himself "Suffering Property Holder," serves Asbury particularly well because it specifically describes Basin Street (later the Main Street of Storyville) as a neighborhood of handsome mansions under siege from the encroaching bordellos. Asbury ratchets up his rhetoric: "[Basin] lay directly in the path of the prostitutes when they started their northward and eastward movement from Tchoupitoulas and the Swamp."[20] Hardly figures of evolving modernity, Asbury's prostitutes here emerge from pre-Columbian history and the primordial ooze to engage, nevertheless, in a modern capitalist competition for prime location. Most were, in fact, poor people pushed from New Orleans's American sector (and the United States generally) as it gained wealth and toward the Creole Quarter as its wealth declined. But this is not a class analysis of diaspora and land use that engages Asbury in his Depression-era, Jim Crow reading of New Orleans underworld.

Instead, Asbury implies that it is racial promiscuity that enables sexual promiscuity. Rather than focusing on the economic struggles of post-War New Orleans, he describes with thinly veiled contempt the consorting of a "black-and-tan Senator" of the Reconstruction legislature with the women at a "mulatto resort"; or the Negro prostitutes of Smoky Row on Burgundy, in the Quarter, grabbing and rolling men and fighting among themselves; or the mixing of white women and negresses in French Quarter bordellos along Dauphine and Burgundy that were patronized by men of all races and classes. Even the scandal sheets were scandalized, he reports.[21] That some of this took place in the 1850s and some in the 1880s does not alter Asbury's conclusion derived from the attitude of the local white press. In fact, the frontispiece of his book is of the White League riots of 1874, an effort his informal history admires for its attempts to restore its version—that is to say, white supremacist version—of racial and class respectability to New Orleans even as it reports on its complicity in continuous political corruption.

Prostitution and miscegenation together inhabit Asbury's New Orleans underworld. He repeats the stories about New Orleans voodoo icon Marie Laveau, herself a woman of mixed race, as an antebellum and postbellum procurer of quadroon and octoroon women for wealthy white men. Fellow informal historian Robert Tallant retells the story that she was also a madam, a "landlady" running the "white house" for wealthy white clients.[22] Storyville, another icon of the city, was also a site where, to the strains of Jelly Roll Morton's piano, prostitution and miscegenation imaginatively if not always physically cohabited. Despite his concern for 1870s white homeowners on Basin Street, Asbury came to believe that in becoming the most celebrated (and legal) red-light district in the United States, Storyville and its "Main Street" Basin, in its heyday, had replaced Congo Square and the quadroon balls as a unique attraction of the city. (The first was the recreation site of slaves and the latter, the high-toned market of young, mixed race women—ostensibly free women of color—for the consumption of wealthy white men.[23]) What Asbury does not say is that race played a role in the setting of Storyville's boundaries, it being understood that prostitution would do the least harm to New Orleanians' respectability if it were located in primarily African American sectors. Within the Storyville boundaries was, for example, the Union Chapel, a substantial African American church, and there was afoot a proposal to move a predominant African American school from Esplanade to within the Storyville boundaries.[24]

In July 1917, just before the forced closing of Storyville by the Navy, the New Orleans City Council adopted an ordinance to clean up the neighborhood, thus hoping to appease reformers but save Storyville.[25]

"Clean up" meant ordering African American and mixed-race prostitutes into a segregated Negro prostitution district just above Canal, but the Navy intervened before this more "modern" American, segregationist approach to race and sex really took effect. Because some of the prominent madams of Basin Street were women of mixed race or claimed to be for the sake of business, and because the Franklin Street area above Canal to which they were being ordered was understood to be the lowest sex district—that is, also mixed race, but far from respectable white people—the change was difficult to institute in any case.[26]

For Asbury, Storyville was the answer to the most prominent threat posed by prostitution: the one to New Orleans property owners by a diasporic, racially mixed population with insufficient respect for single family homes and middle-class mores. In the late nineteenth century,

> as a result of New Orleans's almost universal reputation as the promised land of harlotry, hundreds of prostitutes flocked into the city from all parts of the United States, attended by the "fancy men" and other male parasites who fattened upon the shame of their fallen sisters. . . . The day when a New Orleans family might awaken any morning to find that the house next door had been transformed into a bordello ended with the adoption of the Story ordinance and didn't return until Storyville was abolished.[27]

Asbury does not further observe that Storyville compromised the lives and property of respectable African Americans living in what became the Storyville neighborhood before the city designated it a prostitution zone. Nor does he acknowledge that middle- or upper-class male demand for prostitution services in a sufficiently high-toned brothel setting drove the transformation of the "house next door" into a sex business enterprise.

Wiltz's more recent informal history reports that Norma Badon Wallace, the so-called last madam of New Orleans, entered the "life" in the city in 1916 as a fifteen-year-old and soon set up practice in a house at 410 Dauphine in the Quarter. In Wallace's telling, the Storyville segregated sex district did not control prostitution in the Quarter. Instead, a Quarter district called the Tango Belt in honor of that popular dance operated alongside Storyville, amidst cabarets and theaters, between Iberville and St. Louis, Rampart and Bourbon. If seedier than Storyville—at least before the push for historic preservation—it was nonetheless economically viable albeit threatened by prohibition in 1919 and Huey Long's assault on "landladies" in 1928.[28] In response to the presence of Governor Long's state militia, between 1930 and 1932, Wallace closed the Dauphine house, but, in 1936, as the Louisiana

Constitution was naming the French Quarter a special historic district, Algren was lamenting the critical reception of *Boots*, Asbury was publishing his history of the New Orleans underworld, and Bourbon Street was replacing Storyville as the site of sex sale, Wallace's business was flourishing again in the new administration of Robert Maestri.[29] "With Bob Maestri mayor and George Reyer chief of police [and Huey Long dead], the town was as wide open as at any time in its history."[30]

In the 1930s, as Wallace pursued affairs with an entertainment celebrity and a Chicago mobster and married a local business associate in the "life," she prospered. Successful in the underworld and even outside it, she bought the former house of now-famous prostitute photographer Ernest Bellocq at 1026 Conti in the Quarter and renovated it in accord with the historic restoration movement promoted by the VCC. She later remembered the 1937 threat to the French Quarter as urban renewal and low-income housing developments, not, of course, bordellos.[31] In fact, much of the former Storyville, outside the preservation district of the Quarter, was razed in the 1940s to make way for public housing.[32] By the end of the twentieth century, only two buildings remained.[33]

Wallace succeeded in a nation that had no consistent regulatory system for prostitution and thus no sanitary controls. Tacit tolerance within cities throughout the United States facilitated political and police graft and irregular raids, all of which served to line the pockets of city officials and pimps as protector.[34] The military's campaign to close explicit sex districts such as Storyville, the "most overt since classical Piraeus," only increased the power of the pimps during and after World War I.[35] For it not only intensified the uncertainty of an illegal life without a territorial refuge, but it also transformed the image of prostitutes from "white" slave victims to predatory, diseased whores wholly to blame for prostitution. The federal military campaign goaded city governments to act against this public health menace, stressing that any poorly dressed, unescorted woman on the streets should be detained, incarcerated, and examined without consent. Before the war, thinking about sex commerce involved economic, social, and political questions, if also substantial moral righteousness, but after World War I, the discussion narrowed to the "inherited traits, criminal tendencies and psychological disorders" of the prostitute—and remained that way for the next forty years.[36]

Wallace succeeded in New Orleans because she maintained, almost uninterrupted, a house-based business in the French Quarter. There, she taught her girls how to examine clients for venereal disease, controlled the ambiance of her historical house and thus the prices and the clients, and entered into an alliance with a male bar owner who acted as partner and lookout. In her telling, pimps figure less prominently as the heads of "families" who control their girls. Instead Wallace was the teacher of her employees and the protector of her house—protector of its business, its sex workers, and its architectural character.[37] Even if in her seventies a marriage to a man decades her junior was her emotional undoing, throughout her life she had never been escorted quietly off the stage because of unsanctioned sexual liaisons. When she was infrequently arrested, in 1952–1953, for example, it was front-page news. In old age, she was offered a key to the city.[38]

The story of Wallace's success as a madam stands in telling contrast to the lives of many New Orleans prostitutes. The folk song "Rising Sun Blues" is not *Les Fleurs du Mal*, but it tells a critical story in a song Algren listened to over and over as he rewrote *Somebody in Boots* as *A Walk on the Wild Side*. [39] Some say it was "composed when New Orleans was the prostitution capital of the South" and made popular in the 1940s through Libby Holman's version.[40] But the melody has roots in a seventeenth-century British ballad that Alan Lomax names "Lord Barnard and Little Musgrove." And rising sun as a symbol for brothels appeared in British and US ballads. Still, Lomax pronounces the song "unique." In the liner notes for a Roy Acuff classic collection, John W. Rumble, senior historian with the Country Music Foundation in Nashville, claims the ballad circulated among both black and white southern musicians. The first known recording of "Rising Sun Blues" is by black bluesman Texas Alexander in 1928, followed by Roy Acuff in 1938, and in 1941 by the Almanac Singers—Woody Guthrie, Peter Hawas, Millard Lampell, and Pete Seeger—for an album called Sod Buster Ballads. Lomax first heard and recorded it in Middlesborough, Kentucky, in 1937 sung, poignantly, by a "thin, pretty, yellow-headed miner's daughter."[41] If it is not now remembered as recorded by Bob Dylan, it is remembered, ironically, in the voice of a male character as performed by the Animals. The ballad's more traditional female persona laments

There is a house in New Orleans

They call the Rising Sun

It's been the ruin of many poor girls,

And me, O Lord, for one.

. . . One foot is on the platform,

The other one on the train,

I'm going back to New Orleans

To wear that ball and chain.

A girl would have reason to see herself as a prisoner in a house of "cribs" such as those owned by a major city official in the 1930s and rented to prostitutes for $10 a day.[42] The legal system of the post-Storyville era in which Wallace managed to flourish primarily targeted streetwalkers and such low-class houses. Special courts for prostitutes requiring little evidence, tolerating frequent entrapment, and doling out indeterminate sentences were a national norm.[43] If poor women entered prostitution in the period to avoid the role of servant or a miner's daughter, to try their luck in the city, or to find the cash to purchase the consumer goods they were making in factories but could not afford, many found the rules of the "life" hard to live by, especially as enforced by an "old man" (pimp) rather than an "old lady" (madam) such as Wallace.[44]

Algren Narrates the Wild Side

Nelson Algren's *Somebody in Boots* was published as part of a series about "how misery lives." He dedicates this first novel to "the homeless boys of America," not the girls, yet sexual degradation—prostitution central within it—functions as a barometer of misery.[45] When protagonist Cass McKay's beloved elder sister, Nancy, falls from starvation through humiliation into prostitution, in a series of beautifully rendered scenes of melodrama, Cass can neither forgive her nor himself. If poverty and a jobless, violent father are the cause of his leaving home, the loss of Nancy's gentle voice and sexual virtue are the very definition of homelessness from which he suffers throughout the novel. That voice rises through Christianity into madness before passing over into sexual solicitation.

> Cass had heard [Nancy] sing hymns a thousand time, but never before sheerly out of pain [from starvation]—he tried to close his ears to the shrill madness of her voice.
>
> *"Have you been to Jesus for the cleansing power?"*. . .
>
> [Nancy] paused in the pathway; and her voice changed, till it was like a quick whispering there.
>
> "Y'all kin come in fo' a dolla'," she said in that flat hard whispering [not realizing she is addressing her brother], 'a pahty cost but a dolla'. Hev y'all got a dolla', fella?'"[46]

Without Nancy's voice of virtue, Cass can no longer imagine a childhood home from his place on the road, in the boxcar, or in the prison cell.

That home was in Mexican-town in the Rio Grande Valley. Although Algren, with Studs Terkel, may have seemed, at the end of his life, a Chicago monument as established as the Water Tower, "the driving force behind all [his] work began in Texas."[47] There, from hobo camps and boxcars, he not only first observed his own radicalism in stark contrast to a conservative country and learned, in the Brewster County Jail, how a racial pecking order worked to the terror of most inmates, but he also learned what a borderland means. There the folk of two cultures and languages meet and mix with intermittent communication, frequent scapegoating, and sometime sexual comingling. There the frontier ends, the boom town grows, and the underclass of all races—recognizing their places on the racial pecking order—remain in desperation even as their mingling day to day offers the opportunity of something else. Cass's beginning in the Texas borderland of the 1920s instructs Algren's reader (if not his naive hero) to see this cultural confluence in the cities Cass runs to: New Orleans, then Chicago.[48]

As the freight Cass rides nears New Orleans, he cannot sleep for thinking of tattoo parlors and showhouses and whorehouses "with Creole gals" on every corner, or thousands of people, towering buildings and roaring streetcars. Instead the train enters the city through Gretna on the West Bank, where he sees Negro one-story shacks "much like his own had been." When the shacks give way to cottages but the occupants are still Negroes, Cash brags to his white companion that they have "lynchin bees" at home to keep the population of "jigs" down. His companion concurs that they are on the road because "niggers have all the jobs." Yet, as Cass wanders uptown and downtown, seeing poverty and wealth, only the poor houses of Negroes look like home to him. And the prostitute who lures him into her crib reminds him of the "dark girls" at the Pablona Cafe in his Mexican town, even though she is pale. Unable to pay her the wage she demands, naively imagining some bartering other than a strict wage transaction, Cass receives a beating at the hands of her pimp that scars his face for life.[49] The minotaur of the market in the labyrinth of the city—even the city known by tramps to be the cheapest in the nation—discards Cass in a trash heap.[50] Believing he is weak because his father is poor, his brother sick, his sister ragged, his mother dead, and because he lives in Mexican-town, he returns to the freight in Gretna that takes him back to his home in Texas.[51] New Orleans, which extends prostitution and a beating in welcome, is ringed round by Negro strangers who define the place as Mexicans define home. They frame and punctuate the city, and prostitution lies at the core of the New Orleans Cass can enter. Negroes and prostitutes are Cass's social equals and his other. Back at home, Cass watches a Negro witness tell in his own words the story of a white boy murdering his brother. For bearing witness in public, the Negro is "dragged through the streets behind an automobile and burned."[52] Rather than being the glittering respite, the sensual escape from Mexican-town, New Orleans is part and parcel of the brutality that governs the Texas Valley. In Mexican-town, Cass joins the "life" as a pimp procuring for the whore Pepita at the Poblano Cafe. "1928–29 was a good winter for the tourist trade."[53]

New Orleans reenters the novel with Charlotte Hallem, a young black widow, whose female voice undermines her male disguise put on for the boxcar life that Cass too has reentered. When she confesses to her male fellow travelers that her destination is New Orleans, the city's reputation for prostitution—explicitly the lowest tier racialized prostitution of Franklin Street—is called on to excuse the men's rape of her before the city's name is barely out of her mouth. "'Whoops! She's a-goin' to Noo Awlins to work on *Franklin* Street—Step right up, gen-lment, meet Charlotte, the little travellin' girrul. Which way y'll taken it t'night, gen'lmen?'" Over and over then the men sing the hymn *Long, Long Ago* "but with evil words." Distracted only by the need to burn themselves out of a locked boxcar, once in the open, the men again taunt the woman with proposals of "marriage" and then trap her. The scene ends with the narrative voice saying from some distant orb, "they were men without women." Specifically, they were poor white men confronted with a poor, lone, black woman headed for New Orleans. Algren's own data of race and place make clear the significance of those details. "'White! White! Ma Joe you burnt!'" the widow shouts as they push her to the ground.[54]

Even for the bumbling Cass, barking for burlesque becomes a sell he can imitate. At the novel's close, he is in Chicago, a barker for a burlesque with a white troupe and a black, a place where his lost love Nora once worked. There, in the manner of Dos Passos, Algren mixes Cass's barking with the speeches of President Roosevelt and Mayor Kelly at Chicago's 1933–1934 World's Fair, which was themed "A Century of Progress."[55] Although the politicians' pandering for big business may be the minotaur in the city's labyrinth and the market the goal of the maze, Algren's underworld characters are not headed toward that goal and Cass's sale of sex does not position the prostitute to frame the labyrinth. Instead Nora, a prostitute, is lost to him in that maze. Dill Doak, a black entertainer—part Paul Robeson and part Richard Wright—tries to guide Cass toward a communist vision of equality for all workers, with prostitutes most equal of all. He even takes Cass to the fair as an object lesson, but Cass is only awed by the spectacle. He is the passive cultural tourist in the making. When Cass says to Dill, "'Noo Awlins—that's my town. Lots of life, lots of pep, an' that's what ah go for. Ah kin have a bigger time on six bits down there than ah can on two bucks up here.'" Doak replies, "'New Orleans is a sewer. The South is a sink and cities like that are its sewers. . . . Don't you think it's a sign of decay when women can be *bought?*"[56] Before Doak explains fully how the hustling in New Orleans differs from that in Chicago, his influence is undermined by Nub O'Neill, the principal bully of Cass's prison experience, who resurfaces to remind Cass of the racial hierarchy and thus the prison ethics that run the underworld even on the outside. Doak is thus abandoned. Nub's brutality is an extension of Cass's father's as Nora's gentleness is an extension of sister Nancy's. In the absence of the latter—lost again to prostitution—Cass falls victim to the former, unable to think his way toward the position of Doak or any other coherence. Death-dealing forces of prostitution, narrowly and broadly defined, lie around the city, not just at explicit sites of the market. His barking is in a separate, parallel universe to the promotion at the World's Fair. With it, he does not put a human face on the shanty dwellers outside the walls of the Fair's "Rainbow City" nor gain them an invitation to go inside to see the Fair's fan dancer Sally Rand or what scientific discovery has done for industry and living conditions.[57] His is only an invitation to be transfixed by the sex show, any show, as he was when he first saw burlesque in Louisiana.[58]

The reviewer for *The New Republic* said Algren's Cass was too "weak, inept and sheerly dumb to live."[59] Reading retrospectively, however, it is clear that the novel's many strong scenes of horror, gleaned from Algren's own boxcar travels, are building toward the spleen he let loose in his Chicago books, *Neon Wilderness, Never Come Morning, The Man with the Golden Arm*, in an unpublished novel in a prostitute's voice that he called "Entrapment," and in the farce *A Walk on the Wild Side*. In *Boots*, Algren learned that the "undeserving" poor is his subject and the moneyed classes are off his stage but not off his mind. No meteoric rise for sister Carrie in Algren. No Tom Joad off to speak for the masses with Ma's blessing. Full of folk materials, *Boots* does not turn away from the cruelty of those folk toward one another (Steinbeck) or turn back toward the author himself as a troubled, educated observer of that cruel life (Agee).

Algren's evolving vision of the folk of the urban underworld is one of the central features in the transformation from *Boots* to *Wild Side*. It is also central to the ways New Orleans, that "sewer of the South," is made the principal locale in *Wild Side*. It is central to this chapter's analysis of the relationships among prostitution, historic preservation, and the city of modern progress in the New Orleans of the mid-twentieth century.

By the time Algren published his famous Chicago novel, *The Man with the Golden Arm*, in 1949, he understood the message about prostitution and the underworld folk that he wanted to convey to his middle-class readers. From Alexander Kuprin's *Yama, or The Pit*, a novel set in a Kiev whorehouse, Algren adopted the epigraph for *Golden Arm*. "Do you understand, gentlemen, that all the horror is in just this, that there is no horror!"[60] Those in the "philistine routine" do not recognize as extraordinary the daily devastation in the lives of those who are Algren's subject. When Benjamin writes "that things 'just go on' *is* the catastrophe," he provides a link between Kuprin's declaration and the development of the modern city and a means to distinguish his well-known image of the *flâneur* from the position of Algren. "The concept of progress is to be grounded in the idea of [this] catastrophe. . . . That Baudelaire was hostile to progress was an indispensible condition of his being able to cope with Paris in his poetry." Where the city is seen as "the seat of progress," poetry is feeble. Algren, not so much hostile to progress per se, observes instead that there is no progress for the underclass. There is only recalcitrant if geographically shifting uneven development. Yes, perhaps "redemption looks to the small fissure in the ongoing catastrophe," but while Benjamin implies that this is redemption for the poet or philosopher for whom the whore is an allegory, for Algren redemption for the prostitute or the drug addict as social subjects is the issue and he finds little opportunity for this.[61] His epigraph to *Golden Arm* addresses the gentlemen of the philistine routine, but his novels' lens is consistently, relentlessly, that of the pimp, the prostitute, the gambler, and the addict. Between 1935, when he failed to win the audience he had wanted for *Boots,* and the early 1950s when he was rewriting the novel, a series of events, personal and political, literary and urban, local and national, altered how he would speak for the underclass. In *Wild Side*, he would try to make a dent in the middle class.[62]

Algren became a writer, he said in 1964, because of

> all the whores in New Orleans.... All these thousands of little scenes—sitting around a little kitchen in New Orleans with three other guys trying to sell something .... All these scenes, one after another, piled up into something that made me not just want to write but to really say ... that this thing was all upside down. I'd been assured that it was a strive and succeed world .... You had to reverse everything from what you'd been taught, mechanically as well as morally.[63]

He later also learned from his travels that "we've changed from a first-person to a third-person country."[64] Whereas decolonizing Africans were learning, at mid-century, that they were people, Americans ceased to speak out of their own humanity. The writer, in particular, had been assimilated by business—Hollywood, advertising—becoming its whore, a modern wage whore without the underworld promiscuity that, for Baudelaire, was a worthy alternative to philistine routine.[65]

Algren was bitter about his own early 1950s experiences with the business of Hollywood, specifically in the person of director Otto Preminger, and took every opportunity to complain about Preminger's acquisition of and film of *Golden Arm* and the money he, Algren, had been cheated out of.[66] "*The Golden Arm* movie was used to make [the novel's] cry of anguish something that could be sung on a jukebox, that Sinatra could perform to."[67] But the transformation that registered in his New Orleans fiction between the 1930s and the 1950s was more than the result of personal bitterness. And it was different from a nostalgia for the social realism or naturalism of the 1930s. Algren might agree halfway with Michael Denning that "if the Proletcult died, it was killed by the WPA and Hollywood," but he was less concerned with that particular political and cultural death than with the task of articulating the recalcitrant position of the addict, the whore, and the homeless in a changing US society.[68] When Algren writes in *Boots*, "by the winter of 1931 Cass knew that disaster had come to the world above him," he announces already that his subject is not the Depression and his mode is not documentation of that era.[69] His subject is the world below that continues to exist whether or not disaster and dystopia comes to the world above.

In an early 1950s book-length essay, originally titled "A Walk on the Wild Side," Algren offers his understanding of the changes to the literary and political nation he inhabited. Senator Joe McCarthy figures early and prominently for his well-known "pretense and piety" and for his lesser-known bilking of an airline. Beside him is the press corps "warning me that I better stop saying *Ouch* when McCarthy gives the screw another turn—lest the Kremlin overhear my yip and tape-record it for rebroadcasting to Europe." Gum and detergent promotion, spiritual desolation and fear, all that lies "between pretense and piety, between the H Bomb and the A" accumulate in the essay, pointing to the conclusion that "by packaging Success with Virtue, we make of failure a moral defeat." In response, he exhorts writers to live submerged in an alley, to report life from behind the billboards, to act as underworld guides to "Americans [who] do not like to think that such extremes [as ugliness and beauty, the grotesque and the tragic, and even good and evil] can mingle."[70]

In 1953, after the Rosenbergs were executed, Playboy bunnies appeared on the scene to sanitize sexuality of infectious desire, and Doubleday rejected Algren's "Wild Side" essay perhaps because they thought it too hot to touch, he had reason to turn even more toward the grotesque comedy that had served him well in parts of *Golden Arm*. He could pursue a voice, if not quite a fully realized form, that cut across the identification of success with virtue and failure with moral defeat, a voice that pulled the binaries apart to throw them together again without any pattern that could be called progress. The revision of *Boots,* for all its financial necessity—as Algren repeatedly wrote his lover Simone de Beauvoir—was also an opportunity to write a big book.[71] In it he could take on the superciliousness of the age and mingle the grotesque and the tragic. Mimicking with irony the denizens of the Playboy Club, he could perform as though he had "stopped walking in the first person and started walking in the third. When he got the hang of that, he could find himself *thinking* in the third person instead of the first."[72]

Later, Algren would insist, more than once, that it was *Wild Side,* not *Golden Arm,* the winner of the first National Book Award, that was his best book. Sometimes being supercilious rather than enacting superciliousness, *Wild Side* can be difficult for a reader to admire, even de Beauvoir.[73] But as a literary production, it was a precursor to Joseph Heller's *Catch 22* and Terry Southern's *Magic Christian,* as Algren rightly claimed. That Ralph Ellison's *Invisible Man* (1952) and even Richard Wright's *Savage Holiday* (1954) were *its* precursors is a condition of cultural heritage that Algren, however, did not recognize or did not acknowledge. Ellison understood very well how the grotesque and the tragic cohabit, how one needs to enact supercilious speech in the face of evil superciliousness. If Algren's friend Wright and his agent had seen *Savage Holiday* as a similar satire and not as a Freudian case study, it too could have provided a worthy companion to *Wild Side.* But for all the telling racial details in the folk material collected for *Boots,* Algren, the writer renowned for his depiction of white ethnics in Chicago, did not fully recognize his walk on the wild side of New Orleans as a racial story in a context of mode-shifting, yoke-slipping underworld stories.[74] Instead, the novel more obviously steps in to attempt the critique of national politics and mass media and artistic degradation that its namesake essay was prevented from saying (all this while Algren was being denied a passport to leave the country because of his support of the Rosenbergs).[75] And it locates this critique in New Orleans. As a New Orleans book, the novel and its inherited title are a constitutive part of the old city's reputation for prostitution in a mass media age when New Orleans's Bourbon Street was remaking Storyville as sexual nostalgia for tourists.

Given that more of *Boots* occurs in Chicago than New Orleans, and Chicago was the place Algren staked as his necessary artistic territory, it is curious, on the face of it, that he wrote *Wild Side* as a New Orleans novel. But not so curious when looking behind the face of glib despair that the aging Algren liked to wear. Reading W.J. Cash's 1941 classic *The Mind of the South* provided Algren an economic analysis of what he had witnessed in Texas and New Orleans, North Carolina, and other points south while riding the rails, hitchhiking the roads, and walking the Quarter's streets in the early 1930s.[76] If New Orleans was the cheapest place to be a hobo, it was a fact tied to the preposterously low wages of the Southern working poor, lower than Northern workers would accept. The city was also a near neighbor to the brutality, conservatism, and borderland complexity of Texas, which Algren experienced again in his Army training days.[77] While in post-War Chicago white ethnics were engaged in house-to-house combat with Negroes seeking a decent place to live, Algren pulled away from their story and turned south again to retell stories of streets he had walked twenty years earlier. There he could exploit the city's reputation for prostitution and cheap (literally) thrills. There, in the old city, he could locate his own youthful memories while reconsidering the meaning of the sink in the sewer. There, he just might find the kind of financial and critical success that he craved and that Tennessee Williams achieved in the late 1940s and early 1950s out of his New Orleans material. An admirer of theater generally and Williams and *Streetcar* in particular, Algren had reason to reconsider his own New Orleans material in light of Williams's success.[78]

He did revisit New Orleans briefly in 1948 when he and de Beauvoir traveled down the Mississippi and then to Mexico and Guatemala and again, alone, in 1954. The second time he sought a feel for the place as he struggled to rewrite the book, but, at the time, he only complained that it had changed for the worse, becoming crassly commercial.[79] Yet he stayed with the city in his book. The changing modern city, together with the New Orleans scenes sustained in his memory, provided him insight into a 1950s America fluctuating between pretense and piety.

Patrolling the Historic Wild Side

As Algren was reworking his 1930s memories in the 1950s, the brothels that had once threatened Basin and other genteel downtown streets were struggling through their last decade. They would soon be replaced by clandestine call girls, who could turn a profit as Wallace's workers had done but without the house security. In 1956, a prostitute complained to an undercover investigator for the American Social Hygiene Association working in cooperation with the military, "You can't believe how rough this town got to be." Says one madam of long standing, "I've been run off the 1600 block" of Royal because of complaints of neighbors. "Once upon a time my neighbors would're screamed their heads off [instead of complaining to the VCC or other city authorities?]. . . . Today things are different." A survey of bars and nightclubs may have found "very few unescorted females on hand," but, as always, somewhere, moving surreptitiously, there were the streetwalkers, those palimpsests of the city's past strolling the border of pretense and piety.[80] As the houses closed in New Orleans (and in other US cities), more prostitutes sought clients in streets, or cars, even more dangerous places of assignation for them than cribs or cheap hotels.[81]

Norma Wallace, the so-called "last madam," remembers that after Chep Morrison was first elected mayor in 1946, there were new ordinances requiring mandatory jail terms for prostitutes and a commission on vice was created. Still, police corruption continued. Morrison was a "master of doubletalk," Wallace claimed.[82] For his part, Morrison was motivated by the outrage that followed such incidents as the death of Nashville contractor Robert E. Dunn in January 1950 in a French Quarter bar. Dunn's death and other "Mickey Finn" cases elicited the argument that "B-girls, . . . sidewalk barkers, and call girls who infested the French Quarter" "endangered the local populace and hurt the tourist trade." In March of that same year Morrison created a "citizens' committee to investigate crime in the French Quarter" that included Vieux Carré property owners. Among them, it turned out, was the owner of the bar where Dunn had died. Although it seemed the Quarter was "in the throes of a well-publicized cleanup, . . . actually, the police made token arrests" only. As it happened, Senator Estes Kefauver arrived in the city in January 1951 to conduct a televised investigation into organized crime. But what those proceedings revealed was that the mayor and the police, among others, were enmeshed in local gambling and that the mayor had taken campaign contributions from a pinball gambling operation. So, in 1952, citizens of the city's elite formed their own Metropolitan Crime Commission of New Orleans. After several embarrassing years for the mayor—who publicly defended the city police when the state patrol repeatedly turned in evidence against them—he publicly endorsed the Crime Commission's creation of a Special Citizens Investigating Committee for police corruption in 1953.[83] In turn, this body hired a seasoned investigator who had probed corruption in the Chicago Police Department. But because this experienced outsider then hired as an undercover agent a former New Orleans policeman known by Wallace to be corrupt, and because she was attentive to the information that surfaced in the Kefauver hearings, she became convinced that "from the 1920s to the 1950s, little had changed."[84]

Perhaps little had changed in the way of police corruption, but in the 1950s, things were changing for the sex business. Everyone from bellhops to "notorious madams" told the undercover agent of the Hygiene Association that the city was hot, closed. The purveyors of prostitution were uncertain whether Governor-Elect Earl K. Long, brother of Huey

Long, was going to open up the city or keep it closed, but they felt certain that if Mayor Chep Morrison and Chief of Police Dayries were out of office, things would be different.[85] In 1953, Wallace herself was arrested three times, made front page news in both 1952 and 1953, and in 1954 moved across the river to Waggaman. True, that residence was also soon a brothel, and by the late 1950s she was back at the Conti house in the Quarter.[86] But when Downs was recommending in 1959 that New Orleans economic development remain dually rooted in the Quarter's historic preservation and sex and sin, it was a volatile territory in transition. That transition was, in part, driven by the city's exposure during the Kefauver hearings on live television. The reach of that mass medium ran contrary to the cloistered arrangement of the Old Quarter with its narrow streets, narrower passageways, and intimate walled courtyards.[87] Like Algren, Wallace and other denizens of the city had to reimagine their Old Quarter through the context of mass media.

The VCC may have had the muscle to force the Bourbon Street honky-tonks to conduct their business behind closed doors, but in the post-War years, during the Morrison administration, historic preservation was struggling alongside the neighboring houses of prostitution. "As a result of the war, a tremendous number of 'fly-by-night' bars and night clubs opened up in every block in large portions of [the Quarter]. The character of the Quarter suffered proportionately," preservationists complained, and, as they always advised preservationists elsewhere, a unique character was exactly what one was fighting for.[88] That character received an especially stinging blow in 1946. A city ordinance claimed control of the Quarter's edges, Rampart and the river side.[89] Meanwhile, finances for historic preservation dwindled. Its desperate supporters thought about soliciting the pride and monetary assistance of all states of the Louisiana Purchase to protect their cultural capitol, but by 1951 their coffers were only a fraction of what they had been more than a decade earlier.[90] To its dismay, the leadership of the VCC spent much of its energy in the 1950s urging the courts to uphold—with deliberate speed—VCC ordinances about disputed Vieux Carré properties. They feared the courts did not sufficiently respect their efforts.[91]

Although Buford Pickens, Director of Tulane University's School of Architecture, tactfully wrote Mayor Morrison in 1952 praising his "public improvement program" and soliciting his help in gaining credibility for the VCC and its mission, others among the Quarter's preservationists railed against the mayor.[92] Morrison's motion to City Council earlier that year supporting the $3.5 million expansion of the department store Maison Blanche from Canal Street into the Quarter raised the ire of the VCC, which could not then prevent the demolition of old buildings.[93] Remembering those years, preservationist Clay Shaw later wrote, "Chep Morrison, while a most able and brilliant mayor, had absolutely no interest in the French Quarter. It was his private opinion that it was nothing but a breeding ground for roaches and what New Orleans needed was one more good fire."[94] Feeling that historic preservation was losing ground, and wanting to capitalize on the Downs report, the VCC public relations committee proposed that it change its approach from enforcers to promoters. In 1959, VCC Chairman George M. Leake wrote the mayor and City Council inviting them to take a VCC-led walk on the historic side of the French Quarter.[95]

Renarrating the Wild Side

Although *A Walk on the Wild Side* ostensibly retains its 1930s setting, Algren bridged the years between his 1930s memories of New Orleans and the 1950s scene of encroaching urban renewal and practical piety with music. "[*Wild Side*] was something that happened to me. . . . Something of the lost past gathered momentum—and music—and gaiety—. . . ."[96] In the 1950s book, the folk music of *Boots*, sacred and profane, plays simultaneously with the mass-marketed music of jukeboxes and radios. Algren's biographer Bettina Drew indicates that the title *A Walk on the Wild Side* itself derives from the song "Walking on the Wild Side of Life" that Algren claimed to have heard on the radio in New Orleans during his first visit there in 1932.[97] Whether Wayne P. Walker's country and western song "A Walk on the Wild Side of Life" or W. Warren and A.A. Carter's "The Wild Side of Life" might have been the source of this recollection, it is clear that music motivated Algren's first telling of the New Orleans story and more explicitly guided its retelling.[98] Even the embarrassing editor's title *Somebody in Boots* was preceded by the title "Native Son," which Algren captured from a folk/campaign song and later relinquished to Richard Wright.[99] Whatever the 1930s versions of "Walking on the Wild Side of Life" that Algren heard, by 1952 "The Wild Side of Life" was the biggest hit of country star Hank Thompson, big enough to prompt an equally popular answer song the same year from Miss Kitty Wells: "It Wasn't God Who Made Honky Tonk Angels."[100] Algren's title, *A Walk on the Wild Side*, ultimately tapped a significant folk and popular root, later nourished by Lou Reed. Although popular musicians are not the only users of the phrase with whom Algren shares his title, music—folk and popular—is one telling indicator of the transformation from social realism to farce in Algren's fiction.

But not just music. All the voices that filled the airwaves—evangelists, comedy dramas, lingering minstrelsy, senators, advertisements—create the ebullient emptiness of *Wild Side*. In his 1942 introduction to *Never Come Morning*, Richard Wright praised Algren for giving the reading public "the nerves and brains of boys on the street" as a necessary *alternative* to "feverish radio programs, super advertisements, streamlined skyscrapers, million-dollar movies, and mass production [which] have somehow created the illusion in us that we [Americans] are 'rich' in our emotional lives."[101] But in *Wild Side* he renders even his own memories—the first person—in just such media voices, that is the third person. Algren implies that these voices had become an aural imperative for the American masses like the visual imperative of the simulacra Baudrillard later defined. Algren could easily imitate these voices, as he does in *Wild Side*—he watched a lot of television, even in the early 1950s—but he was less at ease solidly grounding any critique.[102] He frequently told interviewers such things as "the corruption of our times" is, for example, in the television commercial that elicits viewers' concern about whether peanut butter does or doesn't break the bread. "This at a time [the 1960s] when the threat of racial violence and when the flames are blowing from every direction that can set the world on fire. There is something a little bit gruesome if it weren't so comical."[103] The comic stories in media voices that together make up *Wild Side* are more than "a little bit gruesome."

Wild Side opens in the Valley of Texas with town gossips' presentation of Dove's father, Fitz Linkhorn, thus positioning the novel within the technique of Faulkner and Fitz, within the socioeconomic status of the Snopeses. He descends from the Scots hill people whose history of labor in America's South W.J. Cash tells. But when Fitz the preacher speaks from the town square, his is more the radio voice of Father Coughlin or an equivalent Protestant nay-sayer than one as proximate as the store porch of Faulkner's fiction; his bantering with sickly son, Bryon, has the rhythmic lunacy of McCarthy with a recalcitrant but doomed witness. Fitz, who himself had married a prostitute, is against Papists, miscegenation, dancing, the gold standard, and all other sin. Even though he is dirt poor, the teenager, Dove, the son of this Coughlin and McCarthy by a mother once a whore, flees these mean-spirited remnants of his family out of embarrassment rather than conviction or poverty. He finds employment with a Mexican gas station/cafe owner who, instead of falling to prostitution, has pulled away from sexual work herself to lead a solitary life on the edge of town. There, at the end of the expanding American frontier, between the Spanish and the English songs on the jukebox, amid the cafe signs in Spanish, the English reader finds in Terasina a character whose first language is tellingly unfamiliar and whose motivation and feeling are ironically legible. Dove, however, takes to the boxcars to satisfy his wanderlust, but not before raping his employer because she once succumbed to sex with him and later rejected him. Daubing his chin with her handkerchief, he walked toward the Southern Pacific freight that "whooped like a Sioux that has seen too many westerns."[104] Even the freight is a product of mass culture, leaving open the question whether Dove's treatment of Terasina is as well.

The drama of sister Nancy's desperation and the gang rape of Charlotte in *Boots* are replaced in *Wild Side* by the lonely, reserved figure of Terasina on the border. They are also replaced by Kitty Twist, fellow boxcar passenger bound for New Orleans. Raised by institutions, she is a recognizable delinquent of the kind especially feared in the 1950s. She tells Dove "the best kick of all is . . . when you put a gun on grownups and watch them go all to pieces."[105] When Dove saves her from falling through a bottomless boxcar in motion, she repays him with sex and a promise to hustle for him in New Orleans; she "had [already] run off upon the prospect of going into business for herself." Because he supposed he ought, Dove declares he loves her and offers to stay with her.[106] Then, after they commit a robbery and the cops close in, he makes off with the $40 and leaves her to take the rap.

While Kitty is in prison in Texas, Dove steps off the freight in Algiers, across the river from New Orleans. With $40 in his pocket, Dove imagines himself in New Orleans strumming a guitar astride a white horse. The image comes from the romance of Scottish poet Robert Burns, but Dove does soon see something similar—minus the guitar—in the statue of General Robert E. Lee at Lee Circle. Unlike the Negro residents of Gretna that Cass saw, the Negro presence, like the Negro voices rising from the church back home, is now more heard than seen in New Orleans. Near the Desire Street dock, a Negro woman's voice sings, "Daddy I don't want your money/I just want your stingaree" joining the sound of vendors like Tennessee Williams's racially marked but inarticulate blue piano amid the Mexican street merchants. The $40 emboldens Dove to approach New Orleans as a large center of commerce first, beginning with "the wide wonder of Canal" Street. Then, in the Quarter again, he cannot lie to the girls in the cribs who ask him, as sister Nancy asked Cass, "Boy, you got a dolla?" What was a central tragedy in *Boots* is here the comedy of excess. Repeatedly Dove is asked; repeatedly he hands over a dollar and his stingaree. Punctuating this scene is a hipster's narrative voice that relates, over the heads of the book's character, the history of New Orleans "hell" at the center of town. There in the Quarter do-right daddies criminalize and patronize prostitutes. The statutes had loopholes that served the do-righties who owned the peep shows as well. "Pulpit, press, police and politicians pushed the women from crib to crib and street to street—yet never pushed any but diseased ones out of reach. . . . Over the treachery, under the revelry, there hung, that airless summer, a feeling that this was all as sad as hi-jinks in an invaded land."[107]

An enterprising swell in yellow shoes, Dove takes on scams and schemes in the whole of the city, giving away "free" coffee pots uptown and finger waves in Gentilly, making condoms in a Lakefront suburb. Like the exploits of Ellison's invisible man, Dove's adventures take him through a sequence of absurd tales, racially and sexually charged. One tale about a Negro woman and a mosquito who together position Dove to have intercourse as he retrieves a misdelivered coffee pot is worthy of Ellison's Trueblood character who inadvertently impregnates his daughter. "Miscegenation," screams Dove's boss Smiley when he intrudes on this scene.[108] But unlike Ellison's culpable young innocent, Algren's has no desire but survival. Wanting nothing in particular, he learns nothing in particular. His actions are racially provocative only because he is illiterate and cannot read signs that say "for colored only" and does not know that white salesmen do not sell door to door in New Orleans Negro neighborhoods.

After he has learned both of these lessons about urban strangers,

> he walked the endless Negro blocks to home because it was still day. He was suspicious of them by night or by day. What were they forever laughing about from doorstep to door that he could never clearly hear? Their voices dropped when he came near and didn't rise till he was past earshot. Yet their prophecies pursued him—
>
> De Lord Give Noah de rainbow sign—
>
> Wont be by water but by fire next time—[109]

Dove is not a Huck with no more territory to run to.[110] Neither boy is, in fact, an innocent. Both have their moment at Cairo; Dove floats on downstream.

His one talent is for sex. When his exploits in the wider city wear thin, the "hell" at New Orleans center draws him in. The novel then narrows to this locale. Algren's narrator laments the life of streetwalkers and crib girls, but tells the story of a Rampart Street brothel and a related speakeasy. In an ornate, high-ceilinged parlor, Dove reenters the prostitution trade as a producer rather than consumer when he is solicited by the pimp Oliver Finnerty to enact the deflowering of "virgins" in a sex show designed for do-right daddies who want to keep their voyeurism at a safe distance. Once thinking to call the novel "Finnerty's Ball," Algren understands the power of pimps before and after World War II. His Finnerty, standing less than five feet, controls his girls with beatings behind the neck where it will not show and with promiscuous promises of settling down on a chicken farm that set the girls in competition to be this "farmer's wife." Only two "girls" are excluded. One is the mulatto madam Mama who passes as maid because the law forbids a colored madam of a white establishment. The other is a lighter-skinned mulatto prostitute named Hallie who enters prostitution out of the racial limbo of quadroons that New Orleanian Alice Dunbar-Nelson recorded in her stories of the city. Hallie's is a familiar tragic tale. A dark infant son exposes Hallie to her white husband, who deserts her when he sees evidence of her racial heritage. When that son dies, Hallie, once a schoolteacher, enters prostitution. The madam is too old to play the virgin; Hallie is too self-contained. Algren does not say that the do-right daddies would not pay to peep at the deflowering of a dark woman.

The madam controls her house much as the real madam Norma Wallace claims she controlled hers. Each house is not only architecturally grand but also a haven for its workers and their quirks. Algren writes,

> The courts were against them, the police were against them, businessman, wives, churches, press, politicians and their own panders were against these cork-heeled puppets. Now the missions were sending out sandwich men to advertise that Christ Himself was against them. . . . "If it weren't for Mama who'd take *our* side.". . . She took their side against Oliver, ordered him out of her house, and told him not to come back till he could show respect to ladies and forced him to apologize to one or the other at least once a week.[111]

Nevertheless, satisfying the sexual whims of their clients is their business. One of those clients is the Mammy-Freak, a character whose story Algren repeated in both *Nelson Algren's Book of Lonesome Monsters* and in *The Last Carousel*.[112] The Mammy-Freak, a naval commander of old southern stock, can only have an orgasm if he is beaten by a heavyset, Negro woman dressed like Aunt Jemima and wielding a broom. This, he explains, was the signal moment of his young southern life. At first, the Mama of all lost souls refuses to be Mammy to this freak, but Hallie urges her to compassion even for this. Nonetheless, Mama is repulsed by this role, this reversal of power, this inverted minstrelsy. Being an overtly racial game, it is a more dangerous sex game than most. (It may also be Algren's attack on the righteous Secretary of the Navy who closed Storyville in 1917 and thereby increased the dangers of prostitution for its sex workers.)

The "really chaste woman [the real mother] is the whore," Algren claimed, never afraid to be sentimental to make a point. "There is nothing less whorish than an old whore who hasn't gone down the drain . . . The whorish ones are . . . the middle-class prick-teasers, who run in and out, who play with sex."[113] Mama; Dove's own dead mother; and Hallie, later Dove's lover and pregnant with a second child: these three prostitutes are the foundation of the American family that Algren creates, not what he called the "gadget-infested middle-class."[114] When Hallie disappears back to her village where she can wear her hair kinky and embrace her second child, no one knows who is the father of this child. It could be a client or her long-term lover, Legless Schmidt, or her recent lover, Dove. She, the mixed-race woman of integrity, carrying a child of indeterminate paternity, reenters legitimate life outside the city as the best hope for an age between piety and pretense. The lost past inscribed in her prostitute's body is not the one that Algren recorded in the 1930s, that time when unescorted black women were raped on boxcars, and it is not the lost past of Baudelaire's urban prostitute, at once mythic and commodified. Hallie retreats to a segregated nonurban place where white strangers like Dove do not intrude on the laughter of Negroes that he finds so enigmatic in New Orleans's neighborhoods.

Dove leaves the Quarter for parish prison when the house is raided by the police. As with Badon Wallace and other sex business figures of history, Mama, Oliver, and the seasoned prostitutes anticipate the raid and are not at home to be arrested. Only Dove and Kitty, who has followed her grudge against Dove to New Orleans, face the police, who smash the jukebox and carry them off. Prison is not beset by the sounds of jukebox and radio that permeate the rest of this 1950s novel, but the texture of mediated voices and the characters of gruesome comedy do distinguish it from the prisons Algren remembered and imagined in the 1930s. In mock trials, an inmate "judge" presides, sentencing offenders to leap-frog. Jeff and Harry, the arresting police officers, pretend not to know a dead body from a live one as though they had been scripted by Beckett. The prison's most moral spokesperson, an inmate named Country Kline, speaks the truth out of madness. He is like the crazy veteran who advises Ellison's invisible man after he is expelled from his college. "There's no trick in not going down the drain if you don't live in the sink," Country tells Dove when he worries about his failure to rise in this life. Country's model is the prostitute who stays afloat when the water is sucking everyone down. He thus answers Dill Doak, who warned Cass, with Marxist rigor, that the South was a sink and New Orleans, its sewer because there women could be bought.[115]

Unlike in *Golden Arm*, the police in *Wild Side* are not an intimate and complex component of illegal activity throughout the novel. The role of police graft in prostitution and the swinging door between prison and the underworld, at least for its poorest inhabitants, are sometimes stated but not enacted. The novel's comedy does not play against a standing order, even one as absurd and uncertain as *Catch-22*. Instead, there is emptiness. Dove returns to the speakeasy at Old Perdido (Lost) and Rampart Street to discover that the old quarter has no memory of him or any of its other jailbait. Doc, the speakeasy's owner, "had lost track of who was in where and who was out. And didn't much care

which. . . . Nobody was long remembered on Old Perdido Street," once
the site of Storyville's cribs.[116] In the old city where the architecture
remembers its past, the poorest human inhabitants, Algren argues, are
eminently forgettable.

In the old building that houses Doc's speakeasy, amid strange whores
and pimps, Dove and Legless Schmidt, an honorable man, fight to the
death over Hallie. This is not the allegorical bar fight at the end of John
Okada's 1950s novel *No-No Boy*, that explosion of racial confusion
that, if only temporarily, clears the air.[117] But it is also an allegory, one
in which the earned rage of the 1930s welling out of Algren's memory
confronts the third-person insouciance of the 1950s. The result is gruesome but not comic. Legless Schmidt, a man who had been cut in half
by a freight and the treachery of his peers, demands a showdown with
Dove, a man who knows no treachery perpetrated against him or by
him because he knows no conviction. Dove is the indifferent son of his
McCarthyite father in whom ranting has replaced principle. Dove
approaches the fight reluctantly, even cordially, eager for an opportunity to walk away. But in the end he is "the face on the floor . . . no
longer a face, . . . a mere paste of cartilage and blood through which a
single sinister eye peered blindly."[118] Schmidt, in his own despair over
the loss of Hallie, his legs and his humanity, refashions Dove's face until
it tells the truth. That is, Schmidt, whose human depth is greater than
the sum of his body's parts, reduces Dove to a face without distin-
guishing human character, whose benign disinterest is finally revealed as
a sinister eye.

After Dove narrowed his world to Oliver's "family," Mama's house,
and Doc's Dollhouse speakeasy, he ceased to walk the city. He no
longer passed the crib girls who asked, "Boy, got a dolla?" In the end,
when he leaves the city, he turns a literal blind eye to the streetwalkers
(and a deaf ear to the enigmatic laughter of Negroes in their neighborhoods). When Dove, sightless, returns to Terasina and the borderland,
he retreats like Hallie from the city. In such hinterlands, mixed-race
women, once whores, women who teach illiterate white boys to read,
are the operative definition of home. Not precisely a Mammy-Freak,
Dove nonetheless retreats to a Mexican woman he could once rape and
wordlessly leave. Thus he avoids his own first-person subjectivity and
the city of New Orleans where hard questions about social justice
between men and women, among the races, and between do-right
daddies and daddy-o's were waiting around every corner for those who
chose to see something other than Finnerty's peep show. When Dove
entered the city, he imagined he would become a guitar-strumming,
Scottish cavalier on a white horse. In retreat, he is as soundly defeated as
the Confederacy, but the image of his lost cause may be equally intact.
At home he musters compassion for his father, who still survives to

shout piety and pretense at his bemused neighbors in the Texas town. Being grotesque himself, Dove now understands the degradation that has made Fitz grotesque. And yet, if Algren intends this compassion in earnest (and he seems to)—and he gets such an idea from *The Mind of the South*—then in his epilogue of the 1950s he has spun Cash's 1930s analysis of Southern poor whites backwards. Perhaps after the fall of McCarthy, Algren felt he could retreat from his satire of the media voices that created a mean-spirited, ranting Fitz. But, in fact, the mid-1950s saw just the beginning of mean-spirited Southern whites ranting before the cameras against the entry of African Americans into public buses, public schools, and businesses open to the public while elites, directly and indirectly staging the drama, Northerners as well as Southerners, remained off-camera.

Old Perdido and the Vieux Carré

Dove and Hallie leave behind the city that has, says Algren, no memory of the underworld denizens stored in its old, preserved bricks and mortar, edifices built by slave labor, as he noted when he revisited the city in the 1950s.[119] "Nobody was long remembered on Old Perdido Street."[120] For the preservationists in pursuit of the Creole Quarter, memory of its late nineteenth-century decline and of the Tango Belt were not part of the neighborhood character they were after. When the National Historic Trust was founded and when, in 1956, the Quarter was named, *tout ensemble*, a national treasure, the preservationists' choice of history and enforcement was gaining, at least nationally, the credibility the state museum curator predicted twenty years earlier. By 1961, New Orleans was being featured in the National Trust's traveling exhibit called "Preservation: Heritage of Progress."[121] Although in the mid-1950s, the VCC was still struggling to make ends meet and to be heard in the courts, at the time Downs issued his report, they were already embroiled in the fight against the riverfront expressway proposed to run in front of the Place d'Arms (a.k.a., Jackson Square), a fight they eventually won. It appears that their memory of the Quarter's economic and architectural glory days never wavered. The buildings were, unlike Baudelaire's streetwalkers, not a palimpsest but rather a time machine that took the preservationist and the cultural tourist to the date in the past he or she wanted to occupy. One would arrive with the 1850s, say, completely intact. The Downs report seemed welcome news, just the nudge the VCC needed to start promoting the economic development inherent in the scene it was saving. If it feared then that the report would augur a tourist trade so successful that the residences of preservationists would become as marginalized as the brothels, it did not stop the promotion of the *tout ensemble* of the Vieux Carré.

For Wallace, the writing on the wall was fully visible two years after the Downs report, in 1961, when Jim Garrison became District Attorney. When he started arresting the "real dancers" on Bourbon Street, the locals and the dancers got nervous and stopped coming.[122] Exotic dancing that she recognized as genuine was replaced with souvenir shops and, Wallace implies, some form of sex show only Cass McKay could appreciate. Meanwhile, Wallace claims, worse crime was replacing prostitution.[123] And the police were in on it.

New Orleans had a firm reputation for prostitution, solidified by the tales of Storyville, before Algren first set foot in the city in the early 1930s. When he published *Wild Side*, he also had a solid reputation for representing the underworld earned over twenty years. Together, the folkways of the city and the author created the resonance of "walking on the wild side" that in turn clung to both decades afterwards. Throughout the last half of the twentieth century, the phrase persisted in the city's advertisements for itself as a tourist destination, even clinging to the backpages of brochures for tourists after the city was selling itself as family entertainment. Until Algren's death in 1981, many interviews with him were also billed as walks on the wild side. (Interviewers, I think, flatter themselves.)

The 1962 romantic film based on the novel perpetuated the circulation of the title, but by associating it only with high-toned brothel prostitution conducted in the nicely re-created, historically preserved Quarter, never troubling itself with vendors or itinerate musicians, let alone streetwalkers, crib girls, or even a discarded cigarette butt in the gutter.[124] (The title sequence, does feature a credible alley cat stalking to the beat of Elmer Bernstein's music.) In fact, in the film, the Texas scenes and the Mexican Terasina are moved to the outskirts of New Orleans. In the film's French Quarter of elegant private courtyards, there is not even a whiff of satire as the Texas farmer Dove goes to New Orleans to take Hallie, a prostitute and his lost love, as his wife. As alternative to the dark brothel warren of interconnected balconies, he offers her a high-ceilinged artist's atelier with tall casement windows. The only dirt or hunger in the film clings briefly to the person of young Jane Fonda (Kitty Twist), too voluptuous to lend much credibility to the problem. The historic French Quarter, itself a character, functions to elicit a wild side of sexual license but one welcoming middle-class male tourists. In fact, the film provides one, a surgeon, who is surprised to find such a sophisticated girl as Capucine (Hallie) in a "place like this," yet is presumably there himself because its character caters to his class of sex tourists and moviegoers. Ironically, the remaining high-toned brothels like the one the film depicts—the ones that made New Orleans prostitution famous—were being forced to close as the film was being released. The streetwalkers and call girls absent from the film would remain offscreen.

The film is arguably bad enough to justify Algren's never having seen it. It did nonetheless have a sufficient budget to hire Laurence Harvey, Barbara Stanwyck, Jane Fonda, and Capucine to star and Edward Dmytryk to direct, some of whom put in admirable performances under the wrought iron. Stanwcyck, the madam who replaces the novel's mixed race Mama—recast only as a maid for the film—bears a striking similarity to Norma Badon Wallace as she appeared on the front page during her trial in 1952–1953: both trim in business suits, mouths hard with the responsibilities of their work. At the close of the movie, a newspaper's front page features besuited Stanwyck and her cohort when they were swiftly brought to justice after the murder of Hallie, reinforcing the link to the frontpage images of Wallace. The film thus acknowledges that it is depicting an end, but, it implies, the end of murderous corruption in prostitution and political graft even in old New Orleans, not the end of a safe sexual business for a tourist like the good surgeon.

In fact, a surgeon became a principal player in a real-life drama of upscale New Orleans prostitution in 2002. Under indictment for health care fraud, he used his knowledge of a Canal Street brothel—to which he had written more than $300,000 in bad checks—to bargain with federal prosecutors. Algren would not have been surprised to learn that the madam running this franchise of a national operation and that the migratory prostitutes were prosecuted but the johns from New Orleans's business and professional community were never named.[125] Brothel prostitution had clearly found success (1994–2002, at any rate) on a corporate model dependent on nonlocal labor. Yet in less gentile neighborhoods, one could still find streetwalkers who were the palimpsest of the city Benjamin described.

The 1960 musical of Algren's novel, for which he wrote lyrics, was staged for only a short time in St. Louis. Nevertheless, he remembered it as the right characterization of his novel, a kind of Les Miz for New Orleans prostitution. Lou Reed misremembers that "they were going to make a musical out of Nelson Algren's A Walk on the Wild Side. When they dropped the project I took my song ["A Walk on the Wild Side"] and changed the book's characters into people I knew from Warhol's Factory."[126] Some of Reed's characters are drag queens, not Algren's types, but the link to him is still a point of honor with Reed. Algren's Wild Side became, if not famous in the literary sphere of Faulkner and Hemingway, a cult classic among subsequent generations that spawned Joseph Heller, Thomas Southern, and Ken Kesey, as well as Bob Dylan and Lou Reed.[127] Wild side denizens may have changed some over time, but they remained residents of an underworld represented by an art that, like Algren's, went "behind the billboards" to find them.

But could Algren's farce successfully shine a light on the horror between the "piety and pretense" of the 1950s—and of subsequent decades? Does its depiction of prostitution "confront a society's definition of social justice" and explain what becomes of that social justice in a city caught in a struggle between historic preservation and some history of economic progress that could be called modernity? Or instead is Benjamin's 1930s conclusion about his own twentieth-century Paris as distinct from Baudelaire's nineteenth-century Paris applicable to Algren in 1950s New Orleans as well? Benjamin writes,

> Baudelaire had the good fortune to be the contemporary of a bourgeoisie that could not yet employ, as accomplice of its domination, such an asocial type as he represented. The incorporation of a nihilism into its hegemonic apparatus was reserved for the bourgeoisie of the twentieth century.[128]

The nihilism that comes of living in the third person, as mass media and marketing taught Americans to do, does render horror as not-horror. Algren has Legless Schmidt beat a social conscience into Dove and still he turns a blind eye to all but those at home, especially those like himself.

When the Vieux Carré's defenders fully digested the Downs's report and became promoters as much as defenders of their historic vision of the built structures, they too learned to walk in the third person. They never intended to look at the horror behind the billboards anyway, but rather to look beneath cheap modern facades and twentieth-century paint. In the former Storyville, just north of the protected Vieux Carré, the cribs of Old Perdido had been razed with the fancy brothels of Basin Street. And a historic walk in the Old Quarter was not one that commemorated its mixed-race brothels and gay bars, let alone streetwalkers (although it did succumb to the safe sale of virtual sex on its Bourbon Street). In 1997, the hundredth anniversary of the creation of Storyville, a commemorative set of exhibits and tours was mounted and conducted despite only two buildings standing and a community driven underground.[129] Platial scholar Dolores Hayden claims that, in the 1990s, a "kind of urban preservation was emerging . . . in focusing on vernacular buildings, landscape preservation, and commemorative public art. These areas offer[ed] new models of collaborations between professionals and communities, as well as new alliances among practitioners concerned with urban landscape history."[130] The Storyville commemoration was not quite the model of communicative action and

sustained bottom-up memory that Hayden has in mind, yet this effort to
see in the mind's eye even a razed neighborhood might have appeal to
more residents and thinking tourists than some tourism industrialists or
cultural critics imagine. It is closer to the geological formation of culture
that David Riesman thought New Orleans offered Americans as a
significant alternative to most commodities for sale in the 1950s. But
alternatives such as the palimpsest of the prostitute have rarely been
given the chance to challenge the safer sexual nostalgia of a Bourbon
Street shaped over decades and on offer 24/7.[131] In this historically
preserved modern street that enacts sexual nostalgia, the face of the
prostitute is openly visible only on T-shirts and in videos.

In the 1980s, having been given the key to the city, even Norma
Badon Wallace had become a media star and was no longer a force
defending house prostitution. The "hegemonic apparatus" of the bourgeoisie had fully embraced her. Advertisements for New Orleans using
the language of "wild side" have also become increasingly scarce or
sanitized as the city's government and tourist industry have targeted
family visitors.[132] They do not offer a walk behind the billboards, where
indeed crime and desperation and low-paying tourist service sector jobs
do exist.[133] Everyone in New Orleans knows that Bourbon Street is the
safest in the city. Although the spin of walking on the wild side in New
Orleans has thus been significantly contained, the phrase has been
outsourced to southeast Asia, where it is still overtly associated with a
more threatening practice of prostitution.[134]

Except among Lou Reed fans, the phrase is mostly used by those who
promise to safely deliver a prepackaged thrill devoid of horror. "Walk
on the wild side" is a special favorite of ecotourism from Fiji to Kenya
to Puerta Rica and of urban tourism from Berlin to Philadelphia to Port-
land (indeed, every city but New Orleans) and of zoos from Cincinnati
to San Diego. It even advertises astronomical tours, a fungi-spotting
walk in the United Kingdom—"don't forget your leech socks," wildcat
cartridges for high-powered hunting rifles, and, most recently, wireless
Internet learning devices (WILD). To walk on the WILD side is to
"augment physical space" for your students. All elicit the possibility of
risk on the wild side, a place that New Orleans and Algren together
created and city marketers then declared safe. For New Orleans, it was
an image so successful as a tourist venture that it reconfigured the business of sex and sin and then the historic property of residential
owners.[135] Both have been crowded out of their houses.

4

Malaise and Miasms

Dr. Percy's Moviegoer and Public Health in New Orleans Environs

In 1919, with Prohibition upon him, Tom Anderson, the ever-appositized "Mayor" of Storyville, saw the imminent decline of that once-profitable urban neighborhood and diverted his saloon earnings into oil, organizing Protection Oil Company, and later Liberty Oil, which he sold to Standard Oil.[1] As with Standard Oil of New Jersey, which established the subsidiary Standard Oil (Louisiana) in 1909, Anderson was awake at the dawn of Hydrocarbon Man. In 1948, Standard Oil paid documentary filmmaker Robert Flaherty to tell the story of their growing presence in Louisiana. Flaherty's lyric *Louisiana Story* follows a Cajun boy and his pet raccoon at play in the bayou country where they live and in which, by the way, some men are also drilling an oil well.[2] The boy can pull his pirogue up to the platform of the drilling operation and get a full tour of the machine in the swamp, finding less threat there than from the alligator that eats his raccoon. After the drilling is finished and the men wave themselves away, very little visible artifice remains to disturb nature's bounty, beauty, mystery, and charming human inhabitants in south Louisiana's wetlands. At mid-twentieth century, Flaherty retells as a regional story the urban creation myth New Orleanians told themselves, from their beginnings into the nineteenth century, about their relationship to the Mississippi River: "'Nature,' through its agent, the river, favored the city and would nurture it."[3]

Some early New Orleanians, however, also warned the public that if they misused the river, it would strike back.[4] One of the ways it would take its revenge is through disease. Before the advent of bacteriological knowledge, a common belief among physicians and their patients about public health purported that miasmas were the cause of disease.[5] The spontaneous generation of pestilence in response to local conditions produced a rot, the theory went, that poisoned the air and made of it a miasma. Early New Orleans's health community believed that digging in the city not only disturbed the river's accretion of soil on its banks and thus exacerbated flooding, but also gave rise to murderous epidemics. Given the city's location at the center of river, lake, and wetlands, and its extended summer heat, it was especially challenged by what New Orleanians called "miasms." But, throughout New Orleans's history as a port city, in the name of commerce, commercial elites fostered—even sometimes forced—a calm, suppressing public panic about any threat borne over water (or air).[6]

In the nineteenth century, epidemic meant yellow fever. It overshadowed other assaults on New Orleans public health, killing thousands as compared with the hundreds taken by cholera, for example.[7] But in the twentieth century, chronic disease, notably cancers, replaced infectious disease nationally and locally as the principle public health concern. The contentious etiology of these chronic diseases frequently traces a path back to the door of growing industries promoting new products with multiple uses in everyday life: lead for paint and pipes, asbestos for building materials, polyvinyl chloride (plastic) for everything under the sun.[8] Among these modern industries expanding through the twentieth century is the petrochemical industry, producers of vinyl chloride and crude oil. So benign and tidily modern a presence in *The Louisiana Story*, the petrochemical industry has transformed the waterways of the lower Mississippi from sugar plantations and backwater fishing and hunting sites into an extensive industrial corridor, dubbed Cancer Alley in the 1980s by activists for environmental justice.

Dr. Walker Percy of the prestigious Greenville, Mississippi, and Birmingham, Alabama, Percys, came to New Orleans in 1947 with his new wife not to hang up his shingle, but to convert to Catholicism.[9] Though in New Orleans, he never practiced pathology (in which he had done his residency in New York) or psychiatry (which he had planned to pursue), he always referred to his novels as diagnostic and to himself and his protagonists as pathologists on a search for answers.[10] His first and most celebrated published novel, *The Moviegoer*, initiates this medical technique by exploring what it calls malaise, an unconscious despair in the face of everyday life in the 1950s. It does so through the story of Binx Bolling, a young veteran caught in New Orleans Mardi Gras season between the Uptown expectations of his Aunt Emily in the

Garden District and his own suspended animation as a stockbroker and consumer of mass culture in the newer suburb of Gentilly.

This chapter reads Percy's malaise in the context of New Orleans's mid-twentieth-century miasms. It argues that, although the novel is ironically self-aware about despair, poised to diagnose its cause in situ, that self-awareness serves as an end in itself. The novel positions itself between post-Auschwitz ideas about mass death and existentialist ideas about individual death, not acknowledging that the social need for public health resides between the two. All the pieces are in place to recognize his protagonist as Hydrocarbon Man, but Percy's irony only begins to intimate this connection between suburban life and Hydrocarbon Society and between malaise and miasms. A New Orleans public intellectual from the success of *The Moviegoer* in 1962 to his death in 1990, Percy frequently looked into the faces of death, of mass culture, and of the changing South. His fiction and especially his nonfiction of the 1980s more explicitly addresses the relationship between King Commerce and the quality of water and human life on the lower Mississippi, even while it still evaded certain urban details. But his early satire stops shy of giving New Orleanians the details from the local autopsy. This is so, I want to argue, not because Percy was uninterested in social change and immune to environmental effects. The social engagement of his realistic and later fantastic fiction and nonfiction and his insistence on a diagnostic method of plot formation, in fact, make the elision of the changing river and its impact on New Orleans environs particularly curious. Although some of Percy's familial and dispositional qualities play a part in this elision, I am interested in a more platial explanation. I argue that the discursive riverfront of past plantations and the literal built environment at New Orleans's long riverfront in the 1950s contributed to the containment of his analysis of death and despair, making individual psychological malaise out of sociosomatic miasm.

I put formal and informal stories of the river corridor and waterfront in dialogue with Percy's famous first novel. These histories offer a geographic explanation for his failing to acknowledge the developing industrial river corridor in *The Moviegoer*, even though the novel sets the stage for just such a recognition. That explanation is further enhanced by a look at Elia Kazan's *Panic in the Streets*, a film shot on location in New Orleans and one seen by Percy's moviegoer, Binx, at a crucial juncture in the novel. Described by Kazan as a movie of provocative camera work, more about the city than a plot of a plague epidemic, *Panic in the Streets* offers a unique if unsustained perspective on New Orleans's waterfront in 1950, a perspective available to Percy's protagonist, fully relevant to his dilemma, but not absorbed into the logic of the novel.[11] In *The Moviegoer*, Percy explores mass culture— even corporate culture—and scientific method as enticing agents of everyday despair that, in New Orleans, can neither escape local plantation and Mardi Gras traditions nor be fully alleviated by them. Nevertheless, the novel, in the end, relinquishes a postmodern savvy in favor of traditional New Orleans cultural and Catholic beliefs, never turning its world weary wisdom or diagnostic inquiry from malaise to miasm.

Percy further addresses the lure of the local in his role as Southern essayist. There he defines public space within a post-*Brown v. Board* Southern context. He thus provides a regional understanding of the concept public that in part also serves to explain how Dr. Percy as public intellectual remained separate from public health. Product of his place and time and disposition, he served the mid-century's and the city's sense of irony but not a recognition of its place within Hydrocarbon Society.

On the Waterfront from Baton Rouge to New Orleans

The history of oil, writes Daniel Yergin, illuminates how ours has become a "Hydrocarbon Society" and we, "Hydrocarbon Man."

> It is oil that makes possible where we live, how we live, how we commute to work, how we travel—even where we conduct our courtships. It is the lifeblood of suburban communities.[12]

From the first decade of the twentieth century, Louisiana has been a major supplier of that hydrocarbon fix for "we" Americans within our borders and as an exported model of consumption.

Louisiana's first oil well was drilled in 1901 at White Castle, on the Mississippi River just south of Baton Rouge.[13] But it was the establishment of Standard Oil (Louisiana) in 1909 that made Louisiana an oil state. As part of the enormous growth by affiliate refineries between 1899 and 1911, Standard Oil (New Jersey) decided to place its contemplated Gulf Coast refinery at Baton Rouge. Standard Oil determined that that site gave it the advantages of proximity to market, facilities for transportation of the finished product domestically and internationally, and the space for growth. It purchased 213 acres (later expanded to 939) on the first high ground of the Delta, safe from flooding yet serviceable by ocean-going vessels via the Mississippi. In 1909, it immediately began building not only a refinery, but also a pipeline from Baton Rouge through Arkansas, linking it to the Prairie Oil pipeline that extended to Chicago and points east.[14] In addition to these advantages, the canny site choice in Louisiana avoided the new antitrust laws and ill will in Texas precipitated by the monopoly of Waters-Pierce Oil

Company. In 1911, Waters-Pierce still controlled all of the marketing territory of the lower south central states except Baton Rouge and New Orleans; Standard Oil (New Jersey) and its domestic affiliates held 99.9 percent of the stock in the new affiliate Standard Oil (Louisiana), thus controlling that remaining territory and linking it to their holdings further north.[15] Cajun boys in the bayous may not yet have known it, but they were already spoken for.

By 1913 Standard Oil (Louisiana) was second only to Standard Oil (New Jersey) in net earnings. Crude oil had been found in northwest Louisiana, but the main source of success at Baton Rouge was the "vigorous program of expansion and diversification"—paraffin, lubricating oil, asphalt; crude stills and cracking stills—and what historians George Gibb and Evelyn Knowlton describe as unusually good labor relations under the kindly leadership of President Frederick Weller. (This was the assessment even though employees received no raises between 1910 and 1915.[16]) In the years around World War I, Standard Oil also discovered the means to move beyond the production of fuel alone by isolating hydrocarbon chains, thus enabling the production of many synthetic fibers and inaugurating the new petrochemical industry.[17] Despite a 1914 federal regulation requiring separate ownership of oil production and its transportation (such as pipelines), intermittent glutted crude oil markets, a 1917 effort by Louisiana Public Service Commission chair Huey Long to regulate Louisiana Standard Pipeline as a public utility, and Standard Oil's own reluctance to enter into lend-lease agreements with service stations, Standard Oil (New Jersey and Louisiana) were still leaders in their territories in 1926. Standard Oil (Louisiana) flourished, even when faced in the 1920s with Governor Huey Long's new severance tax based on quantity of oil and gas taken from the ground.[18]

By then, it has to be said, kindly labor relations at Baton Rouge were being characterized at a company-initiated work conference for labor representatives as "strongly paternalistic." Not overtly anti-union, Standard Oil (New Jersey and Louisiana) was nonetheless decidedly for an open shop. "The boilermakers' union in the Louisiana Company was not opposed, but rather smothered." At a segregated meeting in Louisiana for Negro labor representatives, one observer noted that management announcements were greeted by cries of "Thank God for Standard Oil! Everybody pray for Standard Oil!" Workers who behaved less pliably were not "rehired."[19]

Diversification, experimentation, and an expandable if unconventional workforce were the hallmarks of the Louisiana operation through the 1930s and, at an accelerated pace, through World War II. In the 1930s, chemical engineer Monroe "Jack" Rathbone became head of the Baton Rouge operation, having gone to work there after World War I.

When he assumed leadership of the massive plant, he was thirty-one. Described by a colleague as "an engineer with a T Square," he was unemotional, decisive, confident, a man of few words. He took refining from a "'combination of guesswork and art' and turned it into 'a science.'"[20] As company historian Charles Popple tells it in 1952, when the government had a need, Standard Oil—especially, Standard Oil (Louisiana)—stepped up to offer timely experimentation and production. Whereas the East Coast plants had a shortage of crude and an excess of labor, the opposite was true at Baton Rouge. By hiring women and over-aged workers and lowering physical fitness standards, the Louisiana operation was able to acquire 1,155 additional workers in 1942 and 2,126 in 1943 and continue to stretch its operation in multiple directions.[21]

With this flexibility, Standard Oil (Louisiana) could participate in the manufacture of a dizzying number of new petrochemical substances. With the patent for hydrogenation to manufacture "synthetic" gasoline bought from German company I.G. Farben in 1929, Standard Oil built two hydrogenation plants, one in New Jersey and another at Baton Rouge. The plant at Baton Rouge took on the experimental hydrogenation of di-isobutylene in 1934 and began an experimental operation to produce acetylene in 1933. In 1935, when the Army Air Corps called for 1 million gallons of 100-octane aviation fuel, Standard Oil (Louisiana) got a third of the commission. (By the end of the War, the Baton Rouge plant was one of only three in the world that had produced 1 billion gallons of 100-octane gasoline.) In 1940, Baton Rouge was one of two locations also experimenting with butadiene, a synthetic rubber. The Baton Rouge site took on a "quickie" butadiene production program for the government in 1942–1943. Then, in 1943, it became the experimental plant charged to work out the bugs in the production of butyl, used for synthetic rubber and other products. Standard Oil (Louisiana) also built a nitration-grade toluene plant at Baton Rouge in 1942, a substance used in the production of TNT (trinitrotoluene). The first indication that toluene could be derived "from petroleum [had] occurred at Baton Rouge some time prior to 1933." Ethyl alcohol, isopropyl alcohol, methyl ethyl ketone, naphthenic acid: all of these chemicals—used for the plastic coating of bombers' noses, the manufacture of penicillin, the coating for fabric, napalm, anti-mildew agents for tents—were produced at the Standard Oil (Louisiana) plants on the Mississippi River.[22]

The river corridor between Baton Rouge and New Orleans has served the petrochemical industry well, offering "oil, gas, brine, sulfur, fresh water drawn from aquifers, and huge salt domes [(some as much as a mile wide and six miles long) that] . . . provided extraordinarily cheap storage for hundreds of millions of barrels of oil and other materials essential for the petrochemical and chemical industries."

By the mid-1950s chemicals and chemical products ranked first in the value of manufactured products in Louisiana. In 1956 Ethyl Corporation began construction of a vinyl chloride monomer plant and W. R. Grace Company [later well known through the story told in *A Civil Action*] built a polyethylene plant in Baton Rouge.

Also in 1956, Dow bought the old Union Plantation, ten miles south of Baton Rouge. On that 1,700-acre site of a former sugar plantation, they built the biggest petrochemical complex in Louisiana and one of the biggest in the world: seven major projects and thirty-five minor ones. With brine from a contiguous salt dome, they produced chlorine that in turn was used to produce ethylene dichloride, "a feedstock for vinyl chloride monomer and other plastics."[23] A 1958 *National Geographic* article about the "Land of Louisiana Sugar Kings" could not help but observe in the end that "chemicals, manufacturing, and processing establishments occupy mile after mile of Mississippi frontage. Steel towers rise and derricks dot the levy edge, until the region from New Orleans to Baton Rouge seems one great chemical-industrial plant."[24]

So how could Walker Percy—a physician, pathologist, and critic of the objectivist scientific method, a man who spent formative years upriver at Greenville, Mississippi, with Uncle Will Percy, a principle player in the famous 1927 flood, and the post-War years in New Orleans and Covington, Louisiana—not take on this waterfront transformation as a part of his hero's postwar malaise?[25] True enough, Percy's disposition, especially after the War years spent taking a rest cure for tuberculosis in a New York sanitarium, turned explicitly toward semiotics, psychiatry, and Catholicism rather than chemistry, ecology and modern-day miasms. Such a prolific essayist as Percy—an essayist before a novelist—does not keep his readers guessing about his obsessions. But there is a geographic explanation as well, one that describes not some individual blinders of Percy, if that they be, but how a collective unconscious gets built in a place. It also describes how an environmental consciousness might be developed instead, as was, in part, true for Percy later in his life.

The 1958 *National Geographic* article explains one relevant geohistorical feature of the river Percy knew. In Harnett Kane's words and Willard Culver's photographs, it tells the stories of sugar plantations along the Mississippi between Baton Rouge and New Orleans: their colonial glories of architecture, landscaping, and cuisine; the plantation heroes who brought the sophistication of Paris to the Louisiana backwater;

and the present heroes from New Orleans who renovate the houses to an antebellum splendor. Peacocks, palm trees, and $10,000 wagers between Louisiana planters and French gentlemen lined the riverfront, as Kane tells it.[26] As with protagonist Binx Bolling's father, who could walk for miles on the upriver plantation levees to alleviate insomnia, or his Aunt Emily, who presided at such an upriver plantation, the real-life plantation owners of the nineteenth and early twentieth centuries enjoyed an expansive waterfront privately owned but often publicly inhabited, a kind of vast Main Street of plantations. Although Binx's father could traverse the levees linearly, by 1958, the public of tourists embarked on and disembarked from the paddle-wheelers at narrow openings where renovated plantation houses and gardens dipped down to the riverfront. Only with careful site selection could one still imagine in 1958 the upriver waterfront as the land of sugar kings.

From *The Moviegoer* to Percy's last novel, *Thanatos Syndrome*, he distinguished working plantation houses with muddy boots on the porch, such as Uncle Will's Trail Lake Farm, from tourist attractions.[27] In *The Moviegoer*, the relatives who have renovated the upriver family plantation for tourists are a fatuous pair tolerated by Aunt Emily only for the sake of blood ties. Nevertheless, Aunt Emily, now in New Orleans, cognitively maps for Binx and the reader the upriver plantation life of books and dignity well kept, of land well managed by its owners, and well maintained by its servants. Percy's character Emily, *National Geographic*'s author Kane, and photographer Culver line the waterfront with memorialized images and colorful stories that quell misgivings inherent in the visual evidence that the region from New Orleans to Baton Rouge is "one great chemical-industrial plant."

Percy learned to see the waterfront not only from his youthful days in Greenville, a Yazoo-Mississippi Delta city on the river, but also from his experience in New Orleans in the post-War years. The New Orleans he entered in the 1940s was one already closed off from its riverfront by the railroad and, most of all, a continuous line of warehouses. In the first years of the twentieth century, the new Dock Board had put its mark on the river by building warehouses along more than two linear miles of the waterfront, including one opposite Jackson Square.[28] Historian Ari Kelman argues that beginning in the late nineteenth century, commercial elites in New Orleans, facing the competition the railroads mounted against their river port, more aggressively defined commerce as the single public use of the waterfront. No more promenades for New Orleanians along the riverbanks or atop the levees. No more using the accretion from the river as publicly accessible fill dirt for New Orleans citizens. The river was no longer sublime nature that destined the city for greatness. Even river commerce, once visible at almost any street corner as a "forest of masts," was, by the early twentieth century, not visible at all. Gone with that view was that popular naturalist metaphor for the commercial scene. The river had instead become a highway for commerce, devoid of "natural," aesthetic appeal. In its place, the new Audubon Park, built on City Beautiful principles at the Uptown site of the 1884 Cotton Exposition, fulfilled citizens' desire for a breath of air by providing a circular promenade beneath a canopy of live oaks and a view of extensive formal gardens. It offered no glimpse of the river.[29] The Percys' first New Orleans house at 1450 Calhoun stood less than a block from the fountains of Audubon Park.[30] When Binx wants to take one of his girlfriends to see the water, they go east toward the Mississippi Gulf Coast and Ship Island. The Percys also took this eastern route to and from New Orleans after they moved to Covington north of the lake, until 1956 when the Pontchartrain Causeway was built across the lake. In fact, they made the trip frequently for the sake of their deaf daughter whose teachers and doctors were in the city. So frequently did they make this trip that in 1957 they bought a second house on Milan Street, Uptown. There Percy, separated from his library at Covington that fueled his essays on semiotics and psychiatry, began to write *The Moviegoer*.[31]

When Percy imagined Binx headed to the Gulf Coast with his latest secretary in his MG, off-shore oil exploration was not yet a prominent feature on the Gulf Coast horizon. Binx and the novel's other Gulf Coast habitues—southern Baptist school children, Army recruits and their girls, Ohioans—could all expect to find the same kind of respite that drew wealthier New Orleanians of the nineteenth century out of the yellow fever–ravaged city east to the resort at Ocean Springs.[32] Only time, responsibilities in the city, and his own encroaching sense of malaise limit the Gulf Coast experience for Binx. The waterfront at New Orleans and upriver is, by contrast, an enclosed site, invisible and memorialized. In one vestigial urban water scene, Binx and Aunt Emily Cutrer promenade up and down the gallery of the Cutrer's Garden District home while a thunderstorm rails. The storm blows in from the river, but they pace above the street, the river invisible to them.

> We come to the corner of the gallery and a warm spray blows in our faces. One can smell the islands to the south. The rain slackens and tires hiss on the wet asphalt. . . . She links her arm in mine and resumes the promenade.[33]

Even those who continued to live upriver of the city after the extensive industrialization at mid-century have been physically enclosed in their own small towns. Streets dead end at the fence of the petrochemical plants. There are no emergency evacuation routes except the winding two-lane River Road that runs between the levees and the plants. In case of a toxic spill at any of the plants, industry officials instruct these contiguous communities to "Shelter in Place"; that is, close all doors and windows and stay inside. "For many of the poor, whose homes were often little more than shacks, Shelter in Place must have seemed a cruel joke, for their homes were rarely airtight."[34] When, in 1958, Kane tells the story of the "Land of Louisiana Sugar Kings," he omits these enclosed towns of mostly African American agricultural laborers who had lost the agricultural enterprises that employed them. Binx's Aunt Emily has brought her Negro "retainer" Mercer with her from the plantation; otherwise, she speaks of no former plantation servants or laborers. The small upriver towns in the industrial corridor are invisible except to their own inhabitants, some of whom find no labor except enacting their former servitude in plantation houses renovated for tourists.[35]

The Waterfront the Camera Saw

When an interviewer asked Elia Kazan why he had opened *Panic in the Streets* with a long tracking shot—why, in fact, much of the film is long or wide-angled shots, Kazan replied that the object was "to keep moving pictorially—to constantly saturate the picture with the feeling of New Orleans."[36] The point was not to make actors look like stars (he chose actors who were not stars) and not to tell a narrative about a threat of pneumonic plague in the city (he and writer Richard Murphy rewrote the script every morning to suit the platial circumstances).[37] Instead, as had John Ford, or Charlie Chaplin before him, Kazan wanted to pull the movie out of the place in a way that exploited the camera and liberated him from his experience as a stage director.[38] While shooting the film, Kazan later claimed, he ran free in the city: Mayor Morrison was a fan, the police were part of his staff, the great restaurants opened their doors, storytellers shared their memories, citizens served as extras, and a tugboat captain took his kids for a ride. Wandering New Orleans after dark, he found streets of "joints" with jazz flooding out, a pulsing sound that he tried to reproduce as the soundtrack, the only really significant sound to accompany his moving pictures of the city.[39]

Kazan's camera saw a New Orleans waterfront not visible in Percy's New Orleans. From the flight of the plague-ridden illegal immigrant pursued by New Orleans toughs whom he beat in a card game, to the discovery of his body, to the final extended scene as police and the public health inspector chase the two thugs exposed to plague, the film breaks the commercial barriers between the city and the river. In the process, it also recalls New Orleans's commercial port as the site of disease.[40] Kochak, the immigrant stowaway, runs back toward the wharf from which he entered the city, the only New Orleans he knows. The local toughs follow him there, a territory they know better still. In a later scene, their leader Blackie (Jack Palance) even chats familiarly with one warehouse security guard. But even as the characters and the camera traverse the built structures of the waterfront, its single-minded commercial use remains inhospitable. In flight, Kochak crosses a series of tracks and in front of a train that narrowly misses him. (Kazan remembers that the actors did all their own stunts, blaming him for trying to kill them.[41]) Although unharmed by the train, Kochak is soon killed by Blackie's men in the shadow of a warehouse and found next morning facedown in the shallow, murky water somewhere between the dock and the shore. The camera pans up to citizens above, behind a narrow rail—real citizen extras, in fact—as they watch police at the crime scene below. They are told to get back, move along.

At the film's end, when the tables are turned, Blackie and Fitch (Zero Mostel) flee from the police through cavernous banana and coffee warehouses where broad-shouldered Negroes—not actors—hoist massive bundles in the half light. Blackie and Fitch fall out of a mechanical chute with the goods as though part of the tonnage measured by the Dock Board. In the climactic scene, Blackie crawls on all fours along the edge of the extended dock while the police run on the wharf just above his head and in front of the wall of warehouses facing the river. Ratlike— Kazan admitted the easy symbol—Blackie then climbs up the rope securing a ship to the shore until he encounters a rat-catching device on the line that he cannot get around. He falls then into the muddy river and must be fished out by the police. All the while, the camera is giving the audience the long and wide view of the warehouses and wharfs unfamiliar to tourists or citizens: across the breadth of freight-line tracks; inside and outside warehouses; above, beside, beneath, the docks; up to the line of ocean-going vessels.

It is not just the film's underworld characters that the camera detects in the commercial space between city and river. There are the workers in the warehouses, the merchant seaman awaiting commissions in their hall, a tugboat captain and his girl who live below deck on their boat beyond the Barracks Street Wharf, and even a merchant vessel in the Gulf (the carrier of the stowaway and the source of the plague) approached by the public health official and police detective (Richard Widmark and Paul Douglas) in a seaplane. Between the city and the river there are also the US Public Health Service doctor and the police detectives themselves, doing their detective work. The dockworkers, who were hidden by the enclosure of warehouses and rail yards in the early twentieth century, are made visible again in Kazan's film. They are an inherent part of the "feeling of New Orleans" Kazan conveys.

"I wanted boats, steam engines, warehouses, jazz joints—of New Orleans—in that picture," Kazan told an interviewer.[42]

The domestic scenes in the film occur, by contrast, in an Uptown cottage, bathed in light and isolated from the river except for the sound of steamboat whistles. There the Public Health Service doctor (Widmark) and his wife (Barbara Bel Geddes) and their son Tommy (Tommy Cook) lead a pleasant, wise-cracking life understood as the object to be protected from the plague and its carriers. The camera sees their lives consistently from the middle distance, one room at a time, the backyard being an enclosed room as are the interior shots. The camera never shows the front of the house or any long shot down the street, where an Uptown wharf might be located, though we do see one glimpse of the back alley that intersects with a street. There are, however, no tracking shots that lead from the source of the whistle to their door. The domestic scene always fades in, a bright surprise after a fadeout on some dark downtown scene. All the advantages of communal and platial interaction gained by the long, wide angle, and tracking shots in the rest of the film depicting the commercial and industrial city, are absent in the domestic location. The camera casts a domestic gaze on these scenes of two-person dialogues, one room at a time. Wife and boy, not surprisingly, appear only in these rooms, separate from the father's investigation on and off the waterfront.

Ironically, other threats enter this Uptown everyday life unchallenged while the good doctor spends his nights in a frantic 48-hour search between French Quarter dives and riverfront haunts for the sources and carriers of plague. In the backyard of the cottage is a chest of drawers, outside for repainting. As a marker of a significant but undeveloped plot, it comes in for visual comment in every domestic scene and verbal comment in most. The camera first fades in on this object when Widmark and the son are introduced. The boy instructs his father how to paint the chest and offers to do the work himself when his father proves inept. Tommy is a good student not only of their neighbor the painter but also of National Lead Company's *Dutchboy Painter*, the company's magazine. From 1918 until 1952, knowing already the deleterious effects of lead paint on children, they ran a campaign to "cater to the children," encouraging kids to be like the Dutchboy and repaint their old toys and furniture with lead paint. The advertisements similarly encouraged parents to paint old walls for a more healthful, modern home.[43] By being an inexpert painter, Widmark is in danger of failing a domestic test of modern, healthful living. The neighbor chides him for two overlapping offenses: not taking the chest of drawers inside sooner to save the new paint job and not spending enough time with the boy.

In the narrative of the script, the chest of drawers might signal the return of the couple's repressed desire to have a second child. But this explanation only begs the unanswered question about the safety of the domestic scene for the living and the as yet unborn. If the father stashes his plague-contaminated clothes in the garage before he comes in the house, does that maintain the barrier between the safe and the unsafe? Does that hold the miasm at bay? The chest of drawers remains in the yard for the boy, the father, and the neighbor to lean on as they converse and for the viewer to ponder.

Infectious diseases such as the plague might be kept from the door of the modern home, but each room of the house cannot be separated from the tenticular radiations that link domestic products to the industries that produce them and to the river that carries industrial wastes and drinking water.[44] Chronic disease is not an illegal alien stowing away on a commercial vessel. It is, like an old chest of drawers, inside everyday life. To see those links, viewers need more than a peculiarly present piece of furniture. They need long shots of the domestic scene, tracking shots from the river to their kitchen faucet, from the petrochemical plant to their paint can. As Laura Mulvey said of the female gaze thirty years ago, the ecological gaze would make visible the miasms of everyday life only if the camera taught the viewer to see differently.[45]

In 1950, the audience would have known without thinking the Dutchboy's advice to boys and their parents, but not many would yet have acknowledged the danger there, let alone from the Mississippi River corridor.[46] The film and its characters do not recognize these dangers either. When the Public Health doctor sees himself as an economic and professional failure, he envies Bill Mosley who works for Independent Chemical Company. Knowing his ambition and his disappointment, his wife teases that the oil companies can't lay a pipeline in Arabia without the services of her husband, the public health doctor. These kinds of professional and economic ambitions are the future in Hydrocarbon Society

Malaise and *The Moviegoer*

Binx and his "cousin" Kate see *Panic in the Streets* at a Tchoupitoulas Street theater. "There is a scene," Binx tells the reader, "which shows the very neighborhood of the theater." Kate, clinically depressed but deliberately chipper, looks around the neighborhood as they leave the theater and remarks, "Yes, it is certified now." Binx explains,

Nowadays when a person lives somewhere, in a neighborhood, the place is not certified for him. More than likely he will live there sadly and the emptiness which is inside him will expand until it evacuates the entire neighborhood. But if he sees a movie which shows his very neighborhood, it becomes possible for him to live, for a time at least, as a person who is Somewhere and not Anywhere.[47]

In his essays, Percy often defined the malaise of everyday life in the 1950s as human beings never having had so much, so much control, and so many reasons to be happy but never having been so miserable. This malaise is temporarily relieved, Binx teaches Kate, through certification by film.[48] Yet the filmic respite for a neighborhood in malaise will give way to public evacuation nonetheless, Binx claims, because of the emptiness inside the individual—rather than to a plague or any other public health emergency. Binx looks to mass culture—movies, television, radio, advertisements, signage, car consumption—to alleviate the malaise, sometimes defined, in the novel, as the pain of loss. At the same time, he experiences the effect of mass culture as tenuous.

When Kazan shot his film and later when Percy wrote his novel, Tchoupitoulas Street ran along the river without providing visual access to it. Railroad tracks and warehouses lined the riverside of the street. But Binx, the narrator and the hero, does not describe any feature of the theater's neighborhood or the film's scene for that matter. Although the characters declare the neighborhood certified, the novel provides the reader no visual evidence to share in this sensation.

Percy does proffer the reader a whiff of the Tchoupitoulas neighborhood where city meets wharf but only in the preceding Mardi Gras parade scene occurring nearby that Kate and Binx witness immediately prior to the movie. As "Negroes from Louisiana Avenue and Claiborne" cross the St. Charles neutral ground to bring their children closer to the parade, Binx observes that "a south wind carries the smell of coffee from the Tchoupitoulas docks."[49] Except for the distinctive Choctaw name itself, here, permeating the parade from off-site, is the reader's only sensory access to, if not certification of, the Tchoupitoulas neighborhood.[50]

> Film scholar Richard Dyer says of movie stars that they matter because they act out aspects of life that matter to us; and performers get to be stars when what they act out matters to enough people. Though there is a sense in which stars must touch on things that are deep and constant features of human existence, such features never exist outside a culturally and historically specific context.[51]

Dyer's familiar contemporary cultural argument takes film's powers of certification as seen in Binx's Kierkegaardian humanist frame and places them inside a "culturally and historically"—and, we could add, geographically—"specific context." Seen through Dyer's assumptions, what matters to Binx and to Percy comes more clearly into focus, as does the failure of moviegoing (as well as television and secretary spectating) to offer Binx sustained relief from the malaise.

The immediate narrative context for viewing *Panic in the Streets* is a description of the parade's flambeaux bearers as rich in visual detail as the neighborhood description is poor. The last days of Mardi Gras season mark the duration of the novel, so Carnival's significance asserts itself in form even as the central characters of the diegesis resist its traditional claims on them.

> Here they come, a vanguard of half a dozen extraordinary Negroes dressed in dirty Ku Klux Klan robes, each bearing aloft a brace of pink and white flares. . . . The bearers stride swiftly along the very edge of the crowd, showering sparks on everyone. They look angrily at each other to keep abreast, their fierce black faces peeping sidewise from their soiled hoods.[52]

If the Negro flambeaux bearers look ironically like besmirched Klan members bearing a burning cross, the white krewe members aboard floats and horses "look [less ironically] like crusaders."[53] To avoid Kate's current fiancé, "royalty" in this krewe, Binx and Kate dart away from the scene and into the showing of *Panic in the Streets,* but the parade is not so easily escaped. The interface of parade denizens and the film—its Twentieth Century Fox title and Binx's brief exposition of its plague-scare plot—begs the question whether the incipient epidemic besetting the New Orleans of the novel is the angry Negroes as passionate as the Klan or the white krewe members besotted by nostalgia and their own vainglorious quest. It is likely both because together they attract the Negroes from Claiborne onto the neutral ground of St. Charles and entice their children to run alongside the parade just on the border of the elite Garden District. In the waning days of segregation, Percy's novel describes a racially inflected panic in the streets both ritualistic and nascent. Kate and the Negro onlookers may laugh at the spectacle, but the flambeaux bearers remain "contemptuous" and the krewe members "strangely good-natured."[54]

The film's plague plot half-heartedly, even comically, references anti-Communist paranoia and xenophobia, but in the local context given to it by the novel, its broad conceit enacts the desperate comedy of racial rituals and pending integration's threat that matter to Percy and his New Orleans characters.[55] Binx may play at some postmodern game of simulacra in which the film's pictures certify the local landscape, but the imbrication of parade scene and film synopsis conveys that in the New Orleans of the novel, Mardi Gras controls the diachronic and

synchronic reality of time and the ritualistic violation of space. And it
conveys—to return to Dyer's terms—that this is what matters to Percy.
Although the photography of Kazan's film reveals a city still intimate
with its river and fearful of that intimacy, Percy references, then
suppresses, those images by omitting any verbal reenactment of the river
view. Instead, in laying the bald, film noir plot like a stencil over the
vivid imagery of the previous parade scene, he both certifies its significance and minimizes it at the same time. On the one hand, the effect of
the interface is to make an announcement: the time peaceably to address
the racial inequities afoot is running out—hardly more than forty-eight
hours remains; each enactment of Carnival ritual in a moment recalls
the repetitions of tradition, but also of the vulnerability of segregation's
borders. On the other hand, the effect is to evacuate that social content,
laugh at both spectacles, and thus identify the true horror as residing
within the individual pathology of Kate. She is playing the role of the
"best buddy," but in fact "she unfailingly turns everything she touches
to horror."[56] Thus ends the chapter. In the desegregating 1950s, Percy
suspends his hero between these two effects.

Within the Cutrer's Garden District household of Aunt Emily, Uncle
Jules, and his daughter Kate, Aunt Emily retains the racial rituals of her
class: she perceives her servant Mercer as a faithful retainer brought
from the upriver plantation so he might remain with the family—hers,
not his. But Binx believes that Mercer knowingly weighs every move.
"My main emotion around Mercer is unease that in threading his way
between servility and presumption, his foot might slip. I wait on
Mercer, not he on me."[57] Although the Negroes from Claiborne may be
approaching, Mercer, who siphons off money from the household
expenses, has already infiltrated the Garden District. Binx has, by
contrast, taken himself off to Gentilly, one of the new suburbs built on
fill dirt in the wetlands north of the river ridge. There he can immerse
himself in mass culture, evading both the past and the future of New
Orleans society. But even in Gentilly, on Ash Wednesday, he encounters
a disquieting although less calculating Negro, a middle-class man with a
cross of ashes on this forehead, a suit on his back, and a recent model
car awaiting him.[58] On the last page of the Carnival season narrative, in
the penultimate chapter preceding the epilogue, Binx asks himself why
this man is here. To come up in the world, to find God at the corner of
Elysian Fields and Bons Enfants? Although Binx cultivates a self-irony
foreign and repellant to Aunt Emily, his self-awareness does not explain
these Negro characters or identify their place in the malaise of everyday
life that he experiences and witnesses. He only waits on their next move.

In the suburbs, Binx plays at being Hydrocarbon Man. He courts his
secretaries on drives to the Gulf Coast in his car. While sitting on the
plastic play equipment of the elementary school next door, he even

contemplates running a service station rather than continuing as a stock broker for Uncle Jules or returning to medical school as Aunt Emily wishes. Aunt Emily has invested some of her plantation inheritance in service stations, but Binx, at twenty-nine, toys with actually entering the social class of his stepfather, who works at a Western Auto. Binx has sold the wetlands of his own inheritance to a developer and has the money to invest.[59] Although this is a whim, an unrealized strategy of his search for a life without malaise, he meanwhile does act on his feelings about American Motors stock, making himself a nice profit.[60] The character Binx may suffer anxiety on a business trip in the vast wind-swept prairie of Chicago or worry about the horror that revolves around Kate, but the bemused narrator Binx claims the middle distance of ironic self-awareness without appreciable deviation from that state of emotional suspension. What has been lost in his everyday world is not the unattainable Caddy Compson of the faltering plantation class who haunts Faulkner's Quentin, but rather the very pain of loss itself from which he is fleeing. In a world where, by mutual consent, Binx and Kate's acting is taken as action: "the thou of I-thou [has] become the thou of 'I netted better than thirty-five thou this year.'"[61]

Critic Richard Pindell, who made this piquant observation in 1975, concludes that Percy's style "says in effect let us now praise filling stations." It thus embarrasses us, says Pindell, but keeps "the right desires active" such that we feel at a loss but not lost.[62] More than twenty years later, Philip Simmons offers a similar but more sweeping conclusion: in the Eisenhower years of spiritual poverty amidst material plenty, the years conveyed in The Moviegoer, mass culture—that is, corporately produced culture—is an alien, colonizing presence rather than the hegemonic one it will become in later, more thoroughly postmodern fictions.[63] The novel's epilogue does indeed find Binx, now a medical student, living in a renovated Garden District shotgun with wife, Kate, whom he delicately leads through life. Local rituals and familiar locales still assert their dominance over mass culture as the parade and Panic scene foretold. And yet the helplessness of Kate and the forbearance of Binx in the epilogue are not a persuasive antidote to the self-directed irony throughout. The epilogue begs for explanation beyond culture—of the colonizing, hegemonic, or local kind.

If throughout the novel, Binx engages mass culture as one who sees its emptiness but filters his emotional life through it anyway, at the end, he seems to have no emotions at all. His relationship with mass culture is so bemusingly portrayed throughout the novel that it tempts readers to dwell there away from the epilogue, to bring the whole retinue of postmodern criticism to bear on Binx as consumer of mass culture. But postmodernism's attention to technologies of communication and representation, of mass culture and consumption, will not in itself explain the circumscribed options of Percy's epilogue. Nor does the epilogue provide a satisfying answer to the questions raised by Binx as mass culture man. The provocation of Percy's novel and the limitation of its epilogue can, however, be better understood if postmodernist fiction is defined as representing the "pluralistic and anarchistic ontological landscape of advanced industrial cultures" in which industrial production and its effects are still at play.[64] In Gentilly, Binx watches the vast sky stretching north and east toward the lake and Gulf and sees not only water fowl but also the service station of his imagination. Just as in Flaherty's *Louisiana Story*, Binx's vision can, for a time, imagine the easy coexistence of the romantic's Nature and Hydrocarbon Society. But not without an ironized relationship to mass culture that recognizes such visions as passing flirtations. The gap between the service station vision and the epilogue leaves unanswered why such a vision is impossible, and the epilogue subsequently squelches any open explanation beyond Binx's (re)turn to traditional upper-class, male responsibility. Inside the wall of Tchoupitoulas Street warehouses that separate the Garden District from the river, Binx's epilogic life, on the surface of verbal play, is as sunny and limited as the doctor's wife in Kazan's film.

Except, perhaps, in his telling of his stepbrother, Lonnie's, death. Lonnie, fifteen, a congenital "cripple" all his life, "dies of a massive virus infection which was never positively identified." The whole of Binx's story exists between his memory of his brother Scott's death from pneumonia when Binx was eight and Lonnie's death at the end.[65] Between the scourge of infectious disease and the mystery of chronic disease, Binx the survivor lives to be a student, a soldier, a moviegoer, a doctor, and a husband. Surrounded by individual death, he, as a veteran of the Korean War, is haunted, however ironically, by the era's experience of mass death.[66] Death and mass death, as much as mass culture, define the malaise and Binx's search for a way out.

In explaining what he calls a repetition, for example, Binx recalls a time when he picked up a German magazine and saw there an ad for Nivea Creme just like one he had seen twenty years earlier in the 1930s. The effect, he says, is to neutralize the intervening years: "the thirty million deaths, the countless torturings, uprootings and wanderings to and fro. Nothing of consequence could have happened because Nivea Creme was exactly as it was before."[67] His language, of course, speaks the horror he claims was neutralized by repetition. Or, another example: "For some time now," chapter nine begins, "the impression has been growing upon me that everyone is dead." He continues, "when I speak to people, in the middle of a sentence it will come over me: yes, beyond a doubt this is death."[68] Ironized, mass culture and the malaise of everyday life collapse distinctions between coincidence and holocaust, social boredom and death.

Writing about mass death not long after Percy, Theodor Adorno describes how

> our metaphysical faculty is paralyzed because actual events have shattered the basis on which speculative metaphysical thought could be reconciled with experience. . . . The administrative murder of millions made of death a thing one had never yet to fear in just this fashion. There is no chance any more for death to come into the individuals' empirical life as somehow conformable with the course of that life. . . . The destruction of nonidentity [the death of death] is ideologically lurking.[69]

The effect of mass death that Adorno calls "absolute negativity" resides in the interstices of Percy's irony. Characters fall out of the novel into individual death as though they were never part of Binx's or the reader's experience. If Lonnie's death is an exception, it is only because Kate takes what Binx calls a "womanish whim" to come see the dying boy. When, distressed, she says to Binx, "he's so hideously thin and yellow, like one of those wrecks lying on a flatcar at Dachau," his reply is to say he shouldn't have let her come and that she is good-looking.[70]

Percy repeated often that the real fear of his alienated era was that the bomb would *not* fall, because then, without the convenient threat of near total annihilation, future everyday life would have to be imagined beyond the breakdown of metaphysical thought.[71] For medical student Bolling, the future of the epilogue is one that brackets the malaise and alienation and reembraces the objective-empirical facts of scientific method. Hepatitis has made Lonnie yellow. An unidentified viral infection has killed him. He dismisses Kate's metonymy that links Lonnie's individual death to mass death, and he laconically manages her knuckle-biting grief.[72] In his nonfiction, Percy repeatedly expressed his doubts about the scientific method of the age.[73] Kate, Percy's bellwether of horror in the scene, confronts Binx's empiricism, calling him "bumptious," "cold-blooded," and "thick-skinned." Her strident sorrow struggles against the objective treatment of individual death and, through her metaphor, against the "banality with which acts [of mass slaughter] are committed and taken note of."[74] But in the final scene, though Kate calls Binx "grisly," she does not question his control of the scene and the future. Her recognition of horror is just another symptom of her neurosis like her inability to ride the streetcar alone without detailed instructions.

Percy's hero lives between the alienated consumption of mass culture and the objective-empirical facts of the scientific method in his attempt to survive an everyday life immersed in individual deaths redefined by the breadth and banality of mass death. Whether as ironic Romeo or cool-headed husband, his self-awareness is its own end. Acting is action. Even in the epilogue, Binx and Lonnie's young siblings play a game of tragedy in response to the brother's death. It is sweetly rendered, less distant and ironical because played with children for whom illness and death are still only vaguely attached to pain and loss. They are easily distracted by an offer of a train ride at Audubon Park and an assurance that Lonnie will be free of his wheelchair in heaven.[75] But Percy's Catholic promise of salvation sits less easily on his reader than his young characters. The reader has been trained too well by Binx's ironic wit to give it up for a quick promise of heaven without wheelchairs. Between individual death and mass death are immanent questions of public justice and public health left unaddressed, in 1961, by Dr. Percy or medical student Bolling.

The Public Intellectual and Public Space

Before Walker Percy was a public figure in New Orleans or even a successful novelist, he already had some notoriety in larger intellectual circles. Robert Coles remembers that he was introduced to Percy's work when Paul Tillich assigned Percy's 1954 essay "Man on the Train" to his class at Harvard.[76] But Percy has been most widely known as the novelist from the South, especially south Louisiana. With the National Book Award for *The Moviegoer* under his belt and nearly a second National Book Award for his second published novel, *The Last Gentleman*, Percy received invitations to teach at the prestigious colleges of the Eastern United States.[77] He taught, however, only at Louisiana State University in Baton Rouge and Loyola of New Orleans. He lectured in Athens, Georgia, where his mother's people were from, and wrote about Mississippi, where he grew up with Uncle Will, but he remained in Covington proximate to "New Orleans: Mon Amour."[78] In "Why I Live Where I Live," with homage to Eudora Welty's sense of place, he wrote about Covington as a useful nonplace in relation to the place, New Orleans. In Covington, on the north side of Lake Pontchartrain, he said he could avoid anonymous nonplacement, exotic misplacement, or totally rooted Faulknerian placement.[79] At Bechac's, a restaurant on the lake's north shore, Percy became, nonetheless, a habitué who nurtured local writers and bookstore owners. There or at his home in Covington he gracefully tolerated burgeoning columns of interviewers, academics, and fans, whether Robert Coles or a boy from Walla Walla.[80] In person or in print, he appeared in New Orleans as needed by friends or required by publishers. Multiple photographs of him presided over the Maple Street Bookstore Uptown. Although never quite a Norman Mailer or a Saul Bellow on the national scene, Percy achieved the status of public intellectual on the local scene.

In a *Harper's* article in 1965, Percy defined "public" in a way that explains, in part, the choices of Binx and of himself. He began his essay comparing the brave Mississippians killed at Cemetery Ridge near Gettysburg to brave Mississippians James Meredith and Medgar Evers by way of boldly introducing the ugly resistance of Ole Miss students to Meredith. Always a keen eye for the South's racial rituals (see *The Last Gentleman)*, Percy was also a good student of Father Louis Twomey at Loyola's Institute for Industrial Relations (later, Institute of Human Relations).[81] That sensitivity—courage even—is evident in the 1965 essay. So he has credibility when in writing of Ole Miss and the federal government, he said that there "was cultural confusion over the word 'public.'" The traditional conviviality among the white student body made it de facto a private school, argues Percy. Meredith was entering "their living room." "It is this hypertrophy of pleasant familiar space at the expense of a truly public sector which accounts for the extraordinary apposition in Mississippi of kindliness and unspeakable violence." The national idea of public space may be a necessary alternative for Mississippi, Percy proposes, because the American Settlement for "alienation, depersonalization, and mass man" is a means to racial impasse. That is to say that "the depersonalized American neighborhood, a Giant supermarket or eighty thousand people watching a pro ball game may not be the most creative of institutions, but at least . . . people generally leave each other alone." Yet, he hopes that the Southern sociable yeast, black and white, may yet find a way to "leaven the American lump," to teach the nation what whites and blacks in the South know about getting along—quite apart from "humbuggery about a perfect love" between Southern whites and blacks—and thus save the nation from itself.[82] Percy's character Binx is poised between the American Settlement and old white Southern sociability without a public place in which to enact the dialectic of public that this essay proposes.

"Like nature, public space in the city has been historically contingent, culturally constructed, *and* material," writes Kelman.[83] Without a space and thus a means to achieve a new definition of "public," without a new location for public space that is neither the Super Dome nor the beautiful enclosure of Audubon Park nor someone's living room, neither Binx nor Percy can conceptualize a multiplex public with shared social and medical needs. Without such public space, there is no room to conceptualize public health. There is only the inevitability of individual death, the abstraction of mass death, and the distraction of mass culture. Or there is private space.

In the 1960s, after the publication of *The Moviegoer*, Percy and other south Louisianians had more overt evidence to prompt their thinking publicly about health. Although, as early as the 1940s, the public of water drinkers complained of an oily taste in the municipal drinking water, the belief remained that the river had a virtual limitless capacity to dilute any pollutants. In 1951, the US Public Health Service reported that the industrial wastes from Baton Rouge may affect the New Orleans water supply, but they focused their analysis on bacterial and biological contamination (as was traditional at the time). Until the 1960s, the state granted discharge permits to all comers and took virtually "no enforcement actions along the lower Mississippi." But even if the general public in New Orleans missed the debates about and studies of the drinking water prompted by public complaints in 1957 and 1960, the 1963–1964 massive fish kill in the lower Mississippi "riveted public attention on pollution."[84]

The dangers to the river and from the river were now not only tastable, smellable, and indeed knowable at the site of the kitchen faucet in all greater New Orleans homes, but, in the 1960s, the river was again visible from the French Quarter. In 1962 the warehouse at Jackson Square was torn down when it was discovered that its weight was too great for the river bank that was eroding underneath it. After the river view reappeared, Vieux Carré opponents of the proposed riverfront elevated expressway gained momentum as they argued with more passion for a renewed spatial relationship between the city and the Mississippi. They saw the possibility to reinstate a public promenade on the riverfront. In 1964, the Louisiana Courts returned the control of the neighborhood's borders—Rampart Street and the riverfront—to the Vieux Carré Commission, and US Transportation Secretary Volpe decided against a riverfront expressway at the French Quarter site, adding authority to the possibility of a new river view. In the mid-1960s, then, New Orleans citizens and tourists got an opportunity to reconsider their relationship with the Mississippi on site rather than simply in Kazan's movie.

One argument for a renewed spatial relationship with the river was launched by Harnett Kane. He urged New Orleanians to reconnect the Vieux Carré with the river and its collective memories, however contested and contingent.[85] It is important to note that depending on which ways the contests and contingencies of those collective memories fell, the reinstated river view and river walk might make Jackson Square another depot on the plantation tour riverboat circuit and not a window onto the geographical and ecological force of the river and the multiple histories in its currents and on its riverbanks. As Percy argued of Ole Miss, traditional cultural practice can maintain a public space as a private living-room.

Although the riverfront at Jackson Square was opened up to public use in the 1970s, from his nonplace home in Covington, Percy never seems to have found the sort of public place implied in his 1965 essay. Even his last novel, *Thanatos Syndrome,* though it contains a stunning description of the Old River area behind Angola penitentiary upriver from Baton Rouge and creates a plot dependent on waterborne contaminants, does not take on the industrial sources and public health effects of the Mississippi's pollution down river. In this last fiction, he foregoes an ecological gaze at the course of the lower Mississippi and instead tells a tale in which the waters of the river are a means to social engineering by malevolent doctors who have deliberately infused the water with a special sodium compound.

When, in 1985, Percy did want to take the state of Louisiana to task, he could write *The Times-Picayune* with the full legitimacy, if not authority, of a public intellectual of that place. What is wrong with Louisiana and how did it happen? he asks. How did a state with mineral resources, the greatest gas production, and the largest port become a place with depleted oil and gas preserves, "marshes plundered and polluted," a yearly loss of fifty square miles of wetlands, one of the highest cancer rates in the country, one of the lowest per capita incomes within the United States, and the worst quality of education (tied with Mississippi)?

> At least part of the answer is no great mystery. Ever since the palmy days of the Perezes fifty years ago, when Judge Leander Perez acquired royalty interests in public land drilled by major oil companies, some Louisiana politicians and the big oil-and-gas corporations seemed to have enjoyed an extended love-in, a mutually beneficial arrangement, but not necessarily beneficial to the people of the state.[86]

In the 1980s, the numbers making this connection were growing even if, as Percy says, boosters took any such inquiry as an assault on the city's economic growth. The comparison of Louisiana's industrial river corridor to Germany's Ruhr Valley was fast becoming a trope, and the name "Cancer Alley" a synonym for south Louisiana. However, Percy's emphasis on the unsavory Perez country bumpkins and his turn to the problems of public education deflect concern away from the more polished politicians and elites in New Orleans and Baton Rouge and the leadership of Standard Oil, Dow, W.R. Grace, and the growing numbers of German and Japanese corporations eager to export their most toxic industries to Louisiana. He decries the inferior public education of poor Louisiana children, mostly African American children, but does not follow his own logic and denounce, as well, the assaults on this public's or any local public's health.

Even physicians and scientists who make it their business to study disease in industrial settings and proximate sites can find threats to local public health as difficult to prove if not to diagnose as did Percy, the last gentleman physician, the pathologist who distrusted scientific method. One problem lies in that method itself: "the inability of epidemiology, toxicology, and statistics to demonstrate very small effects"—local effects.

> As one physician who studies disease in industrial settings puts it, "I'm usually the last to know when there's an environmental problem. Even then I can only find anything of significance when virtually everyone in a community or factory already knows the problem exists."[87]

Given these conditions of scientific knowledge production (and legal demands for a particular positive proof of toxicity), Percy's turn to philosophy and fiction might have provided a better opportunity to diagnose Kierkegaardian malaise as a response to the miasms besetting the bodies of the public than would have a career in pathology. He was poised to make such a connection. But his vision, as with that of other New Orleanians, was directed inward, away from the transforming river, contained by the wall of levees, warehouses, and railroads.

5

The Spectacle Between
Piety and Desire

The Place of New Orleans's Black Panthers
and Ishmael Reed's Neo-HooDooism

Harnett Kane was the guest speaker when the Young Men's Business Club (YMBC) met on September 9, 1970, at the Fairmont Roosevelt Hotel. He was there to defend the legal boundaries of the French Quarter from city council members and developers who would "strip away" the valuable riverfront. But before Kane spoke, the YMBC had some other business to conduct. They passed a resolution opposing the use of student, state, or federal funds to pay "leftist revolutionary speakers" on local college campuses. Visits to New Orleans by Yippie leader Jerry Rubin, Black Panther leader Bobby Seale, and attorney William Kunstler did not, they said, reflect the desires of the majority of students, and, they stressed, "laid a foundation for radical activity this fall."[1] Two shootouts at the Desire Housing Development the next week between New Orleans Police (NOPD) and the National Committee to Combat Fascism (NCCF), the vanguard of the Black Panther Party (BPP), and another confrontation at Desire on November 19 were among the more spectacular events confirming the YMBC's fears. But not everyone believed these events corroborated the YMBC's analysis of where the foundation of violence lay. When NCCF member Tim Pratt spoke that fall at Louisiana State University of New Orleans, he sited the cause for confrontation in the city itself rather than in incendiary outsiders. "Wherever black people are oppressed in the city of New Orleans, there will be a chapter of the NCCF."[2]

It is hardly news that a business organization dedicated to economic development such as YMBC and a political organization committed to social justice such as NCCF would have offered these disparate theories on the violence in the city that fall and on threats to the city's sustainability. But the architectural metaphor of YMBC and the urban promise of the NCCF together do share a significant preoccupation with place. This chapter turns again to the particularities of place—New Orleans generally and the Desire Housing Development specifically—to explore presumptions and concerns of organizations such as the YMBC and NCCF about the brewing conflict in 1970. With the help of Ishmael Reed's 1972 novel *Mumbo Jumbo*, this chapter brings New Orleans HooDoo folkways and their penchant for spectacle into reciprocal relation with the 1970 spectacle of police and Black Panther standoffs at the Desire Housing Development.[3] By doing so, it emends the substantial scholarship about Reed's work and the equally substantial memoirs and retrospective analyses of the Black Panthers, in both of which the place of New Orleans is absent. The chapter argues that platially specific analysis across the spectacles of Reed's narrative collage, the NOPD, and the NCCF of the BPP in New Orleans enables a richer understanding of Panther/police confrontation. In the end, the Panther/police binary gives way to a different and important distinction between politics as reportable spectacle and politics as singular action.

Although the former was its own national genre in the late 1960s and early 1970s, the latter is enmeshed in local folkways and local sites. The national debate over "1960s" Panther/police confrontation—what Nikhil Pal Singh has called "the Panther effect"—is still a subject of ongoing critical attention that obscures the local circumstances of those events.[4] It is true that, inevitably, the local events are enmeshed in the national discourse and national policy. But the complicating details of their locality are necessary to a reading of the city's sustainability as both cultural memory and economic and sociopolitical viability. The details of locality are also, more tied to international intercommunalism, as the Panthers called their alternative to Communism, or Neo-HooDooism, as Reed called the cross-platial multicultural aesthetic driving his satire, than they are to a national narrative of conspiracy and security. Singh's essay on the Black Panthers turns theoretically toward questions of locality by tracing the translocal and transnational circulation and accumulation of BPP political strategies and cross-cultural reasoning. But whereas Singh attends to what Arjun Appadurai has defined as the "mediascapes, ethnoscapes and ideoscapes" of the postcolonial "global cultural economy," this chapter focuses on the sustainability of the local site, a place where desires were in motion before (and after) the BPP arose there as a force to enact "highly localized, spatially defined demands for communal autonomy."[5] As New Orleans community leader Bob Tucker said recently, "What they [the Panthers] were doing—all that military stuff—was no problem because it was just another phase of a foundation that had already been laid. It was just another group in the neighborhood."[6]

A Casebook Example

On September 14 and 15, 1970, NOPD twice engaged in gun battles at the 3500 block of Piety Street, the site of NCCF headquarters, across from the Desire Housing Development. Having been evicted from a building in the Uptown area of the St. Thomas Housing Development the previous summer and under threat of eviction from their new headquarters on Piety Street, the NCCF had dug in their heels, sandbagging the building where they held meetings and stored a cache of weapons and Panther literature.[7] Purportedly, the gun battle at Desire on the 14th and 15th ensued after the NCCF "tried" two police infiltrators who later claimed they ran to local grocery stores to spare themselves beatings from the "People" in the street. More than one hundred police personnel armed with automatic weapons and backed by a helicopter and armored car borrowed from the state police entered the Desire neighborhood in response, police later said, to reports of sniper fire, some aimed at uniformed police on regular duty, and to reports of fire bombings. After an extended exchange of gunfire that resulted in the wounding of seven people and the removal and arrest of sixteen NCCF members from the Piety address, the police withdrew, only to return in force hours later, in response, they said, to reports of a firebomb threat to Broussard's grocery. Broussard, a black man, was the owner of the Piety house and also a grocer from whom the NCCF asked (demanded?) contributions to their free-breakfast-for-children survival program. During a second gun battle, four men were shot in front of the grocery. There was one fatality—a man named Kenneth Borden. Eventually, an angry crowd forced the police across a drainage canal bridge, just as the police had marched the NCCF members across the bridge earlier that day and had them lie spread-eagled in the grass. After midnight, the police withdrew a second time.[8]

The sixteen were arraigned that night on charges of attempted murder, and bail was set by Judge Bernard J. Bagert at $100,000 apiece.[9] State charges of criminal anarchy were later brought by District Attorney Jim Garrison against five Panther members from out of state, only one of whom was in custody. (Anarchy was defined by Louisiana as an attempt to overthrow the state government.) Four of the five purportedly fled the city before the police raided the Piety Street

headquarters, although some Desire residents claimed several days after
the raid that they were sheltering and caring for wounded Panther Steve
Green of Oakland.[10]

When Howard Odum collected rumors of race in the American South
at the start of World War II, he found that white Southerners were
telling each other stories of an impending race war: African Americans
in the South were stockpiling weapons, drilling outside New Orleans;
domestic workers were whispering of insurrection.[11] Although psychol-
ogists Gordon Allport and Leo Postman explained in 1947 that rumors
circulate with greatest frenzy on the brink of momentous events—
meaning, in this case, World War II—people spreading rumors in New
Orleans in 1970 seemed to long for and even produce a decisive event.[12]
Before the YMBC publicly ever voiced their fears of impending violence,
the police chief and mayor were strategizing based on information
about the Black Panthers relayed to them by the Federal Bureau of
Investigation.[13] Police Chief Clarence Giurrusso met with newspaper
editors before the September 14 and 15 events, alerting them to the
news before it happened.[14] Even some of the wounded were apparently
victims of curiosity rather than commitment (as police claimed). Donald
Sneed, a Vietnam veteran, and Jefferson McCormick were drawn to the
Desire neighborhood the evening of September 14 because "we were
curious. . . . Everyone else in the city was curious, I guess."[15] History
teacher Peter Woislawski (injured in the fray) and his wife, Evelyn
(dragged from their car), also went to Desire in response to a rumor.
White witnesses needed to get to the project area before police got
"carried away," they were told.[16]

Summarizing for *The New York Times* the events at Desire on
September 14–15 and Panther/police battles in other cities, Martin
Arnold described the New Orleans incidents as a "casebook example"
of the mutual fear between police and Panthers nationwide that trig-
gered these confrontations.[17] But were the incidents on Piety Street a
casebook example of a deadly national binary? What defined the state
of dread expressed by the YMBC? The "reign of terror" that Mayor
Moon Landrieu perceived at Desire?[18] The "climate of hostility and
repression" that a committee of three prominent black citizens saw
threatening a fair trial of NCCF members?[19] Would the incidents at
Desire in November bear out the *Times* thesis of October?

The National "Panther Effect"

The organization the twenty or so young New Orleanians joined in
1970 was founded in 1966 by Huey Newton and Bobby Seale in
Oakland, California. Inspired by Malcolm X, who had recently been
assossinated, the Black Panther Party for Self-Defense soon replaced

Malcolm's Black Nationalism with the international, class-based political analysis of Frantz Fanon, Che Guevara, and Mao Ze-dung. As a display of resistance to the state, Newton and Seale advocated openly (and legally) carrying guns. In 1967, they won national press when, with a total of 29 Panthers in full regalia, they occupied the California State-house as it voted on the Melford (or "Panther") Bill to criminalize the open display of firearms. That same year, after Newton was accused and then convicted of manslaughter in the death of an Oakland police officer, the national and international notoriety of the Panthers was assured. Local demonstrations and international messages demanded that California "Free Huey," who many believed had been unjustly arrested and tried. In July 1970, Newton was released on bail pending a new trial, but not before the Party leadership and purpose fractured in his absence.[20] Whether or not his absence was the cause of rupture is a matter of ongoing debate.

During those three years, Geronimo ji Jaga (Pratt), a Vietnam veteran, was recruited from Los Angeles to provide military training for the Panthers. Meanwhile, the East Coast BPP, together with the Black Liberation Army, joined the Revolutionary Action Movement in its commitment to armed resistance on the part of all US colonial subjects.[21] After a meeting in Detroit in 1968, 500 Black Nationalists, together with some Black Liberation Army members, initiated a Republic of New Afrika movement designed to found a Black nation-state in the territories of Mississippi, Louisiana, Alabama, Georgia, and South Carolina (an agenda, it seems, at odds with the founding vision of the Panthers).[22] Also, in 1968, eight BPP members, including Bobby Seale, were arrested in Chicago, accused of inciting riots during the 1968 Democratic Convention.[23] The following year, a police raid in Chicago resulted in the notorious killing (with excessive force) of BPP members Mark Clark and Fred Hampton. In New York, police sweeps raked in twenty-one Panthers, arraigning them on various conspiracy charges.[24] Unlike the New Orleans story, the stories of the Chicago Eight and the New York 21 permeate the memories of and the scholar-ship about the BPP.

It was during the three years that Newton was in prison that J. Edgar Hoover decided the BPP was the greatest risk to the nation's security, and in collaboration with local police departments, infiltrated BPP membership with multiple informants. So many, in fact, that the BPP formed a separate recruiting wing: the NCCF. Some argue that government repression was central in the transformation of BPP policy away from armed resistance, always advocated by BPP Minister of Informa-tion Eldridge Cleaver, to a weakened reformism. Others, supporters of Newton, emphasize that the *display* of arms was initially legal and always a *strategy* designed to police the police.[25] Newton spoke for intercommunalism, defined by BPP member David Hilliard as a set of dispersed communities within the system opposed to "one empire-state authority, the reactionary circle of the United States," but understood by Newton's opponents within the BPP as selling out Cleaver's "revolution now."[26]

Historian Philip S. Foner introduced *The Black Panthers Speak* (1970), with the observation that the BPP, like the International Workers of the World more than a half century earlier, had received much press about its conspiracies of silence but little articulation of its beliefs, although these had been published in their newspaper *The Black Panther* since the spring of 1967.[27] Whatever the policy on revolution now, Foner found the BPP's value in its reminder to black Americans that their future is tied to their past, such as the actions of the slave rebels per Marriam-Webster Toussaint Francis-Dominique-L'Ouverture, Gabriel Prosser, Denmark Vesey, Nat Turner, and Frederick Douglass, who, by his own telling, was transformed when he fought back against the slaveholder.[28] The BPP ten-point program calling for black self-determination, decent housing, a jury of true peers, relevant education, and a United Nations–supervised plebiscite held throughout "the black colony" was published in Foner's collection and was publicly reiterated that same year when Huey Newton spoke to an interracial audience in early September 1970 in Philadelphia at the BPP's Revolutionary People's Constitutional Convention. New Orleanians could read Newton's words in their local (white and black) press. Among the articulation of beliefs was a direct address to the racial composition of his audience: "Black people have been looking for such white allies [committed to revolutionary struggle for change] in America for 300 years."[29]

Only 4,500 of the 6,700 convention registrants, half of them white, could fit into the hall at Temple University where Newton laid out the Panther agenda. Another 1,000 were left at the door.[30] Although the previous week, in an apparent effort to discourage convention attendance, Philadelphia Police Commissioner Frank T. Rizzo had ordered raids on three Panther centers in the city that resulted in the search of members as they stood nude on the sidewalk, his tactic had the opposite effect.[31] Attendance was beyond expectations. Registrants attended fifteen workshops in churches and community centers throughout the city, discussing sexual self-determination, health and drugs, control and use of the military, educational systems, and political power.[32]

While police spectacles like the one in Philadelphia increased the support for Panther objectives, the Federal Bureau of Investigation and local police found encouragement in federal legislation. A 1968 amendment to the Civil Rights Act—the so-called Rap Brown Amendment—had "made it a crime to cross state lines with intent to incite a riot," and, in October 1970, four bills that garnered complete bipartisan support were aimed against "urban terrorism." The NOPD's support of these bills was significant.[33]

We Do the Police in Different Voices

Some New Orleanians claimed that before the September violence, they had heard off-duty police officers in bars saying that they were going to "get the Panthers."[34] Desire residents said that when people in Desire needed the police, they would never come; residents had to wait four or five hours for an ambulance. But now that the Panthers were in Desire, the police were interested.[35] Others reported that one of the Desire regular patrolman, Raymond Reed, who had grown up in the "project," was "overly tough in handling cases." Panthers referred to Reed and the other Desire patrolman as "Uncle Tom's."[36] But Desire resident Linda Francis, age fourteen in 1970, remembers the "black cops assigned to the development" as people "who would stop and talk with folks as they walked their beat."[37] Cecil Carter, New Orleans's deputy director of human relations and one of the first blacks to hold a high position in the city in the administration of Moon Landrieu, tempers Francis's memory with the observation that the first wave of black cops were "conscientious super-cops, good guys," but the second wave "felt it necessary to out-cop the cops, . . . to be bad ass."[38]

For his part, Police Chief Clarence Giurrusso proclaimed the two young black undercover policemen who infiltrated the NCCF "heroes" who were terrorized by a Panther "trial" when they were discovered. To the contrary, former Panther Malik Rahim and a Desire community leader claim that some six weeks before the mid-September events, two boys selling *The Louisiana Weekly* tipped off the Panthers that the two with the big "bushes" were police officers. Rather than expose the two, who would then surely be replaced, the Panthers, Rahim remembers, decided to "feed them with a long-handled spoon." Only one member of the group—later discovered to be an undercover federal agent—said, "kill them." Rahim claims that on September 14, police snipers and the helicopter overhead were present *before* the Panthers acknowledged that they knew the true identity of the police agents. When they sent the two agents out into the crowd surrounding the Piety Street headquarters, the two ran to Broussard's grocery where the police were already in place.[39] The two undercover policemen had told reporters in September 1970 a different story: they ran to two separate groceries after being pistol-whipped and sent outside to face an angry mob.[40]

At a Southern University banquet on September 22, 1970, top-ranking black police officer Deputy Chief for Administration Sidney

J. Cates told graduating security guards that police institutions were deteriorating and police officers were seeing themselves as a "persecuted minority" rather than "servants or protectors of society." Because police departments lack sufficient money to attract qualified candidates, he said, they are instead attracting "individuals whose intellectual shortcomings and psychological defects would, under better circumstances, disqualify them for service."[41] Although the NOPD of 1970 had more training and better equipment than the self-armed, self-appointed volunteers who expanded the New Orleans police force in 1900 to find and capture Negro Robert Charles, an incident of white vigilantism and police unpreparedness that Ida Wells-Barnett wrote about in *Mob Rule in New Orleans*, the past did stand as fair warning about the future.[42] A police force such as the ones Cates and Carter described risked what historian William Ivy Hair called, in his 1976 analysis of the Robert Charles events, "a carnival of fury." Explicating that 1900 episode of mob rule, Hair gleans from the local press vivid verbal images of Negroes pulled at random off streetcars and out of the French Market or invaded in their homes, then battered beyond identification and of the dead body of Robert Charles dragged into the street for all law officers and bystanders to shoot or otherwise abuse.[43] New Orleans's own past and present police culture were present together in *The Louisiana Weekly*'s placement of Deputy Chief Cates's words on the same page with the extended coverage of the two undercover agents.[44] A similar rhetoric of juxtaposition was in play when they later ran headlines on the Panthers' trial and deplorable prison conditions at New Orleans Parish Prison continuously across their front page.[45]

Although in the press of 1970 there is little verbal or photographic evidence of rapport between Desire residents and the police, in 2003, Desire community organizer Henry Faggen did remember with respect the restraint of Police Chief Clarence Giarrusso when Faggen was taunting one threatening officer among the many lining the streets.[46] But such restraint is not visible in the record of patrolmen's behavior when they were confronted at the hospital by the brothers of Kenneth Borden, the seventeen-year-old young man killed by police gunfire on September 14. The two brothers were immediately arrested for battery and resisting arrest when they allegedly used obscene language as they sought information about their brother.[47]

The excessive firepower used in Chicago in the raid on Panthers Mark Clark and Fred Hampton two years earlier and other police spectacles in cities such as Philadelphia and New York stood as further provocation for the possible "fire next time" that *Louisiana Weekly* editors wanted to avoid.[48] New Orleans's history, however, forged a somewhat different political desire from that motivating the black migrants and their descendents in the cities of the North, Midwest, and

West. In 1973 the publication of John Blassingame's *Black New Orleans, 1860–1880*, reminded readers that New Orleans experienced large numbers of rural Negro in-migrants more than a century earlier during and after the Civil War, doubling the Negro population between 1860 and 1880. As early as September 1862, large groups of slaves armed with knives, clubs, and old guns eluded rebel pickets and marched to the city, where they fought pitched battles with police even as New Orleans maintained an established population of African-descended people "more articulate, literate, and cosmopolitan than blacks in most other Southern cities."[49]

Desire

Richard Nixon's 1970 government retained two federal policies from the Johnson Administration that US city-makers, like those in New Orleans, wanted to exploit. One of these was the Model Cities Program, originally called Demonstration Cities, that promised federal funds for a comprehensive renovation of the physical and social inner city in relation to an entire metropolitan area. In 1966, Lyndon Johnson signed the Demonstration Cities and Metropolitan Development Act amid rhetoric that the Act initiated "a complete shift in the form of federal housing assistance from that which was started in 1932" under Herbert Hoover.[50] Among other incentives, the Act offered to cover 80 percent of the planning costs for a model neighborhood in those cities whose proposals demonstrated "an understanding of the conditions of the neighborhood area selected, how these conditions have developed, and what will be necessary to overcome them"—assuming conditions exist to be "overcome." A subsequent act in 1968 announced a "ten-year timetable for providing a suitable living environment for every American family."[51] In September 1970, anticipating $9.2 million of the Model Cities money, the city of New Orleans hosted a presentation by the Department of Housing and Urban Development (HUD). There, local teachers heard that neither "community schools" nor any other project under the Model Cities Program would be instigated without the involvement and approval of those in the community. That said, teachers could anticipate $400,000 to pay for breakfasts for 18,000 of the city's children.[52] On November 12, 1970, Mayor Moon Landrieu signed the first ten of thirty-five Model Cities contracts that would deliver the $9.2 million. With those ten contracts in hand, the city could recruit and train residents of beleaguered neighborhoods, initially providing jobs for 845 people and eventually creating jobs for thousands more, the administration claimed. Local credit unions, local day care, local contractors—these were among the promises of the Model Cities Program in New Orleans.[53]

In addition to the desiderata of Model Cities, the other HUD watchword circulating in New Orleans in 1970 was "scattered sites." At the time, scattered public housing sites, which would disperse the urban poor, were a necessary condition for any local housing authority to receive federal funds. Thus in early September 1970, New Orleanians read in local newspapers that the City Planning Commission had approved the Housing Authority of New Orleans's (HANO) request to build an additional 196 "scattered housing units," even though 120 of those were in a block backed up against the Industrial Canal in the territory of the already existing Desire Housing Development.[54] The difference between the promise of "scattered sites" outlined in federal policy and the local practice of "scattered sites" came clearly into focus after the police encountered opposition on Piety Street beside the Desire Housing Development and then, in November, on the public housing grounds themselves. *The Louisiana Weekly*, the city's African American newspaper, ran an opinion piece on October 31, 1970, criticizing HANO for neglecting the large Desire "project" as more isolated than scattered. Surrounded by an interstate, industrial canal, freight rail tracks, wetlands, and major arterials, Desire received no visits from HANO authorities who "speak authoritatively about Scattered Site Housing," accused Furnell Chatman.[55] Constructed in 1957 in the Upper Ninth Ward as 1,860 dwelling units, principally for large families, by 1970, Desire contained many units—whole buildings—abandoned to disrepair. "The failures of public housing have been less in the area of housing . . . than in the area of expectations," argues Alexander von Hoffman in Fannie Mae's *Housing Policy Debate*—expectations he describes as mostly "environmental determinism." Less dispassionate observers of the same phenomenon have referred to US public housing as "subnational institutional space," internal colony within the city. Desire was an example of these paradigms, but, as a local example, was also more than the case study for a model.[56]

After the confrontations between the police and the BPP on Piety Street across from Desire on September 14 and 15, J. Gilbert Scheib, executive director of HANO, seems to have indulged some of those stereotypes even as he offered reassurance to Desire residents. As Scheib praised the NOPD for halting what he called "wanton savagery," he referenced the city's history of violence, but not, it seems, the white mob rule that appalled Ida Wells Barnett. In Scheib's rhetoric, that history had been displaced by "barbarous acts" understood, implicitly, as perpetrated by blacks.

> As seems to be usual in these cases, there was no valid reason for the barbarous acts that were committed, and others attempted but

thwarted. Also, as usual, the victims and intended victims were innocent black citizens.[57]

Happy that no Desire resident or any New Orleanian was injured—teenager Kenneth Borden, not an NCCF member, was killed by police gunfire—Scheib expressed HANO's "vital interest in the safety and welfare of project residents. [We] will spare no effort, at any time, in their behalf."[58]

In time for the year-end holidays, *The Louisiana Weekly* found reason itself to celebrate improved prospects at Desire. A new area office of HUD situated in New Orleans agreed to foot the bill for a survey of Desire residents aimed at assessing the problems and needs there. HANO chairman Tommy J. Heier, Jr., repeated that chief among the project's problems was its "location, which insulates the tenants, to some extent, from the surrounding community." It is, he said, difficult to police, even though off-duty officers are paid by HANO to augment regular police oversight. The survey, he assured readers, would attend to issues of density, family privacy, garbage handling and other health conditions, as well as employment and general modernization.[59] But two years later, when the New Orleans Family Service Society board made their first onsite visit, they still found a "bleak, depressing atmosphere . . . [and] isolation."[60] "Desire was a slave-like community" remembers Lolis Elie, an attorney for the New Orleans NCCF, "a neo-colony of spatial apartheid," claims New Orleanian Orissa Arend retrospectively.[61]

Desire is a feeling that is nothing in itself because—for Lacan, at any rate—it cannot be represented wholly by any one thing or rather because it can only be represented by something else, one thing at a time. If indeed this is so, then when Bernard de Marigny platted his plantation naming one of his new faubourg streets Desire, and Tennessee Williams responded dramatically to that name on the brow of a French Quarter streetcar, they were performing a service for the paradox of desire. That is, they provided it a host, a particular location, just as the loa (spirits) of HooDoo find a host through which to express themselves.[62] The housing "project" that took on the name from the street where it resided also pulsed with this paradox. In each case, desire was all the greater for being called out by its name.

But desire can also be measured and mapped by what transportation planners call desire lines, the most efficient and frequented commuter route between here and there.[63] If this is so, then desire is as much about everyday rhythm and pacing, direction, and speed as it is about a coveted object, nameable or not. Traffic engineers with their can-do, modernist inclinations do miss the desires for the pleasing detour and the cultural center hub, let alone the ineffability of unconscious human desires, but the psychoanalysts also miss something: the pressures of everyday life that push people to chart a direct course and adopt an efficient speed to the extent that they are materially able. By any means necessary. Revolution now. When Desire was named in the press or the police station, HANO applications or the mayor's office, the public housing site against the Industrial Canal was the emplacement of a dialogic relation between a force of desire unnamable in itself, but attachable to something else and a line of desire created by the momentum of necessity. If street names may be read as speaking the drama of a neighborhood, then we can say that the complexity of desire/ Desire exceeded the piety of nationalism enacted in September 1970, whether conducted by the nation-state through its local law enforcement representatives or by any black nationalist opponents.

For *New York Times* reporter Martin Arnold, Desire Housing Development was a typical city within a city with its 14,000 residents, encircled by a sewage-fouled canal, railroad tracks, and superhighways, with access to few buses, no taxis, and minimal sanitation, and with its school barricaded by wire fences. For Arnold, New Orleans was distinguished only by its being "this rather lazy and unconcerned city, where the blacks are not so militant as they are in the North, [even though] there is still more black militancy than most New Orleans whites like to think."[64] Another battle reported in *The Times-Picayune* on September 13, 1970, the day before events at Desire, did not figure in Arnold's typifying description of the city: a commemoration at the newly restored Liberty Monument on the 96th anniversary of the White League's Battle of Liberty Place. Among those scheduled to attend the event that afternoon to honor the White League overthrow of carpetbag rule were a councilman, former mayor, national representative F. Edward Hebert, and a Catholic priest. Reading the names of the dead, laying a wreath and the playing of taps would be followed by a dinner at Antoine's restaurant.[65] Arnold's analysis does not look to this commemoration of New Orleans locality for understanding. However, Reed's *Mumbo Jumbo* does place the spectacle of whiteness—or more precisely, a dominant univocalism he calls *atonism*—in the same narrative collage as the stories of folkways coming out of desire. Specifically, through his use of New Orleans in a novel enacting an extranational, multicultural Neo-HooDoo aesthetic, the local place of New Orleans in the Panthers' movement for translocal intercommunalism, and the state's—that is, the State's—resistance to translocal alliances can better be imagined.

Spectacle

Subversive spectacle as a means of flushing out the legal and extralegal spectacles of hegemonic power is a strategy that the Panthers and Ishmael Reed share. The police raids create publicity, observed Arnold in the *Times,* and without publicity the Panthers would collapse and not be the symbol that they are for American youth, white as well as black.[66] But the police raids did occur and the publicity did continue. As they had in Philadelphia, at Desire the police raids had indeed only enhanced the reputation of the Panthers, especially among children. By full display of their military might and state authority, they did cooperate in their own exposure. To hold a mirror up to police actions, "to stage an encounter that would dramatize, through disciplined resistance to violent policing, the repressive, naked brutality of the state," in fact, to "reveal the state's own spectacular and performative dimensions" as a monopoly on violent social theater, was a primary strategy of the Panthers.[67] But the Panthers' theatrical excesses referenced as well the extralegal spectacles of white terrorism: the lynch mob celebration and the "carnival of fury" that was white mob rule. In doing so, they complicated the past and present articulation of the state as itself a unified player in the confrontation.[68]

If Panther rhetoric ("kill the pigs," "power to the people"), the clothing (combat boots, berets, black leather), and the acquisition of guns and fortified headquarters together provoked J. Edgar Hoover's fears for the nation's security, for "many black intellectuals the black literature and theater and art of the near future would grow largely out of the Panther experience."[69] Although the Panthers and Reed share a talent for "great restive" performances, these arose not as reaction of one to the other but synchronically out of "the American slums and fringe communities."[70] In fact, Reed recalls the performance of the Black Panthers emerging explicitly from a theater movement in San Francisco.[71] His own performative *Mumbo Jumbo* enacts the 1970 theater of opposition through a pastiche of indirection and fragmentation that emerges instead from New Orleans, a city "like Hoodoo [that] is all over place and time."[72] In doing so, it performs a folk-based commentary on the police/Panther casebook examples, the "Panther effect."

The novel's collage of verbal text, iconic signs, and images tells the histories of the 1920s Jazz Age, the presidency of Warren Harding, and the US occupation of Haiti by way of a HooDoo detective story that takes an excursion through Egyptology and anachronistic asides about 1960s black militancy and the Vietnam War in its pursuit of Neo-HooDooism's lost text, *The Book of Thoth.* It is a spectacle of necromancy (the past as predictor of the future) as discontinuous and fast-paced as television, advertising, or popular film, one in which the speed and rhythm of performance—the verbal and iconic riffs—bear meaning beyond the accumulation of verbal denotation and connotation.[73] Just as mass media delivered the Panthers' performance—if not always their message—technicways can be the vehicles for folkways in Reed's aesthetic, not always their opposition.

Although scholars now call Reed's work postmodern, he defined his Neo-HooDoo Aesthetic as one founded on

> original tall tales and yarns. . . . —the enigmatic street rhymes of some of Ellison's minor characters, or the dozens. . . . A spur to originality, which prompted Julia Jackson, a New Orleans soothsayer, when asked the origin of amulets, talismans, charms, and potions in her workshop, to say: "I make all my own stuff. It saves me money and it's as good. People who has to buy their stuff ain't using their heads."[74]

Mumbo Jumbo, Reed insisted, was not a response to Beat novelist William Burroughs, but rather to gris-gris dolls.[75] The novel's initial critical success, its critical legacy as the model for Henry Louis Gates's influential Africanist theory in *The Signifying Monkey* in 1988, and its popularity among current postmodern and Black Atlantic critics has ensured the novel's visibility among literary professionals in the last thirty years. Its influence among subsequent generations of writers is reaffirming that prominence.[76] But neither the strategies of spectacle it shares with the Panthers nor its sense of place have ever figured in the attention given to its treatment of narrative and history. Yet the trans-local syncretism of Vodun and the emplacement of those religious and social folkways in New Orleans have been a central feature of his Neo-HooDoo Aesthetic. New Orleans provides Reed the means to define Neo-HooDooism, and he provides the city a means to understand its racial spectacles.

Already in the early 1960s in New York, he had not only met New Orleans in the person of fellow Umbra Workshop poet and New Orleanian Tom Dent, but he also had learned from another Umbra poet, David Henderson, the rich possibilities of voodoo and the significance of New Orleans in an archipelago of black-centered, multicultural sites. In the poetry collection *De Mayor of Harlem*, Henderson embeds thirteen poems about New Orleans between the covers of two sets of poems about New York. When reviewing *De Mayor of Harlem*, Reed notes that, for nomad New Yorker Henderson, "New Orleans is 125 1/2 Street."[77] In *Mumbo Jumbo*, Reed reverses and refracts the picture and the frame, beginning his novel in New Orleans and moving the principal action to New York. Although New York and Oakland (even Chattanooga), places of residence for Reed, figure in his nonfiction and in his fiction, poetry, and other art, he specifically evokes New Orleans—its HooDoo, its gumbo, its carnival—as models of the multicultural,

African-inflected concoctions capable of evading the piety of American cultural and political hegemony, and of the expected black nationalist oppositions to it.

In Reed's usage, New Orleans folkways, outside American binaries, arise in the everyday present with the spectacular past in tow, moving toward an open future. In one early example, "hoodoo poem in transient" within the collection *Conjure*, Reed offers his readers the opportunity to rub elbows with HooDoo queen Marie Laveau—if, in following their own desire lines, they happen to get the timing right. If not, well, there is Lake Pontchartrain to consider while you wait.

1nce a year marie laveau

arises frm her workshop

in st louis #2, boards

a bus & rides dwn to

the lake. she threw

parties there 100 years

ago.

some

lake[78]

Laveau's public, lakeside extravaganzas that attracted white participants and threw the white establishment into a frenzied defense of Victorian values could reappear if conditions are right. Circulating underground and overground, as rituals or cures, dance or blues, collage or comedy, this energy is the spiritual, multicultural folk force Reed calls Jes Grew in *Mumbo Jumbo*.

New Orleans in *Mumbo Jumbo,* Mumbo Jumbo in New Orleans

The federal "Rap Brown Amendment" said to the Panthers that they could not travel from one site of the black archipelago to another to organize. To speak intercommunally across dispersed communities against the nation-state was, in the government's words, crossing state lines to incite a riot.[79] For the authors of the amendment, each location had to be its own isolated entity, a "scattered site" as Desire had been and not as the HUD policy had originally intended. In "Shrovetide in Old New Orleans," an essay about his experience of Mardi Gras, Reed imagines, for a moment, another less determinedly oppositional opportunity for intercommunalism: distribution of every city's theater of "local histories, legends, and gossip," one of those "multi-media spectaculars . . . a co-ordinated coast-to-coast Mardi Gras by video hookup." But in the next breath, he is "over-floated with this Mardi Gras" and asks a "brother," a fellow traveler, to corroborate that Mardi Gras is "an obscene Confederate pageant." (Reed never presents himself as one who pulls his punches.) "'I don't know nothin about that,' he said. 'Mardi Gras, to me, is gettin together with your friends and eatin and drinkin.'" Everyday local experience, for its moment, derails not only binary political analysis, but also techno-translocal cultural performance. The essay ends when Reed stops the proliferation of possible interpretations of New Orleans carnival that began with the rumors on the plane flying in and multiplied in descriptions of Mardi Gras events. Mardi Gras, as with HooDoo, he concludes, is a spirit.[80] The technological connection of multiple local folkways might be a possibility, just as the essay itself publishes the multiplicity of the local New Orleans carnival. But the less explicit circulation of some force of Mardi Gras and HooDoo for which New Orleans is a key, if not altogether original or unique, site is already in effect. "Shrovetide" sees the needs for atonement and festival as they coexist on site in New Orleans and imagines this spirit of "New Orleans" set in motion among a translocal community by old-fashioned gossip and, possibly also by 1970s, newfangled technology. As Reed says in *The Last Days of Louisiana Red*, the "business" of Neo-HooDoo cannot have a single, central location if it is going to evade opposition, but it has no spirit without the practice of local folkways.[81]

New Orleanians struggle to explain their distinctive racial spectacles. "'There was always an underlying feeling in Louisiana of some kind of comradeship between blacks and whites. . . . We had worked out our own pace [by 1970], and things were going to generally get better, but it was not on a national time," said Harvey Britton, NAACP Louisiana field secretary. The Moon Landrieu administration, elected by 90 percent of the black vote in 1970, was moving the system, placing African Americans in positions of authority.[82] But Catherine Giarrusso, wife of Police Chief Clarence Giarrusso, evaded the possibility of local exceptionalism as she reconsidered events of 1970 from the vantage point of the twenty-first century: We're "too American" to be "a rioting kind of city," she said. Cecil Carter, deputy director of human relations under Landrieu, surmised instead that if New Orleans had fewer riots in 1970 than other US cities, it was because "poverty was so severe," too severe for the presence of hope. Uprisings occur, he reasoned, in communities where there is hope but an inadequate rate of change or the suppression of change. Bob Tucker, Landrieu's special assistant, added that Mardi Gras gave people an annual occasion to "go act out." Carter and Tucker concluded, in New Orleans "we are all kin."[83]

In what Gates calls the "false start" of *Mumbo Jumbo,* the pandemic Jes Grew is placed in New Orleans. These five pages that begin the novel, before it begins again with another title page, copyright page, and epigraphs, announce through a mock panic both the mystery and the resolution to the mystery that drives the novel. Where has this spiritual energy Jes Grew come from and where is it going? Where is the text that will explain it? The false start, extratextual to the novel of the second start, is itself the explanation for Jes Grew, the text that is not a text, the desire that is located not wholly in any one place but some place, New Orleans. When New Orleans's cartoon mayor of a parodic Jazz Age and his manic minions try to stop Jes Grew, they discover its infection is not confined to Place Congo, the former recreation site of slaves. During the 1890s outbreak, when the Wallflower Order fumigated Place Congo to arrest the pandemic, they too learned that Jes Grew was an antiplague that enlivened its host. Even those who, in the 1920s, attend the infected victims in St. Louis Cathedral are not safe from this syncretic infection. It is leapfrogging from neighborhood to neighborhood, threatening, says the doctor, "the end of Civilization As We Know It." Those subject to it "feel like the gut heart and lungs of Africa's interior . . . the Kongo: 'Land of the Panther.'" They hear "shank bones, jew's harps, bagpipes, flutes, conch horns, drums, banjos, kazoos" coming together from multiple cultures and they must dance. As with the "second line" who follow the parade of a jazz funeral in New Orleans, as Louis Armstrong describes it in a quotation Reed cites, "The spirit hits them and they follow."[84] Even if Jes Grew is driven underground, as it was in the 1890s, "broken-hearted and double-crossed," that double cross (++) is a sign of continuity from the HooDoo knowledge of the HooDoo greats, such as Marie Laveau, into the present. These are the orange crosses that adorn her gravestone in St. Louis Cemetery #1. My people know the signs anywhere, says Reed.[85] Note that these crosses are not subaltern mimicry of a hegemonic tradition. Rather, they prefigure the very idea of double cross before it finds its modern meaning in broken (colonial) promises.

Reed gives the definition and Mandingo etymology of "mumbo jumbo" as the "magician who makes the troubled spirits of ancestors go away," (mama, grandmother+gyo, trouble+mbo, to leave), but if Gates is right and the etymology may also lie in Swahili Jambo (hello) and mambo (its plural), then mumbo jumbo also signifies a coming together as much as a departure.[86] In "Neo- HooDoo Manifesto" Reed claims,

All "Store Front Churches" and "Rock Festivals" receive their matrix in the HooDoo rites of Marie Laveau conducted at New Orleans' Lake Pontchartrain and Bayou St. John in the 1880s. The power of HooDoo challenged the stability of civil authority in New Orleans and was driven underground where to this day it flourishes in the Black ghettos throughout the country. Thats why in Ralph Ellison's modern novel *Invisible Man* New Orleans is described as "The Home of Mystery." "Everybody from New Orleans got that thing." Louis Armstrong said once.[87]

In "Shrovetide," Reed is less romantic about New Orleans's carnival spectacle in which the flamboyance of white supremacy, white mob rule, syncretic "Mardi Gras Indians," and black parody coexist. When *Mumbo Jumbo* begins a second time, there are also powerful forces amassed against Jes Grew.[88] As the city sweeps up the mess left by Jes Grew exuberance, the Atonist Hierophant 1 and his/its Wallflower Order determine to stop the pandemic as they have in the past. They begin this process by putting on trial the New Orleans mayor, now infected by the Jes Grew pandemic that threatens to overcome "the saving Virus in the blood of all Europe." "A man wearing a mask that reveals only his eyes and mouth [such as those worn by all traditional Mardi Gras krewes] calls the meeting to order" where they decide quickly to kill the mayor. As the actions of the novel prepare to leave New Orleans (by name), Reed's narrative overvoice observes the following.

> When an extraordinary antipathy challenges the Wallflower Order, their usual front men, politicians, scholars and businessmen, step aside. Someone once said that beneath or behind all political and cultural warfare lies a struggle between secret societies. Another author suggested that the Nursery Rhyme and the book of Science Fiction might be more revolutionary than any number of tracts, pamphlets, manifestoes of the political realm.[89]

With these words, the action moves to New York City, where the novel's hero detective, PaPa LaBas, HooDoo houngan, carrier of Jes Grew, son of a New Orleans Root salesman, takes up the defense of Jes Grew and the pursuit of its *Book of Thoth*.

LaBas can read the signs of Jes Grew, whether in newspaper headlines about the Voodoo generals of Haiti opposing US occupation or in the parties of Harlem or in the possession of his assistant Earline by the loa Erzulie or in the lore of its "origins" in Egypt, although he needs the counsel of Black Herman to see The Work in the blues and other contemporary cultural sites. Earline had heard LaBas say about voodoo in Haiti, "If I don't visit Haiti perhaps Haiti will come to me." But a younger generation feels there is no place for LaBas's concern with Haitian loas or his articles about "lost liturgies in New Orleans."[90] They instead pursue justice through an organization of multicultural art students who call themselves the Mu'tafikah. Their strategy of internationalism is to liberate Latin American or Asian or African or Native American art from Centers of Art Detention so they can return it to its original cultural sites. It is understood that objects that travel as Ikons of culture under the aegis of European colonialism do not participate in the sort of subversive circulation that propels Jes Grew, but neither do the Mu'tafikah's efforts to return material objects, such as the enormous Olmec head, grasp the significance of spiritual transmission. The younger generation's commitment to the Nation of Islam, in the character of Abdul, is also doomed. While the Mu'tafikah are undone by a tragic Faustian white member who succumbs to the arguments of an Atonist he guards, a betrayal that results in the murder of the group's leader, Abdul's loyalty to the Nation of Islam prompts him to destroy part of the *Book of Thoth* when it comes into his hands because the ancient text strikes him as lewd. Just the same, he too is murdered by the Atonists seeking the Text. The young men are mourned; the old ones and old ways survive and evolve. When, in the end, the young men are dead, a young woman, Earline, decides to head to "New Orleans and Haiti, Brazil and all over the South" to learn The Work, and LaBas gives an annual lecture to an academic audience on the eve of the new Mumbo Jumbo holiday.[91]

A part of the diegesis of that lecture are two images on opposing pages. One is US cartoonist Thomas Nast's 1870 drawing of the pope and Vatican leaders in full vestments on the dome of Europe's Christianity after the declaration of papal infallibility that same year. Their telescope and fingers gesture toward the new world across the Atlantic as the bearers of the battle axes behind them remain invisible. The other image is of carnival revelers, dark devils and white damsels, cavorting down a street of iron balconies hanging above sidewalks alive with a multiracial audience moving toward the revelers in anticipation of a "second line." Both architecture and inhabitants mark the Latin territories of the new world.[92] The credits identify the place as Brazil and the language of a sign is Portuguese, but the architecture speaks New Orleans as much as other sites in the HooDoo archipelago. *Mumbo Jumbo's* final words, "freeze frame," offer no single closing frame that returns to New Orleans. Instead, it opens to a "New Orleans [that] like HooDoo is all over place and time." What Amiri Baraka (LeRoi Jones) said of David Henderson's poetry could be said of Reed's novel as well. It is "the world echo, with the strength and if you are conscious, beauty of the place tone."[93]

Mumbo Jumbo geohistorically deconstructs the familiar rhetoric of binary opposition between Panthers and police in New Orleans or other US cities in 1970 by representing the conflict necromantically all over

space and time. In the process, the novel satirizes nationalist claims.
While those possessed by Jes Grew feel like the "heart and lungs of
Africa's interior," like "the Kongo: 'Land of the panther,'" Atonists fear
"the end of Civilization As We Know It," a "threat [to] our National
Security, survival and just about everything else you can think of."[94]
When LaBas appears in court, part of ongoing intimidation, he remembers other incidents of the teens and twenties, among them the case of
an Indiana man who murdered another for shouting "To hell with the
United States." In two minutes, the jury acquitted the murderer. LaBas
remarks through the narrator that "fear stalks the land. (As usual; so
what else is new?)"[95] The BPP appears per se in the diegesis only in a
single anachronistic photograph of young black men marching in
rhythm in support of the New York 21 as police trot alongside like a
would-be second line that missed the groove. Above the photograph—
not as caption but as collage—is the Atonist creed ending with the line,
"Lord, if I can't dance, No one shall."[96]

Humor always figures in Reed's art, especially where and when the
political positions are rigid and fear stalks the land. Humor has been, he
says, a part of multicultural art for thousands of years, teaching
humility through fool stories, "little men" stories, animal fables.[97] His
resentment of editors and critics who romanticize the Black Panther
prisoners and expect him to behave like them is as consistent as his
humor in the face of predictable political pieties.[98] But he also can turn
that resentment directly on those whites, to the political right and left,
who abused and used the Panthers "as cannon fodder."[99] His claims
return, nonetheless, to the centrality of folk art and oral tradition that
use comedy, as does he, in the manner of "satire, hyperbole, invective
and bawdiness."[100] "The whole idea is when state magicians fail, unofficial magicians become stronger," as Eldridge Cleaver did and writer
Calvin Hernton before him.[101]

On the one hand, Reed works this magic through the technique of
historical pastiche and the subject of textual dissolution; that is, the
division and scattering of the Book of Thoth. The resolution to the
mystery of the missing text, as with the exegetical answer to *Mumbo
Jumbo* itself, is its dismemberment and distribution, not its recovery.
The inclusion of visual material in the novel also enhances the spectacle
of the form, inviting readers to "construct narratives that lie outside or
alongside the ones that the text explicitly develops."[102] To stimulate
such constructions is the goal of the novel.

On the other hand, Reed's fiction has an aggressive relationship with
its reader, demanding what Lorenzo Thomas has called "a willing
disruption of belief."[103] Reed refuses allegiance to the "political correct-
ness" of feminism or black power as much as he does to the dominance
of the state or western cultural tradition. In doing so, he cannot be

assimilated or understood as oppositional in any given debate. His is a satire neither normative nor corrective, argues Patrick McGee.[104] But within its restive form, Reed's art has clear values about transformation, I am arguing. Within the fiction of the novel, Reed works his mumbo jumbo to purge New Orleans of the Panther/police binary and "replace" it with the folkways already in place, folkways that resite "New Orleans" in black gossip in black ghettos across the nation and the world as their performance is needed. As such, this hand works with the first to construct the text's active reader.

And yet, within the essay "Shrovetide" that describes his own visit to the city at Mardi Gras, Reed tells his reader that he himself felt compelled to leave New Orleans by the sheer force of spectacle that was as much enacting white power as the Neo-HooDoo aesthetic. As with several BPP members who came to assist in establishing an NCCF chapter in New Orleans and Martin Arnold of *The New York Times* who found a casebook example at Desire, Reed was back home when the carnival was over and the spotlights were off. For some observers who call New Orleans home, the Panthers there seemed to share with Reed a devotion to a theatrical disruption without an "objective."[105] But if we use Reed's spectacle as a model for reading the Panthers, we can perceive that their spectacle may have enabled instead not only the exposure at a specific locality of legal and extralegal hegemonic nationalist performances, but also singular local political acts alongside that spectacle that could only be performed by local actors in place.

The Second Line of Singular Acts

In 2003, the story New Orleanians told themselves about the BPP in New Orleans was primarily the story of November 19, 1970, not the casebook example of September 14–15. On that November day, the week before Thanksgiving, hundreds of police and their armed "war wagon" surrounded the new headquarters of the NCCF in an abandoned Desire housing unit as three helicopters circled overhead. Their purpose was to serve an eviction notice, despite the fact that this was usually the purview of the Civil Sheriff's Office; that the Board of Faith and Action had approached HANO about paying the rent; and that other, white-run poverty programs had used public housing units rent-free.[106] HANO claimed the NCCF did not constitute a family and had to go; an NCCF spokesman insisted instead that Desire belonged to the people who granted them permission to stay there. "This is our home," the people's property, they declared, reformulating comparisons of Desire to the slave past and distant apartheid.[107] The hundreds of police were met that day by more than 1,000 Desire residents and supporters—men and women, but mostly teenagers and children. They surrounded NCCF headquarters, shielding members who waited silently inside. When NCCF members told mediators they preferred suicide to surrender even though the trespassing charge was only a misdemeanor, the crowd outside shouted "Power to the people" rather than move as instructed by a voice from the "war wagon."[108] After an extended standoff and negotiation, the police retreated without having entered the building and without any shots having been fired. Although the next week police arrested NCCF members at a roadblock when they attempted to get to a BPP constitutional convention in Washington, DC, in cars rented for them by Jane Fonda, and the remaining members were taken into custody when they were tricked into opening the door at Desire by police officers dressed as Panthers, postal workers, and a priest, on the night of November 19, there was celebration at Desire.[109] The people at Desire that night were celebrating their belief that NCCF, mostly local people themselves, provided a "safe zone" from the genocide they defined as drugs plus capitalism.[110] With the presence of NCCF, children could play openly in the courtyards at Desire. NCCF especially garnered the support of mothers whose children they promised to feed. (Mothers were in fact the principal defense witnesses at the trial of those arrested in September.) These acts, together with their suicide stand against eviction from their "home," gave them a gravity and moral purpose greater than the "project" rivalries that usually plagued New Orleans's poorest citizens.[111] NCCF attorney Ernest Jones surmised retrospectively that it was the survival programs, not the "off the pigs" rhetoric and spectacle, that turned the establishment against the Panthers. When the Panthers, people with no resources, said that they could feed the hungry people in their community without the central institutions and Model Cities program of the United States, then the government declared war on them.[112] The Desire community, in turn, rallied to their side. Like Buddy Bolden's legendary wailing trumpet, the Panthers' loud call for survival, however impure, attracted curious and impassioned citizens from Desire and the city at large, especially when that call was under siege. In 1970, they set in motion a spectacle of survival; the community leaders in place at Desire then turned that energy from violence and victimization in September to the second line of singular acts in November.

On November 19, the angry crowd was held in check fewer than thirty feet from the police not so much by the presence of police weapons or by a tradition of nonviolent civil disobedience. "They were being restrained by leaders of the project who locked their arms together to prevent the crowd from advancing as other project leaders met with [Police Chief] Giarrusso." While the NCCF members hunkered inside were telling mediators that they were the vanguard of the revolution and as such were prepared to die for their beliefs, one of the community leaders outside amid the crowd said to Giarrusso, "This is our world here. We live by our own code."[113] Under escort of community leaders, Giarrusso entered the "project" to dismiss his men, who then left the area, some of them directing racial epithets at the Chief. For a day, the local and the translocal leadership together achieved a self-determination hard-won in Desire, where poverty and poverty programs ruled.

The next week when the crowd was gone and the police used subterfuge to gain entrance to NCCF headquarters, one of those leaders, Johnny Jackson, director of the Desire Community Center, was among those arrested for interfering with the police.[114] In an open letter, he claimed that he and other community leaders had been used as a shield on the quiet, Thanksgiving Day raid when NCCF members and other citizens of Desire were, as he puts it, "kidnapped."[115] His outrage was echoed by New Orleans clergy, who also objected to the priest's garb used in a police ruse that involved shooting one Panther, a woman, in the chest.[116] Retrospectively, other Desire leaders described themselves as marked men after the "Panther thing." Mayor Landrieu's executive assistant Bob Tucker remembers that after the incidents of November 1970, "they [police] did a big raid, a big drug bust down there in Desire. They swept up everything that was Black." One of those arrested was Henry Faggen, a community member known as Desire's unofficial mayor, one who negotiated with Giarrusso on the 19th. He was convicted on drug charges and sentenced to sixty years, reduced to twenty-five, then to eight and finally to six. "He ended up serving two and a half years. 'They played with me,' claims Faggen."[117]

Although these arrests went on without fanfare, undermining the hope achieved on November 19, the August 1971 trial of those Panthers arrested on charges of attempted murder in September 1970 was an extension of the local action that drove events on the 19th. Unlike at the trial of the Chicago 8, New Orleans Creole Israel Augustine presided over the trial and a black-majority jury rendered the decision. Judge Augustine may not have been sufficiently radical for William Kunstler or sufficiently supportive of blacks living in poverty for the attorneys of the New Orleans Panthers, but through his conduct at the trial, in the courtroom, and in the corridors of the courthouse, he earned a place in that part of the New Orleans Creole legacy that has always spoken for racial equality. The jury, too, truly reflected the New Orleans demographics in place since the Civil War. The mothers from Desire who testified to the presumptions of some police in seizing their private living quarters and to the innocence of young bystanders presumed guilty also served the defendants well. This, the ambiguity about who fired first, and the anti-Panther rumors given public credence by Governor

McKeithen before any violent confrontations, convinced the jurors that those in NCCF headquarters were acting in self-defense. Although it took long weeks to find the right local citizens to render the decision in this final singular act, the trial itself was short, cleanly argued, and decisive.

Reconciliation and Hope

Thirty-three years later, New Orleanians remembered the events of 1970 and 1971 as "a miracle . . . of peace" in "the City that Care Forgot." It is a memory sustained by the triumph at Desire on November 19, in which the pieties of binary opposition were replaced by the massive participation of local citizens second lining a notorious Panther spectacle that had literally been interiorized. The two forces, the local and the translocal, had become mutually dependent. As some told it in 2003, the police too were a local force that, through restraint, shared in the triumph. Only the betrayers, the two black undercover police agents, refused to participate in the newly reconstituted circle of local esteem. A September 2003 commemorative event drew a standing-room-only crowd with more outside in the street. Former Mayor Landrieu said of the Panthers, "God Bless Them"; Panther Malik Rahim said of Landrieu, "My hat goes off to you." The former mayor, former Desire community leaders, and former New Orleans Panthers embraced. South Africa's word, "reconciliation," was in the air.[118] The site of Desire, in memory, was reclaimed as a space of hope.

In his book by that name, David Harvey calls for an optimism of the intellect that moves beyond the confines of Antonio Gramsci's binary "pessimism of the intellect and optimism of the will," an intellect thinking its way to spaces of hope.[119] Before it could be argued that Desire had become a space of hope supportable by the intellect, a lot of concessions would have to be made. In the twenty-first century, the Desire Housing Development has been razed as part of a massive HOPE VI project there and at other public housing sites in the city. In some New Orleanians' judgment, the familiar effect has been to move the social and economic problems and the unrequited desires of the poor around. There are those who remember events of 1970 or simply their own lives at Desire who may see that ground as sacred. But it will not remain bare. Low-rise, mixed-income, lower density housing is being built, and those set flowing are in competition for affordable housing. "Now we've gone back to tribalism," said a former Panther. He added that recently, "Fifty people have been killed in this city behind Hope 6," as though the federal policy were itself a place, specifically a place for violence to hide.[120]

Concessions would also have to be made to some outcomes of events in 1970. In that year, Donald Rumsfeld took over as head of the Office of Economic Opportunity (OEO) and orchestrated a retreat from the programs established in the Johnson Administration. Among those programs was legal aid for indigent clients. When it became known in Washington that the New Orleans Legal Assistance Corporation (NOLAC) was defending the Panthers, the greatest risk to national security, Rumsfeld set changes in motion. He fired Frank Jones, deputy director of Legal Services, and Jones's boss, Director Terry Lenzner, who had wired NOLAC approval of their defense of NCCF. Rumsfeld established a policy of providing legal aid through OEO only in noncriminal cases.[121] The skill of NOLAC attorneys Ernest Jones, Lolis Elie, Robert Glass, and others made the case for the Panthers once there was a jury in place willing to listen. But this would not happen again under the auspices of NOLAC and the OEO. Glass resigned from NOLAC so that he could continue to defend the Panthers after the first trial. One could argue that the Rumsfeld decision was one lasting, demonstrable effect of the Panthers in New Orleans. "The Administration apparently believes in bargain basement justice for the poor," said Lenzner. "What we feared has come to pass," said Frank Jones. "The OEO, and particularly Legal Services program, is now effectively being run by Southern bigots and right wing politicians across the country."[122]

But it is not only the presence of a right-wing national agenda that must be conceded. The Landrieu administration "moved the system" within the city in a more liberal direction, employing African Americans such as Cecil Carter and Bob Tucker in more substantial influential positions and giving credence to the Human Relations Council. But when John Pecoul submitted to Landrieu the Human Relations Council's assessment of Panther activity in New Orleans, "he was furious. . . .That showed the limitations of the committee.... It marked the beginning of the end of the feeling that a committee like this could really bring about change. It really did not have power."[123] Carter, Tucker, and Faggan were all still agreeing in 2003 that Landrieu was the one white man they trusted, but the system did not move far enough to give the Human Relations Council or these community leaders authority to frame the city's relationship to its citizens at Desire.

Former Police Chief Clarence Giarrusso was also honored in 2003 as one of the men who restrained a police force eager to get the Panthers who taunted them. But Cates's warning at Southern University in 1970 and Carter's further analysis about generations of police officers have found sad corroboration in subsequent manifestations of New Orleans police culture. Although by 1987, 45 percent of the police force was African American, some in their numbers had extended corruption to new and yet more dangerous areas. A *New York Times* article from

1996 claims that because the white officers had established control of "clean corruption," such as shaking down brothels and French Quarter bars, the newer cadre of black officers were left the "dirty corruption" that feeds off the illegal drug trade. With a starting salary of $17,000 in 1994, officers were forced to other employment if not corruption. As off-duty, private policing agents, lieutenants were often the bosses of captains, undermining the chain of command in the NOPD. Attempts to hire reform in the persons of outside police chiefs did not go well either. New Orleans's first African American (Creole) Mayor Ernest Morial hired James Parsons in 1978 to reform the police department. Then, on his watch, in 1980, after a police officer was killed, a white police mob killed four and injured fifty in a black neighborhood, dragging some to the swamp where they were tortured in a mock execution. Police culture was again complicit in extralegal as much as legal spectacle. A generation later, when Ernest Morial's son, Marc, became mayor in the 1990s and hired respected Washington, DC, Police Chief Richard Pennington to again reform the NOPD, local skeptics were dubious.[124]

Once this much is conceded, what can be left for the optimism of the intellect? At least one force that can sustain the hope for sociopolitical and economic justice is the synergy of the translocal spectacle and the singular actions of the local second line, those in place who know the local folkways, catch the translocal spirit, and have to move. Even the piercing Marxian analysis that Harvey serves so well is not necessarily a system, an order, that moves. In his search for spaces of hope, Harvey turns from his solitary walk among the ruins of Baltimore to a utopian fiction willing to imagine the future. In his last chapter, the space described contains him, alone, reading. Reed's Neo-HooDoo aesthetic has always reminded the single individual that he is that by using 1 for one rather than a more conventional I/eye Cartesian word-play. This 1 is not just Hierophant1, who is at the central command center of the Atonists; this 1 is Reed or Marie Laveau or Papa LaBas, everyone whose prejudices are best spoken rather than hidden under the good will of any system, right or left. But the 1 does not simply reference solipsism or individualism or the limits of the observant flâneur. Rather, it also signifies the originality of each person who can make his or her own gris-gris, yet be part of a translocal, multicultural, spiritual vision of identity-as-community. For Reed, this community of originals will always be performing in excess of order, but not in isolation from other producers of spectacle at other sites.[125] Seen as a translocal archipelago across space, this matrix of the past tells the future. If it is space, not time, that hides consequences from us, it is also space that can reveal those consequences. To look into the local place and see across translocal space is an act of intellect and a reason for hope in hard work.

Those who crowded into the Ashe Cultural Center in New Orleans on September 17, 2003, and those who spilled over into the street were attracted to something in the performance of reconciliation enacted by the former mayor, Panthers, and Desire community leaders and organized by returned New Orleanian Orissa Arend. If the South African spectacle of reconciliation provided the spirit, those in place in New Orleans on that night caught the groove. Meanwhile, singular acts go on beyond the spectacle, such as youth from the former Desire hired as construction industry apprentices to rebuild historic homes of New Orleans's musicians.[126]

6

The Vampires' Middle Passage

The World of Anne Rice and the Promise of New Orleans's Coast

"Neo-HooDoo never been to France," wrote Ishmael Reed in his "Neo-HooDoo Manifesto" of the late 1960s. Instead,

> Neo-HooDoo is the 8 basic dances of 19-century New Orleans' *Place Congo*—the Calinda the Bamboula the Chacta the Babouille the Conjaille the Juba the Congo and the Voodoo.... "Everybody from New Orleans got that thing," Louis Armstrong said once. ... Neo-HooDoo borrows from Ancient Egyptians. ... Neo-HooDoo borrows from Haiti Africa and South America.[1]

But Anne Rice's vampires do go to France. In the process, she sublimates New Orleans's Africanist gothicism—rooted in voodoo, slavery, and the city's evolving conditions of race, culture, and location—even as her vampiric gothicism calls on it. Louis, a French-born human and the New Orleans–created vampire who tells his story in Rice's 1976 vampire debut, *Interview with the Vampire*, finds in Paris sophisticated vampires of his own kind. In this way, Rice submerges the New World Africanist element in her vampiric gothicism and also emends the traditional quest for origins in the Anglo vampire genre, locating them not in eastern Europe, but in Paris, the capital of the nineteenth century. Although this emplacement is ambivalent—because the Parisian Theatre

des Vampires proves to be fatal, and not just to humans—in the narrative
Louis tells, Paris is nonetheless the strongest platial desire emanating
from his Francophilic New Orleans home site. This Francophilia is itself
ambivalent. It keeps alive the particular colonial foundations of New
Orleans. And it also displaces the economic, political, and moral conditions of that colonialism and of nineteenth-century Paris, replacing them
with a devotion to the aesthetic culture of the European capital.
Although conflicted about the French—and, implicitly, also the
Spanish—colonial and postcolonial conditions in New Orleans, Rice's
vampirism specifically evades the geopolitical nation of the United
States, that is to say the US empire as Thomas Jefferson tried to build it
at the turn of the eighteenth century and as it was understood at the
nation's bicentennial when Rice's novel was published.[2] It instead
reworks New Orleans translocal gothic traditions that have their own
emplacement, first in the Middle Passage from Africa to the Americas
and subsequently (inevitably) in the circulation of voodoo and what
Reed calls Neo-HooDooism through the coast of the Caribbean and
Spanish America.[3] I make this claim with the caveat that New Orleans
subaltern Africanisms are hidden in plain sight in Rice's *Interview* like
the open secrets in postcolonial literatures from other locations
concerning other minoritarian groups.[4] Also, just as her novel's flirta-
tion with homoeroticism, the beautiful male body, and 1970s
androgyny invites queer or feminist readings that it never quite satisfies,
its foundation in Africanist gothicism invites an emplaced racial reading
that remains unfulfilled.[5]

Rice published *Interview*, the first of her successful Vampire Chronicles, in 1976 while, on the one hand, the United States was celebrating
its bicentennial as a nation and, on the other, it was recovering from the
loss of imperial power in Vietnam and the loss of stable leadership at the
Watergate in Washington, DC. Nina Auerbach reads Rice's beautiful
vampires as aestheticized creatures of independent self-indulgence
arising in a late 1970s leadership vacuum.[6] Rob Latham also historicizes
the appearance of Rice's characters, but specifically within the evolution
of the Marxist metaphor of vampirism as capital's exploitation of wage
labor. In 1970s late capitalism, he argues, the vampires' consumption of
luxury goods as well as blood, like the consumptive habits of a youth
subculture, is a less predatory than empowering role, even if it remains
ambivalent.[7] I argue here for a platial reading of Rice's first vampire
saga, one that inflects such historical arguments by repositioning the
national and global geographic scales they presume. Whereas later
Vampire Chronicles take on a variety of global sites, in this the first of
the series, the alternative scale to US national borders is explicitly transatlantic and implicitly the circum-Atlantic and third coast—that is to
say Gulf Coast—territory of French and Spanish colonialism and the

slave trade. Central to this territory and to the novel is New Orleans, Capital of the (Other) Nineteenth Century, as Kirsten Silva Gruesz has described it in her study of nineteenth-century trans-America.[8]

I say nineteenth century because this is when Rice's vampires find their place in New Orleans, when they seek their roots in Paris, and when Paris not only flourished as an affluent cafe society, but also became a model of revolutionary promise and a monument to its political martyrs.[9] The significant duration of Louis's narrative begins just downriver of New Orleans in 1791, moves to New Orleans in 1795, and leaves the city for Europe in 1860, spending most of the final pages in Paris. Being undead, vampire Louis lives into the twentieth century, granting the interview that frames the tale he tells in the 1970s in the Castro District of San Francisco. This enfolding of a long nineteenth century inside the pocket of the twentieth that has prompted historical readings on a national and global scale also enables my local and regional reading of 1970s New Orleans and its coast. In this decade, some New Orleanians—architectural historians, urban designers, historic preservationists, and Catholic activists among them—were rethinking their place among their colonial cousins in the Western hemisphere. Rice's reemergence on the New Orleans scene, first textually and then literally—with all the gothic flamboyance of voodoo queen Marie Laveau arising from Lake Pontchartrain—and the inaugural voyage of her popular vampires, which has subsequently drawn legions of fans to the gothic city, entered local folkways and a contemporary, local dialogue about the intraurban and trans-American mapping of New Orleans.

Inside the World of Anne Rice

As all Rice fans know, she was born in New Orleans in 1941, upriver of Canal Street, on the fringe of the wealthy Garden District. She was raised in this neighborhood designated in the antebellum nineteenth century as the American Sector for the well-heeled migrants from the upper United States who built mansions there to rival the architectural opulence of the creole Vieux Carré downriver of Canal. But these preserved mansions were affordable to Rice and her family only after the success of her Vampire Chronicles. Just as Louis narrates from Divisadero Street in San Francisco's best known gay neighborhood, Rice wrote her early vampire novels from that West Coast site, re-creating New Orleans from research and memory of her first sixteen years. In 1988, she finally returned to the city that acknowledged her status as the vampire queen by giving her a plot in St. Louis Cemetery #1, the oldest of the city's cemeteries, where Laveau is physically buried and Louis's virtual brother comes to rest in *Interview*. Rice and her family relocated to New Orleans's Garden District the next year, bringing with them an attention to its architectural preservation although not to its specifically Anglo American origins.[10]

Although New Orleans's St. Alphonsus School, St. Mary's Assumption School, Redemptorist School, and Holy Name of Jesus School made the rules that governed Rice's formal childhood education, on her return, she bought and recreated Catholic sites, as well as a Garden District mansion, in the secular and gothic images she chose. Rice's spectacular practices in New Orleans's Garden District in the 1990s became an unavoidable lens through which to read *Interview*'s 1976 platial promise of a third-coast consciousness. The sprawling St. Elizabeth's Orphanage for girls at 1314 Napoleon Avenue, for example, became, under Rice's ownership, a museum for her massive doll collection and for religious and secular art, especially that of her husband, Stan Rice.[11] The Orphanage also served as the site of the annual Memnoch Ball, the Gathering of the Coven of some 6,000 fans whom Rice rewarded with hundreds of cases of chardonnay, thousands of bottles of Abita Red Ale, and amalgamated New Orleans gothic party favors: "burlap voodoo bags filled with gris-gris and Spanish moss, Memnoch plastic mugs, and Mardi Gras beads."[12] In addition to St. Elizabeth's, Rice bought St. Alphonsus Church at 2045 Constance on Ecclesiastical Square; the church had merged its shrinking congregation with St. Mary's in the late 1970s. By having it deconsecrated, Rice could preserve its building and redefine its sanctuary as an art and cultural center. Our Mother of Perpetual Help Chapel at 2521 Prytania Street was also deconsecrated after purchase so it might be converted into a Rice family residence.[13] These acts of deconsecration that were steps toward architectural preservation in the material world of the Garden District also resonated with Louis's existential crisis in St. Louis Cathedral where he does not find God and comfort, but rather the recognition that "*I* was the supernatural in this cathedral. I was the only supermortal thing that stood conscious under this roof!"[14] He subsequently drinks the blood of the priest. If voodoo queen Laveau's ambiguous relationship with Catholicism evolved from syncretic voodoo practice to a more traditional Catholicism in late life as her Victorian eulogies claim, Rice, a visible heir of Laveau's gothic spectacle, has foregone her traditional Catholic education for New Orleans's cultural Catholicism and a commitment to its architectural monuments while promoting a supernatural vision as laced with sensuality, violence, and subcultural engagement as any exoticized tale of voodoo. Rice's Garden District gothicism and her vampires' supernaturalism eschew open identification with voodoo's spectacle and its orientalist presentation by nonbelievers, let alone with voodoo's sustained minoritarian subversion of traditional religious and political powers. Yet Rice and her texts evoke these folkways of New Orleans Africanist gothicism nonetheless.

After Rice bought Our Mother of Perpetual Help Chapel, the third purchase with a Catholic past, the Garden District neighbors rebelled, according to Anne Reifenberg, writing in 1996 for the front page of *The Wall Street Journal*. Reifenberg reports that the neighbors did not balk at Rice's arrival at a book signing in a coffin within a mule-drawn hearse, or her use of skeletons and anatomically correct dolls with teeth marks in their necks to decorate her mansion, or the nun's costume for Halloween. But they did believe that the Catholic purchases and renovations were "making a mockery of the church." Reifenberg presumes that New Orleanians have a high tolerance for eccentricity, but also a commitment to a "'[Catholic] cultural history in this part of Louisiana ... older than the United States by dozens of years.'"[15] And that Catholic culture had been offended, Reifenberg's story goes. But comments by Rice's cousin, William Murphy, who worked for Rice's tourist enterprise, Kith and Kin LLC, suggest a different story. He implied that it was the threat of Africanist gothicism within the World of Anne Rice that most unsettled the neighbors. "'They've even spread rumors that Anne's going to perform voodoo rites in the chapel at midnight.'"[16] Neither Murphy nor Reifenberg make clear that such voodoo rites that challenge "the church" are themselves rooted in a religious and cultural history "older than the United States by dozens of years." Instead, Reifenberg explained neighborhood dismay through the history of European colonial Catholicism, and Murphy turned rumors of an Africanist element in Rice's vampiric texts and practices into a parody of Africanist culture. "'We've talked about putting on grass skirts and sacrificing a watermelon on the front lawn just to satisfy [the disgruntled neighbors],'" he quipped.[17] Rice did not, in fact, enact this minstrelsy suggested by her cousin, but instead reinstated her link to voodoo's syncretic spectacle by holding the next book signing near the altar of St. Assumption dressed in a beaded headdress, red cape, and lace gloves.

Her own claim was that the complaining neighbors were elitist. They refused to attend mass at the nearest church because it was proximate to a public housing development, she argued. She countered this elitism, as she saw it, with her devotion to historic preservation, specifically preservation of Catholic sites significant in her own New Orleans Catholic girlhood. (Her mother's funeral mass was said at the Chapel, for example.) The wealth acquired through her gothic vision preserved at least a portion of the Garden District as a memorial to her modest middle class kith and kin. Although the neighborhood had been a tourist destination long before Anne Rice was a name anyone recognized, the neighbors said they objected to this old sector of American mansions becoming "the Anne Rice Business District." Meanwhile, the city was reluctant to decide whether or not Kith and Kin LLC had failed to acquire an appropriate permit for its exclusive walking tour Inside the World of Anne Rice.[18]

As with her vampire Louis, who is unnerved by the passage of time in place, Rice welcomed the unchanging facades of many of the city's buildings, whose function she redefined even as she retained or enhanced their ornate substantiation of class status. She committed herself to historic preservation not only of her re-created familial past, but also of her virtual New Orleans, installing her elegant vampires in buildings already in place. A dozen years before Rice returned to New Orleans in person, her character Louis was already saying that New Orleans is remarkable, if for nothing else, for its monuments of

> marble and brick and stone that still stand; so that even when the gas lamps went out and the planes came in and the office buildings crowded the blocks of Canal Street, something irreducible of beauty and romance remained; not in every street perhaps, but in so many that the landscape is for me the landscape of those times [1790s–1860] always, and walking now in the starlit streets of the Quarter or the Garden District I am in those times again.... The moon that rose over New Orleans then still rises. As long as the monuments stand, it still rises. The feeling, at least here ... and there ... it remains the same.[19]

The feeling of beauty and romance sustained by the facades of preserved buildings is unchanged, Rice implies, whether their function is religious or secular; whether the contemporary technology is the steamboat or the jet; and whether occupants are human or vampire, day creatures or night creatures, straight or gay—as long as their owners have the wealth to maintain and enhance them.

If the feeling is irreducible, as Louis claims, then the historic preservation of the architecture is also locking in place an ideology (of class and race) that is laid in these buildings' foundations and that Rice as wealthy patron can retrospectively claim for her Irish-American family, once of modest income. Rice's particular rededication of Catholic sites for secular purposes further suggests, on the one hand, that the irreducible ideology of beauty and romance may be extended to redefine the past functions of these buildings and, on the other hand, that the shadow of their former functions—especially religious functions—sustains their gothic ambience in the evolving present. What was once conventionally religious is redirected to an underground supernaturalism tunneling through the gris-gris of voodoo. But in Rice's New Orleans, as in Laveau's, this underground is not maintained as a secret too sequestered for the growth of economic and cultural capital. Instead, Rice's public presence in print and in person has made the shadow the act; powerful gris-gris has become camp party favors at spectacles of gothicism such as the Memnoch Ball or any of Rice's novels about vampires or witches.

Unlike Rice's more academic critics, her fans identify her with and in the city of New Orleans just as did the fans of George Washington Cable a century earlier. Fan Joy Dickinson's *Haunted City: An Unauthorized Guide to the Magical, Magnificent New Orleans of Anne Rice* went into a second edition in 1998. With an innocent Texan persona such as Algren's Dove Linkhorn, Dickinson claims that through reading Rice's fiction, she "knew New Orleans far better than any part of Texas."[20] Although Rice's fan and biographer Katherine Ramsland has mapped the world of the Vampire Chronicles, of which New Orleans is a part, for the particular tourist fans, the city of New Orleans is uniquely "Rice-inflected," as Dickinson puts it.[21] With the impetus of her texts, Rice and her fans' virtual place-connectedness to New Orleans have renovated geographic sites—which have their own traditional and evolving religious, gothic and spectacular practices—as sites of vampires or witches. This virtual place-connectedness has enhanced Rice's own ambiguous public identity as subcultural outsider and family woman in her home neighborhood. It has also enhanced her books' geocultural appeal and the city's palimpsest of cultural tourism even as Rice and the city have struggled over whether Rice's world is a neighborhood of New Orleans or New Orleans is a city inside Rice's world. Readers who find ambivalence in Rice's presentation of feminism, queer culture, or, as in my case, colonial conditions, can locate that tantalizing but frustrating irresolution in New Orleans's preserved architecture where, in the equivocal World of Anne Rice, gothicism and traditional family values coexist.

The River at the City's Edge

In the mid-1970s, while the nation of the United States was stumbling abroad and in its capital even as it celebrated the close of its second century, the young National Endowment for the Arts (NEA) was promoting City Edges projects around the country.[22] In 1973, New Orleans's leaders in the Vieux Carré Commission (VCC) and the Tulane University School of Architecture took advantage of this NEA initiative and city funds, proposing to study the Mississippi River Corridor. Their purpose was to understand what forces had developed and were developing the Corridor in the New Orleans Metropolitan Area, what the effects of this development were or might be, and what strategies might be formulated to guide future development now that the proposed Riverfront Interstate Expressway had been defeated. The city had weathered the intensive commercialization of its riverfront that closed virtually all of it to public use from the late nineteenth century until the mid-1960s. It had survived city officials' post–World War II attempt to wrest control of the Vieux Carré's edges from the VCC from 1946 to 1964, including its riverfront, thus permitting further large-scale commercialization. It had also outlasted the 1960s sustained battle over an elevated or street-grade interstate along the riverfront at the Vieux Carré that eventually resulted in the defeat of this highway plan. It even survived the 1960s fish kills in the Mississippi that announced the upriver petrochemical industrialization of the riverfront. Anyone who cared about the city and its river had good reason to look hopefully toward the proposed City Edges project. In its draft report of 1973, the project investigators state the case emphatically by remarking that, even in that year, without a map no one would know New Orleans is on the river. Because the river was walled off from the city by the port, the levee, and the railroad, they observed, it became an object of "fascination," "terror," and thus "ambiguity."[23] To address the city's edge along the river was to begin to reopen the place and the view to the present public and to the layers of time and human use embedded in the river silt and the mud of the batture.

In announcing the grant winners, the NEA explained that their main objective in City Edges projects was to focus attention on neglected or misunderstood dividing lines, both real and psychological, between different areas and activities in cities. It has to be said that the New Orleans project leaders and the architecture student-investigators they advised primarily addressed the need to manage large-scale riverfront development and offered their drawings and analysis with an implicit belief in the beneficial effects of physical design. From the conversion of Jax Brewery to retail space to the use of a riverfront streetcar for tourists, many of the 1973 City Edges design ideas have, in fact, been realized and in a way that retrospectively seems anything but controversial. This said, the project's investigators were also implicitly reopening New Orleans riverfront as a fascinating, terrifying, and ambiguous historic site of intracoastal and transcontinental Middle Passage. Without claiming too much for it, I want to propose that the City Edges Project at least introduced the possibility of connecting, through the river, the city's folkways and technicways translocally to southern upriver sites as well as to other former colonial sites in Haiti, Cuba, the rest of French and Spanish America and to the west coast of Africa.

Rice's New Orleans vampire Louis begins his interview in the 1970s with the story of the 1791 French colonial plantation society at the Mississippi River's edge and thus, in her virtual New Orleans, introduces the same promise emergent in the City Edges Project. That is, she opens up gothic secrecy to public scrutiny on the coast, as the novel calls the territory downriver of the city.[24] If fantasy says what realism (and civic projects) dare not say, then to understand just how much Rice's first vampire novel does and does not exploit this opportunity at the river's edge, it is helpful to punctuate its reading not only with civic projects, but also with her subsequent novel, the 1979 historical fiction of the city's *gens de couleur libre, Feast of All Saints*. It too presents the riverside plantation society that drives the economy of artisanal and cultural New Orleans; it too approaches the reading public in the latter 1970s as the nation and the South are recoiling from civil rights and black power and as the nation and the city are responding to the revolts against feudal plantation society in Spanish America.

"I was talking about the plantations. They had a great deal to do with it, really, my becoming a vampire," Louis tells the boy at the start of the interview.[25] On the face of it, Louis means that it was the opulence and money-making system of the plantations in 1791 that attracted the vampire Lestat to him. But details of the colonial plantation society enhance this simple logic of the plot. On the two indigo plantations in his namesake Louisiana, the boy Louis and his French family find a life of luxury greater than any possible for them in eighteenth-century France, a life in which the rosewood furniture is all the more precious for residing in a swamp. When Louis becomes master of the plantation Pointe du Lac, he retains his equilibrium and his pleasure in colonial life by confiding to his beloved and devout younger brother "the difficulties I had with the slaves, how I distrusted the overseer or the weather, or my brokers."[26] But then his serene brother upsets this routine by claiming to see visions of the Virgin, who commands them to sell all the Louisiana property and use the money to do God's work in France to "turn the tide against atheism and the Revolution."[27] When Louis's brother subsequently dies from a fall as he looks to the heavens from the head of the gallery's brick staircase, Louis blames himself for doubting the visions. With his brother buried in New Orleans St. Louis Cemetery, Louis roams the city streets, a drunken "invitation ... to sailors, thieves, [and] maniacs ... but it was a vampire [Lestat]" who attacked him.[28] As his mortal body lay dying, he confesses his distress about his brother to a priest, but the cleric rejects Louis's guilt, insisting instead that his brother was possessed by the devil, that the French Revolution is the devil's work, that all of France is under the influence of the devil. "He went on talking about the devil, about voodoo amongst the slaves and cases of possession in other parts of the world. And I went wild ... nearly killing him."[29]

Ironically, the priest and Louis's brother share the same (implicitly monarchist) assessment of the French Revolution and its implications for traditional Catholicism. If Louis nearly kills the priest, ostensibly to defend his brother's religious honor, he is not also defending his brother's ideological position. Instead Louis's place at Pointe du Lac suggests that he violently rejects both his brother's vision and the priest's judgment because both disrupted his isolated luxury in the swamp. On the one hand, to reenter the polis of France would require him to take up a position dictated by (undistinguished) hereditary position or to take responsibility for his new capitalist position as a land and slave owner. On the other hand, to acknowledge the devil's work in the new world through the voodoo of slaves such as those on the unnamed San Domingue (or Santo Domingo [Haiti])—those people who revolted in 1791 when their masters did not grant them the liberty claimed for all French people—would be to threaten his oasis of colonialism on the coast of the Mississippi.[30] But a third hand of composed inaction is no longer an option either, for his brother is dead and Louis lay dying. Enter the fantastic in the form of Lestat: at Louis's impasse between death and rage, the vampire reappears to transform the young planter into a vampire. Having suppressed his complicity in two scenes of political horror—one in France and one in San Domingue—Louis instead reluctantly joins a gothic world of vampiric horror in New Orleans and its riverside plantation society.

The Feast of All Saints provides Rice's commentary on the Haitian revolution, a more extended analysis of New Orleans Francophilia, and more direct reference to the US plantation system, all largely undeveloped in *Interview*. Unlike Charles Chesnutt's New Orleans novel *Paul Marchand, F.M.C.*, or Caryn Cosse Bell's history of the Afro-Creole protest tradition in Louisiana, *Feast* does not finally endorse the liberatory effects of a Parisian political education on New Orleans men of mixed race; in fact, it concerns itself primarily with the aesthetic education to be had there.[31] Instead, its young protagonist Marcel, son of a white plantation owner and his Haitian mistress, learns to relinquish his yearning for Paris by discovering a history of San Domingue as told by its mixed-race survivors. He finds these texts at San Souci, the plantation of his "aunt," a woman of color valorized by the text despite her having stolen his beautiful dark mother from her own African mother during the Haitian revolution that pitted free mulattos against African slaves more often than it sustained their alliance against plantation-owning whites. In this mixed-race plantation culture is a "noble" and "horrible" past that joins San Domingue and Louisiana and roots him in the trans-American world rather than in France. But Marcel's position in relation to slavery is nonetheless ambiguous. Through the history lessons, he discovers sympathy for "his people," those of mixed race, and does not act on his awareness of the slaves in their quarters on his aunt's plantation. Tante Josette exploits his newfound but circumscribed compassion, telling him that the lives of *gens de couleur libre* are threatened by Northern abolitionists even as she explains that there will be no slave uprising in the United States because the American nation's system of domestic slavery, like a cotton gin, has, "in its precision ... ground the slaves utterly and completely into the dust."[32] Having said this, the mistress of Sans Souci offers her slaves no alternative to plantation economy. Instead, she recommends "passing" for "her people," these "flowers of the French and the Spanish and the African" doomed by the boots of the Americans. As a visibly mixed-race body, Marcel could not himself take this advice if he were inclined. What he does do is enter the artisanal class of New Orleans *gens de couleur libre*, burying his response to slavery—including to his own half-sister—inside his angst about his own identity and his attraction to the new technology of the daguerreotype. Meanwhile the novel's melodrama directs his half-sister slave to dupe Marcel's elegant light sister and lead her into a den of voodoo where she is drugged and made the object of gang rape by five wealthy white men. The victimization and virtue of the *gens de couleur libre* beset by the slaves and their gothic Africanist culture on one side and the powerful whites and their Creole colonial culture on the other could hardly be made more explicit. This liminal position is not unlike the geosocial one occupied by the child Anne Rice living on the edge of New Orleans's Garden District.

As does Walker Percy's fiction, *Feast* distinguishes between good and bad plantations. Just as for Percy, the working plantation with muddy boots on the porch is to be distinguished from those dressed up for tourist consumption, in *Feast,* San Souci succeeds specifically because of the hands-on management of its Afro-Creole owners while Marcel's white father's plantation struggles under his absentee management and his lavish spending in New Orleans. (Just the same, its occupants maintain a haughty white supremacist attitude that rejects Marcel.) These distinctions between good and bad plantations ask readers to locate evil in white arrogance and pretension that rejects adequate managerial oversight rather than in a system of labor and social arrangement that entraps some people in a physical regimen (and punishment) over which they have no control and in which they earn little or no reward. This, Huston Baker reminds us, as he meditates on plantations, ships, and black modernism, is the fundamental etymology of "plantation." Whether the "farm" in question is Booker T. Washington's Tuskegee Plantation, Louisiana's Anglo State Penitentiary, or Rice's virtual San Souci and Pointe du Lac, the same definition applies and the same immobility and insecurity of black bodies—literal and virtual—results.[33] Marcel's Tante Josette is not the victim of what Baker calls American punitive disciplinarity; as a plantation-owning, mixed-race trans-American, she is nonetheless its carrier.

More than the antebellum "French-speaking" Afro-Creoles of *Feast*, *Interview* evades American national disciplinarity and other US ideology by positioning its plantations in a pre-1803 Louisiana and imbricating the gothicism of slavery and voodoo with that of its fantastic white vampires (who get all the whiter when they are hungry for blood). With these strategies, it implies more about the river's edge from which the City Edges Project might have learned something than does its historical cousin *Feast*. Although these implications are provocative for what they promise, it is important to repeat from the outset that Rice does not sustain an ideological critique grounded in New Orleans colonial past, only a gothic spectacle attached to the city's historical facades. The nature of the promise and the failure are nonetheless instructive for an analysis of New Orleans's place on the coast.

In describing his slaves to the boy who is the auditor of his twentieth-century interview, Louis overtly turns away from the US South.

> In seventeen ninety-five these slaves did not have the character which you've seen in films and novels of the South. They were not soft-spoken, brown-skinned people in drab rags who spoke an English dialect. They were Africans. And they were islanders; that is, some of them had come from Santo Domingo [San Domingue/Haiti]. They were very black and totally foreign; they spoke in their African tongues, and they spoke the French patois; and when they sang, they sang African songs which made the fields exotic and strange.... The slave cabins of Pointe du Lac were a foreign country, an African coast after dark.[34]

In fact, Louis explains, in the four years (1791–1795) that he and Lestat lived at Pointe du Lac as vampires, "the work of the plantation produc[ed] little."[35] In part, this is because his is an indigo plantation at a time when technology perfected the growing and refining of sugar cane, thus making that product the extraordinary cash crop of south Louisiana. Louis reflects nostalgically on the changes sugar brought to the plantation territory of the river's edge and its market in New Orleans.

> There is something perfect and ironic about ... this land which I loved producing refined sugar. I mean this more unhappily than I think you know. This refined sugar is a poison. It was like the essence of life in New Orleans, so sweet that it can be fatal, so richly enticing that all other values are forgotten.[36]

Not only did his indigo plantation produce little because it was outside this sweet addiction, but also because he turned his attention to investing Lestat's gambling earnings in New Orleans real estate. Although Louis feared his African slaves when he was a mortal, as a vampire he gives over the management of the plantation to those who have no reason to promote its economic growth.

Ironically, he had more to fear from them as a vampire than he did as a mortal. When the slaves charged with domestic service inside the house recognize the peculiarities of their masters' sleeping and noneating habits and put this together with the killing of slaves and animals in the swamp, they gather with slaves from along the river's edge not to plan their own escape, but rather to plan the murder of these devil creatures, the vampires.[37] The Africans' gothic system of voodoo recognizes another (and evil) gothicism and determines to defeat it on ground they claim implicitly as their own: an "African coast" in trans-America despite their enslavement within the plantation system of colonialism. Though in fiction and in fête Rice weaves her vampires into the fabric of New Orleans folk gothic traditions rooted in plantation slavery and voodoo practices, in this foundational novel she also sets them up as enemies in the colonial world. They cannot coexist because their strategies for physical and cultural survival are at odds.

If the vampire Louis expresses sympathy for the foreign syncretic culture of his slaves, it is not consciously or unambiguously so. Louis knows that from the beginning of Lestat's life on the plantation, he seeks food primarily among runaway slaves whom he finds encamped in the swamps. And when both vampires are discovered and realize that their survival is in doubt, they attack the Africans, beginning with Daniel, the man Louis trusted as his overseer. Rice gives to the vampires the supernatural speed and strength whites historically feared in their black (male) laborers. When the vampires are found out, these powers enable them to murder many of the slaves and burn Pointe du Lac, making of it a funeral pyre. Louis tells his interviewer that he "had had enough of Pointe du Lac and Lestat and all this identity of Pointe du Lac's prosperous master."[38] What he does not say is that in relinquishing the role of feudal lord for that of investment capitalist, he reasserts his power to destroy the persons and the memories of those who were the plantation's imprisoned laborers, thus victimizing them twice. Their bodies are not a necessary part of Louis's real estate investments nor of the vampires' effort to secure their own survival. Louis's principal regret is that some slaves escaped and with them the secret of the vampire masters at Pointe du Lac.

Louis fears his slaves will run to the neighboring Freniere plantation, a site of romantic fantasy for him, another good plantation to his bad one. His idealization of the Freniere family is implicitly consistent with the ideology of the US South that he explicitly rejected in his description of Pointe du Lac's slaves. It belies any cross-gothic insight and subcultural identity he might have achieved at his own plantation. This idealization in itself makes the Freniere plantation scenes, together with the Pointe du Lac scenes, an important stage for the vampires' lives in New Orleans and Paris, but Louis's romantic vision is even more intensified by Lestat's disdain for it and violence toward it. Although Louis's more squeamish human voice controls the narration of the interview, Lestat's vampiric passion, especially in the Freniere episodes, ambiguously intuits a potentially more humane because more broadly transgressive practice than the romantic fantasy of the US South that Louis shares.

The two vampires teeter on either side of the questions of race and purity that shape Donna Haraway's signal essay about vampirism and US racism. Haraway claims that

vampires can be vectors of category transformation in a racialized, historical, national unconscious. A figure that both promises and threatens racial and sexual mixing, the vampire feeds off of the normalized human: and the monster finds such contaminated food to be nutritious. The vampire also insists on the nightmare of racial violence behind the fantasy of purity in the rituals of kinship.[39]

It is precisely "the fantasy of purity in the rituals of kinship" that so compels Louis's preoccupation with the Frenieres; it also drives Lestat's desire to destroy them.

The Frenieres are a colonial French family of five sisters and one brother on a plantation that participates in the new sugar refining technology. "All depended upon the young man. He was to manage the plantation" and all the dowries of the marriageable sisters.[40] For these reasons, the young Freniere is what Lestat likes in a victim and what Louis most wants to defend. When the young man is pulled into a duel, Lestat fumes that he will be cheated of the kill, whereas Louis feels for the "agonizing position" of this plantation family completely unlike the inhabitants of his own "unnatural" Pointe du Lac. So Louis intervenes in the duel to save Freniere, but Lestat seizes the opportunity to drag the young man into the cypress groves, drain his blood, and leave his body to sink into the swamp until "the water rose over his face and covered him completely."[41] In his interview, Louis interprets Lestat's motive for killing Freniere as revenge against life itself, but the Freniere family is not life itself. It is a particular construction of purity and kinship, what Haraway sees at the core of the American racialized unconscious.

Through the figure of Babette Freniere, Louis fights Lestat's violent assault on the bloodlines of her family. Louis urges Babette to take her brother's place, and, for the sake of "family, a line ... [that] meant something to Babette," Louis advises her to arrange a Catholic charity affair to win over New Orleans Creole society to her new position in the plantation economy. Louis tells her that in this endeavor, "it was confidence and purity which were all-important," and she agrees. "Babette was to me ... an ideal human being," Louis confides to his boy auditor.[42] She in turn perceives Louis as an angel of advice if not annunciation, until the night he and Lestat seek refuge from his slaves. The stories of Pointe du Lac have preceded them, and Babette now believes Louis is an agent of the devil. Although Lestat wants only a carriage in which they can escape to New Orleans, Louis lingers to indulge his distress that she will doubt his earlier advice and thus her "rich and good" life that, as he sees it, she must not question.[43] For human life at the river's edge to be defined as anything other than a collection of pure racial kith and kin is unbearable to Louis. Apparently, he cannot leave the plantation coast behind until he has tidied up the dark coast of Africa for the new nation of the United States. The novel enables a reading that exposes the national racialized unconscious conventionally situated in the US South. At the same time, it evades an explicit US national context and instead represents a colonial context troubling in itself yet more syncretic, more creolized, in its trans-American reach. But it also ambiguates the reader's sympathies, forcing an impossible choice between Lestat's overt vampiric violence and Louis's human racial violence. If the boy auditor interviewing Louis is meant to speak for the reader, then his aversion to Lestat's merciless killing of Freniere pulls us away from Haraway's transformative hope for vampires, that they will mingle bloods and thus races and thereby undo a national racial violence predicated on racial purity. Louis does indeed save Babette's mortal life from Lestat's quick and voracious appetite, but then he cannot save her from a psychic unraveling after she believes she has seen the devil's agents. The commitment to pure bloodlines Louis sought to defend at the Freniere plantation through its mistress Babette does not survive after she looks into his vampiric face of evil and doubts her own sanity, if not her own racial entitlement. Haraway concludes her essay, "I am on the side of the vampires, or at least some of them. But, then, since when does one get to choose which vampire will trouble one's dreams?"[44] Haraway's nightmare of racial violence is Babette's angelic visitation of family purity; Babette's nightmare of blood violated is Haraway's visionary community of transgressive vampires. Rice, it seems, has both visions at once.

Rather than resolve this conundrum, the novel moves into the city, replacing the family of pure bloodlines and the slavery of the coastal plantation system with vampiric alternatives in the space of eighteenth-century and antebellum nineteenth-century New Orleans, where cosmopolitanism masks rather than resolves the socioeconomic order on the coast. Although, in the novel, purity and slavery are left at the river's edge, the figurative and literal refined sugar they produce quietly underwrites the opulence and the economic violence of the city. Pointe du Lac's slaves, whose agency is left damaged but not destroyed, are replaced by the denizens of the mongrel city. "A vampire richly dressed and gracefully walking through the pools of light of one gas lamp after another might attract no more notice in the evening than hundreds of other exotic creatures." The "town gave [Louis] an endless train of magnificent strangers" on which to feed for company and for blood. And there is a new advantage for vampires when they move to the city of the Gulf Coast: "never in New Orleans had the kill to be disguised. The ravages of fever, plague, crime—these things competed with us always there and outdid us."[45] In this sugar capital on the river, Louis tries to bury the ashes of his own unconventional coastal plantation and set aside the ideal of the other pure plantation he cannot sustain. He thus kills humans again, beginning with a five-year-old orphan named Claudia. After Lestat transforms the dying girl into a vampire and adopts her, the two grown male vampires and the child who matures but does not age become an alternative family. But theirs is a family in which Claudia and Louis see themselves as slaves to their vampiric nature and to Lestat, their maker.

Rice's representations of family have been a source of much ire. The novel's critics have argued that the vampiric family is created by Lestat's rape of Louis and Louis and Lestat's pedophilic attack on Claudia. The 1980s proponents of family values—that is to say, "family values"—kept the novel off the movie screen until 1994, and yet scholars of queer studies see in the vampiric family not an opening for the gay family, but a condemnation of one.[46] This ire, however disparately provoked, can be usefully situated in the platial context of the plantation households at the Freniere place and at Pointe du Lac. These colonial conditions resonate significantly in the novel's New Orleans, especially through the development of the character Claudia. Herself the daughter of poor immigrants brought into the port of New Orleans where they find sickness and death, Claudia, like a perverted Dickensian orphan *cum* heiress, returns to the riverside at the "Irish Channel" of Rice's Garden District to find a family—but so she might consume it rather than embrace it. As a wealthy beautiful vampire, she is a second generation of colonial capitalism without any code of familial ideals or any worries such as those that beset Louis as master of Pointe du Lac. "Poverty began to fascinate her; she begged Lestat or me to take a carriage out through the Faubourg St.-Marie to the riverfront places where the immigrants lived ... Claudia had a family there which she took one by one."[47] Her desire does not attempt to re-create a family of her own (past) kind; rather she steals their bloodlines for her own alternative survival, later mixing it indiscriminately with the homeless drunks that she kills in the cemeteries. Lestat relishes Claudia's extraordinary appetite for conventional families (and material wealth) that follows his own and uses it to tweak Louis about the undoing of the Frenieres. "'Claudia has a taste for families' [he taunts Louis]. Speaking of families, I suppose you heard. The Freniere place is supposed to be haunted; they can't keep an overseer and the slaves run away.'"[48]

Lestat may gloat, but Claudia is yet more fierce than he. She plots his death to free herself and Louis from his control, not knowing that in the code of the vampires, to kill one's own kind is unforgivable and punishable by vampire death. The novel may introduce to Haraway's dreams vampires who disrupt the pure bloodlines of racialized humanity, but the sanctity of one's own kind is preserved in Rice's world nonetheless. Meanwhile, it is important to note, the history of race slavery is displaced by the language of slavery applied to the vampires' condition. "'I'm not your slave,' [Louis] said to [Lestat]. But even as he spoke I realized I'd been his slave all along. 'That's how vampires increase ... through slavery. How else?' he asked."[49] It is the fuller understanding of what they call their slave condition that prompts Claudia to revolt against Lestat. Claudia tells Louis,

> "The vampire [that created Lestat] made a slave of him, and he would no more be a slave than I would be a slave, and so he killed him. Killed him before he knew what he might know, and then in panic made a slave of you. And you've been his slave."
>
> "Never really.... Not a slave. Just some sort of mindless accomplice."
>
> "No, slave," she persisted...." And I shall free us both."[50]

The economic and physical conditions of plantation slavery in transAmerica that produced gothic horror in slave markets and ships' holds, and in cane, cotton, and tobacco fields as well as the gothic threat of syncretic voodoo practices of the circum-Atlantic journey developed to survive and reject the terror of slavery are here set aside. Spanish and French colonialism built on the river's edge and the hovering racial logic of the Anglo American empire sink into the swamp like the head of the Freniere boy. In the city behind the levees, in a new Spanish townhouse, the vampires (enslaved and enslaver) live lavish lives on their real estate investments. The physical realities of colonialism and Anglo American ideology might be said to reemerge from that swamp, as does the battered body of vampire Lestat after Claudia and Louis attack him, leaving him for dead. But mostly these realities and this ideology survive, in the novel, in the guise of preternaturally white creatures trapped in immortal luxury and predatory distaste if not always guilt.

After Claudia and Lestat try to kill Lestat a second time, leaving him in the burning New Orleans townhouse, they flee the city for Europe. The year is 1860, by my reckoning. Katherine Ramsland makes it 1862. In either case, it is the beginning of the Civil War and the gateway to the Emancipation Proclamation, and neither national US event is acknowledged in the text. In the novel, these and subsequent national acts that promise African Americans liberation disappear in a vacuum between the nineteenth century of Louis's story and the mid-1970s of his narration when civil rights and black power are again issues off the national stage. Although the 1994 Neil Jordan/Anne Rice film of *Interview* has the vampires complain of Yankees—that is, Americans—polluting the pre-American Creole Louisiana that they remember and shows the city enveloped by a conflagration as Louis and Claudia's ship leaves the dock—the fall of New Orleans? the fire next time?—the novel is silent on the Americanization of New Orleans in 1803 or 1861 or, through desegregation, in 1960. The lights of the city dim, and then "in moments we were carried downstream past the piers of Freniere and Pointe du Lac."[51] Rice makes clear that the plantations are the vampires' points of departure from the New World, even if they are suppressed in the ongoing consciousness of Louis's narration.

Their passage past the coast, out of the river, through the Gulf, and across the Atlantic to the Mediterranean to reclaim the birthright they believe Lestat denied them and to move fully beyond the veil of humanity skirts the islands of the Caribbean and the shores of Africa. As their trans-atlantic vampire voyage to their roots continues to reconceptualize the gothic tales of slavery, the Middle Passage remains, in the novel, a "repressed signifier of American [and trans-American] historical consciousness."[52] On the vampires' voyage, Claudia preys on the *Mariana*'s wealthy passengers, whereas Louis survives on its rats. "Amazingly clean of vermin," the ship is still a vessel of death for some human passengers who can only surmise that a fever has struck the unfortunate.[53] These words elicit comparison to the slave ships of the reverse voyage on which it was the wealthy plantation owners waiting in the Americas who preyed on the slaves. Their confinement as cargo in the pestilential hold

> produced copious perspiration, so that the air soon became unfit for respiration, from a variety of loathsome smells, and brought on a sickness among the slaves, of which many died ... and [there was] the filth of the necessary tubs, into which the children often fell, and were almost suffocated. The shrieks of the women, and the groans of the dying, rendered it a scene of horror almost inconceivable.[54]

For all their talk of vampiric enslavement, Louis and Claudia, of course, want no part of abjection of this sort. They completely reject the devastated bodies of the vampires as zombies that they find in eastern Europe. These hollow, ugly monsters devoid of free will are not their kind. Instead, the New Orleans vampires are identified by an English human victim of the zombie vampires as his kind: "The same blood flows in our veins, you and I. I mean French, English, we're civilized men, Louis."[55] Louis is immediately won over to this argument for civilization—of nineteenth-century empire—being of his kind. He and Claudia kill the vampire of the "Old World," rejecting both its physical abjection and its bald violence beyond the control of the creature himself. In their civilized world, neither this kind of corporeal enslavement nor this kind of unsavory victimization of others could be true of them. Louis becomes convinced that they have taken the wrong route. Not that they should have remained in the New World seeking the sites where Africa and America met to produce the new patois and new gothicism of his Pointe du Lac slaves—and also zombies such as those in the Caribbean described by Zora Neale Hurston.[56] Rather, "we need our language, our people. I want to go directly now to Paris."[57]

Latin Roots

New Orleanians have been turning to Paris to verify their civilization from the beginnings of their colonial city. New Orleans's local colorist Grace King rooted her post-Reconstruction retort to George Washington Cable's attack on racist Creole culture in a comparison of the city of New Orleans to a Parisian woman.[58] Spanish rule of Louisiana from 1763 to 1801, the Spanish reconstruction of the original old city after it was destroyed by fire, diocesan leadership located in Havana— New Orleans's closest architectural cousin—and New Orleans's position as the gateway to Spanish America before, during, and after the Mexican-American War of 1848 did not squelch the identification of the city and its (Euro- and Afro-) Creole population with French culture and language. (New Orleans's relationship to France, and Paris in particular, provides a telling contrast to the relationships inherent in the ideologies of design governing later French colonial urbanism in Morocco, Indochina, and Madagascar.[59]) As Rice's vampires were turning away from colonial trans-America, making the traditional pilgrimage to Paris in her 1976 novel, the City Edges project was, nevertheless, setting the table for another NEA-initiated civic project, a more geographically and organizationally ambitious idea called Latin Roots in the Built Environment. Touted as the first project of its kind in the United States, the resulting Latin Roots conference scheduled for April

1978 was sponsored by the NEA, the National Register of Historic Places, the Organization of American States, the US Department of State, and Partners for Livable Places.[60] Because the NEA's Robert McNulty saw New Orleans as the bridge between the French and Spanish language of architecture arriving in the United States through the Caribbean and the dominant Anglo American culture to the north, he specifically chose the city as the "perfect metaphor," "the stage set," for the agency's new Latin Roots initiative. Whether or not he went so far as to agree with Louis Armstrong that "everyone in New Orleans got that thing," McNulty approached VCC Director Lynda Friedmann about hosting a Latin Roots conference in New Orleans.[61] This project imagined New Orleans as a staging area for twentieth-century trans-America, even if no longer its capital. The circum-Atlantic gothicism abandoned by Rice's vampires at the river's edge was here to be reconsidered if not through emphasis on the Middle Passage, at least in recognition of the interface of architectural history, folkways, and modern problems in urban sites throughout trans-America.

Its proposal announces that the project arose at the conjunction of several events: the US bicentennial emphasis on ethnicities, the declaration of 1978 as the year of architectural heritage by the Organization of American States, and the debate over the US return of the Canal Zone to Panama. The sponsors and these cited events might suggest a program as controlled by US interests as a new version of the Good Neighbor Policy. Indeed, the chairman of the NEA does seems to miss the geographic implications of the conference and speak from within the Washington, DC, Beltway when he sends his regrets to New Orleans organizer Lynda Friedmann. He declares the conference part of President Carter's initiatives "to implement cooperation among federal agencies to solve the problems of cities."[62] Despite this national view of the conference, the organizers' mailing list reached out to other Latin cities—not only within but beyond the United States—and to a variety of nongovernmental participants as it evolved from a conference about architecture to one about community art and action as well. Community artists, World Bank employees, Catholic liberation theologians, architectural historians, urban design experts, consuls, and urban officials from Chile to Haiti, from Columbia to Brazil, from Mexico to Florida were invited to participate.[63] Conference organizers pursued not only trans-American participation, but also Latin American press coverage.[64]

Four conceptual units were proposed: folk architecture, urban design, community problems, and strategies for the future. In a press release from November 1, 1977, these issues had become four themes that enabled a translocal approach outside the Cold War dichotomy dominating US political debate about the region: Changing Conditions in Latin Cities, Environmental Arts, Community Action, and the Historic Built Environment. While a national photography exhibit of Hispanic Architecture in the United States was mounted in New Orleans, organizers also pursued funding to acquire and mount other trans-American exhibits, such as one from Bogotá, and called on local experts to create a local Latin neighborhood tour of the city that focused on the "heart of the Latin area" in the Uptown neighborhood of the Garden District. Another New Orleans tour of the Vieux Carré pointed to the hybrid Spanish-, French-, American-, and Caribbean-inflected roots in many of its buildings.[65] The intraurban mapping of the local city tours focused on the architecture of the place, but the trans-American connections asserted at the conference gave renewed sanction to this US city's past and present emplacement within trans-America and the history of the coast that Rice's vampires leave behind. The conference was one dependent on US federal funds and one with considerable faith in the social power of "amenities"—that is, the features of physical design. The founding visions of its organizers and of it sponsor Partners for Livable Places make this very clear. It also bracketed any overt recognition of the remaining feudal struggles in the region in the waning 1970s. It nevertheless invited overt testimony to the geography, culture, and social history linking New Orleans's river's edge to the Gulf, and the city in the swamp to the Latin American isthmus.

New Orleans and Louisiana's ongoing connection to Spanish America had been visible in the 1970s, principally in their relations with political and financial leaders. In June 1975, for example, Governor Edwin Edwards (again) invited Nicaraguan ruler Anastosia Somoza for a visit. Edwards's administration told the press that "the President [Somoza] recognizes the natural ties that exist between Nicaragua and Louisiana. He has expressed an interest in establishing a closer relationship between Nicaragua and Louisiana."[66] New Orleans's major white newspaper, *The Times-Picayune*, the banner of which describes itself as "Serving America's International Gateway Since 1837," routinely recorded the anti-Communist Cuban anxieties of syndicated columnists and the repetitions of Franklin Roosevelt's declaration that Somoza (father and son) were s.o.b.s, but they were our s.o.b.s. But the views of witnesses in Nicaragua, Guatemala, and El Salvador who returned to New Orleans to tell their tales of torture were also reported alongside the consuls' insistence on stable, favorable relations. Local protestors against Spanish American dictators and US support of them found their place in the newspaper's pages, as did Spanish American exhibits in the lobby of the International Trade Mart and city trade delegations' determination to make New Orleans's economic links to Central America as strong as Miami's or Houston's. *The Times-Picayune*'s own editorial position tried to accommodate New Orleans business interests, its citizenry of Central American origins, and its tradition of Catholic charity (if not activism) by consistently calling for US aid to "responsible opposition in Nicaragua," which was the most unnerving because the most successful of the anti-feudal revolutions in Spanish America.[67] Still, the 1970s were not a decade when New Orleanians could take for granted familiar ties between Central America and Louisiana that the governor was counting on. The New Orleans Latin Roots project emphasized intraurban and intercoastal connections to Spanish America not usually so explicitly acknowledged.

As the VCC and the city's architectural community were contemplating the city's edges and its Latin roots in the 1970s, the local Catholic community was in the midst of changes that can be traced in their relation with the nations of the Central American isthmus. On the one hand, the archdiocese's very visible response to the earthquake in Managua, Nicaragua, in 1972; a devastating hurricane in Honduras in 1974; and another powerful earthquake in Guatemala in 1976 reflect a traditional charitable relationship between New Orleans Catholics—many of them immigrants from these nations—and the Central American Catholic nations, whose clergy often had ties to New Orleans. On the other hand, the growing social justice movement among Sisters in the United States and clergy in Central America reveals a reaction to Central America focused on political repression and terror rather than natural disaster. This movement which presented a challenge to the Pope, and to the New Orleans archbishop, was reconfigured in the local Catholic press as women's bid for the priesthood or their flight from spirituality.[68] But while Sisters were defending the spiritual basis of work for social justice, even the mass media was beginning to see the link between the natural disasters that called for the city's traditional charitable responses and the political and economic injustice apparent in a dictator's control of the distribution of that charity among the people of their own nations.[69]

Amid the Cold War rhetoric that dominated US discourse about Spanish America, *The Times-Picayune* and the local Catholic newspaper, the *Clarion Herald*, told stories of individuals acting on extranational initiative for motives of their own. Their activities gloss the goals of the Latin Roots project and the narrative trajectory of Rice's *Interview*. One is a former US soldier who had become a soldier of fortune in Central America's civil wars. Another is a New Orleans small businessman so impatient with federal, local, and diocesan response to the hurricane in Guatemala that he finds effective alternatives. Teachers, nuns, and purveyors of New Orleans trade all journey to Central America and return with stories that confront or evade the national leadership in the United States and in Central America as well.[70]

The evasion of the US nation in Rice's 1976 presentation of New Orleans and its coast enters this discourse. In doing so, the novel leaves undeveloped the national fate of US slavery and plantation society, as I argued, but it also promises to join these 1970s stories that try to define the trans-American experience outside the smothering and dichotomous assumptions of the Cold War. (We must side with our s.o.b. Somoza, or face a Nicaragua controlled by Cuba and the Soviet Union.) Although the editors of *The Times-Picayune* do not propose to act outside the authority of Washington, they do try to reclaim New Orleans's status as the capital of trans-America. It is fitting, they argue, that negotiations among Great Britain, Belize, and Guatemala to decolonize Belize and resolve its dispute with Guatemala over sea access should take place in New Orleans.[71] It is right that New Orleans should be the conduit for material aid in times of Central American natural disaster. New Orleans should speak for a rational position in Nicaragua between the Cold War extremes emanating from the Washington of President Carter and his substantial political enemies. If Rice's beautiful vampires arose at a time without national political leaders, as Auerbach has argued, they also emerged in a trans-American world at a site where and in a time when alternatives to colonialism and even nationalism are in play. But then they go to Paris.

The Vampiric Theater of Paris

Anyone who knows Rice's novel, or the Jordan-Rice 1994 film of it, also knows that the theater scenes in the Paris portion of the story are an interpreter's dream. In these scenes, the vampires stage the real murder of a human woman by male vampires for a human audience unclear about what they are witnessing and for a vampire audience of Louis and Claudia who have no doubts. In this performative world, in an unidentified Second Empire Paris (1851–1870), Louis meets his superior in sophistication, the vampire Armand. Their homoerotic relationship and elegant night life promise to sanction a queer culture that the novel never quite embraces. At the same time, Rice reintroduces Lestat to seek revenge specifically against the girl vampire, Claudia, and her new-found mother–friend (and thus disillusions feminists). All of this occurs amid the Bosches and Boticellis that vivify a conjunction of beauty, sexuality, and violence. The wealthy colonial vampires from New Orleans immerse themselves in the expensive cafe society without any reference to the imperial politics underwriting the Paris of the Second Empire or its physical transformation under the direction of the city prefect, the Baron du Haussmann. In the world of the novel, nineteenth-century Paris has no politics, no citizens displaced by urban modernization, no class conflict, and no barricades because the vampires' wealth renders them immune to such effects. They might even be in Paris as it succumbs to the 1870 siege by the Prussians or as the government at Versailles slaughters thousands of Parisians—Communards, as they were called—in their defense of a republican city; the novel does not specify. But it does not matter in the vampires' world because they are among those few elites who enjoyed "the luxuries of cafe life which were kept going, supplied by hoarding merchants at exorbitant prices."[72] In 1970s terms, they are among the Somozas of the colonial world, enjoying extraordinary wealth. If meanwhile "the common people were [literally] consuming their ancestors [in the form of bonemeal from the cemeteries baked into the bread] without knowing it," this use of the Parisian cemeteries was not the vampires' concern.[73] Rice's Paris is an elite, aesthetic place that, as it happened, sympathizers with the Communards themselves identified as vampiric. When, in the 1890s, a republican Paris had found its feet and taken a stand against the building of the grand Basilica of Sacré Coeur on the Butte Mont Martre as a monument to traditional Catholicism and its earlier alliance with the monarchy and as a desecration of the Communards killed there, they depicted the building in progress as a vampire.[74]

Paris both gives Louis a kind of life—the life of art—and takes it away through the murder of Claudia enacted by the trickery of Armand and the vengeance of Lestat. Despite their wealth, beauty, and life beyond mortality, the vampires—particularly the vampires in Paris—are self-destroying. When Armand tries to recuperate the curiosity and passion Louis had when he met him, he takes him back to New Orleans. "'I thought something would quicken and come alive in you if you saw him [Lestat] ... if you returned to this place.'" But Louis rejects, even mocks Armand's effort to bring him back to life. Revenge, passion, hatred, love, a return to a New Orleans home site are not possible for Louis after the murder of Claudia in Paris. Armand complains that Louis has become as cold and distant as a modern painting, "as alien as those hard mechanical sculptures of this age [the twentieth century now] which have no human form.'" Whether or not he has indeed become as modern and mechanical as Haussmann's design for Paris, Louis leaves New Orleans because he does have feelings there, sorrow attached to "that old house where Lestat was dying" and because he realizes the goal of his quest was not Paris, he says, but his own death.[75]

Rice's fans know that, of course, Lestat does not die, and this devolution into meaningless despair is undone by subsequent, if retrospective, Vampire Chronicles and Rice's enormous financial success writ large in the gothic world of New Orleans and her own vampiric Garden District. The spectacle of her gothic presence, underwritten by a diffuse reading public, many of them countercultural tourist-fans, promised substantially more than despair in material and virtual New Orleans. It provided the opportunity to infuse the city's Africanist gothicism into the affluent, former Anglo American sector. And it provided the opportunity to rearticulate the formation of these Africanist folkways in the trans-American plantation culture and the traditional Catholicism of French and Spanish colonialism. Readers of Rice might look back through her success to the mid-1970s of *Interview* and the promise of New Orleans's coast. There they could see the invitation to understand New Orleans's colonial past and the African American roots of its gothicism in its trans-American context specifically as that volatile context was changing quickly and being reseen in the city. But even the first of the Vampire Chronicles turns from this promise on the coast to an ideal of Parisian aestheticism devoid of that city's lessons, for good and ill, in revolutionary politics and modernist urban design. And what was subsequently sustained in New Orleans into the 1980s and 1990s—after the 1980 assassination of Somoza in Paraguay and subsequent regime changes in Washington, for example—was the spectacle of Anne Rice that rewarded fans with provocative posturing, buildings preserved for virtual history, party favors of syncretic gothicism, and colonial secrets of New Orleans Coast still hidden in plain sight. Rice's repeated implicit invitation to goths, gays, and other fans young and not so young, issued through her official Web site as well as her novels and through the publicity surrounding her performances of herself, has been to find a home inside New Orleans gothicism. But it turns out that the World of Anne Rice, for all its tourist reach into New Orleans plantation environs, its virtual reach into global space, and even its deployment at a local annual function to raise money for AIDS research, was not prepared to make good on its platial, gothic promises. Rice could create a public character as vampire queen to rival the marketing success of Laveau's voodoo queen because she built on New Orleans gothic traditions facilitated by historic preservation and local folkways—those marketed to tourists and those held closer to the local heart. But for all its infusion into the place of New Orleans, that public character has remained mostly enclosed inside the virtual mass media world of Anne Rice, shaping the local sites to the demands of that world.

The Latin Roots of the Built Environment also promised more than it delivered. Lynda Friedmann remembers the 1970s, under the administration of Moon Landrieu, as "heady times for New Orleans." People were moving into the city, and the Vieux Carré was on an economic upswing. There was, she recalls, no reason to make compromises. So, though she was young and inexperienced, it seemed reasonable to take on the Latin Roots conference proposed by McNulty at the NEA. It was an opportunity for the VCC and the city residents generally to "broaden their horizons" and become less "provincial." It was a chance to educate the public. But, by 1978, when the conference was held, a change in mayoral administrations was under way and "things were in flux." The conference itself was poorly attended and not the prestigious event it promised to be. Feeling it had been too ambitious in looking outside the city, the VCC turned its attention to historic preservation of other New Orleans neighborhoods, the lower Garden District in particular. Focus remained on this expansion of preservation districts such that, Friedmann argues, it went too far, producing too much gentrification. Meanwhile, in 1985–1986, the bottom fell out of New Orleans's economy.[76] As New Orleans's turn to preservation and tourism sharpened, Rice came back to the neighborhood of her birth, in 1988, riding on the capetails of her vampires. Embracing both preservation and tourism for her own purposes, she could use her economic success amid the city's economic decline, claiming New Orleans—or at least its Garden District—as Inside the World of Anne Rice and not the other way around.

7

Mapping the Spirit Region

Sister Helen, the Dead Men, and the Folk of New Orleans's Environs

[We are in a] "battle for the soul of the city."

—Police Superintendent Richard J. Pennington[1]

In 1852, a man sentenced to die was taken to the scaffold outside New Orleans Parish Prison just behind Congo Square in full view of the public, as was the custom. Just as the gallows opened and the noose began to tighten, the execution went awry. An enormous black cloud that had blown overhead let loose with a tremendous storm. The frightened spectators, running amok, charged the scaffold, and were further terrified by being entangled with the hanging man. Somehow the condemned man continued to live. Later, within the walls of the prison, this man was hung—again—and the law was changed so that all subsequent death sentences were carried out within the prison away from the public's eye. So recounts Herbert Asbury in his 1936 book about the New Orleans underworld[2] and Robert Tallant in his 1946 book about New Orleans voodoo.[3]

After this interrupted execution, many claimed that voodoo queen Marie Laveau caused the storm, for she was the condemned man's spiritual advisor.[4] Repeated stories say that between the 1850s and the middle 1870s, Laveau, a free Creole of color, not only nursed the victims of yellow fever with her herbal remedies and whatever other powers were at her disposal, but also acted as spiritual advisor to men awaiting execution in Parish Prison in the French Quarter.[5] According to an 1881 obituary,

> she would sit with the condemned in their last moments and endeavor to turn their last thoughts to Jesus. Whenever a prisoner excited her pity Marie would labor incessantly to obtain his pardon, or at least a commutation of sentence, and she generally succeeded.[6]

This obituary further observes that "the cultivated" appreciated her knowledge and skill in medicine and herbal healing; only "the ignorant attributed her success to unnatural means and held her in constant dread." Although Asbury concurs—her spiritual advising was wholly Roman Catholic—prolific stories indicate that she was widely remembered as the voodoo queen endowed with the power to produce interrupting storms.[7] Another of the several, conflicting obituaries, this one from the *New Orleans Democrat,* declared that "with her vanishe[d] the embodiment of the fetich (*sic*) superstition" of "old Louisiana," but stories of her work and life were not so easily laid to rest.[8] In New Orleans environs, not only all subsequent voodoo practitioners but also all subsequent spiritual advisors enter the discursive legacy of Laveau when they approach their work. The most famous late twentieth-century heir to Laveau is Sister Helen Prejean, spiritual advisor to men on death row in Louisiana State Penitentiary at Angola and author of her own story about the experience, *Dead Man Walking.*[9] How she participates in the regional folkways evolving from the stories of Laveau and maps a spiritual territory emerging from her own time and place and how some folk of that place compete to define its scope and contours are the subjects of this chapter.

Defining the Spirit of the Region

Although Asbury and Tallant and some of the oral storytellers who inform them may see a need to distinguish Catholic, European-defined practice from voodoo, African-defined practice, the syncretism of voodoo ritual and belief in the Western Hemisphere is everywhere obvious, not least in the stories about Marie Laveau. Not only mutually influential, Catholicism and voodoo together shaped other systems of belief and practices of faith. One such religion is the woman-centered, largely African American Spiritual Churches of New Orleans.[10] Spiritualism in the city attracted a large following in the 1920s and 1930s and maintained it through much of the twentieth century.[11] "Mother

Laveau," according to one theory of spiritualist origins in New Orleans, is said to have focused worship on the Holy Mother, adoration of the Saints, and the sacramentals and to have distinguished herself from common gris-gris users. In time, some say, the practice of the Laveaus, Marie the mother and Marie the daughter, was incorporated into Catholicism.[12] Yet, of the many Spiritual Church ministers who were also spiritual advisors in New Orleans neighborhoods in the late twentieth century, some still used conjure paraphernalia.[13] In Laveau's role as advisor to condemned men, she was participating in—perhaps, in some cases, even initiating—a set of syncretic spiritual traditions that continued to influence New Orleans spiritual advisors through the twentieth century.

Battles to control the Laveau legacy destabilize any precise political claims for her work. We know that the period in which she visited prisoners was one of dramatic changes in New Orleans. 1852, the year assigned to the aborted hanging, was an especially traumatic one for free Creoles of color such as Laveau. In that year, the 1836 partition of the city into three separate municipal districts, two Creole and one American, ended. With that reunification, free Creoles of color and slaves as well lost their relatively safe haven in the autonomous Creole districts where "enforcement of almost all laws was notoriously lax. ... For many years after the Civil War, creole black leaders recalled 1852 as the year of the breakdown of their sheltered and privileged order in New Orleans."[14] Circumstances of 1852 required a spiritual if not supernatural power such as that attributed to Laveau. Policing of the city also underwent peripateic change in the years of Laveau's prison work, seeing both the first significantly integrated police force after 1868 and a violent white reaction to that reform in the 1870s.[15]

Stories of her building altars, hearing sins, and conducting prayers present her as usurping the authority of the priests even as they recover her as a devout Catholic. Although a laudatory *Daily Picayune* obituary paints a sentimental tableau of nurse Laveau at the side of Père Antoine (who died in 1828), Fray Antonio de Sedalla—popularly remembered as Père Antoine—was himself often a renegade defying his Church superiors. He maintained power in New Orleans from 1785 to 1790 and from 1795 to 1828 by aligning himself with independent-minded laymen of St. Louis Cathedral and by offering information to the Spanish crown in exchange for the patronage of King Charles IV—even after the United States bought the Louisiana territory.[16] Publicly, American Governor Claiborne vowed to stay out of the battle with Sedalla when, in 1805, the newly appointed pastor of the Cathedral appealed to him to oust the old priest. Privately, he wrote President Jefferson describing Sedalla as a powerful and dangerous man.[17] If the young Laveau was aligned with Sedalla, then she would not have been the demure and docile Victorian female envisioned by the *Picayune* in 1881. She would instead have been an apprentice to a master who knew how to manipulate the volatile colonial situation and retain the overwhelming devotion of his frontier flock. It can be no surprise that stories describe her as a confessor who functioned as a visible ally of condemned men rather than a conventional, veiled intermediary between God and man. As a spiritual advisor, she was not, by all accounts, a prison chaplain serving at the pleasure of Church and state.

White, middle-class, and a member of the Congregation of St. Joseph, Helen Prejean began her twentieth-century Catholic practice in south Louisiana without immediate access to the creolized spiritual tradition of Laveau that she later entered. She instead found her place within the traditional beliefs and governing structures of the Catholic Church and the more European-influenced catholic cultural practices of south Louisiana.

> "All New Orleans is Catholic," remarks a local Catholic school Principal. If New Orleanians are not Catholic, they are in a sense catholic with a little 'c.' Regardless of who you are, you live in a parish, not a county; you stroll St. Peter, St. Ann, and St. Philip Streets; your neighboring parishes are St. Bernard, St. Charles, St. John, St. James, Ascension, and Assumption ... Catholic names, feasts, and traditions are simply part of life in New Orleans and South Louisiana.[18]

The Catholic colonial heritage *is* obvious everywhere in New Orleans and environs. Not only do the street names evoke its presence for any peripatetic observer in the city, but its sequestered archives house the official records of the colonial enterprise, records that reflect emergent categories of residents. "The earliest use of the term *Creole* [in south Louisiana] for which we have written evidence are descriptions of individual settlers in the baptismal, marriage, and death registers of the Catholic church in Mobile and New Orleans, the two main outposts of the fledgling French colony on the Gulf Coast."[19] Transferal of the territory to Spain, if anything, tightened the imbrication of Church and state. "I ... appointed ... swear before God, on the Holy Cross and on the Evangelists, to maintain and defend the mystery of the Immaculate Conception of Our Lady the Virgin Mary, and the royal jurisdiction to which I appertain in virtue of my office," intoned all public officials intending to work in the Spanish colony after 1769.[20] Yet, to attract Americans and English and their capital, the Spanish crown held the power of its colonial Church in check.[21] The official Church in New Orleans evolved in accord with the sociopolitical customs of the territory. In the nineteenth century, Irish, Italian, Latin American, and

Spanish immigrants "drew solace from the well-rooted Catholic church in New Orleans."[22] Although the Church "long resisted the complete racial segregation of its congregations ... well before the Civil War, the diocese had forbidden racial intermarriage, denied the entrance of black men into the priesthood, and implemented segregation in its schools, cemeteries, and lay societies." Some churches had segregated pews, and the Church prelates were supporters of the Confederacy and so, of course, sanctioned slavery.[23]

New Orleans street names do immerse residents and passers-by in a Catholic world extending from France and Spain. But in the new world, the saints—St. Ann, for example—are the addresses of New Orleanians such as Laveau, whose syncretic spiritual practices made them pilgrimage sites. St. Louis Cathedral sheltered the obdurate and irremovable Père Antoine who ruled by a vote of his (male) parishioners when his church superiors would not support him. The saints of the city and the region take their meaning as well from their proximity to precolonial names such as Mississippi and Atchafalaya and African diasporic names such as Angola. In the territory of the lower Mississippi River and the Atchafalaya Basin, these and innumerable other encounters have defined many and multiple catholicisms. African American inmigrants of the nineteenth century did bring with them American protestant religions, and the cosmopolitan city saw immigration from Asia, eastern Europe, and other corners of the world's religious practices. But it is the resonance of those earlier colonial encounters that define the cultural conditions in which and the field of faith on which Laveau, then Prejean, did her work. If there is a soul of the city, a spirit that can grasp the "wholeness of being" that architecture scholar Christine Boyer seeks as a respite from the fragmentary citations of postmodernity, then it must be mapped and remapped as needed onto this field of faith.[24]

Crises and Decisions in Place

From her home on St. Ann, Laveau visited Orleans Parish Prison a short walk away. Built in 1834, the prison remained at the site contiguous to Congo Square until well after her death in 1881.[25] In 1895, it was moved to Tulane Avenue away from the Creole Quarter.[26] When execution was later confined to the state penal institution, any spiritual advisors for prisoners awaiting execution would have to make their way outside New Orleans to the Louisiana State Penitentiary.

The first Louisiana State Penitentiary was built in 1835 in Baton Rouge, purportedly as a modern replacement for the "vermin infested jail in New Orleans" described by Alexis de Tocqueville after his two-day visit to the city at the New Year 1832.[27] But after nine brief years of prison reform, Louisiana's legislature—then controlled by Americans rather than Creoles—decided running a prison was too expensive. So, from 1844 to 1901, except when controlled by Union troops, the prison was privately run. Continuing the pre–Civil War system, the black and white post-War Republican legislature contracted with former Confederate Major Samuel James to act as lessee. James "maintained for twenty-five years the most cynical, profit-oriented, and brutal prison regime in Louisiana history."[28] Convicts, a majority of whom were black in the post-War period, could never be found at the Baton Rouge penitentiary itself. Their labor was sold to build the New Orleans Pacific Railroad and the levees and to work the plantations. Of most consequence for the future of the Louisiana State Penitentiary, James sent inmates up river to build levees and work the land at his 8,000-acre plantation called Angola for the African home of the slaves who once worked it. In 1901, after reports of numerous abuses under the leadership of James and his son, who succeeded him, the Louisiana State Penitentiary at Angola was reestablished as a state-controlled institution but one that maintained the convict lease system. Historian Mark Carleton claims that the state reasserted its control of the penitentiary not because of egregious abuses of the lease system, but because in the 1890s James, who had always functioned by bribery, dared to split the Democratic party.[29] Political gamesman and ruthless lessee, James left an indelible mark on Angola.[30] When major floods in 1903, 1912, and 1922 left their own marks, driving away neighboring plantation owners, the Angola penal site he developed acquired the land and increased "the farm" to its present size: 18,000 acres.[31] Made nationally infamous by its brutality—"the bloodiest prison in the South" or "the bloodiest prison in America"—and nationally famous for its rodeo, for the anti–death penalty work of Sister Helen Prejean, and for the social and spiritual reforms of current warden Burl Cain, Angola became the sole site of execution in Louisiana.[32]

Hanging at Angola was the method of execution until 1940, when the state legislature replaced it with electrocution. Then, from June 1961, when Louisiana suspended death as a punishment, until December 14, 1983, when Robert Wayne Williams was killed by electrocution at Angola, there were no executions at the prison.[33] During that hiatus—specifically, in July 1982—Sister Helen Prejean, C.S.J., first drove from New Orleans to Angola to receive approval to visit Elmo Patrick Sonnier on death row, the first step toward her inheritance from Marie Laveau.

Prison officials gave Sonnier the choice of designating his pen pal Sister Helen a friend or a spiritual advisor. She claims not to have known at the time that his decision for spiritual advisor granted her status as one of the few eyewitnesses permitted in the Death House.[34]

What she does know, at least in hindsight, is that this decision allowed her access to intimate knowledge about sequestered execution crucial to the formation and influence of her opposition to the death penalty. It is the category "spiritual advisor" that drives the book's plot and the political action of its author. That category also places the controversy evolving from Prejean's spiritual advising and her written story squarely within what Southern regionalist Howard Odum called "folkways," which circulate in the New Orleans region through stories about "Mother Laveau."[35]

In her narrative, Prejean presents herself as a recognizably religious woman. Her gender, independence from the demands and pleasures of being a wife and mother, and interpretation of Vatican II as a mandate for political action on behalf of the poor come to define how she occupies the category "spiritual advisor." Her self-definition as religious woman provokes a criticism in kind: her activity as spiritual advisor is a threat to the pope's, the priests', the middle class citizenry's, the government's, or the Bible's rules. Some believe she consorts with the devil. Some suspect that romantic feelings for her Death Row advisees motivate her action. Some accuse her of being a Communist. Prejean's written narrative folds the stories that arise as her work becomes public into her larger story, shaping their presence to her purpose. But that purpose is to demonstrate the learning curve of spiritual advising rather than to arrive precisely on a dime; multivoiced controversy, mistakes, irrepressible dissent, and uncontainable moral challenge are a necessary part of that long-term process. These forces keep the multiple stories within her text alive—if not altogether on their own terms, then at least in a semblance of the moral panic the topic of execution demands. (Rather than following Stuart Hall in defining moral panic as a media-hyped public response in excess of the purported cause, I imagine its inverse: a necessarily acknowledged moral confusion in need of public debate and political action.[36])

Although urban folkways synchronically link the stories of Laveau and Prejean, the government's technicways of execution locate the two women, each at her particular moment, in the continuum of historical time and progressive innovations. Thus these progressive technicways of execution seem to draw them apart as they mark the passage of time. Hanging in a central state institution replaces hanging in parish prisons. In deference to the federal standard limiting cruel and unusual punishment and in response to the modern inventions of electricity and then precisely dosed deadly drugs, electrocution replaces hanging, then lethal injection replaces electrocution.

We have already seen the government practice of execution change within the Laveau stories themselves: public chaos is said to have driven the process of hanging into seclusion in the New Orleans of 1852. The process of execution and the response of the public were thus contained. Prejean's rhetoric as well often returns to this distinction between public and private—ancient and modern—punishment, so central in Michel Foucault's familiar arguments in *Discipline and Punish* about controlling the subjects of the state.[37] If execution is not excessive punishment in violation of the Eighth Amendment to the US Constitution, then why is it hidden away in the bowels of death row at Angola? she asks. If it deters violent criminals, relieves the anguish of crime victims, and quells the fears of the public at large, why not put executions on television so that the whole of society might benefit? If the purpose of secluded execution is to shield the general public from horror, is the production of that horror—the enactment of execution—in fact for the public good? How remote should the citizenry be from punishments inflicted in its name?

Resisting Remoteness: Defining the Spirit Region

It is the relevance of remoteness to the formation of morally and politically accountable regions that most interests me, not the debate about the death penalty per se. The life and death issues of that debate do, however, crystallize the link between remoteness and accountability within regions in a way that is instructive for less stark but no less crucial public concerns. The concept of remoteness as developed by bioregionalists and clarified by ecological feminist Val Plumwood provides perspective on the death penalty and other public moral issues as it also speaks to the difference between the geography of Laveau's spiritual work and of Prejean's.[38] Bioregionalists claim that small-scale human communities with close ecological relationships to the nonhuman world around them are in the best position to make good ecological decisions about that region. Those remote from the region are less sensitive to signals from nature and to the effects of their daily productive and consumptive habits on the region.

Plumwood argues, however, that proximity to nature does not necessarily preclude insensitivity to its signals, and so spatial remoteness is not the only or the best means of understanding the term. She defines three additional kinds of remoteness:

> consequential remoteness (where the consequences [of actions] fall systematically on some other person or group leaving the originator unaffected), communicative remoteness (where there is poor or blocked communication with those affected…), and temporal remoteness (from the effect of decisions on the future).[39]

If we include human relationships within our definition of ecology—as we should—then we can say that when the hanging was moved inside New Orleans Parish Prison in 1852, the public became more spatially and more communicatively remote from the consequences of official actions taken in its name. When the site of execution moved from Parish Prison to Angola and the means of execution changed from hanging to electrocution, from electrocution to lethal injection, the practice of execution and its effects on a human body became increasingly remote from the citizenry of New Orleans and environs. What was once obviously subject to urban folkways became an ever more private and remote ritual. With each move, the state performed the ritual through yet more precise technicways designed to eliminate mistakes that would leave the executioners and any who witness the execution open to moral panic.

Warden Frank Blackburn tells Prejean "that a guard, matching the inmate's height and weight, does a dry run from the cell to the chair to make sure the 'Tactical Team' can 'contain' the condemned prisoner should he put up a fight."[39] The prisoner approaching electrocution remains in leg irons and handcuffs until he is strapped into the chair—later, with the method of lethal injection, a "bed." These precautions are taken not because the prisoner is in any position to hurt anyone physically. Rather, if the prisoner could struggle free or if the method of execution failed to hide his—usually, but not always, his—pain, witnesses behind the Plexiglas who came to see a man die would be wrenched from their remote position by a dead man walking.[41]

Although those Laveau ministered to were housed and hung within her own neighborhood, Prejean's advisees are a half-day's drive from New Orleans. About her first drive to Angola, she writes, "I have a poor sense of direction, so I have carefully written down the route to the prison, which is at the end of a circuitous road, about three hours from New Orleans." This drive takes her out of her present home in New Orleans's St. Thomas public housing development and through a varied topography.

> It feels good to get out of the steamy housing project onto the open road, to see the sky and towering clouds and the blue, wide waters of Lake Pontchartrain.
>
> Highway 66, which dead-ends at the gate of the prison, snakes through the Tunica Hills, a refreshing change of terrain in pancake-flat Louisiana. It is cooler and greener in the hills, and some of the branches of the trees arch across the road and bathe it in shadow.[42]

Prejean is not exaggerating the beauty of the landscape approaching Angola; it is, for good reason, the site of J. James Audubon's paintings of Louisiana wildlife—made after he had already killed his subjects, it has to be said. She relishes this physical and aesthetic distance from the New Orleans public housing development where she has been working and living while she is also still some distance from death row within Angola. Here in Audubon country she is "close to nature" and physically remote from St. Thomas and Angola in a way Laveau was not.

But she then counters these details of spatial and (human) ecological remoteness with a willed resistance to consequential, communicative, and temporal remoteness.

> I think of the thousands of men who have been transported down this road since 1901, when this 18,000-acre prison was established. About 4,600 men are locked up here now, half of them, practically speaking, serving life sentences. ... In 1977 ... the life-imprisonment statute was reformulated [in Louisiana], effectively eliminating probation, parole, or suspension of sentence.[43]

Unable to act as a spiritual advisor to condemned men within her neighborhood, Prejean begins here to deviate from the directions she has written down. That is, she maps what I will call a spirit region, a spatial territory within which consequential, communicative, and temporal remoteness can still be effectively resisted despite the prison's location outside the neighborhood and even the city limits. In this newly mapped spirit region, a moral decision as grave as state-sponsored execution can best be adjudicated by the citizenry of those environs. I use the language of law and politics deliberately. Inside a consciously mapped spirit region their definitions of justice and public participation are subject to the scrutiny of principles deriving from different premises. Someone with a self-described "poor sense of direction" may seem an unlikely cartographer, but it may be just this inability to retain prescribed direction from designated authorities—be they professional cartographers, highway engineers, or governors—that enables Prejean to create a map undaunted by city, parish, or state boundaries.

The subtitle of Prejean's *Dead Man Walking* is *An Eyewitness Account of the Death Penalty* in the United States (emphasis mine). The book's national and international reception and the national and global reach of Tim Robbins's movie inspired by it leave no doubt that the book's influence has been on a scale in excess of the spirit region.[44] The 1995 film starring Sean Penn as the man awaiting execution and Susan Sarandon as Sister Helen propelled Prejean's book to the *New York Times* nonfiction bestseller list for weeks.[45] Available in Japanese, Spanish, French, Italian, and Greek, it is not hard to imagine that the book has entered debates on the death penalty not only in every state in the Union, but also in most nations in the world. In fact, Prejean's

Web site records her global travels in the service of abolition.[46] E.E. Schattschneider, author of *The Semisovereign People*, the classic 1960 analysis of postwar US democracy, would applaud Prejean's enormous success at expanding the scope of the conflict by gaining some control over its visibility.[47] So I am swimming against the tide of traditional political analysis when I argue, as I emphatically want to do, that her book's effectiveness lies not in any claims—even her claims—for a national scale or a global reach, but in its ability to map a spirit region in which the moral decision can best be considered by its diverse public. Those in Iowa or Rhode Island, Israel or Indonesia, who want to replicate its impact need to re-create its cartographic work in their own territories. Otherwise, this narrative of New Orleans and environs is likely to be read only as a condescending cautionary tale. Do WE want to sink as low as Louisiana with its debased justice system that allows corrupt governors to walk on the wild side and executes indigent prisoners?

Schattschneider concedes that "there is nothing intrinsically good or bad about any given scope of conflict. . . . A change of scope makes possible a new pattern of competition, a new balance of forces and a new result, but it also *makes impossible a lot of other things.*[48] National antiexecution forces have found in Prejean, her book, Robbins's film, and now an opera of her story and a PBS documentary about the making of that opera, greater visibility for their cause.[49] But I question the power of this enlarged scope and greater visibility to substantially change conditions and sustain those changes in south Louisiana. It is conditions there that are my subject. Without attention to the scale of the spirit region, we risk making a lot of important things impossible.

By law, capital punishment is, of course, a state decision facilitated by rulings of the US Supreme Court. Prejean's narrative traces the decisions by the high court, by the Louisiana state legislature, and by the governor that have enabled the reinstatement and continuation of the death penalty. Those jurisdictions matter. The authority of the court and the legislature is enacted within those federal and state territories. But as Denis Wood reminds us in *The Power of Maps*, maps construct the world; they do not reproduce it. If one wants to resist the purposes for which one map is drawn—the boundaries of Louisiana map the boundaries of an execution zone—then one must produce an alternative map drawn from a different perspective, for a different purpose. We need "dueling maps," as Wood argues.[50]

Mapping the Spirit Region

The alternative map Prejean constructs is of a spirit region centrifugally capacious enough to welcome humanity—however corrupt or condemned—and yet centripetally compelling enough to demand atonement from each individual in turn. Such a space requires permeable boundaries rather than rigid and patrolled borders. The map of a spirit region creates a territory better understood if compared to a bioregion rather than a geopolitical territory such as a city, parish, state, or nation-state. In "Living by Life," a much-cited 1981 essay by bioregionalist Jim Dodge, he urges readers to let definitions of bioregion emerge from practice, specifically an anarchic governing practice that he pointedly defines as "out of *their* control," rather than simply outside of any controlling idea.[51] The spirit region I propose draws on this idea of the impermanence and permeability of borders and the ways they emerge from practice as needed.

Daniel Kemmis elaborates this kind of organic proposal in his preface to the 1999 *Bioregionalism* collection. He argues that the forces of globalization favor the recognition of organic forms at all levels: global, continental, ecosystem, city-region and "organic subcontinental level of regions." He further argues that regionalism reflects the "devolution of power downward from the national government."[52] Citing a familiar analogy between the growth of the nation-state in the eighteenth century and the mechanical predictability and control of Newtonian physics, he perceives, at the end of the twentieth century, an analogy between the new evolving regionalisms and the radical unpredictability of quantum physics, an unpredictability with its own order derived from mutually influential fractals reproducing patterns at different scales. "From situations which appear to be utterly chaotic, order is constantly emerging not on our terms, but on the terms of the emerging order itself." No one can tell a place it is a region, he declares. "Either it is a region inherently, by its own internal logic, or it is not a region at all."[53]

But Kemmis leaves unexplained how the "devolution of power downward from the national government" does or will occur. In defining the regional city in the book by the same name, Peter Calthrope and William Fulton insist that the metropolitan region must have an agreed-on border as a way of responsibly managing sprawl. The conventional pro-growth perception of an inherent city-region might be one radiating outward indefinitely into sensitive ecosystems and important agricultural land to the detriment of community building (and public health, I would add).[54] Gerald Frug in *City Making* proposes the formation of a regional government that has significant power to make competing contiguous cities work together for the common good of all their citizens, residents, and visitors.[55] These concerns for the design of a region's built environment and its governance are crucial to the realization of a regional vision. But these efforts to imagine and create the right balance of environmental health, economic viability, and social justice need, I am arguing, the fourth leg of spiritual motivation, felt wholeness, to build a sustainable region. So I return to the question arising from the bioregionalists. What is a region's "own internal logic"? Who will discover it? Apprehend it? Use it? And how?

These questions find useful answers in Denis Wood's assertion—familiar to humanists—that all maps are constructions by someone for a purpose, and that we do well to know the creators of a map and their purpose in order to read the rhetoric of the map. In *Seeing Like a State*, James Scott conveys just how tragic the consequences can be when a society is made legible—mapped—for the purposes of social engineering.[56] Although the legibility promoted by the modern state grounds our freedoms as much as our unfreedoms, Scott argues, when we find it linked to high-modernist top-down desire, an authoritarian state determined to act on that desire, and an incapacitated civil society, large-scale disaster is the consequence. This formula for catastrophe applies to global capitalism in the present world as much as to any governmental state now or in the past. For anyone wishing to avoid such tragedies, the task is clear: capacitate civilians possessed of what Scott calls *metis* (knowledge from practical experience) and what, after Odum, I am calling regional folkways.

Wood, a human geographer, does not stop in encouraging us to read official maps as constructions. He wants to inspire map-making in all of us.

> Freed from the tyranny of the eye (the map never was a *vision* of reality), the map can be returned to . . . *the hand* (that makes it) . . . *the mind* (that reasons with it) . . . *the mouth* (that speaks with it). Freed from a pretense of objectivity that reduced it to the passivity of observation, the map can be restored to the *instrumentality* of the body as a whole. Freed from being a thing to . . . *look at*, it can become something . . . *you make*. The map will be enabled to work . . . *for you, for us.*[57]

Wood distinguishes between mapping, which is the mental order that all humans must give the world, and map-making, which is a conscious effort to construct a territory of whatever scale for a specific purpose.[58]

Prejean engages in map-making for the purpose of defining a territory in which the most intellectually and emotionally informed consideration of the death penalty can occur. Her stories of her eyewitness experiences defy the technicways meant to keep citizens remote from state-sponsored execution. In doing so, those stories participate in the local folkways of spiritual advisors, an "internal logic" from which the permeable spirit region emerges. Her map also emerges, as it happens, from the "internal logic" of the lower Mississippi's hydrology, which is constantly making and rearranging south Louisiana. It is fitting for Prejean's purposes and mine that the site where the US Army Corps of Engineers forces the Mississippi into the channel they have built for it and away from the Atchafalaya Basin is at Simmesport, Louisiana, on what the locals call Old River, just across from Angola. This shifting lower Mississippi River region, so cunningly depicted by Anuradha Mathur and Dilip da Cunha in photographs, texts, maps, and artistic prints, is the precarious territory on which the ecological, economic, social, political, and spiritual life of south Louisiana resides.[59]

Prejean never does actually draw the map that her stories make; what she does provide is a journal that renders the map-making process as narrative. Emboldened on the one hand by Odum's assertion from the 1930s that the "first essence [of regionalism] is to be found in the geographic factor" and, on the other hand, by Mathur and da Cunha's juxtaposed scientific and artistic depictions of the shifting region, I have taken the liberty of rendering Prejean's spirit region on a series of maps that the river runs through.[60] I mean them as a modest beginning to what I imagine as a greater New Orleans Atlas of Love and Hate drawn by any and all inspired map-makers of the region.[61] Such an atlas would approach a dialectic that could address the concerns of James Scott described above and of David Harvey, who observes "that maps are typically totalizing, usually two-dimensional, Cartesian, and very undialectical devices with which it is possible to propound any mixture of extraordinary insights and monstrous lies."[62] I can say that my maps and text are mutually constitutive, that both reach back to the texts and ontological objects that are their subject and their concern. But perhaps the necessary dialectic—or trialectic of time-space-society, as Edward Soja would have it—can best be iconographically represented, even on amateur maps like mine, by the battle between the Mississippi River and the Army Corps of Engineers visible on any map of south Louisiana.[63] This standoff produces a fragile ecology (and economy) not often handled with subtle perception and a delicate touch. Mapping of this dialectic conveys, in the moment of visual intuition, the complexity, and yes, the lies, of this spirit region.

Three major, intersecting categories of place make the space of the spirit region visible and, in this sense, define Prejean's map-making. One is the category of sites relevant to the politics of state execution: the crime scenes near St. Martinville and Franklinton; Death Row in Louisiana State Penitentiary at Angola; the offices of the Prison Coalition in New Orleans; the meeting rooms of the Louisiana Pardon Board in Baton Rouge and at Angola; the Governor's office in Baton Rouge; the Death House at Angola; and the office of Pilgrimage for Life, a grass-roots anti–death penalty organization, at Hope House, which is contiguous to New Orleans's St. Thomas public housing development.

The courtroom, so crucial to crime drama, does not figure on Prejean's map. Her rhetoric does not rely on the law's binary of guilt and innocence and its assertion of its power in specific jurisdictions. She meets both Sonnier and Robert Willie after they are convicted of gruesome murders and sentenced to death. Even as she meticulously records her education in the laws that permit the death penalty and the processes that could stay an execution, she is not riveted on the law's dichotomy. This is not a story of the innocent unjustly convicted. It is a story of the poor unjustly punished, a story with a long legacy at Angola. This is a problem solvable only through massive participation of regional citizens. She thus brackets the legal binary so as to recognize guilt and innocence in virtually everyone she encounters in the course of her work as spiritual advisor—herself included.

The second category of selection follows from the first. It is areas of socioeconomic need within the parameters mapped by the politics of execution as she experiences them. So, St. Thomas in New Orleans and the homes of Sonnier in St. Martinville and Willie in Covington are significantly located relative to the sites mapped by political execution. Sonnier's mother lives in a small public housing development in St. Martinville; Willie's mother and stepfamily are working class. The absent fathers of the two comdemned men—a sharecropper, a prisoner—were poorer still.

The third category that defines the spirit region Prejean maps are sites of Roman Catholic presence. They run the political gamut: from the conservative Archbishop Philip Hannan's archdiocese office in New Orleans to the liberal Bishop Stanley Ott's diocese office in Baton Rouge; from the office of the pre–Vatican II chaplain at Angola to "my community," the international Congregation of St. Joseph of Medaille, and to Hope House, the Catholic social service agency run by nuns; and from the office of New Orleans' Catholic, pro–death penalty District Attorney, Harry Connick, Sr., to the New Orleans home of the Quigleys, a former priest and nun, now married, whose backyard potlucks serve as a meeting ground for any and all local economic justice workers.[64] The governor, the pardon board president, the head of corrections, the warden and other prison workers, as well as crime's victims and their families, its perpetrators and their families, and, of course, Prejean's own family all come from or meet at sites of Catholic—or, in a few cases, simply Christian—presence.[65] These three categories of place together form an internal logic from which the boundaries and purposes of Prejean's spirit region emerge.[66]

Telling the Story; Making the Map

Prejean begins her book with an epigraph from *Huckleberry Finn*, the bad American boy who decides he will "go to hell" to protect Jim, a slave. Huck's social deviance for the sake of this moral commitment announces the faith-based approach to Prejean's subject that the bioregionalists would call organic.

> I went right along, not fixing up any particular plan, but just trusting to Providence to put the right words in my mouth when the time come: for I'd noticed that Providence always did put the right words in my mouth, if I left it alone. [67]

When, in 1982, Providence in the form of the Louisiana Coalition on Jails and Prisons sends Prejean the name of a potential pen pal on Death Row, this initiation to her work with the death penalty is, as she tells it, an aside in the drama of her daily work at Hope House within St. Thomas. The lines of her map begin from that site. "Not death row exactly," she says, "but close."[68] Each recollection of that first appearance of Sonnier's name and address is juxtaposed to a paragraph about conditions for the then 4,000+ residents of St. Thomas. Following the 1971 synod of bishops who "declared justice a 'constitutive' part of the Christian gospel" and the 1980 decision of her religious order to "stand on the side of the poor," Prejean moved to 519 St. Andrew Street to join the neighborhood of St. Thomas. It is not Sonnier, the Prison Coalition, or the death penalty per se that propels her into a position as known spokesperson against execution; it is instead "my community's" decision for social justice and their facilitation of her "radical" recognition that Jesus's good news to the poor had been an admonition to resist their poverty and suffering and that his challenge to the nonpoor had been "to relinquish their affluence and share their resources."[69] She enters the political map of official execution through the socioeconomic map of the St. Thomas neighborhood and enters St. Thomas through the interaction of the local, national, hemispheric, and global scales of her Catholic community.

"Now, here in St. Thomas, I am learning plenty about systems and what happens to the people in them, here in a state whose misery statistics are the highest in the nation."[70] To draw a new map of socioeconomic justice requires knowing well who has drawn the official maps that serve these systems. [71] Prejean's first chapter, then, locates St. Thomas within the scale of the city, the state, and the nation-state.

> According to a 1984–1990 US Department of Justice survey, New Orleans logged more complaints against its police than any other city

in the country. . . . Meanwhile, I watch Reagan slash funds for prenatal and child care, low-income housing, employment training, and food subsidies. And as social programs are slashed, new prisons are built. Between 1975 and 1991 Louisiana expanded its adult prisons from three to twelve, with prison populations increasing by 249 percent. Throughout the 1980s Louisiana ranked first, second, or third in the nation as the state incarcerating the greatest number of its residents. . . . Between 1981 and 1991 the federal government cut its contribution to education by 25 percent (in real dollars) and increased its allocation for criminal justice by 29 percent.[72]

As of October 1, 1980, 3,167 of the 4,813 total residents of St. Thomas were minors.[73] A 1990 survey showed 70 percent of the St. Thomas residents were younger than fourteen years of age and only 7 percent were older than twenty.[74] As late as 1996, residents of St. Thomas had an average household income of less than $5,000 per year, and through the 1980s and 1990s, the police district for the area reported the second-highest rate of violent crime of the city's eight districts.[75] A 1999 study still showed New Orleans with the second highest poverty rate in the United States next to Detroit and containing the second highest number of hyperpoverty census tracts (i.e., more than 60 percent of the population existing at or below poverty level) next to Chicago.[76] The years 1979–1996 also saw all of New Orleans public housing stock languish in what the federal department of Housing and Urban Development (HUD) designates as a "troubled" condition, and saw the Housing Authority of New Orleans (HANO) constantly under threat of takeover by HUD.[77]

Prejean's first chapter not only compares incarceration at Angola with entrapment in St. Thomas, but also situates St. Thomas in relation to another Saint, St. Martin. A quiet small town in Southwest Louisiana—Cajun Country—St. Martinville is the home of the Sonnier brothers, and the LeBlanc and Bourque families whose teenage children the Sonniers killed near the town at the local lovers' lane where they had attacked a number of teenage couples over several weeks. This shocking violence notwithstanding, St. Martinville seems remote from St. Thomas and the problems that beset its African American residents, but Prejean's opening chapter draws a line between the two and lines from each to Angola, creating a triangle (see Figure 7.1.)

Questions of socioeconomic inequality ride the lines. While examining the Sonnier case file, Prejean learns of the LeBlanc and Bourque victims and their families from *The New Iberian*, a newspaper close to St. Martinville, yet she has observed that "when residents of St. Thomas are killed, the newspaper barely takes notice."[78] By contrast, the murder of whites in New Orleans is often a front-page story. Similarly, the

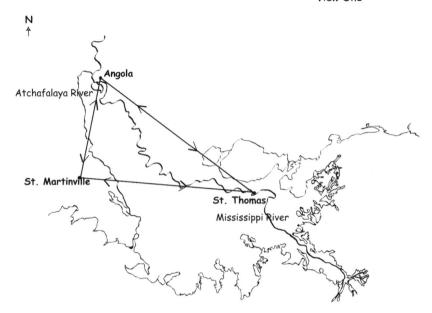

Figure 7.1 Map of the spirit region, view one. (Property of the author, rendered digitally by Kelly McLaughlin)

LeBlancs and Bourques are strangers to the criminal justice system and to the prison at Angola until their children are murdered, yet "almost every family [Prejean] meets in St. Thomas has a relative in prison."[79]

The area of the map's triangle frames not only socioeconomic inequalities, but also Catholic presence. Of "the information about the Bourque and LeBlanc families [that] filters through the news articles," Prejean specifically notes that David LeBlanc and Loretta Bourque were murdered after attending the homecoming game at Catholic High School. Both of their families regularly attended mass and sent their children to Catholic schools. The Bourques are described as particularly devout, as evidenced by the way they care for God's "special angel," a youngest, brain-damaged child.[80] In letters from Angola, Sonnier writes that he too went to Catholic schools. Bemused at the fact of writing to a nun, he remembers that nuns hit him with a ruler in the process of teaching him catechism.[81] Multiple manifestations of Catholic practice define the territory stretching from Prejean on St. Andrew St. to Sonnier on Death Row to the LeBlancs and Bourques in St. Martinville.

Imbricated with the challenges of offering spiritual advice to a condemned man and entering the battle against government execution are two additional challenges emergent in this territory Prejean embraces. One is to articulate a Catholic spiritual practice—spiritual folkways—capacious enough to include diverse individuals in diverse positions and compelling enough to draw boundaries around a coherent region. The other is to enhance her knowledge of socioeconomic justice through intimate engagement with the murders of middle-class white Catholics by a lower-class white Catholic so that she can illuminate, on the regional map, the socioeconomic, political, and spiritual position of St. Thomas and its urban residents, very nearly 100 percent African American. The three primary sites or objects of the map that I have drawn do not exist in empty space; the geometry of the triangle and the vectors that connect its points can only be a crude beginning to the supple map-making demanded by these challenges.

Even later, when Prejean has devoted most of her energy to Death Row inmates and the abolition movement and thus moves out of St. Thomas, she returns in the narrative to crime victims and their families in St. Thomas and other New Orleans public housing. St. Thomas is both a beginning and an ending of the journey that she maps. Although Jesus's instruction propels Prejean into sociopolitical work, it is her living and working in St. Thomas that "liberates her spirit." There, proximity to poverty means not only proximity to nature's intense heat and humidity and thus a lesson in the signals of nature—the small breezes and "company of trees" that define the essentials of the region—but most essentially the friendship of black people.[82] Don Everard, director of Hope House and resident of the neighborhood, explained in 2001, "It's important to us to be in a neighborhood rather than being a city-wide organization because you're not thinking of yourself as a social worker but as a neighbor."[83] The presence of Prejean (and her coworkers) in the community of St. Thomas illuminates by contrast the racial and class remoteness in which both Prejean and the St. Thomas residents had been living.[84]

The capacious and compelling spirit region that emerges from the experiences as recorded in Prejean's narrative elaborates the triangulation of St. Thomas, St. Martinville, and Angola. Although she describes her first trip from New Orleans to Angola as one across the appealing terrain of Lake Pontchartrain through the Tunica Hills and describes her journey away from Angola after her first meeting with Sonnier as a "road open before me,"[85] subsequent journeys acknowledge what highway engineers would refer to as the desire line, the presumed most popular route from New Orleans to Angola through Baton Rouge. This "desire line" insists trips to Angola from St. Thomas—and from St. Martinville—are most expeditiously made on the interstate highway that runs through the state's capital. And indeed, it is there that the Pardon Board or the governor commute or uphold death sentences. The mapping of a spirit region must acknowledge the pull of this desire line drawn by the state and federal governments out of their

interpretation of the "people's will." When the Fifth Circuit Court of
Appeals in New Orleans denies Sonnier's petition for a new trial,
Prejean has no alternative but to follow the course of the law into
Baton Rouge.

On March 27, 1984, with Sonnier's new legal counsel, Millard
Farmer of Atlanta, Prejean travels to Baton Rouge to meet with
Governor Edwin Edwards, recently inaugurated for his third term.
Prejean pointedly prefaces the narration of this meeting with a story
about another authority, Archbishop Philip Hannan of New Orleans.
She tells of Hannan's equivocation on the death penalty, his deliberately
sending priests to counter Jesuit George Lundy's plea for clemency in a
death penalty case and then later writing the Pardon Board himself to
seek clemency for the same man.[86] The juxtaposition of the two Catholic authorities of church and state, Hannan and Edwards, invites the
reader to observe the level of their sanctioned authority, the territorial
scope of that authority, and the degree of their indecision about governmental execution. "John Maginnis, a Louisiana political writer, calls
this pardon power of the governor the last vestige of the power of
kings" in a democracy.[87]

Rather than grant the witnesses for Sonnier the private meeting they
anticipated, Edwards greets them from behind the lights of television
cameras. He has just come from a meeting with Catholic bishops to
clear up a public misstatement he had made about the resurrection of
Jesus that had gotten him into trouble. So he first tells the press that he
and the bishops have "cleared up this matter of the resurrection.'"[88]
Prejean imagines the governor's appointment calendar: "Tuesday,
March 27: noon, resurrection; 2:00, execution. Inverse order exactly of
the Gospels of Matthew, Mark, Luke, and John."[89] In this inverted spiritual universe of television spectacle, Prejean and the other witnesses
testify on behalf of Sonnier.

When the hot lights are turned off, Prejean chases after the governor
to plead again for Sonnier and identify herself as the spiritual advisor
who will accompany him to the death chamber. "'Can you do that?' he
asks me. 'Can you watch that?'"[90] Having just included Prejean in a
hyperpublic spectacle of moral evasion, he then expresses concern that
she will witness the resulting private spectacle. Although the state
affords all citizens what Plumwood calls consequential remoteness by
sequestering execution, the governor, with his regal power, must
consciously develop a strategy of irresponsibility. In a familiar act of
circular logic, he defers to the law, which he characterizes as the "will of
the people," people who are in a position of communicative remoteness
from the full information about state execution. Prejean cannot tell
whether the governor's forehead sweats with concern for her plight or
only because of the television lights.[91]

The witnesses must return to Baton Rouge to plead Sonnier's case again, this time with the Pardon Board on Mayflower Street. In this space, no one may enter without declaring whether she or he is on the side of the state or the defendant. Still, Prejean and Farmer think they have an ally in Howard Marsellus, the Board chairman, a black Catholic who has previously shared with them his views on the racial inequalities in the use of the death penalty. Having heard both sides, the Pardon Board retires to make their decision, and the witnesses for and against Sonnier move out onto the sidewalk, into the sunlight.[92] There, Lloyd LeBlanc, father of the murdered boy, confronts Prejean when she offers her condolences. "Sister, I'm a Catholic. How can you present Elmo Patrick Sonnier's side like this without ever having come to visit with me and my wife?'" Although the Bourques' faces silently register hurt and resentment that she believes is directed at her betrayal of her proper role as a representative of the Church, LeBlanc voices his pain and frustration as he and Prejean "walk up and down the sidewalk talking" in an awkward but countervailing rapprochement, undoing the dichotomy established by the hearing room.[93] Baton Rouge finds a place on Prejean's regional map as the necessary site of official authority and its jurisdictions underwritten by the people's will, but it also emerges as a public meeting ground of diverse opinions. On this ground, the public sidewalk, can be discovered a principle of democratic practice "outside of *their* control." (See Figure 7.2.)

As it has the power to do, the state of Louisiana kills Sonnier, and Prejean, Farmer, Bill Quigley, Mr. LeBlanc, Mr. Bourque, and the warden are all there to witness the event. The governor and Pardon Board are not.[94] After the execution, driving away from Angola down Highway 66, Prejean must ask Quigley to stop the car so that she can vomit; the consequences of the execution lie within the bodies of any who refuse to be remote. For them, a clean getaway down the open road is not possible. "Freed from a pretense of objectivity that reduced [the map] to the passivity of observ[ing the execution territory], the map can be restored to the *instrumentality* of the body as a whole."[95] Now Route 66 leads back to Baton Rouge, the burial, and then the publicity in New Orleans. And it leads on to the Sonniers' home in St. Martinville to deliver Sonnier's last effects.

After Sonnier's execution, the press fully takes on the story of Sonnier and Prejean, creating a mass media–driven lore, a popular history like that which surrounds Marie Laveau, but with the technological power to radiate quickly beyond a meaningful spirit region. These stories arise as early as the funeral, where television cameras cover the event. As the mourners and the press leave the cemetery, one reporter pulls Prejean aside and asks "'Were you in love with Elmo Sonnier? ... I mean, his last words, "I love you"—he said he loved you, didn't he?'"[96] The headline

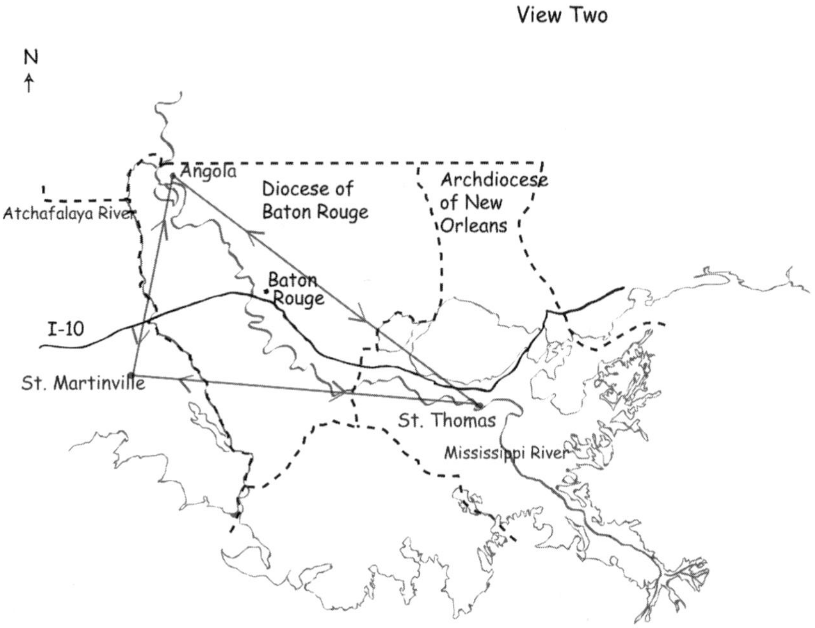

View Two

Figure 7.2 Map of the spirit region, view two. (Property of the author, rendered digitally by Kelly McLaughlin)

of the Associated Press story on Sonnier's burial reads, "Executed Killer Blessed with Burial for the Elite," interpreting as a hero's farewell the burial clothes and coffin and grave site fellow nuns had cobbled together from their various communities of sisters. A barrage of outraged letters issues from the pages of the *New Orleans Times-Picayune* and the *Daily Iberian,* accusing Prejean of betraying good Catholics and of being one of those nuns who are "naive, frustrated women who know nothing of the real world."[97]

When Prejean later returns to Death Row to become spiritual advisor for Robert Willie, she feels the impact of *these* gendered stories competing with any she tells about herself as a religious woman. The new warden, Frank C. Blackburn, has heard some "pretty bad things" about her, that she was "emotionally involved" with Pat Sonnier, that she caused "'a lot of trouble' with the fainting episode,'" (when, forbidden to eat in death row, she had passed out from hunger). On the advice of two priest chaplains at Angola, the prison is thinking of barring women from serving as spiritual advisors there. "Women, they are saying, are just too 'emotional' to relate to death-row inmates."[98]

For the reader, Prejean now defends herself by recalling Sonnier's response when asked about last rites from the priest chaplain. "'No, I don't like that man. All of you, my friends who love me, you make

me feel close to God. Sister Helen, when it is all over, you receive
communion for both of us.'"[99] Although Sonnier confessed his sins to
the priest at Angola before Prejean became his spiritual advisor, in the
end, she reports that he chose the spiritual community she offers out of
her two communities—the established community of the Sisters of Saint
Joseph and other nuns and Catholics committed to serving the poor
and, also, the evolving community created of legally educated and politically motivated opponents to the class-biased death penalty[100]

Expanding the Scope of the Spirit Region

Ignited by the mysterious final hours and secluded execution, the stories
by reporters, by writers of letters to the editor, by church and state officials at the prison, and by Prejean as well, transform the intense relationship between a condemned man and a female spiritual advisor into
a legend. They are like the multiple tales of Laveau, propelled and
sustained by the life and death mysteries of voodoo practice, that have
made her a legend. Both mysteries elicit stories of romance conjoined to
political power, of syncretic and democratized spiritual power
displacing the sanctioned power of the priests and the official power
of the state. Even a headline for an article in a Catholic newspaper
intending to clarify Prejean's work—"Controversial Nun Takes Christ's
Directive Literally"—contributes to the folkways that follow
public women such as Laveau and Prejean who dally with the poor, the
dark-skinned, and the powers of recrimination and redemption.[101]
There is no stopping these stories or any stories. The question is, can
one map a spirit region that emerges from the stories, a territory in
which moral and political decision-making can be more just?

Prejean engages controversy by forming with others a death penalty
abolitionist organization called Pilgrimage for Life based at Hope
House. Seeking a means to involve more of "the people" in the death
penalty debate, the organization follows the advice of "Barbara Major,
a black woman who knows about marches and their role in history.
[She] says, 'Let's walk. Let's walk big-time. From here to Baton
Rouge.'"[102] One of the organizers of the New Orleans–based national
organization, People's Institute for Survival and Beyond, and later
director of the successful St. Thomas Health Service, Barbara Major is
as important in planning New Orleans's future maps as she is in remem-
bering history.[103] On October 26, 1984, on Barbara Majors's advice,
forty people leave New Orleans and begin the eighty-mile walk to Baton
Rouge. "Along the road [Prejean] uses every media opportunity to
provide facts about the death penalty" for statewide consumption.[104]
In this way, and by eliciting thumbs up or down from passing motorists,

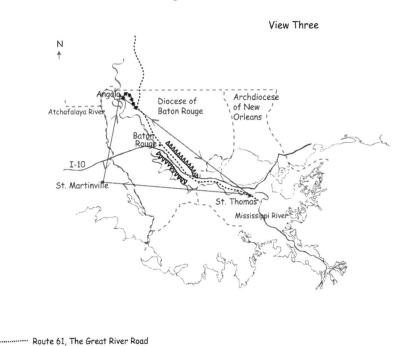

View Three

Route 61, The Great River Road
Route 66, to Angola
direction of message expanding the spirit region

Figure 7.3 Map of the spirit region, view three. (Property of the author, rendered digitally by Kelly McLaughlin)

the walkers expand the territory of discursive democratic engagement through the issue of death penalty abolition. Moving together at pedestrian pace they claim, from cars barreling by, a part of the open road, the Great River Road, Route 61. Risking the impact of sound bites, faster and more relentless than cars, they walk to shape the storytelling into a moral and political dialogue. (See Figure 7.3.)

The three-day pilgrimage ends at the steps of the Capitol in Baton Rouge, where they are met by counterdemonstrators led by Vernon Harvey of Covington, stepfather of the teenage girl murdered by Robert Willie. When, with trepidation, Prejean accepts his invitation to talk, he ticks off his favorite proexecution arguments. Prejean responds in kind. Such familiar arguments and stories produce many a jaded politician, planner, and political activist. Yet it is in listening for the defamiliarizing surprise in these stories (as de Certeau describes the essence of story) that the potential for human-based, regional democracy can be realized.[105] Who is telling the familiar story this time and *where*? What are his purposes or hers?

Setting the Boundaries of the Spirit Region

Prejean asks Harvey if she might visit him and his wife at their home. Although the Pilgrimage for Life is designed to broaden the spirit region and expand citizen-involvement in the moral decision, its reach cannot extend beyond boundaries within which a potent and intimate link to specific crimes and punishments is possible. Thinking of Vernon Harvey's understandable desire for revenge, Prejean quotes Susan Jacoby's words on retribution from *Wild Justice: The Evolution of Revenge.*

> A society that is unable to convince individuals of its ability to exact atonement for injury is a society that runs a constant risk of having its members revert to the wilder forms of justice.[106]

Furthermore, I am arguing, a society that is able to convince its citizens of its ability to exact appropriate atonement for injury is one that understands *geography* as a constituent part of its definition. I am not simply saying that a global scale or a territory the size of the United States is too large to contain a coherent moral society. Rather, maps at different scales must emerge from stories of the particular dilemma at issue and these must be read as interacting—the reproducing fractals that Kemmis uses to define a region, the different scopes of conflict that Schattschneider uses to define democracy, the "mutually inclusive" time-space configurations (chronotopes) that M.M. Bakhtin's dialogic imagination uses to define narration—to frame the problem and therefore suggest possible solutions.[107] Although the Pilgrimage does the work of expanding the region as far as the information of its work and message will carry, Prejean restrains that reach with face-to-face meetings with central players in the drama. For a society to be credible in the way Jacoby identifies, the expanse of its territory cannot exceed the ability of its participants to confront the emotional core of the problem they are defining. Eighty miles of River Road must be juxtaposed to a climb up the Harveys' front steps and the passage through their front door. "In the front living room, I sit where I can see their faces and ask them to tell me about their daughter."[108]

There are two other thresholds within Prejean's map-making that insist on the passage of one individual at a time entering a space where the faces and voices of all participants can be seen and heard. At the invitation of the Harveys, Prejean "stands outside the door and looks down at the doorknob," prepared to enter a meeting of Parents of Murdered Children. The horror stories of this all-white, middle-income group ("My little 12-year-old daughter was stabbed to death in our back yard by my son's best friend. . . . When our child was killed, it took over a week to find her body. . . . Our daughter was killed by her ex-husband in our front yard. . . . I lost my job. Just couldn't pull it together") are juxtaposed to another emotional node of the problem. "One evening in January 1991," Prejean writes, "I'm facing another doorknob and taking a deep breath before I turn it." Inside this meeting room at Loyola University's law school is one of the weekly gatherings of Survive, a group of New Orleanians—mostly poor, African American women—whose family members have been murdered. ("How do I introduce myself—as the mother of six or the mother of four?. . . . My son was abducted and shot twelve times. . . . Well, they know me at City Hall, yes, they do. . . . I keep wanting to stay in bed and sleep. . . . I keep waitin' for my boy to knock on the door. . . . My eighty-three-year-old father was shot in cold blood."[109]) Added to the emotional immediacy of Prejean's meetings with Sonnier and Willie in their final months and minutes are these stories in the book's final chapter. They are not simply the other side of the aisle at the Pardon Board Hearings. They are embedded within the internal logic of the spirit region and as such they set limits on the breadth of the territory that can be mapped for the consideration of this moral dilemma and effective action in response to it. Participants engaged in public decision-making within the region must be able to articulate the relationships among the relevant scales, linking the intimate stories to current actions in public spaces. (See Figure 7.4.)

If a spatial region is going to overcome the problems of consequential and communicative remoteness, if its participant-residents are going to ensure socioeconomic justice and protect the bioregion itself from destruction, then those who map it must also attend to temporal remoteness, the consequences of actions on the future. In Prejean's narrative, the future becomes a phenomenological condition marked by the word "later." What at first seems a flaw in the narrative—later I was to learn x—denotes instead the text's distinction between those who have a later and those who do not. The reader is never kept in suspense about the impending executions of Sonnier and Willie; we are told their outcomes before we are told the stories of their appeals. In contrast, throughout the book, Prejean signals her ignorance, her mistakes, by telling us what she will learn or correct "later."

> I assume that by now the Bourques and LeBlancs have tried to put the pain behind them and want nothing to do with someone befriending their children's murderer. Later, Lloyd LeBlanc will berate me for not seeking him out at the beginning, and the Bourque family will be outraged and hurt over the "Church's" attention to their daughter's murderer.[110]

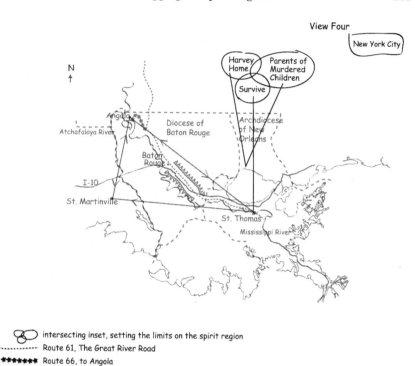

intersecting inset, setting the limits on the spirit region

·············· Route 61, The Great River Road

✦✦✦✦✦✦✦ Route 66, to Angola

▲▲▲▲▲▲▲ direction of message expanding the spirit region

Figure 7.4 Map of the spirit region, view four. (Property of the author, rendered digitally by Kelly McLaughlin)

By including two examples of her spiritual advising work with Death Row inmates, Prejean can demonstrate, as she could not with just one example, the extent of her naive ignorance and the distance she traveled through time to atone for errors of judgment and omission. More than just extending the horror to an isolated cave south of Franklington where Willie and another man raped and stabbed the Harveys' daughter, Faith Hathaway, and then, also extending the grief to the Harveys' home in Covington, the second example puts the two victims' advocacy meeting rooms on the map. It also introduces an advisee less palatable than Sonnier, who strains the bonds of faith that hold the spirit region together.

Willie presents himself to the press as a follower of Hitler. A former white supremacist gang member at Marion Federal Prison in Illinois, he uses nineteenth-century racial logic to specify his identity. "I can't stand people who act like victims. That's why I don't much like niggers. They're always actin' like somebody owes 'em somethin.' Not just niggers. Chinks and spics, too.'"[111] The spirit region that contains not only the survivors of Willie's victims, but also the African American residents of St. Thomas must be capacious enough even for this man, as man.

The text, which repeatedly enacts Prejean's learning process and the consequences of her current mistakes in the future, begs the question of whether or not temporal remoteness is best countered by killing Sonnier and Willie, thus separating their murderous acts from their consequences. Vernon Harvey argues that execution is the righteous consequence of rape and murder, but within the spirit region that Prejean maps, everyone, even criminals like Willie, must have a later in which to recognize their culpability and pursue atonement. She turns to the Gospel of John to persuade Robert Willie and authorize her conviction for the reader:

> I lay down my life
> in order to take it up again
> No one takes it from me;
> I lay it down of my own free will.[112]

But even the authority of the Christian Gospel depends for its impact, if not its legitimacy, on specific ground, in this case the geohistorical understanding that execution reifies temporal remoteness for criminals, victims, witnesses, and the public. In execution territories, no one is asked to engage the long-term consequences of his or her actions. It is no surprise that Vernon Harvey is as enraged and frustrated after Willie's execution as he was before.

Among those who have a "later" in which to atone is Howard Marsellus, chair of the Pardon Board under Edwards, and Governor Edwards himself. The narrative pauses near its conclusion to consider the divergent futures of these two men, both tried for corrupting the offices they held. Prejean recalls a 1991 telephone conversation with Marsellus, after he has served eighteen months in prison for accepting bribes. In her reckoning, Marsellus displays great remorse for his role as Governor Edwards's loyal subject appointed to uphold death penalty sentences so the governor would not have to. A man who, by his own admission, once voted to execute an inmate he believed was innocent, Marsellus later participates in abolition efforts, speaking, for example, at a Loyola University of New Orleans forum on July 7, 1993.[113] Governor Edwards was also on trial in 1986, for racketeering, but was not convicted. He gave two to one odds that he would be acquitted. In a 1991 interview with Errol Laborde for *New Orleans Magazine*, as Edwards gears up for a fourth run at the governor's office, he confesses only to the mistake of overestimating others' acceptance of his obvious integrity and honesty.[114] When in 2000 he was again on trial, this time for extorting payoffs from Louisiana riverboat casino applicants, he was convicted but not contrite. On the stand, he declared to the prosecutor, "I can look at you and this jury and my maker, who knows my heart." Sentenced to ten years in 2001, he was released pending appeal.[115] Throughout his career, Edwards has deferred that later time of accountability and atonement, a luxury he, as monarch of the execution territory, denied other convicted criminals.

After the execution of Willie, Prejean leaves the building and "walks into a blur of television camera lights outside the prison." In front of those cameras again, less adept than Edwards in this medium, Prejean and the Harveys play out the dichotomy of their positions, only for a moment looking across at one another. The next afternoon she receives a call from *ABC World News Tonight* in New York to appear that evening. From the studio of WBRZ in Baton Rouge, she talks to Peter Jennings, who has called her to balance the feature they are doing on the Harveys. She follows the Harveys and precedes political commentator George Will. Prejean remembers Will asserting that the American people favor capital punishment because it satisfies a "deep moral intuition," that "vengeance ... can be noble." Although the execution occurred in private, he says, it "expresses the community's vengeance ... the whole community of Louisiana."[116]

Will's suggestion that vengeance is noble unnerves Prejean, but it is his conceptions of the familiar "American people" and "the Louisiana community" that intrigue me. Here are two groups of people ostensibly defined by territories within which occupants share enough common ground to be understood as coherent bodies. But in fact "the American people," as articulated here, is only that majority of individuals polled who, when given a binary choice, favored execution over whatever else was offered. The two-party system so defines choice on the scale of the American nation-state that all political opinion, which is to say also all public moral opinion, is most often rendered as one of two prescribed options. This is not a citizenry emerging from a region or a region emerging from the moral dialogue of consequentially, communicatively, and temporally proximate individuals. "Louisiana community" here can mean no more than those residents of a territory whose boundaries contain the legality of execution, a territory whose authorities have made one of two choices proffered by the federal binary logic. Although Prejean grabs this and every opportunity to speak on the death penalty, in this national context, her words are circumscribed by their position as ballast for the weighty views of victims and survivors. On the national news, the Harveys and Prejean are not even in the same room at the same time. Their words and images, not even in sync with one another, are beamed in from Baton Rouge and Angola and only appear together on the millions of television screens across the nation. Their shared passion to address this moral conundrum is lost in some placeless space where two bodies called "the Louisiana community" and "the American people" are said to reside.

In her commitment to the abolition of the death penalty, Prejean too speaks of "the American people," this body that must be persuaded of the economic and moral cost of execution. Throughout, she believes knowledge about execution, the eyewitness truth, will shame "the people" into abolishing the death penalty.[117] But consequential, communicative, and temporal remoteness coupled with an inattention to the effects of spatial distance shield any remote body of people from shame or accountability and thus from committed action. The task before her, to undo the remoteness of the American people, is enormous, an enormity compounded by any presumption that the speed and breadth of mass media will solve the problem. Prejean's own forays into the national media raise serious questions about the communicative purposes served by those technicways isolated from folkways.[118]

Prejean herself signals the loss of the region that she has mapped when she pauses to observe that Jennings practices the pronunciation of her name before going live. Acadians from New Iberia to Baton Rouge to New Orleans know the name as /pray-zshawn/; those from the Tunica Hills area nearer Angola, such as some of the guards there, say /pre-jeen/, but no one within the region Prejean maps pauses "to get it right." Pray-zshawn or pre-jeen, the name is a part of the territory.

This said, Prejean is only one map-maker of that territory. Not only is every map through someone, as Wood insists, but every map, "every view, is taken *from* somewhere."[119] Prejean's view begins from St. Thomas in New Orleans and rivets on the death chamber at Angola, but it is *from* Mama's house in Baton Rouge, the vantage point to which Prejean repeatedly returns. When, after Willie's execution, she wants to do something "natural," she puts on jeans and washes the car in her mother's driveway.[120] Her family home is where she stays on the day of the executions and after they have occurred. When she must leave Sonnier and Willie alone in their isolated cells, she can rest in her mother's embrace. It is often through analogy with the reactions of her own mother should violence take one of her children away that Prejean imagines the anger and pain of victims' families. Although her narrative ends where it began with the locations of the two saints, with her return to the families of murdered relatives at St. Thomas and other poor neighborhoods in New Orleans and with Lloyd LeBlanc at the St. Martin of Tours chapel in St. Martinville, she enters this last place through her family home in Baton Rouge. For her protection, her brother Louie accompanies her in the night drive through Acadiana to the 4:00 A.M. vigil at St. Martin's.[121]

Mapping Death and Life in the St. Thomas Neighborhood

The St. Thomas Residents Council (STRC) has imagined a different map, one drawn from their view in the oldest of the New Orleans public housing developments, contiguous to the historic Garden District, near the port and moving upriver away from the tourist sites, and in the corridor of riverside warehouse-district renovation. In 1982, the same year Prejean began corresponding with Sonnier, "STRC organized a takeover of HANO's main office to protest poor living conditions" and then organized a rent strike that ultimately resulted in a $21 million rehabilitation grant from the federal department of HUD.[122] From 1979 through 1996, when they reached an agreement, HANO and HUD battled to determine who would control the publicly owned homes, occupied by a tenth of the city's residents. Amid this struggle between the city and the nation, STRC, originally, by necessity, a group composed exclusively of low-income *women* of color, organized on a different geographic scale: their neighborhood.[123] With the assistance of Barbara Major and the People's Institute for Survival and Beyond, STRC reached outside their island of public housing to form the St. Thomas/Irish Channel Consortium, "an organization made up of the STRC and about a dozen social service and community organizations [such as Hope House] that serves as a mechanism for resident participation in decision making affecting the community."[124] From this political and geographic base, residents of St. Thomas could work to avoid the fate of Iberville public housing residents. They had mostly been excluded, in the 1980s, from top-down land development decisions about their desirable location proximate to the French Quarter and the Central Business District.[125] STRC could instead participate—with savvy—in the map-making of developer Joseph Canizaro, who planned to extend the transforming and lucrative downtown warehouse sector up river to the Garden District and the neighborhood of St. Thomas. STRC and the St. Thomas/Irish Channel Consortium became participant-cartographers in this now familiar central city exercise in urban economic growth and redevelopment. On their emergent map—to put it in my terms—STRC sought to erase the vectors linking them to Angola and to the sorrow of the Survive group by working to undo their isolation from their immediate wealthier Garden District neighbors and from the scale of local and national funding necessary to change their residences and their lives.

Prejean's map frames one moral and political choice emerging from the socioeconomic conditions of her spirit region. STRC's map strives to redraw those socioeconomic conditions in one urban neighborhood of the region. It shifts the vantage point from which mapping occurs and the scale on which the map is drawn. Thus it challenges the specific routes and boundaries that, for Prejean, define spiritual motivation and moral choice alongside economic viability and social justice. In this way, the maps of STRC and Prejean are engaged in an important duel. But STRC's map also complements the goals of Prejean's mapping of the spirit region. They are two interactive scales of a holistic vision for renewing urban neighborhoods, severing their literal and metaphoric link to prisons, and encouraging the political engagement of citizens and residents of regions by calling upon their articles of faith.

A part of that vision for STRC has been the creation of a community as family, a family base with as much power to heal and protect its members and to hold them accountable as Prejean's middle-class family or the Congregation of St. Joseph. Speaking of struggles within the Consortium, Barbara Major explained in 1993, "The consortium is a family and no one is prepared to leave. We will struggle through. That's what families do."[126]

Within the neighborhood, family was not to be just a metaphor for political organization; it was to be constitutive. STRC has expressed commitment to dealing with the children and elders of residents and a commitment to including black men heretofore "deemed invisible" by federal housing policy, welfare policy, school policy, health policies, and police practices.[127] Seeing men as part of the neighborhood rather than as victims of crime or Angola-bound reconfigured their role in the spirit region. Men in the neighborhood formed Black Men United for Change in 1992.[128] And in 1994, Fannie McKnight of STRC asserted,

> Our young men are talking about wanting to stop the violence in our community. They say they're tired of it. ... We're taking a spiritual approach to dealing with all this violence. We're not crying and complaining, we're pulling ourselves up to fight. There's a spiritual grieving process going on. This city was dead but the people in this community is not. Shame can't be used against them anymore.[129]

This approach and all STRC strategies were articulated as long-term relationship-building: a future long enough for atonement and proximate enough for accountability. They stipulated a challenging holistic strategy in defiance of consequential, communicative, and temporal remoteness.

The insistence on seeing urban challenges in terms of whole systems, urban renewal in a regional context, and the processes for change from the ground up became the key strategies of HUD in the later 1990s.[130] STRC's participation in neighborhood map-making and Prejean's regional map-making, which arose amid some of the worst years for public housing residents in New Orleans, subsequently became more fashionable. Since the HUD/HANO Cooperative Endeavor Agreement of 1996 has been in place, HANO claims that HUD's HOPE VI programs (Housing Opportunities for People Everywhere) have been rebuilding the structures and the decision-making practices in New Orleans neighborhoods.[131] St. Thomas has been one such program. STRC, HANO, and the private developer Historic Restorations, Inc. (HRI)—chosen by HUD—have engaged in a HOPE VI–induced, mixed use, $320-million, public-private transformation plan for St. Thomas.

This pricey revitalization process promised ultimately to improve conditions for some residents, but not all.[132] Whether these mixed results signal STRC's successful partnership in the map-making process that controls land use in the city became difficult to determine after most of St. Thomas had been demolished; 775 families, all of the former residents, had been removed to other public housing developments or non-HANO housing where they could use Section 8 vouchers. In 2001, they were awaiting the new construction: 73 new homes (average price $160,000) with 15 reserved for first-time owners eligible for assistance in acquiring and financing a mortgage; 300 garden apartments, with 60 reserved for low-income residents not asked to pay more than 30 percent of monthly income on rent; 100 condos ($300,000–$400,000); 290 units in doubles, four-plexes and rowhouses, with 116 specified for low-income residents with the same rent and possible rental subsidy as applies to the apartments; a 67-unit low-income residence for the elderly sponsored by the Archdiocese of New Orleans and awaiting grant funding; a 2.75-acre park; and retail space in the 1941 original, renovated public housing structures. Adjacent to these properties, in the warehouse riverfront area, a Wal-Mart was planned, one whose size and facade was to be commensurate with the remaining warehouses under renovation, reported HRI.[133] If HANO's claim for restructured buildings and decision-making processes were borne out, HRI and HANO's plan for St. Thomas's redevelopment and HUD's mandates for HOPE VI funding would have the potential to foster the communities as designed. But the HRI and HANO plan/the map for St. Thomas begs the key question: did the certainties of the image render epistemological objects (digital representations of spatial objects produced through a model) as though they were ontological objects (as close to the real thing as we can get)? In other words, did positivism replace realism?[134] What is the economic and political ground truth, for professional and amateur mapmakers?

The examples of Prejean and STRC's stories suggest that the $320 million redevelopment plan for St. Thomas could live up to its promise *as a mixed-income community* only to the degree that its private and public developers and future residents recognized their place within spirit regions that emerge from diverse folkways; multiscale regions mapped by diverse people with vision, will, organization, and faith broadly construed. At least as early as January 1996, St. Thomas residents were invited by HANO executive director Michael Kelly and HANO administrator Peggy Landry to envision with potential developers the transformation of their neighborhood. At that time, I imagine, many drew in their mind's eye and on newsprint the physical maps that would change their lives and enlarge their futures. But by October 2001, STRC president Barbara Jackson lamented, "'This definitely didn't work out the way we had planned. It wasn't what we pictured.'"[135]

In 2001, HANO still listed themselves, HRI, and STRC as *partners* in the St. Thomas project.[136] HRI, however, described the collaborative effort this way:

> The St. Thomas Re-Development in New Orleans is a massive project currently underway that will transform land previously occupied by public housing developments into a vibrant community set in a historic area.[137]

HANO and HRI both clearly understood HUD's priorities and the stipulations for HOPE-VI funding, yet in embracing those new urbanist ideas, HRI also announced that it would build from bricks and mortar a community where there were once (only) public housing developments—that is, presumably, no community.[138]

In 2001, HRI was announcing other ambitious plans for community-building in the region. Pres Kabacoff, head of HRI, was cochair of "Project Top 10 by 2010," "a comprehensive, citizen-based initiative [led by twenty civic, business, and community groups] to make the New Orleans Region one of the nation's top 10 communities in which to live and work by the year 2010."[139] In March 2001, Project Top 10 announced that it would spend the next eighteen months measuring economic, environmental, social, and health indicators of the region. Collecting these data and displaying them digitally surely could produce measures of rank for the region. Just as surely, local elites can renovate and erect buildings, and Wal-Marts can move into urban markets, "the last frontier" of retail growth.[140] But when this happens, the result is not just economic uneven development. The networks of sustainable communities and the capaciousness and coherence of spirit regions are, if not "made impossible"—to use Schattschneider's logic—made something very close to impossible.

Calthorpe and Fulton—themselves advocates for physical design as a core constituent of the regional city—claim that we live at neighborhood and regional scales (more than at city, state, and national scales), but lack political structures to take advantage of the opportunities inherent in these scales. Thus, instead of inhabiting "communities of place," we inhabit "communities of interest," "gated communities of the mind"[141]: I'll hang with my coworkers, class, age, and ethnic group; you hang with yours. In contrast, resident-organizers in the St. Thomas neighborhood attempted, over time, to build not only a political structure, but also a spiritual community "inclusive of built structures, collaborative policies, and, most importantly, human relationships based on an acceptance of struggle and conflict, an appreciation of culture, and an ethic of accountability."[142] But those residents, and others like them, have become part of an intra-metro diaspora separated from the evolving neighborhood place that gave rise to their active community. In such platial circumstances, it is hard to be anything but a community of interest. Ironically, Hope House remained on St. Andrew Street, in 2001, next door to the barbed wire enclosing the demolition site that was once the dilapidated housing for 700 families. In 2001, Hope House workers still stayed in touch with 600 of those families through "Keeping the Ties," a weekly newsletter devoted to dispelling misinformation about St. Thomas.[143] If, in their dispersed state, the former St. Thomas residents who worked to build their community could meet the substantial challenge of sustaining it across the metropolitan region from Westwego to Slidell[144] while also addressing the personal, social, and financial challenges of dislocation, then perhaps they could reconstitute a community of place whether in their redeveloped old neighborhood or in a different site or on a different scale. Out of their disparate locations could emerge the map of a spirit region on the scale of the metropolitan area no less crucial than Prejean's lower Mississippi delta map in defiance of an execution zone.

Epilogue

When Andrei Codrescu wrote "between New Orleans and New York stretches the fifteen hundred miles of frontline in America's meanest war: that between time and timelessness," neither he nor the world had yet witnessed the events of September 11, 2001, and the subsequent retaliations.[1] While the world ponders just what is America's meanest war, it is instructive to reconsider the relationship between New Orleans and New York and the role assigned New Orleans in the post-9/11 nation. On Sunday, September 30, 2001, New Orleans occupied center page in the Travel section of the *New York Times*. Two large photographs from New Orleans stretched the width of the newspaper: one, a folk art mural of diasporic yet celebratory inclinations that hangs in a Magazine Street gallery: the other, City Park's Ladybug roller coaster bearing happy riders and emerging from the boughs of a live oak tree laden with Spanish moss. The mural piques the viewer's curiosity, presenting not only music, dance, and toasts to camaraderie, but also pilgrimage, or at least movement, across an enigmatic landscape. The City Park photograph draws the viewer into the luscious treetops where neither she nor the metal ladybug need concern themselves with gravity and other events on the ground. Between the two photographs is the headline: "New Orleans, Without the Beads." Above the photographs under the category, Air Travel, is the headline "In a Changed World, Passengers Face New Sets of Hurdles," and beneath this headline two articles are noted: "With flights cut, you may not be able to get there from here" and "At Airports, anxiety is consistent but security levels vary." To the right of these titles is a modest-sized photograph of black-clad airport security in Atlanta, one man with a large dog and another on a bicycle. Beneath the two large New Orleans photographs is the category, Getting Home, and the headline, "After the Attacks, Odysseys."

In this feature, on this page, *Times* travel editors and New Orleans own tourist industrialists offer the city's folkways and romantic, subtropical foliage to traumatized readers of the *Times*. The *Times* promises its readers a New Orleans without the chaos of Mardi Gras, outside the crowds of the French Quarter, too familiar to New Yorkers or other *Times* cosmopolitans anyway. This promise is not only consistent with some local wisdom that says New Orleans's visitors should be directed away from the tourist-beleaguered residential Vieux Carré,[2] but it also assigns New Orleans the role of providing US families international sights within the patrolled borders of the post-9/11 nation. In one article, "The Big Easy, Child Size," grandmother Frances Frank Marcus describes just how well the city of Bourbon Street can entertain a child, offering nothing more frightening than the "sinister shadows" of "moss-draped bald cypress trees," a Komodo dragon under glass, or a tradition-clad Galatoire's waiter bearing a grilled cheese sandwich and a smile. Jennifer Moses, in "Shopper's Street of Dreams," meanders with her daughter down Magazine Street, indulging in desires for European antiques, Caribbean courtyard restaurants, the colors and shapes of Latin American folk art, the tastes of southern latitude coffee, and yes, some unusual undergarments. Although this sell of the city may well have been prepared before the New York tragedy, its effective placement within the unfolding warnings for American travelers confirms the sustained memory of New Orleans as the other US city. In this context, that otherness may be deployed to serve a new wave of US isolationism and self-protection, for it offers cultivated, unfamiliar sites without the need of a passport. In a time when great devastation has been wrought right in the foyer of the front door to the United States, these articles and photographs say never mind the old fear that New Orleans's port is the dangerous backdoor to the nation. Here, in the literature of travel, the cultures and the horticulture of Africa, the Mediterranean, the Caribbean, and the Spanish American isthmus have seeped into the city without any threat.

If *Times* travelers are too experienced to be lured by the familiar French Quarter, the midwestern traveler is expected to yearn after the iconic images of the Vieux Carré's St. Peters Street and Jackson Square, and of the St. Charles streetcar. These were the photographs on the front page of the travel section of the *Des Moines Register* for Sunday, October 28, 2001. Although the New Orleans "Cajun Carnival" feature occupied two thirds or more of the front page, the bottom section was devoted to an article entitled "Warnings, advisories alert Americans planning overseas travel." As with the *Times* sell of New Orleans, this coverage also offered that other place within the borders of the United

States where travelers can forego the precaution of appearing not to be Americans.

Although the *Register's* layout implied a thesis about New Orleans in the post-9/11 world comparable to that implied by the *Times*, it did so with some significant differences. Although the *Register* piece also presented a New Orleans that is "more than Mardi Gras," it deployed all the central tropes about the city to accompany the iconic images.

> From its tropical courtyards and flickering gas lamps amid charming 18th and 19th-century Spanish and French architecture, to its loose liquor laws and history of decadence and crime, New Orleans is likely to leave you with a lasting impression. ... It has such a distinctly European and Caribbean ambience and feel, you may forget you're in America altogether.... First-time visitors especially might be better served by focusing on travel destinations indigenous to the Crescent City [unlike Harrod's Casino].

Topping the list of these indigenous destinations is "the tomb of voodoo queen Marie Laveau."

The familiarity of the *Register's* advertisement for the city provokes again the recognition that these tropes and icons of New Orleans have been sustained in public memory both because they are lived and constructed as timeless in situ and because they have been created and recreated as simulacra of the city's history. The photographs in the *Register*, unlike the ones in the *Times*, were provided by the New Orleans Metropolitan Convention and Visitors Bureau, Inc., an arm of the tourist industry that threatens often to succeed at the expense of the lived place. In a time of terror, amid a war on terrorism, what is that industry and those it attracts expecting of the city? Gregory Shriver's article for the *Register* first compares New Orleans with New York and Las Vegas, two other party towns that never sleep. Yet he distinguishes New Orleans from these places and from its own "well-deserved reputation as a party town" by observing, "because its many points of interest are so naturally incorporated into the fabric of the landscape, and because the natives are likely to treat you with a heavy dose of Southern hospitality, you may feel more like a resident than a tourist." Forgetting you are of the United States, forgetting you are a tourist, you can, the argument implies, dwell (safely) in an intriguing place unlike the one where you live. New Orleans's timelessness will sustain you.

Yet the photograph of the French Quarter street at night betrays nothing of the countercultures alive there, or of tourists enjoying too well the law that allows them to carry open alcohol on the street, let alone the underpaid service industry workers "behind the billboards," as Algren put it. This street scene, at dusk, is serene, giving little evidence of automobile traffic and only enough evidence of pedestrians—mostly at a distance and under gaslights—to suggest security within familiar community. A balcony in the foreground is a viewing platform for several diners who overlook the street, framing the scene with their surveillance the way small-town porches provide a focal place and porch sitting, an activity for their communities. Although many conventional French Quarter architectural photographs point to the wrought iron railings of these porches built decades after the buildings' original construction, in this photograph that French detail is not visible in the dim evening light. The effect is, in fact, to render the Quarter visually proximate to small towns of the US Midwest (East, West, or South, for that matter). The other within is rendered as like us after all.

Already miniaturized in scale compared with most US cityscapes and even to more modern two-story buildings, the Quarter, in the perspective of this photograph, offers, as Main Street, the kind of security of the diminished scale deliberately built into Disneyland's Main Street, USA. On this French Quarter Main Street, Midwesterners would indeed feel like residents rather than tourists if the Quarter were as it appears here. Disney banked on this sense of nostalgic belonging as the real Main Streets were abandoned at mid-century by Americans moving to the automobile suburbs.[3] Although the text of the *Register*'s travel essay promises "a distinctly European and Caribbean ambience," the photograph reassures readers that they will recognize the "*tout ensemble*" as part and parcel of the United States.

The small photograph of the St. Charles streetcar, rolling amidst live oaks and not multistoried buildings of the Central Business District, looking every bit the National Historic Monument that it is, and the headline, "Cajun carnival"—not Creole carnival—further suggest that the Midwestern traveler will find the country in the city of New Orleans, an historical, nonurban nation. As with the *Times* piece, the text in the *Register* steers the reader away from Mardi Gras. But here the would-be tourist is led back to the "party town," qua "town." In the New Orleans nonurban nation depicted here, there is no ostensible evidence of scrabbling for that global economy that more naturally exists, as Codrescu claims, in New York time. In this New Orleans, there are also no places as targets, because the Mediterranean and Caribbean village is as tame as Ottumwa.

The most iconic building in New Orleans, St. Louis Cathedral, is the object of the third photograph in the *Register*. In this rendering, the Cathedral, with Andrew Jackson's statue centered below its highest central spire, stands alone. Neither the Cabildo nor the Presbytere, those late-eighteenth-century buildings that evidence the Spanish colonial past and flank the Cathedral, nor the mid-nineteenth-century

Pontalba apartments, which form the other two sides of the open square, are visible. Instead, the setting sun illuminates the cathedral and statue in a relation like that of Walt Disney's statue to Cinderella's Castle, the Disney World copy of Disneyland's Sleeping Beauty's castle that is positioned as the destination of his Main Street USA. Neither the architecture of the castle nor of the Cathedral is distinguished, but both are indicative of their European origins put to specific New World uses.

I do not mean to imply that Jackson's imagineering conjured up the remodeling of the cathedral in the 1850s as Disney's did his castle. On the contrary, Jackson came to the city in 1840, a quarter of a century after the Battle of New Orleans, only to lay the cornerstone for the statue. It was not completed until 1856, and the Place d'Armes was not even renamed Jackson Square until 1851. Historian Christina Vella claims that the Creole First Municipality procrastinated on the project in typical fashion until Baroness Micaela Almonester de Pontalba returned from France, shaming them into completing both statue and cathedral work by the expeditious building of the Pontalba apartments in 1850 under the direction of an American contractor. The cathedral renovation even copied some of the new, machine-made ironwork that she introduced from France.[4] Although Pontalba and the First Municipality were at odds on other matters, she was eager to work with them in a private-public venture to make Jackson Square a place des Vosges in New Orleans. That meant leveling dilapidated structures to build her apartments, and it meant hustling the loiterers out of public Jackson Square. It was her imagineering, not Jackson's, which created the square. But it is his image that fronts the cathedral.

In the *Register* photograph, the Pontalba legacy is largely absent, as is the colonial past. All the battles throughout the twentieth century—over automobile traffic around the square, the fence, and, of course, the proposed Riverfront Expressway that would have separated the square from the river—are also absent. What remains is a foundational US past conjoined to a Christian icon, however fancifully rendered by the especially sharp trio of spires. Former Archbishop Philip M. Hannan asks with pride, "Where else in the United States do you have the picture of a cathedral as the signature of the city?"[5] In this iconic photograph, that signature endorses the cross at the top of the middle spire, visible in the late evening clouds, whereas much else is not. The Christian church and the gallant equestrian leader of a valiant rag-tag army preside over the public square, isolated here from the mimes and musicians, tarot readers and artists, local school children and overheated tourists, talking birds and homeless men, history museums and local residences that occupy the place.

If you stand in the square and look up at Jackson, chances are good that a local will hasten to tell you with self-deprecating pride that the

Battle of New Orleans was won only after the War of 1812 was over. Though the specifics of military history may argue for the significance of this battle nonetheless, in this familiar local story, New Orleans is proud to be out of sync with the national norm. It did not leap to rename its French Colonial Place d'Armes after a US military hero and president and complete the square that newly bore his name. Ironically, it did so only on the eve of secession.

If St. Louis Cathedral has been sustained as the signature of the city, as Archbishop Hanna claims, then Jackson Square is the document on which that signature is inscribed. But the interpretation of the two together need not be confined to a recognition of the United States post-Colonial wedding of church and state and the tamed Disneyfication of that powerful union that the *Register* suggests. Although this imagery can easily be deployed nationally with all the meanness of war and all the insouciance of amusement, the local view has more to offer. Hannan goes on to say that "the church is recognized as the focal point of the city. We have natural opportunities here for the church to be involved in the life of the city."[6] If we take the broad horizontal perspective of local metropolitan New Orleans, as I have aimed to do historically and spatially throughout this book, the "natural opportunities" arising from this extended frame of reference, for good or ill, inflect the cropped photographic rhetoric offered to readers of the *Register* in a time of trauma. Visible on the ground is, for example, the Moon Walk: the Riverfront Promenade, named for former Mayor Moon Landrieu but echoing the eighteenth-century promenade, which historic preservation-ists had in their mind's eye as they fought the Riverfront Expressway. With this transformation of its fourth side, Jackson Square approaches the colonial design it had—and the memory of colonial society—before entry into the US enterprise. From along this site, at the beginning of the twenty-first century, resident pedestrians, visitors, homeless people, musicians, and lost dogs can view the world's massive ships (grain vessels and oil tankers) and the treacherous Mississippi or turn and act as audience to Jackson Square. Whether the individuals on the prome-nade face the fraught hydrology, frail ecology, and geoeconomic uncer-tainty in one direction and turn their backs on the determinedly preserved longevity in the other or reverse their spectating, it is hard to escape the physical reality that one is in place between the two. Some visitors breast the levee, get a glimpse of the Mississippi, and turn on their heels back to the Square. Others breathe a sigh of recognition when they see the boiling river that comes from Minnesota, Iowa, or Illinois (as the tourists often do). Residents, homed or homeless, are eager to take a chance on a breeze. But all, together, must sense the instability of their location on this site of New Orleans and the mystery of the city's longevity, at the indistinct edge of the nation, on the eroding shores of the continent. This is one horizontal perspective in a horizontal landscape, open to an interpretation that the vertical spires of the cathedral and rearing horse of Jackson do not afford.

Another is in the breadth of the Square itself. The less architecturally vertical colonial church presided—eventually with the Cabildo for the Spanish governing body and the Presbytere intended as a rectory for the church—over the military parade ground and site of public hangings. Instead of one equestrian statue, there were multiple men on horseback and more in line on foot ostensibly to enforce all colonial governing measures. In familiar images of the colonial Place d'Armes, the spectators inside the frame turn their complete attention to the parade ground and the figures in control and turn their backs on the river that brought them or their people to that place. Neither do most attend to the small buildings that flanked the Square before the Pontalba apartments were built. Even if the colonial city lacked the literal ramparts often drawn into images of its design throughout the eighteenth century, frontier citizens were depicted as at ease with the French inclination to buy native peace with European wares or with the military might on display.

Pontalba's First Municipality reclamation of the Square, in the mid-nineteenth century, enclosed it on three sides and gave it a central US icon at the intersection of its axes, reconfiguring the hierarchies governing this central urban public place. With the money and impetus of a local elite, returning home with architectural and engineering innovations from France, the Square took on the design that subsequent historic preservationists have been sustaining. Yet neither they nor Pontalba herself could completely eradicate the loiterers and other undistinguished denizens of her square (even if photographs can be made to suggest their absence). If not inside the fence, then just outside it on the broad sidewalks, they gather in an array Colonial Creecy would have recognized as the "infernal motley crew." Although this public square has derived from the needs of the hierarchies that flank it—church; state; and private, local elite investment (the US powers replacing the European forces that first extended their empires on this ground)—the public remains in Jackson Square.

And that public is not all tourists. Even the cathedral building functions other than as the shell of it architecture. One "natural opportunity" is Archbishop Schulte's annual Mass for victims of violence. On this solemn occasion, the cathedral is put to use to address a continuing threat to the sustainability of the metropolitan region.[7] Nor, for that matter, are the visitors all passive tourists of one sort, looking for the produced fix on the city.

In their use and in their symbolism, New Orleans's most familiar icons do not evoke the power of contemporary global wealth, despite the fact that some would wish it so. The local icons—the Superdome, notwithstanding—are unlikely targets of international ire. So, in the fall of 2001, the city's many sensory entertainments could be offered as respite to aggrieved New Yorkers and citizens of the United States generally. Its spirituality, as syncretic as the scene in the folk art mural, could be offered as solace. If its multiple folkways, imbricated populations, and confluence of coastal cultures are, however, also offered as safe intranational alternative to international, translocal engagement (of a nonmilitary sort), then those who spin New Orleans legends should take heed for the sake of their city and of the larger world.

Notes

Preface

1. Baraka is cited on the back of David Henderson's *The Low East.*
2. Wilson's comment is recorded in Baumbach and Borah's *The Second Battle of New Orleans: A History of the Vieux Carré Riverfront Expressway Controversy*, 52.
3. Baumbach and Borah's *The Second Battle of New Orleans* also contains the excerpt from Lowrey's letter to *The Washington Post*, 64.

Chapter 1

1. In fact, this balancing act is as old as the city. One such mid-twentieth-century comment that I pursue in Chapter 3 came from economist James C. Downs Jr., speaking to New Orleans businessmen in 1959 at their request. He recommended just this balance of sex and history to preserve New Orleans downtown business district. "Don't turn over your French Quarter to the history buffs. They'll kill it. But so could the entrepreneurs of sex and sin. It's the balance between history and honky-tonks that makes the Vieux Carré what it is." See Iris Turner, "Night Life, Past Vital To Quarter," *New Orleans States*, June 15, 1959, 11.
2. Searight, *New Orleans*, 9.
3. Searight, *New Orleans*, 29.
4. Richard S. Weinstein offers the familiar description of the sprawling or extended city that he claims is "The First American City," in *The City: Los Angeles and Urban Theory at the End of the Twentieth Century*, 22, 26, 28.
5. Searight, *New Orleans*, 140.
6. Rotella, *October Cities.*
7. Tuan defines topophilia in *Topophilia: A Study of Environmental Perception, Attitudes, and Values*, 4, 93.
8. See Odum and Moore's *American Regionalism: A Cultural-Historical Approach to National Integration*. For a view of how the war nationalized his regionalist vision, see *In Search of the Regional Balance of America*

(Westport, CT: Greenwood Press), written with Katherine Jocher. John Friedman and Clyde Weaver are unusual in recognizing Odum within the circle of US regional planners (*Territory and Function: The Evolution of Regional Planning*, 5, 35–40).

9. Odum's folkloric work among Negroes was met with skepticism in some quarters. In Hurston's judgment, he and his collaborator Guy Johnson were particularly "presumptuous in their confidence that they understood fully the black folk material" that they had collected for *The Negro and His Sons* (1925). Arnold Rampersad, Foreword, in Zora Neale Hurston, *Mules and Men*, xviii.

10. Hirsch and Logsdon, "Introduction to Part III: Franco-Africans and African-Americans," in *Creole New Orleans: Race and Americanization*, 189.

11. Simon, Introduction, in *Race and Rumors of Race*.

12. To elicit the Africanist circulation within New Orleans folkways, Joseph Roach calls on Ngugi wa Thiongo's term orature. "Orature," explains Roach, "comprises a range of forms, which, though they may invest themselves variously in gesture, song, dance, processions, storytelling, proverbs, gossip, customs, rites, and rituals, are nevertheless produced alongside or within mediated literacies of various kinds and degrees. In other words, orature goes beyond a schematized opposition of literacy and orality as transcendent categories; rather, it acknowledges that these modes of communication have produced one another interactively over time and that their historic operations may be usefully examined under the rubric of performance." *Cities of the Dead: Circum-Atlantic Performance*, 11–12. In a crucial move, orature joins "high" and "low" culture in understanding folkways but Roach's performative emphases stop short of placing these modes of expression in a dialectical relation to the technicways also crucial to the production of space and sustainability of place.

13. See Scott's *Regions and the World Economy: The Coming Shape of Global Production, Competition, and Political Order*, 3–4.

14. Scott, *Regions and the World Economy*, 6.

15. From a distinctly anticapitalist position, David Harvey also voices reservations about the leap to think globally. He warns against the inclination, in critical debates, to mount analysis of narrative or society or economics on the scale of the individual human body or the global economic system. For this bias of scale effaces the scales that lie between. Harvey writes in *Spaces of Hope*, "that so many of us took the concept [globalization] on board so uncritically in the 1980s and 1990s, allowing it to displace the far more politically charged concepts of imperialism and neocolonialism, should give us pause," 13.

16. In my final chapter, I argue that urban scholars and practitioners should include a fourth term, spiritual well being, in their thinking about and practice of sustainability.

17. See Wheeler and Beatley's introduction to *The Sustainable Urban Development Reader*, 2.

18. Campbell, "Green Cities, Growing Cities, Just Cities? Urban Planning and the Contradictions of Sustainable Development," *Journal of the American Planning Association*, 297.

19. Bakhtin, "Forms of Time and of the Chronotope in the Novel," 84–258.

20. Kammen, *Mystic Chords of Memory: The Transformation of Tradition in American Culture*.

21. Campbell, "Green Cities, Growing Cities, Just Cities?," 302.

22. Buell, *Writing for an Endangered World.* In addition to Buell's more unusual platial analysis, postcolonial theory is replete both with questions about the intermingling of cultures, the mutual mimicry of colonizers and colonized (or postcolonizers and postcolonized), and about the urban conditions governing the diasporic lives of exiled or unemployed outsiders in the complex entity called the cosmopolitan city. Frantz Fanon, Albert Memmi, Edward Said, Homi Bhabha, Azzedine Haddour: the roll call is long and distinguished.

23. In making this argument, I call on Finnegan's articulation of "common urban narratives" "locally grounded" found in *Tales of the City: A Study of Narrative and Urban Life.*

24. Boyer, *The City of Collective Memory: Its Historical Imagery and Architectural Entertainments,* 322–23.

25. Kammen explicates the passage of the Historic Sites Act of 1935 (459–60, 470), and the Vieux Carré Commission (VCC) records, especially the file Preservation Activities in Other Cities, 1957–1964, in the box VCC Correspondence and Subfiles, housed in the City Archives of the New Orleans Public Library, confirm that cities from Montreal to Boston to Philadelphia to San Juan to Berkeley sought to replicate the success of the VCC in the French Quarter. In addition, a letter from Helen Duprey Bullock, director of the Department of Information of the National Trust to Fred P. Wohlford, director of the Vieux Carré Commission, dated August 29, 1961, informs him that New Orleans will be featured in a National Trust traveling exhibition entitled Preservation: Heritage of Progress. See the file VCC Records Subject Files National Trust for Historic Preservation 1955–1967 in Box VCC Correspondence and Subfiles, available in the City Archives of the New Orleans Public Library. The history of Vieux Carré organizations and the documents drafted to protect the neighborhood appear in Box 2 VCC Records, 1952–1979, File Organizations (before Vieux Carré Com).

26. Riesman, "Abundance for What?," 305.

27. The failure of the Vieux Carré Commission to achieve a full-blown Williamsburg makeover for the Quarter may be due, in part, to their failure to attract the money and interest of John D. Rockefeller, Jr. Two letters from Dana S. Creel for Rockefeller, dated May 31, 1946, and June 10, 1946, twice deny the VCC the support it requests citing Rockefeller's large commitment to "the restoration of Williamsburg" (File VCC Records Rockefeller, John D. 1946; Box VCC Correspondence and Subfiles; City Archives, New Orleans Public Library).

28. Hirsch and Logsdon note that "between 1950 and 1975, the built-up area in New Orleans and its surrounding suburbs doubled in size. The metropolitanization of New Orleans finally wrote into the city's spatial relationships the same uncompromising racial dualism that had conditioned political and legal rights for the past century. New Orleans came to resemble other American cities, both North and South, with an increasingly black core surrounded by a ring of white suburbs." See "Introduction to Part III: Franco-Africans and African-Americans," *Creole New Orleans: Race and Americanization,* 198–99.

29. Anuradha Mathur and Dilip da Cunha quote Marryat's *A Diary in America with Remarks on Its Institutions* (New York: D. Appleton, 1839) in *Mississippi Floods: Designing a Shifting Landscape,* 5. Searight also cites the Captain. Mathur and da Cunha's arguments for seeing the lower Mississippi as a "working landscape," a set of ideological sites both made by and making human life, informs my understanding of the region's distinctiveness.

30. See Part 4 of Colten, *Transforming New Orleans and its Environs: Centuries of Change* for four analyses of the river's quality and its effect on human and aquatic health.

31. Barry tells this story especially well in *Rising Tide: The Great Mississippi Flood of 1927 Flood and How It Changed America*. Morris argues, in "Impenetrable but Easy: The French Transformation of the Lower Mississippi Valley and the Founding of New Orleans," *Transforming New Orleans*, 22–42, that in the eighteenth-century Louisiana colony the reverse was true. The French fought to save the agricultural lands of the plantations and sacrificed the fledgling city in times of flood.

32. Manthur and da Cunha, *Mississippi Floods: Designing a Shifting Landscape*, 73.

33. In "The Trouble with Wilderness," *Uncommon Ground: Rethinking the Human Place in Nature*, Cronon urges attention to urban nature and not just that territory conventionally understood as wilderness.

34. When Buell writes of place-connectedness, he advocates conscious attention to inhabiting of multiple sites simultaneously, the entire archipelago of places affected by the decisions we make as consumers and by the emotional ties we accumulate, even as he acknowledges the impossibilities even pitfalls of full environmental consciousness. When Lyn Lofland writes of person-to-place connections, she traces the trajectories and rhythms of familiar paths, habitual haunts, pursuing the home sites and desire lines that make a human life in public space as well as private.

35. Dupont, "New Orleans: The Case for Urban Exceptionalism," *Journal of Urban History*, 881–93.

36. For this reasoning about oral history see Portelli, "The Death of Luigi Trastulli: Memory and the Event" in *The Death of Luigi Trastulli and Other Stories*, 1–26. Hurston's liars are in *Mules and Men*.

37. DeCerteau, *The Practice of Every Day Life*.

38. Although Laveau's death in 1881 elicited obituaries in the major (white) New Orleans newspapers, which speak of her fame in the city, a search of thirty-three major American periodicals between 1800 and 1925 produces a scant three entries about Laveau. Most hits refer only to George Washington Cable's *Old Creole Days*. This confirms my suspicion that it is primarily twentieth-century writers—Lyle Saxon, Robert Tallant, Herbert Asbury, Ishmael Reed, Francine Prose, Anne Rice, even Helen Prejean—who deploy New Orleans Laveau legends for their own purposes.

39. Brady, "Foreword," in *Literary New Orleans*, vii.

40. U.S. Official Register for 1851.

41. Creecy, "Introduction," *Scenes in the South and Other Miscellaneous Pieces*, 7–8. Evidence suggests Lippincott of Philadelphia published the book later that year. Patricia Brady's foreword to *Literary New Orleans* cites the story of the Congressman and a stanza of Creecy's poem.

42. "Mustee" is a corruption of "mestizo" and refers to the offspring of a white parent and a quadroon parent. It is traceable to 1699, according to *The Oxford English Dictionary*.

43. Creecy, "A Duel in New Orleans, In 1829," in *Scenes in the South and Other Miscellaneous Piece*, 275–79.

44. The examples are myriad. Take an Associated Press story from July 23, 2002, "Big Easy Cracks Down on Graft," reprinted in the *Iowa City Press Citizen*. Contextualizing the new mayor Ray Nagin's initiatives to eliminate bribery in the auto inspection and taxi licensing agencies, the journalist writes, "the city

has long had a reputation as a place of excess—from food and drink to prostitution to graft." The infernal motley crew of mixed-race residents is not mentioned, of course, but this legacy shadows, I submit, this reputation of excess, despite the mayor's being an African American.

45. Saxon, *Fabulous New Orleans*, vii. The book was reprinted three times before January 1929.

46. Among the many treatments of New Orleans class and race politics as enacted through Mardi Gras celebrations, see Mitchell's *All on a Mardi Gras Day* and Roach.

47. Asbury, *The French Quarter: An Informal History of the New Orleans Underworld.*

48. Kane, *Queen New Orleans: City by the River.*

49. In "Home by Way of California: The Southerner as the Last European," *Southern Literature in Transition: Heritage and Promise*, 55–70, Lewis P. Simpson argues that "the literary destiny of the American South has been to assimilate the West to the historical vision of America as an integral part of the Atlantic and Mediterranean worlds, or, in short, the historic European culture" (p. 63). He locates this imperative, distinct from that of New England, not only in Thomas Jefferson, but also and emphatically in Mark Twain, Robert Penn Warren, William Faulkner, and Walker Percy, all— excluding Jefferson—sometime residents and neighbors of New Orleans.

50. Carter, "An Introduction with Love," in *The Past as Prelude: New Orleans 1718–1968*, 15–16.

51. Carter, "An Introduction with Love," 9.

52. This said, neither Hurston's work of the late 1920s and early 1930s, nor Saxon's 1928 claim for a fabulous New Orleans, nor Asbury's fascination with New Orleans noir convinced every occupant of New Orleans's attractions. In "New Orleans (1946)," in *Literary New Orleans*, Capote wrote that the city was nothing but a "spiritual bottomland" without any of the reputed "old charm." Estes's contrary celebration of the city appears in "The neo-African Vatican: Zora Neale Hurston's New Orleans," *Literary New Orleans in the Modern World*, 66–82, 75.

53. Codrescu, "The Muse Is Always Half-dressed in New Orleans," in *The Muse Is Always Half-dressed in New Orleans and Other Essays*, 196.

54. Douglas, *Terrible Honesty: Mongrel Manhattan in the 1920s*, 3, 8, 18, 483.

55. Codrescu, Introduction to *Hail Babylon: In Search of the American City at the End of the Millennium*, xx–i.

56. Codrescu, *Babylon*, xx.

57. Codrescu, *Babylon*, 3–4.

58. Codrescu, *Babylon*, 4.

59. Cronon, *Uncommon Ground*. Raymond Williams, "Between Country and City," in *Second Nature*.

60. Codrescu, *Babylon*, 6, 7.

61. Williams, "Between Country and City." In *Second Nature*, 219.

62. Codrescu, *Babylon*, 53.

63. Codrescu, *Babylon*, 11.

64. Codrescu, *Babylon*, 14–7.

65. King, Introduction to *New Orleans: The Place and the People.*

66. Boyer, *The City of Collective Memory: Its Historical Imagery and Architectural Entertainments*, 18.

67. King, Introduction to *New Orleans*, xv.

68. The Mechanics Institute riot is analyzed in Hollandsworth's *An Absolute Massacre: The New Orleans Race Riot of July 30, 1866.* The White League receives attention from Asbury, Roach, and many others. Barnett's "Mob Rule in New Orleans," in *On Lynchings* and Hair's *Carnival of Fury* are two definitive voices describing the race riot of 1900.
69. Bryan, *The Myth of New Orleans in Literature: Dialogues of Race and Gender,* 7 and throughout.
70. Habermas, *The Structural Transformation of the Public Sphere: An Inquiry into a Category of Bourgeois Society,* 31.
71. Carter, "An Introduction with Love," in *The Past as Prelude: New Orleans 1718–1968,* 11.
72. For further analysis of this feminine imagery, see *The Sphinx in the City: Urban Life, the Control of Disorder, and Women* by Elizabeth Wilson (Berkeley: University of California Press, 1991), especially "The City of the Floating World: Paris," 65–83.
73. http://www.mcadams.posc.mu.edu/garrison.htm
74. File, "Shaw, Clay, Preservation Proposal," in VCC records box 2, City Archives, New Orleans Public Library.
75. Dominguez, *White by Definition: Social Classification in Creole Louisiana.*
76. See note 1.
77. Estes, "The Neo-African Vatican: Zora Neale Hurston's New Orleans." In *Literary New Orleans in the Modern World,* 78, 80, 82.
78. In Houston Baker's analysis of Hurston's *Mules and Men* ("Workings of the Spirit: Conjure and the Space of Black Women's Creativity," *Workings of the Spirit: The Poetics of Afro-American Women's Writing*), he argues that the voodoo women of the book's last section serve to heal the wounds that divide African Americans from one another as demonstrated earlier in the book; he does not, however, speak directly to the New Orleans locale where this healing occurs.
79. Jeannine DeLombard's "'Eye-Witness to the Cruelty': Southern violence and Northern Testimony in Frederick Douglass's 1845 *Narrative*," appears in a special issue of *American Literature* on the topic Violence, the Body and "The South," 245–75.
80. Hearn's "The Last of the Voudoos" (1885) is reprinted in *The World from Jackson Square: A New Orleans Reader,* 301–06, from *An American Miscellany,* collected by Albert Mordell (New York: Dodd Mead, 1920). Gwendolyn Midlo Hall argues in "The Formation of Afro-Creole Culture" (Hirsch and Logsdon, 85–86) that this set of cultural and religious and medicinal practices came to eighteenth-century New Orleans from the west coast of Africa before the substantial in-migration from San Domingue (Haiti) in the early nineteenth century.
81. Douglas, *Terrible Honesty: Mongrel Manhattan in the 1920s,* 4.
82. Saxon, *Fabulous New Orleans,* 242, 243.
83. Hurston's review of Tallant appears in the October-December 1947 issue of the *Journal of American Folklore.* See also Carla Kaplan, Introduction to *Every Tongue Got to Confess: Negro Folktales from the Gulf States.*
84. Tallant, *Voodoo in New Orleans,* 3.
85. Tallant, *Voodoo,* 121, 122.
86. Bryan, 102–113, for an explanation of Christian's contribution to Tallant's book, his disagreements with Tallant, and his own contribution to New Orleans letters. Christian's papers are held at the Earl K. Long Library of the University of New Orleans.

87. Bell, *Revolution, Romanticism, and the Afro-Creole Protest Tradition in Louisiana 1718–1868*, especially note 62 on 214.
88. "The Mulatto" first appeared in *La Revue des Colonies*, 1837, and was reprinted in *The Norton Anthology of African American Literature*, edited by Henry Louis Gates, Jr. and Nelly Y. McKay (New York: W.W. Norton and Company, 1997): 286–299. Beaumont's *Marie* was translated by Barbara Chapman, and reissued by Stanford University Press in 1958. *Paul Marchand, F.M.C.*, Chesnutt's tale of New Orleans free man of color, found a publisher in Princeton University Press in 1999 through the efforts of editor Dean McWilliams.
89. Tallant, *Voodoo*, 95.
90. Not content to tell Laveau's story within the book on voodoo, Tallant wrote a novel about her, *The Voodoo Queen*. Francine Prose took up Laveau as the subject of an early novel, *Marie Laveau*. Both received national reviews.
91. Tallant, *Voodoo*, 87, and Leavitt, *A Short History of New Orleans*, 121.
92. Leavitt, 122.
93. Tallant, *Voodoo*, 68.
94. Although all compilers and interpreters of Laveau stories place her in Parish Prison as a spiritual advisor between 1852 and 1875, none note that the city was occupied by federal troops from 1863 to 1876. It appears that the Laveau legend was not much a subject of print discussion during the antebellum period or the occupation but only after white New Orleanians, and Orleanians of color were in open if intermittent battle for the social and political control of the city, especially in the twentieth century.
95. Asbury, *The French Quarter: An Informal History of the New Orleans Underworld*, 270–76.
96. Tallant, *The Romantic New Orleanians*, 162.

Chapter 2

1. *A Streetcar Named Desire* won the Drama Critics Circle Award on March 31, 1948, and the Pulitzer Prize on May 3, 1948. The Desire Line was initiated on October 17, 1920, and last ran on May 29–30, 1948. Roundtrip, the Desire route covered 7.358 miles. If one got on at Canal and Bourbon, one could ride down Bourbon through the French Quarter to Esplanade, then riverward to Decatur, then off Decatur to Elysian Fields and into the Faubourg Marigny on Chartres and Desire, heading toward the outer terminus in the Industrial Canal area at Tonti and France, and finally returning to the Quarter on Royal that extends up river back to Canal. For a description of this (and all the New Orleans streetcar routes), see Hennick and Charlton, *The Streetcars of New Orleans, 1831–1965*, 216, 226–27.
2. Benjamin, *The Arcades Project*, 459.
3. Beauregard investigates the interaction of public discourse and planning in *Voices of Decline: The Postwar Fate of U.S. Cities*. Rotella expands public discourse to include literature in the dialogue between the city of fact and the city of feeling in *October Cities: The Redevelopment of Urban Literature*.
4. Spoto, *The Kindness of Strangers: The Life of Tennessee Williams*, 129.
5. For coverage of the Parades of Progress see *The New Orleans Times-Picayune*, July 8, 1937, and January 9, 1955.
6. See Edwin Quinby's self-published broadside, 1946, housed in the New York Historical Society; and Lewis Mumford, "The Highway and the City"

(reprinted from 1958) in *The Highway and the City* (New York: Harcourt, Brace & World 1963): 234–46.

7. Quinby urged readers to seek transit advice from the Transit Research Corporation located in New York City. For the attack on Quinby, see Ross Schram, "Queer Case of Quinby," *Mass Transportation* 42 (1946): 62–5.

8. The City Lines consortium was originally convicted in 1949 of anti-trust violations in the monopolization of the motor bus business. To follow both the civil and the criminal cases of U.S. v. National City Lines see 7 FRD 456, 334 US 573, and 337 US 78. For decisions see also 118 F Supp 465 NIL and 134 F Supp 350 NDIL.

9. St. Claire, *The Motorization of American Cities*, 56–62.

10. The quotation from page 172 of the President's Research Committee for 1933 is quoted in James J. Flink, *The Car Culture*, 2. Between 1946 and 1967, whereas the average profits for all manufacturing corporations were 6.64 percent rate of return on total assets and 9.02 percent return on net worth, the auto industry averaged 11.51 percent rate of return and 16.67 percent return on net worth. See Flink, 200, and Lawrence White, *The Automobile Industry Since 1945*, 248. Defense machinery as well as domestic transportation might account for this considerable profit margin. For example, in December 1958, New Orleans Congressional Representative F. Edward Hebert, chair of an investigating subcommittee of the House Armed Services Committee, exposed that GM (Buick Division) had overcharged the Air Force $18,000,000 in a jet contract and yet continued to receive government contracts despite procurement regulations forbidding such contracts with a company suspected of fraud by the comptroller general's office. Hebert charged the Justice Department with failure to collect the $9,000,000 compromise offer from GM before the statute of limitations had run out on the fraud case, a charge the Justice Department later denied. For coverage of the Hebert charges see *The New Orleans Times-Picayune,* December 12, 18, and 24, 1958, as well as *The New Orleans States-Item* December 17, 1958. GM President Alfred P. Sloan's best-selling autobiography, *My Years with General Motors* (reprinted from 1964; New York: Doubleday/Currency, 1990) never mentions U.S. v. National City Lines; in fact, it never mentions motor buses, trolley coaches, or streetcars.

11. Rose, *Interstate: Express Highway Politics, 1939–1989,* 3.

12. Rose, *Interstate,* 117.

13. Bottles, *Los Angeles and the Automobile: The Making of the Modern City.*

14. Mumford, "The Highway and the City," 234–46.

15. Smerk, "The Streetcar: Shaper of American Cities," *Traffic Quarterly,* 569–84.

16. Carson, *What Ever Happened to the Trolley? A Micro Historical and Economic Study of the Rise and Decline of Street Railroads in Syracuse, New York, 1860–1941,* 88, 90; original emphasis.

17. Beauregard, *Voices of Decline,* 6, emphasis mine.

18. Beauregard, *Voices of Decline,* 6.

19. Perez, *The Last Line: A Streetcar Named St. Charles,* 34; and Guilbeau, *The St. Charles Street Car or The History of The New Orleans and Carrollton Railroad,* 3rd edition, 95.

20. Hennick and Charlton, *The Streetcars of New Orleans,* 212.

21. *Taken for a Ride,* documentary film directed by Jim Klein. I am grateful to Martha Olson, *Taken for a Ride* researcher, for leads she gave me during our phone conversation in the summer of 1997.

22. "Middle South Utilities, Inc.," *Moody's Public Utility Manual,* 257.

23. *The New Orleans Times-Picayune*, March 17–24, 1962, and *The New Orleans States-Item*, March 16–22, 1962.
24. Robert Moses, director, *Arterial Plan for New Orleans*, Andrews and Clark, Consulting Engineers (June 24, 1946): 9, 31. The arterial plan is available from the Williams Research Center of the Historic New Orleans Collection.
25. Haas, *DeLessups S. Morrison and the Image of Reform: New Orleans Politics, 1946–1961*, 57.
26. Boyer, *The City of Collective Memory: Its Historical Imagery and Architectural Entertainments*, 47.
27. Michael Kammen specifically locates this passion in the interwar years (*Mystic Chords of Memory: The Transformation of Tradition in American Culture*, 423), but the 1948 parade still calls on that earlier commemorative tradition.
28. *The New Orleans States*, February 11, 1948.
29. Brownell, "A Symbol of Modernity: Attitudes Toward the Automobile in Three Southern Cities during the 1920s" *American Quarterly*, 28, 30.
30. *The New Orleans States*, July 9, 1948.
31. *The New Orleans Times-Picayune*, July 10, 1948.
32. Haas, *DeLessups S. Morrison*, 54.
33. *The New Orleans States*, July 10, 1948.
34. *Moody's Public Utility Manual* for 1954 shows that between 1947 and 1953, NOPSI increased its number of motor buses modestly from 333 to 348, decreased its number of streetcars substantially from 242 to 100, and significantly increased its investment in trolley coaches from 69 to 212. NOPSI put real money behind the narrative this Magazine Street parade tells in 1948, money well spent, by St. Clair's analysis. Yet by 1965, just as there remained only one streetcar line—St. Charles—there remained only one trolley coach line—Magazine. Some set of forces made the company abandon its commitment to trolley coaches. Was it that other manufacturing companies followed GM's Yellow Coach and quit making trolley coaches? Did National City Lines practice of no trolley coaches as conversion vehicles influence the decision?
35. Joseph G. Tregle, Jr., "Creoles and Americans" in *Creole New Orleans: Race and Americanization*, 131–88, 172–73.
36. Haas, *DeLessups S. Morrison*, 68. For more extensive treatment of Mayor Morrison's paternalistic relationship with black citizens and supporters, see Arnold R. Hirsch, "Simply a Matter of Black and White: The Transformation of Race and Politics in Twentieth-Century New Orleans," in *Creole New Orleans*, 273–83.
37. Logsdon and Bell, "The Americanization of Black New Orleans, 1850–1900" in *Creole New Orleans*: 201–60.
38. Drummond et al v. New Orleans Public Service, Inc., Civil District Court, Parish of Orleans, Docket 4. 18 December 1943. Taken from the NAACP Papers in the Manuscripts Division of the Library of Congress, the documentation of this court case narrates the ill treatment of Negro citizens, including veterans, by a NOPSI bus driver.
39. New Orleans planned to spend "an estimated $157 million to restore streetcar service to Canal Street...., a project that [was] expected to be completed by 2004," reported Rick Bragg ("New Orleans Journal: City Plans to Revive Romance with a Streetcar," *New York Times*, August 5, 2001). The Canal line has since been completed.
40. *The New Orleans Times-Picayune*, May 12, 1963, provides the NOPSI position, and *The New Orleans States-Item* ran a series of short articles in

May 1963 acknowledging group endorsements of the NOPSI Canal conversion plan: the Cosmopolitan Club, May 7, 1963; the Chamber of Commerce, May 15, 1963; and the Junior Chamber of Commerce, May 16. A *States-Item* editorial, May 22, 1963, entitled "Transit Realities," defines "reality" as elimination of streetcars. Clarence Doucet, "History of Orleans Transit Changes Reveals Reluctance," in the *Times-Picayune*, May 5, 1963, compares the 1960s citizen fight for the Canal streetcar to the 1893 resistance to give up mules for electricity. In both instances, he chides New Orleanians for being among the last urbanites to accept new technology. Lakeview residents echoed the editors and endorsed the NOPSI plan in letters to the *Times-Picayune*, May 19, 1963, and May 20, 1963. Apparently, 1960s Lakeview residents were descendents of the modern thinkers its developers had tried to attract with their 1907 brochure that commanded, "tear down the old and make way for the new" (quoted by Hirsch and Logsdon, "Franco-Africans and African-Americans: Introduction" in *Creole New Orleans*, 189–200).

41. For an image of the motor buses, driving in formation and arriving on Canal Street in 1964, see the documentary *Streetcar Stories,* a documentary film written and produced by Michael Mizell-Nelson (University of California, 1995) in conjunction with the New Orleans PBS station, WYES.

42. *Streetcar Stories.*

43. Hennick and Charlton, *The Streetcars of New Orleans,* 187.

44. In *Streetcar Stories*, one man recalls that the violent 1929 strike broke the union; however, another man observes that the strike was never over. Whatever the feeling of workers through the conversion years of the 1930s, 1940s, and 1950s, the union did not strike again until 1973 when the two-man rule was abandoned, thus replacing the old fare boxes and the conductors on the remaining St. Charles line with automatic, exact-change fare machines.

45. Hennick and Carlton, *The Streetcars of New Orleans,* 183.

46. Haas, *DeLessups S. Morrison,* 55–57.

47. *The New Orleans Item*, February 7, 1948. As part of this future work, Utilities Commissioner Earhart planned to convert Rampart and St. Bernard Streets and to remove the neutral grounds praised by the arterial plan.

48. Kammen, *Mystic Chords of Memory,* 513–14.

49. New Orleanians could hardly have missed the extraordinary success of the play. By February 1948, the play had already paid for itself and was on its way to rewarding investors—Irene Selznick and Cary Grant among them—with big dividends. So reports Philip Kolin in *Williams:* A Streetcar Named Desire, *Plays in Production,* 6. Kolin goes on to explicate the unique conditions of this success: two years of headlines in national newspapers resulting in two national tours (p. 33); a 1948 Mexico City premiere supported by Diego Rivera; a 1949 Rome premiere directed by Luchino Visconti and designed by Franco Zeffrelli; a London premiere in 1949 directed by Laurence Olivier; a Gothenburg City Theatre production in 1949 directed by Ingmar Bergman; a 1949 adaptation by Jean Cocteau in Paris; the 1951 Warner Brothers film. The list goes on.

50. *The New Orleans Item,* April 7, 1948.

51. *The New Orleans Times-Picayune,* April 27, 1948.

52. Clay Shaw summarizes Morrison's opinion of the French Quarter in a Preservation Proposal that he wrote the Vieux Carré Commission during the later (1970s) administration of Moon Landrieu. "Chep Morrison, while a most able and brilliant mayor, had absolutely no interest in the French Quarter.

It was his private opinion that it was nothing but a breeding ground for roaches and what New Orleans needed was one more good fire" (in the Vieux Carré Commission Records, Set 1, Box 2, File: "Shaw, Clay" in the City Archives of the New Orleans Public Library). Further evidence of the rift between Morrison and the Vieux Carré supporters can be seen in the 1946 city ordinance that restricted the jurisdiction of the Vieux Carré Commission, allowing the mayor to foster modern development at its borders. This 1946 ordinance was declared unconstitutional in 1965 by the Louisiana Supreme Court because a 1936 Louisiana Constitutional Amendment had granted special status to the Quarter and defined the boundaries of that district. Although mayor for four consecutive terms, by 1965, Morrison was gone.

53. This reasoning was consistent with their belief that artists in the Quarter had been instrumental, in the 1920s, in turning it away from blight. This familiar version of the Vieux Carré history is contained in, for example, *Plan and Program for the Preservation of the Vieux Carré*, Historic District Demonstration Study, conducted by the Bureau of Governmental Research, New Orleans, for the City of New Orleans (December 1968). Architectural historian Samuel Wilson, Jr., consultant for the Bureau's study, is credited with this history of the Quarter.

54. Even before tourists went in search of Basin Street, they wandered New Orleans, text in hand, in pursuit of the sites described in George Washington Cable's fiction. Tregle, "Creoles and Americans," 177.

55. *The New Orleans Times-Picayune*, April 12, 1948.

56. In a June 1997 interview, John Waters explains that he comes to New Orleans because of Tennessee Williams. "And every time I go there it still makes me crazy because I ride on the 'bus named Desire,' which just doesn't have that ring. Somehow it just stumbles off the tongue" (John Waters, interview with Rich Collins, *Gambit*, June 3, 1997).

57. Friends and scholars of Tennessee Williams know that his was a restless talent. In working on a play, he frequently changed the title, the setting, the characters' ethnic identities and virtually every other feature of the work. *Streetcar* was no exception. From 1945 to 1947, pieces of the story were variously titled "The Moth," "Port Mad," "Leafless Block," "Portrait of a Madonna," "Blanche's Chair in the Moon," and "The Poker Night." Earlier drafts were set in Chicago, then Atlanta. The Kowalskis were, in one version, an Italian-American family instead. See Spoto, *The Kindness of Strangers*, 112, 118, 132; Lyle Leverich, *Tom: The Unknown Tennessee Williams* (New York: Crown Publishers, 1995): 332, 437, 580–81; and Ronald Hayman, *Tennessee Williams: Everyone Else Is an Audience* (New Haven, CT: Yale University Press, 1993): 110–17. I make no claims for the prescience of Williams's individual genius. I am interested instead in the effects of the final title and setting and then the plot of the produced play—via the collaborative genius of agent Audrey Wood, Kazan, Brando, Tandy, Leigh and others—as they entered the New Orleans and national public domain in the immediate post-World War II years.

58. In the documentary *L'Abecedaire de Gilles Deleuze* with Claire Parnet and directed by Pierre-Andre Boutang, 1996, Deleuze reaffirmed his belief that desire occurs in an aggregate, a domain of desire.

59. For a history of this and all New Orleans street names, see John Chase, *Frenchmen, Desire, Good Children*. For a popular history of the Faubourg Marigny neighborhood through which Desire runs, see Mel Leavitt, *A Short History of New Orleans*.

60. Christine Boyer, 335, gathers these fragments from Walter Benjamin quoted by Peter Szondi in "Walter Benjamin's City Portraits," *On Walter Benjamin: Critical Essays and Recollections*, edited by Gary Smith (Cambridge, MA: MIT Press, 1988): 26, and quoted by Richard Sieburth in "Benjamin the Scrivener," Benjamin: Philosophy, History, Aesthetics, Gary Smith, ed. (Chicago: University Press, 1989): 13–37.
61. See the inferno in *Taken for a Ride*.
62. Kammen, *Mystic Chords of Memory*, 573–4.
63. Haas, *DeLessups S. Morrison*, 82–3.
64. *The New Republic*, June 1947.
65. *Time*, November 1947. In a letter to the *New Republic* (September 15, 1947), New Orleanian John H. Bernhard corrects the *New Republic's* misinformation about a Morrison Rhodes Scholarship and other facts about prostitution, crime, and the mayor's union station project. Bernhard concludes that Morrison is no liberal but rather an "affiliate of [a] little circle of wealthy men."
66. The play had undergone successful tryouts in Boston, New Haven, and Philadelphia before the Broadway opening. Kolin, Plays in Production, 1.
67. Hayman, *Tennessee Williams: Everyone Else is an Audience*, 120.
68. Murphy, *American Realism and American Drama, 1880–1940*, 194.
69. Brenda Murphy, *Tennessee Williams and Elia Kazan: A Collaboration in Theatre*, 27.
70. In the introduction to *Tennessee Williams' Letters to Donald Windham, 1940–1965, 1940–1965*, edited by Donald Windham (New York: Holt, 1977): vi, Windham remarks, "When I read the stories he put together from these scattered pages, they were accurately observed portraits of other sentient beings, in accurately observed milieux, performing a multiplicity of activities which he gave no hint of knowing anything about in his daily behavior. And from this contradiction, I had the strong impression . . . that his entire manner of behavior at that time was the result of his having such a backlog of emotional material stored inside him, so much accumulated 'byproduct of existence' pressing on his heart, that he dared not receive any more, only release the complex images and insights he was packed with, until the pressure of his observations and involvements with the world was poured out in carefully dramatized works of art."
71. Boyer, *The City of Collective Memory*, 74.
72. See Atkinson, "*Streetcar* Tragedy: Mr. Williams' Report on Life in New Orleans," 52–53.
73. Spoto, *The Kindness of Strangers: The Life of Tennessee Williams*, 96.
74. Spoto, *The Kindness of Strangers*, 121.
75. Spoto, *The Kindness of Strangers*, 121.
76. Cited in Peter Drucker's *Concept of the Corporation*, 137.
77. Murphy, *Williams, and Kazan*, 33.
78. Kolin, *Plays in Production*, 15.
79. Kolin, *Plays in Production*, 14, and Kolin, "Reflections on/of *A Streetcar Named Desire*." Confronting Tennessee Williams's A Streetcar Named Desire: Essays in Critical Pluralism, 2. In the later work for the Cambridge Plays in Production series, Kolin describes a more extensive collaboration that also included producer Irene Selznick, costume designer Lucinda Ballard, and music creator Alex North, in addition to the actors, writer, and director, 5, 18.
80. Lott, *Love and Theft: Blackface Minstrelsy and the American Working Class*.
81. New Orleans WPA writers Lyle Saxon and Robert Tallant produced an array of books about New Orleans that sold well in the 1940s: *Fabulous*

New Orleans (reprinted from New York/London: Century, 1928 and 1939; New Orleans: R.L. Crager, 1947), *Gumbo Ya-Ya* (Boston: Houghton Mifflin Co., 1945), *Voodoo in New Orleans* (New York: Macmillan Co., 1946). They offered to the nation a city unlike any other in the United States, a mysterious place of the past existing in the present. Much of that mystery revolved around the culture of African-descended people. According to Hale, "Two On a Streetcar," *Tennessee Williams Literary Journal*, 31–43, when Williams first came to New Orleans, most of Saxon's coterie were working on projects with African American culture at the center. Yet, as Bryan points out in *The Myth of New Orleans in Literature: Dialogues of Race and Gender*, WPA researcher and poet Marcus Christian, a black man, was not acknowledged for his research on which Saxon and Tallant depended.

82. Kelly, "The White Goddess," in Kolin, *Confronting Tennessee Williams's Streetcar*, 121–32.

83. Kazan, "Notebooks for *A Streetcar Named Desire*," in *Directors on Directing: A Source Book of the Modern Theater*, 371.

84. Haas, *DeLessups S. Morrison*, 68.

85. Coming out of the social consciousness of Group Theater and establishing the post-War method acting through participation in the Actors Studio, Kazan imagined Blanche and Stanley as social entities, social modes, and these at the source of the play's stylization. Kazan, "Notebooks," 365.

86. Kazan, "Notebooks," 375–76.

87. Gerber, "Heroes and Misfits: The Troubled Social Reintegration of Disabled Veterans in *The Best Years of Our Lives*." *American Quarterly*, 545–74.

88. The promotion for the 1951 film told audiences how to see Stella: "She took a lot because she loved a lot," Kolin, *Plays in Production*, 151.

89. Spoto, 136, writes that Williams wanted his audience to feel "tragic ironies and shifting identifications" and that he so liked Brando because he captured the idea that the play was about misperceptions. In *Rebel Males: Clift, Brando and Dean*, 97, Graham McCann reminds us that 1951 censors forced Williams to chide Stanley in the film version of his play. In that film's end, Stella with the baby ascends the stairs away from Stanley.

90. This undoing of the gender binary is visible, with a different tone, in *Belle Reprieve*, a cross dressing, camp commentary on the play that premiered in London but is echoed every Mardi Gras season in the French Quarter. Kolin Plays in Production, 142–48, for a description of the *Belle Reprieve* production.

91. Cited in Stamberg and Arnold, "Streetcar Anniversary: Part II."

92. Drucker, *Concept of the Corporation*, 136, 140.

93. Drucker, *Concept of the Corporation*, 137, 139.

94. Drucker, *Concept of the Corporation*, 138, 148–49.

95. Uta Hagen, a taller, more robust Blanche, played the role in the summer of 1948 while Tandy was on vacation and in one of the two touring companies the next year. Her Stanley on the road was Anthony Quinn, taller, but less taut than Brando. Together, Hagen and Quinn were a more balanced set of adversaries, Kolin, *Plays in Production*, 38.

96. Adding to the effect of Mielziner's set, Alex North's offstage, urban sounds permeated the play suggesting a crowded world, Kolin, Plays in Production, 17–8. George Lipsitz, *Rainbow at Midnight: Labor and Culture in the 1940s*; Hirsch, *Making of the Second Ghetto: Race and Housing in Chicago, 1940–1960*; Sugrue, *The Origins of the Urban Crisis: Race and Inequality in Postwar Detroit*; Branch, *Parting the Waters: America in*

the King Years, 1954–63; and Moses's comments quoted earlier in the arterial plan for New Orleans explicate these spatial and racial post-War conditions.

97. Williams, *Streetcar,* scene four. Subsequent references to scenes from the play are noted in the text.
98. Perhaps Williams shared Blanche's aversion to buses. When his agent Audrey Wood acquired for him a $250 per week job in Hollywood, a substantial boost to his income of the War years, she telephoned him to explain the terms. "Audrey exclaimed happily, he should simply come to New York to sign the contracts and ... then proceed at once by train—by train!—to Los Angeles. He had taken, she assured him, his last bus ride" (Spoto, 95).
99. Young and Lebrun, "Blondie," Cartoon, May 21, 1999.
100. Lowenthal, "Identity, Heritage, and History" in *Commemorations: The Politics of National Identity,* 50.
101. Kwitny, "The Great Transportation Conspiracy: A Juggernaut Named Desire."
102. Pickrell, "A Desire Named Streetcar: Fantasy and Fact in Rail Transit Planning," *Journal of the American Planning Association,* 158–76.
103. Connerton, *How Societies Remember,* 61–104.
104. Gronbeck-Tedesco, "Ambiguity and Performance in the Plays of Tennessee Williams," *Mississippi Quarterly,* 735–49.
105. Paglia, "Brando Flashing." In *Sex, Art, and American Culture,* 91–5. She pans Richard Schnickel's biography, *Brando: A Life in Our Time* (New York: Atheneum, 1991).
106. Conroy, "Acting Out: Method Acting, the National Culture, and the Middlebrow Disposition in Cold War America" *Criticism,* 242. The Actors Studio began in 1947.
107. Levinson, *Written in Stone: Public Monuments in Changing Societies,* 247.
108. April 25, 1978, internal memo of the Department of Art, Historical and Cultural Preservation to the Accessions Committee regarding the proposed gift of the Tourist Development Commission, Louisiana State Museum in New Orleans.
109. May 24, 1978, letter of Robert Macdonald, Director of the State Museum, to Robert LeBlanc, Director of the Louisiana Tourist and Development Commission, Louisiana State Museum in New Orleans.
110. The stationary Desire car also commemorated the March 1983 death of Tennessee Williams, by then one of America's most famous writers and also an openly gay man who had found in New Orleans as much of a home as he ever claimed anywhere.
111. James R. Amdal's April 3, 1987, letter to Museum Director G. Rollie Adams, Louisiana State Museum in New Orleans. State Museum Board minutes of December 4, 1991, include the belated agreement to transfer the Desire streetcar to the Regional Transit Authority (RTA, now separate from the utility company) for use on the Riverfront Transit Line, a route useful to tourists and similarly inclined shoppers. However, the reinstitution of the Canal Line, although also serving tourists, facilitates residents' movement as well.
112. Rick Bragg, "New Orleans Journal: City Plans to Revive Romance with a Streetcar," *New York Times,* August 5, 2001.
113. Boyer, *The City of Collective Memory,* 67.
114. Kammen, *Mystic Chords of Memory,* 576.

Chapter 3

1. Iris Turner, "Night life, Past, Vital to Quarter," *New Orleans States* (June 15, 1959).
2. Walter Benjamin, "Central Park," *New German Critique* 34 (Winter 1985): 40, 52–3, and Charles Baudelaire "Allegory," *Les Fleurs du Mal*, 132. Also, Bell, *Reading, Writing, and Rewriting the Prostitute Body*, 43 especially.
3. Benjamin, "Central Park," 42; Reichl, "Historic Preservation and Progrowth Politics in U.S. Cities," *Urban Affairs Review*, 513–35.
4. Hobson, *Uneasy Virtue: the Politics of Prostitution and the American Reform Tradition*, viii.
5. *Somebody in Boots* gets some attention from Rotella in *October Cities: the Redevelopment of Urban Literature*; in Peddie, "Poles Apart? Ethnicity, Race, Class and Nelson Algren" *Modern Fiction Studies*, 118–45; and in Ward, "From the Vagrant to the Fugitive: Institutional Models in Nelson Algren's *Somebody in Boots*," *49th Parallel*.
6. *Daily Picayune* (October 20, 1855); King, *New Orleans, the Place and the People*, 70; File: "Jackson Square," VCC notes, in City Archives, New Orleans Public Library (NOPL).
7. Asbury. *The French Quarter: an Informal History of the New Orleans Underworld*; Tallant. *The Romantic New Orleanians*.
8. File: "Riverfront Expressway #2 News Clippings," VCC Box 3, in City Archives, NOPL.
9. See also File: "Ordinances-VC," VCC1.htm Box 2, in City Archives, NOPL.
10. "Public Control of Property Seen as General Law," *New Orleans Times-Picayune* (March 25, 1937) in File: "Organizations (before Vieux Carré Com.)," Box 2 VCC Records 1952–1979, in City Archives, NOPL.
11. VC Ordinance #14, 538 in File: "Ordinances VC," VCC1.htm box 2, City Archives, NOPL.
12. "Public Control of Property seen as General Law."
13. File: "Ordinances VC," VCC1.htm Box 2, in City Archives, NOPL.
14. Morrison to Joseph Scheuering, chief of police (May 22, 1953), File: "VCC Records Correspondence Mayor and City Council 1947–1956," Box VCC Corespondent and Sub files; Frank S. Scott affidavit and letter to Lee C. Grevemberg (August 20, 1958), File: "VCC Records Correspondence—Director, 1952," Box VCC Correspondence and Sub files, in City Archives, NOPL.
15. Long shows New Orleans shrinking prostitution districts in *The Great Southern Babylon: Sex, Race and Respectability in New Orleans, 1865–1920*, especially 108.
16. Hobson, *Uneasy Virtue: the Politics of Prostitution and the American Reform Tradition*, 148.
17. Asbury, *The French Quarter*, 351–52.
18. Benjamin, "Central Park" 51–53.
19. Asbury, *The French Quarter*, 353–57.
20. Asbury, *The French Quarter*, 360.
21. Asbury, *The French Quarter*, 364, 388, 390.
22. Asbury, *The French Quarter*, 266; Tallant, *Voodoo in New Orleans*, 121, 122.
23. Asbury, *The French Quarter*, 433.
24. Long, *The Great Southern Babylon: Sex, Race and Respectability in New Orleans, 1865–1920*, 134–37.
25. Long, *The Great Southern Babylon*, 191.
26. Asbury, *The French Quarter*, 451–52.

27. Asbury, *The French Quarter*, 424, 454.
28. Wiltz, *The Last Madam: A Life in the New Orleans Underworld*, 7, 18, 24, 33, 44.
29. Between 1859 and the 1870s, Bourbon Street in particular transformed from a residential and conventional commercial street to one on which prostitution flourished. The foundation of Storyville restored Bourbon to much of its former use, but the close of Storyville changed Bourbon Street again. By 1925, it was a site of musical and dance clubs. The war brought back illegal prostitution. When Downs reflected on Bourbon Street in 1959, legal and illegal sex was sold there. It was already the nostalgic recreation of Storyville for tourists that is the subject of Vesey and Dimanche's study in the late twentieth century, but not yet the site of safety and surveillance that it later became when the clubs were regulated and the prostitutes evacuated. They were replaced by sexual souvenirs, and shopping replaced illicit sex. Vesey and Dimanche, "From Storyville to Bourbon Street: Vice, Nostalgia and Tourism," *The Journal of Tourism and Cultural Change*, 54–70.
30. Wiltz, *The Last Madam*, 51. Hobson explains, "How big a city was, who ran the local government and whether a segregated zone existed all shaped the prostitution economy," *Uneasy Virtue*, 146.
31. Wiltz, *The Last Madam*, 66.
32. Long, *The Great Southern Babylon*, 232.
33. Vesey and Dimanche, "From Storyville to Bourbon Street: Vice, Nostalgia and Tourism," 9–10.
34. Hobson, *Uneasy Virtue*, 144.
35. Wimick and Kinsie, *The Lively Commerce: Prostitution in the United States*, 132–33.
36. Hobson, *Uneasy Virtue*, 165, 183.
37. Heyl, *The Madam as Entrepreneur: Career Management in House Prostitution*, 107.
38. Wiltz, *The Last Madam*, 107.
39. Drew, *Nelson Algren: A Life on the Wild Side*, 254–55.
40. Wimick and Kinsie, *The Lively Commerce*, 25.
41. Alan Lomax, *The Folk Songs of North America*, 280, and John W. Rumble, liner Notes to *Country and Western Classics: Rog Acuff*.
42. Wimick and Kinsie, *The Lively Commerce*, 163.
43. In New York, in a ten-year period, only 67 of 1,782 arrests for prostitution violations were of men (Hobson, *Uneasy Virtue*, 160).
44. Heyl, *The Madam as Entrepreneur*, 18–22.
45. Algren, *Somebody in Boots*.
46. Algren, *Boots*, 97, 221.
47. Bettina Drew, Introduction, *Texas Stories of Nelson Algren*.
48. One might call this borderland experience cosmopolitanism, because Drew does in her introduction to *Texas Stories*, but this implies an urban multiculturalism and not the social horror that was always Algren's subject.
49. Algren, *Boots*, 55–57.
50. Drew, *A Life*, 35.
51. Algren, *Boots*, 76.
52. Algren, *Boots*, 83.
53. Algren, *Boots*, 100.
54. Algren, *Boots*, 128, 137, 136. Algren or his 1950s informants know Franklin Street as a low-level prostitution district employing mostly Negroes.
55. Algren, *Boots*, 352–355.

56. Algren, *Boots*, 361–362.
57. http://www.chicagohs.org/history/century.html and http://www.japan.park.org/guests/286.
58. Algren, *Boots*, 146.
59. Otis Ferguson, "Review of *Somebody in Boots*," *The New Republic* (July 17, 1935).
60. Kuprin, *Yama, or the Pit*, cited in Drew, *A Life*, 128.
61. Benjamin, "Central Park," 50.
62. Donohue, *Conversations with Nelson Algren*, 94.
63. Donohue, *Conversations*, 56–7.
64. Donohue, *Conversations*, 191.
65. Donohue, *Conversations*, 253.
66. Drew, *A Life*, 260–65.
67. Donohue, *Conversations*, 294–95.
68. Denning, *The Cultural Front: the Laboring of American Culture in the 20th Century*, 227.
69. Algren, *Boots*, 151.
70. Algren, *Nonconformity: Writing on Writing*, 11, 14, 33, 42, 50, 53, 76.
71. De Beauvoir, *A Transatlantic Love Affair: Letters to Nelson Algren*, 491, note 2.
72. Algren, *Who Lost an American?*, 295. Simon notes that Algren and Benjamin both called on Whitman's *Democratic Vistas* for their understanding of superciliousness (*Nonconformity*, 78). An essay as allusive as Benjamin's but with quick turns from high-brow to low and back again, "Wild Side" has been well served by Daniel Simon and C.S. O'Brien who tracked down the allusions and published the essay with exegesis.
73. De Beauvoir, *A Transatlantic Love Affair*, 487.
74. Algren's closest friend in 1930s Chicago, Wright remained Algren's supporter even in Paris and wrote the introduction to *Never Come Morning*. In the 1950s, even as their romance turned to ash, de Beauvoir frequently wrote Algren and reported on the Wrights' lives in Paris—in fact, as though Algren's letters were asking for such reports. Ellison, for a time Wright's most intimate friend in New York, was a part of the literary world Algren occupied. In any case, the reception of *Invisible Man* was even apparent to de Beauvoir in Paris, although she herself did not much like the book. See Rowly, *Richard Wright: the Life and Times*, and de Beauvoir, correspondence from 1948–1961, 108–9, 131, 159, 201.
75. If the essay was an attempt to best Sartre in the role of the engaged artist and thereby win de Beauvoir away from him, as *Nonconformity* editors Simon and O'Brien suggest, it failed as an act of intellectual wooing. De Beauvoir tactfully reports on August 20, 1953, that they found the essay impossible to translate for their journal *Temps Moderne*, 487. But as a staging for the spleen necessary to enact a vicious comedy in the novel *Wild Side*, the essay, specifically the failure of the essay, could enable another success.
76. Donohue, *Conversations*, 97.
77. Drew, *Texas Stories*, xiii.
78. Donohue, *Conversations*, 97.
79. De Beauvoir, letter of August 1954, 503–4.
80. Report of the American Social Hygiene Association, "Commercialized Prostitution Condition in New Orleans La." (April 1956): 2, 3, 7 in City Archives, New Orleans Public Library.

81. There crazy clients and pimps and disease are least controllable, notes Wallace (Wiltz, *The Last Madam*, 235–36). David concurs in *Prostitution: An International Handbook on Trends, Problems, and Policies*, 315.

82. Wiltz, *The Last Madam*, 87.

83. Haas, *DeLessups S. Morrison and the Image of Reform: New Orleans Politics, 1946–1961*, 181–84, 194.

84. Wiltz, *The Last Madam*, 82.

85. Preoccupied with secrecy, the investigator who files this report expends as many pages explaining the need for secrecy as he does on the purported subject of the report. He also converts all references to the governor, governor elect, mayor, and chief of police into code. Hygiene Association V2 code sheet, in City Archives, NOPL.

86. Wiltz, *The Last Madam*, 125.

87. Halberstam, *The Fifties*, 188–94.

88. Letter from Jacob Morrison, president, Vieux Carré Property Owners Association April 15, 1952, to William Kearney, president, Texas Wire and Cable Company, regarding a liquor license for a new restaurant on Bourbon, File "VCC records Correspondence—commission Members, 1946–1952," VCC 1.htm.box 2, in City Archives, NOPL.

89. This city ordinance was overturned by the Louisiana Supreme Court in 1964, File: "Vieux Carré Property Owners Association 1946–1959," VVC 1.htm.box 2, in City Archives, NOPL.

90. Letter from Marion McClure, VCC field director, to Caye Nelson, executive director of the Louisiana Economic Development Commission, July 6, 1945, Vieux Carré Property Owners Association Letter from Jacob Morrison president of the YMBC, September 21, 1951, City Archives, NOPL.

91. Report by certain members of the Public Relations Profession to the VCC June 29, 1959, File: "VCC records Correspondence Gen., 1948–1965," VCC Correspondence and Subfiles, in City Archives, NOPL.

92. Letter from Pickens to Morrison, November 11, 1952, File: "VCC records Correspondence Gen., 1948–1965," VCC Correspondence and Subfiles, in City Archives, NOPL.

93. Pickens to Morrison.

94. A Proposal for the Preservation, Restoration and Development of the French Quarter, n.d., File: "Shaw, Clay, Preservation Proposal," VCC1.htm Box 2 in City Archives, NOPL.

95. Letter to Mayor Morrison from VCC chairman George M. Leake July 8, 1959, File: "VCC records correspondence commission members, 1958–1962," VCC Correspondence and Subfiles, in City Archives, NOPL.

96. The Crystal Palace in Gaslight Square in St. Louis in 1960 did make it into a musical Nelson Algren admired. "Nelson Algren Talks with NOR's Editor at Large," *New Orleans Review* (1969): 130–2.

97. Drew, *A Life*, 35.

98. Lyrics for the two songs may be found at http://www.chordie.com and at http://www.bluegrasslyrics.com

99. Fabre, *The Unfinished Quest of Richard Wright*, 175. The lyrics to the campaign song "Native Son" went,
The miners came in forty-nine,
The whores in fifty-one,
They jungled up together
And begot the Native Son.

100. Discographies of Thompson and Wells in the music guide at AMG, www.allmusic.com.

101. Wright, Introduction to Nelson Algren's *Never Come Morning*, ix–x. Rotella writes, "Neighborhood novels of Farrell, Wright, and Algren (before *Golden Arm*) together launch a critique of exactly this numbing, easing effect of mass culture, arguing for the cultural impoverishment of the industrial proletariat inhabiting the neighborhood order," 84.

Donohue, *Conversations*, viii. DeBeauvoir remembers watching US television with Algren in a letter dated January 17, 1954, 490. Gelfand, *The American City Novel*, praises Algren's description of Chicago city life but criticizes the absence of urban analysis.

102. Donohue, *Conversations*, 271.

103. Algren, *A Walk on the Wild Side*, 42.

104. Algren, *Wild Side*, 85.

105. Algren, *Wild Side*, 75–7.

106. Algren, *Wild Side*, 40, 92, 94, 108–11.

107. Algren, *Wild Side*, 125.

108. Algren, *Wild Side*, 144–45.

109. Algren's suggestion regarding Huck was picked up on by Giles, *Confronting the Horror: the Novels of Nelson Algren*.

110. Algren, *Wild Side*, 144–45.

111. Algren, *Wild Side*, 218–231. Also, *Nelson Algren's Own Book of Lonesome Monsters* (New York: Bernard Geis Associates/Random House, 1963) and *The Last Carousel* (New York: Putnam, 1973).

112. Donohue, *Conversations*, 160.

113. Pelongo, Interview with Nelson Algren, *Arizona Quarterly*, 101–06.

114. Algren, *Wild Side*, 322; *Boots*, 361.

115. Algren, *Wild Side*, 337.

116. Okada, *No-No Boy*, 245-251.

117. Algren, *Wild Side*, 342.

118. Drew, *A Life*, 193.

119. Algren, *Wild Side*, 337.

120. Letter to Fred P. Wohlford from Helen DuPrey Bullock, director, Department of Information. National Trust (August 29,1961), VCC Subject Files: National Trust for Historic Preservation, in City Archives, New Orleans Public Library.

121. Wiltz, *The Last Madam*, 148.

122. Wiltz, *The Last Madam*, 85.

123. Dmytryk, *Walk on the Wild Side*, film.

124. See coverage of the story in the *New Orleans Times-Picayune* from April 3, 2002, through May 1, 2003, by staff writers Michael Perlstein and Bruce Eggler and by columnist James Gill.

125. For example: "Holly came from Miami, F.L.A./Hitch-hiked her way across the USA/Plucked her eyebrows on the way/Shaved her legs and then he was a she/She says, Hey babe/Take a walk on the wild side/She said, Hey honey/Take a walk on the wild side." http://www.lyricsvault.net /songs/718.html

126. Giles, *Confronting the Horror*, 74.

127. Benjamin, *The Arcades Project*, 385, J91–5.

128. Vesey and Dimanche, "From Storyville to Bourbon Street: Vice, Nostalgia and Tourism," 61.

129. Hayden, *The Power of Place: Urban Landscapes as Public History*, 228.

130. Vesey and Dimanche, "From Storyville to Bourbon Street: Vice, Nostalgia and Tourism," 61–68.
131. One can still find the wild side lurking in a New Orleans publication such as *Offbeat* in the form of advertisements for wild chat (i.e., phone sex).
132. Gotham, "Marketing Mardi Gras: Commodification, Spectacle and the Political Economy of Tourism in New Orleans," *Urban Studies*, 1735–56.
133. Horn, "Walk on the Wild Side," and also Algren's own *Notes from a Sea Diary: Hemingway All the Way*.
134. Mardi Gras has been an ever-expanding source of fantasy marketing as the city has turned more exclusively to tourism to support itself. Kevin Fox Gotham marshals the misery statistics to argue that "the transition to a tourism-dominated economy has paralleled population decline, white flight to the suburbs, racial segregation, poverty and a host of other social problems including crime, fiscal austerity, poor schools and decaying infrastructure." It is not only French Quarter residents who have lost their homes.

Chapter 4

1. Asbury, *The French Quarter: An Informal History of New Orleans Underworld*, 435.
2. In a letter dated November 9, 1949, and addressed to Nelson Algren, Simone de Beauvoir admires Flaherty's documentary, The Louisiana Story, in *A Transatlantic Love Affair: Letters to Nelson Algren*, 300.
3. Kelman cites this traditional opinion in *A River and Its City: The Nature of Landscape in New Orleans*, 37. Lewis later described New Orleans as "an impossible but inevitable city" because of its relationship to the river and the deltaic plain in *New Orleans: The Making of an Urban Landscape*, 17.
4. Kelman, *A River and Its City*, 38, 42, 73, 230, note 54.
5. Melosi, The Sanitary City: Urban Infrastructure in America from Colonial Times to the Present, 12.
6. Kelman, *A River and Its City*, 91, 38–9, 94–5.
7. In the worst epidemic year, 1853–1954, 10,000 died from yellow fever; 600 from cholera. After the summer's yellow fever scourge that could, in the end, not be denied, the fall onslaught of cholera, though severe by any measure, went completely unreported in the press. News spread only by word of mouth. Kelman, *A River and Its City*, 88, 116.
8. Markowitz and Rosner, *Deceit and Denial: The Deadly Politics of Industrial Pollution*, xv.
9. Samway, *Walker Percy: A Life*, 148.
10. Montello, "From Eye to Ear in Percy's Fiction: Changing the Paradigm for Clinical Medicine," in *The Last Physician: Walker Percy and the Moral Life of Medicine*, 46–58. Montello cites Percy's "The Diagnostic Novel," *Harper's Magazine* (June 1986), 40. One might also cite his "Diagnosing the Modern Malaise," "From Facts to Fiction," and "The State of the Novel" in *Signposts in a Strange Land*, edited by Patrick Samway (New York: Farrar, Straus, and Giroux, 1991): 139–52, 186–90, and 204–21. Though Howard Odum was in his heyday at the University of North Carolina when Percy was a premed undergraduate there in the late 1920s, Percy never embraced Odum's studies of regional folkways and technicways so visible in the school's newspaper, according to Tolson, *Pilgrim in the Ruins: A Life of Walker Percy*, 110–11.
11. Ciment, *Elia Kazan: An American Odyssey*, 72; and Young, *Kazan: The Master Director Discusses His Films: Interviews with Elia Kazan*, 67.

12. Yergin, *The Prize: The Epic Quest for Oil, Money, and Power*, 3.
13. Markowitz and Rosner, *Deceit and Denial*, 234.
14. Hidy and Hidy, *History of Standard Oil Co. (New Jersey): Pioneering in Big Business 1882–1911*, 401–12.
15. Hidy and Hidy, *History of Standard Oil Co. (New Jersey)*, 418–20.
16. Gibb and Knowlton, *History of Standard Oil Co. (New Jersey): The Resurgent Years 1911–1927*, 33, 129, chart 167, 140, and 150.
17. Markowitz and Rosner, *Deceit and Denial*, 235.
18. Gibb and Knowlton, *History of Standard Oil Co. (New Jersey)*, 495; Markowitz and Rosner, *Deceit and Denial*, 235.
19. Gibb and Knowlton, *History of Standard Oil Co. (New Jersey)*, 171–72, 414–15, 464–65, 585–87.
20. By 1960, he was chairman of Standard Oil (NJ) and facing not Huey Long but the leaders of the oil exporting countries whom he saw no reason to consult. Yergin, *The Prize*, 520.
21. Popple, *Standard Oil Company (New Jersey) in World War II*, 217–218. I have no figures on the incidence of illness or injury among these employees.
22. Popple, *Standard Oil Company (New Jersey)*, 10, 23–4, 51, 48, 54, 67–9, 108, 98–9, 123–26. Tankers, privately owned, then government owned, moved many of these products away from the refineries, 89, 250.
23. Markowitz and Rosner, *Deceit and Denial*, 237. In the post-War years of the Louisiana story, off-shore drilling also began in earnest. Markowitz and Rosner, *Deceit and Denial*, 239–40.
24. Kane, "Land of Louisiana Sugar Kings," *National Geographic*, 531–67.
25. See Barry, *Rising Tide: The Great Mississippi Flood of 1927 and How It Changed America*, and Percy, *Lanterns on the Levee: Recollections of a Planter's Son*.
26. The intense mechanization of cane harvesting at mid-century left the African American farm workers in the river corridor without agricultural jobs. Between 1937 and 1959, sugar cane plantations decreased from 10,260 to 2,686, whereas acreage increased from 28 to 101, and most plantations were mechanized between 1940 and 1955. Markowitz and Rosner, *Deceit and Denial*, 237–38. Kane mentions in passing this transformation of the river corridor.
27. Tolson, *Pilgrim in the Ruins*, 110–11.
28. Kelman, *A River and Its City*, 143, 145–46. The Board of Commissioners of the Port of New Orleans, known as the Dock Board, was created in 1896.
29. Kelman, *A River and Its City*, 60, 155–56.
30. Tolson, *Pilgrim in the Ruins*, 200–01.
31. Tolson, *Pilgrim in the Ruins*, 269; Samway, 186.
32. Kelman, *A River and Its City*, 102–03.
33. Percy, *The Moviegoer*, 47–8.
34. Markowitz and Rosner, *Deceit and Denial*, 276, 286.
35. The rural people in New Orleans environs have been disregarded more than once, most dramatically when, during the 1927 flood, the city's elite forced the dynamiting of a crevasse below the city, flooding Saint Bernard Parish and its trapping industry. Barry, *Rising Tide*; Kelman, *A River and Its City*, 179. When faced, decades beyond the 1950s, with charges of racism, petrochemical officials would argue that the market determines where poor people live. Corporations do not choose to build chemical plants in African American neighborhoods and towns; rather, the plants deflate housing costs and this attracts the poor. Markowitz and Rosner, *Deceit and Denial*, 289.

36. Young, *Kazan,* 66.

37. Kazan, *Elia Kazan: A Life,* 378–79.

38. Young, *Kazan,* 63; Kazan, *A Life,* 378.

39. Kazan, *A Life,* 379, 381. Making *A Streetcar Named Desire* the next year on a California set was a retreat to stage work, the play being perceived at the time as too fine a literary thing to alter in place. *On the Waterfront* (1954) was the serious film that exploited what he learned about image and place in shooting *Panic,* his most "naturalistic" film. Adrian Danks, "In the Waterfront," http://www.rottentomatoes.com.

40. On the one hand, immigrants were most vulnerable to yellow fever and cholera, because they had no immunity from exposure to the first nor clean living conditions to protect them from the second. On the other hand, native New Orleanians blamed immigrants for their encounters with epidemics and were inclined, wrongly, to see themselves as immune. Kelman, *A River and Its City,* 96.

41. Young, *Kazan,* 66.

42. Young, *Kazan,* 65. Kazan, director, *Panic in the Streets.*

43. Markowitz and Rosner, *Deceit and Denial,* 64–107, 93.

44. Buell names one dimension or model of place-connectedness "tenticular radiations" in *Writing for an Endangered World.* Melosi tells the story of New Orleans unsafe drinking water, *The Sanitary City,* 392–93.

45. Mulvey, "Visual Pleasure and Narrative Cinema," *Contemporary Literary Criticism: Literary and Cultural Studies,* 422–431. Helfand and Gold's *Blue Vinyl,* documentary film, produces the ecological gaze, following the tenticular radiations from the blue vinyl installed on Helfand's parents' home to the production of vinyl in Louisiana and in Venice, Italy, and subsequent public health effects and battles.

46. Even knowing the danger from lead, the South and the West of the United States were still not exploiting federal funds for lead abatement in 1981. Markowitz and Rosner, *Deceit and Denial,* 106.

47. Percy, *Moviegoer,* 55.

48. See, for example, Percy, "The Delta Factor," in *The Message in the Bottle.* Coles, in his introduction to *Walker Percy: An American Search,* records that Percy felt like Kierkegaard after he finished reading Hegel: he explains everything except how to live as a man who must die.

49. Percy, *Moviegoer,* 54.

50. It could be an anywhere neighborhood, except for the name "Tchoupitoulas" that Percy chooses to use. In his essay "Naming and Being," *The Personalist: An International Review of Philosophy, Religion, and Literature,* 148–57, he argues that if one thinks of naming "as a sound calling forth a thought or referential activity, one misses the point. . . . A name does not call forth something, it names something" (149). That is, for example, the word "water" named that wet substance for Helen Keller, as Percy often repeated, and thus allowed her to enter the human race of symbolic language users. But a name like Tchoupitoulas is one, as Benjamin said of street names in particular, that does both name something and call forth a reference. The word pulls vertically into the deep human history of that riverside geography quite apart from Kazan's expansive horizontal filming across the barriers at the waterfront and in spite of Binx's existential malaise. After its habitation by native people, the dockside street, Tchoupitoulas, was an area of prostitution.

51. Dyer, *Heavenly Bodies: Film Stars and Society,* 19.

52. Percy, *Moviegoer,* 54.

53. Percy, *Moviegoer*, 55.
54. Percy, *Moviegoer*, 54–55.
55. Young, *Kazan*, 67.
56. Percy, *Moviegoer*, 55.
57. Percy, *Moviegoer*, 24–5.
58. Percy, *Moviegoer*, 184–86.
59. Percy, *Moviegoer*, 92, 95.
60. Percy, *Moviegoer*, 56, 165. Richard Pindell, "Basking in the Eye of the Storm: The Esthetics of Loss in Walker Percy's The Moviegoer," *Boundary* 2 (Fall 1975): 219–30, calls this transaction rather than action.
61. Pindell, "Basking in the Eye of the Storm: The Esthetics of Loss in Walker Percy's The Moviegoer," 221–22.
62. Pindell, "Basking in the Eye of the Storm: The Esthetics of Loss in Walker Percy's The Moviegoer," 228.
63. Simmons, *Deep Surfaces: Mass Culture and History in Postmodern American Fiction*, 26.
64. Brian McHale, *Postmodernist Fiction* (New York: Methuen, 1987): 38; quoted in Simmons, *Deep Surfaces*, 8.
65. Percy, *Moviegoer*, 11, 187.
66. Another of Binx's half-brothers dies off-stage from drowning; his depressive father dies in the War; Kate's first fiancé dies in an auto accident. Death and disease were common place in young Percy's life as well. His grandfather and then his father committed suicide when he was a child. Soon after, his mother died in an odd auto accident that he perceived, frequently, as another suicide. He left his pursuit of a medical career because of tuberculosis, from which he slowly recovered during World War II. But respiratory weakness and depression dogged him throughout his full, ironic life. Samway, *A Life*.
67. Percy, *Moviegoer*, 69.
68. Percy, *Moviegoer*, 83.
69. Adorno, *Negative Dialectics*, 362.
70. Percy, *Moviegoer*, 188–89.
71. Percy, "The Man on the Train" in *Message*, 83–100; see also Coles's introduction, *Walker Percy*, where he links Percy to Paul Tillich.
72. Percy, *Moviegoer*, 188–89.
73. "The Fateful Rift: The San Andreas Fault in the Modern Mind," "Physician as Novelist," and "Diagnosing the Modern Malaise" in *Signposts*, for example.
74. Percy, "The Delta Factor," *Message*, 21–22. Percy has observed in his essays that at mid-century though 50 million have been killed in Europe, no one seems surprised. "Instead there is more [meaningless] talk than ever of the dignity of the individual." "Novel-Writing in an Apocalyptic Time," *Signposts*, 156.
75. Percy, *Moviegoer*, 189–90.
76. Coles, *Walker Percy*, Introduction.
77. Samway, 279; Tolson, *Pilgrim in the Ruins*, 290–92; Robert Cubbage, "A Visitor Interview: Novelist Walker Percy," in More Conversations with Walker Percy, edited by Lewis A. Lawson and Victor A. Kramer (Jackson: University Press of Mississippi, 1993): 183–188.
78. "Going Back to Georgia," "Mississippi: The Fallen Paradise," and "New Orleans: Mon Amour" in *Signposts*.
79. "Why I Live Where I live" in *Signposts*.
80. Samway, *Walker Percy*, 411.
81. Samway, *Walker Percy*, 155, 207, 270, 272.

82. "Mississippi: A Fallen Paradise," *Signposts,* 49, 51.
83. Kelman, *A River and Its City,* 13.
84. Colten, "Too Much of a Good Thing: Industrial Pollution in the Lower Mississippi River," in *Transforming New Orleans and Its Environs: Centuries of Change,* 141, 143, 147, 150. Rachel Carson's *Silent Spring* (1962) had alerted the nation to the dangers of agricultural pesticides and that source was assumed the culprit in 1963–1964. When the USPHS investigated, however, the source of the fish kill was found to be the Velsicol Chemical Company in Memphis, reports Melosi. The USPHS concluded that the problem was specific to Velsicol's waste disposal practices, to the relief of the petrochemical industry along Louisiana's industrial corridor. They could then conduct business as usual. It was 1973 before an Environmental Protection Agency study officially "detected sixty-six potentially carcinogenic organic chemicals in New Orleans drinking water" corroborating the USPHS's study of 1970 "which stated that many water-supply systems failed to meet the 1962 PSPHS Drinking Water Standards," 393, 392.
85. Kane cited in Kelman, *A River and Its City,* 204.
86. "A Better Louisiana," *Signposts.*
87. From an interview in New York City with Dr. Craig Zwerling, July 5, 2000, quoted in Markowitz and Rosner, *Deceit and Denial,* 291.

Chapter 5

1. "YMBC Step Hits Radical Talks," *New Orleans Times-Picayune,* September 10, 1970.
2. Carolyn Kolb, "Exceptional Incidents: The Black Panthers in New Orleans 1970–1971," Division of Urban Research and Policy Studies Working Paper Number 57, (New Orleans: College of Urban and Public Affairs, University of New Orleans, 1999), 18–19 citing *NOLA Express,* October 2, 1970.
3. Reed, *Mumbo Jumbo.*
4. Singh, "The Black Panthers and the 'Undeveloped Country' of the Left," in *The Black Panther Party [Reconsidered],* 57–105.
5. Singh, "The Black Panthers and the 'Undeveloped Country' of the Left," 64, 66.
6. Arend, *Showdown in Desire,* 43.
7. Specifically, eleven shotguns, two revolvers, one M1 rifle, one training rifle, and a Bowie knife plus some 887 live shotgun shells.
8. "11 Shot: 16 Arrested," *New Orleans Times-Picayune,* September 16, 1970; "Police, Hold It; Don't Do It, Said Warning to Victims," *New Orleans Times Picayune,* September 17, 1970; and Harold Lee Bethune, "Black Community Is Victim In Reign Of Terror; 1 Life Lost," *The Louisiana Weekly,* September 19, 1970.
9. "Bonds Totaling $1.5 Million," *New Orleans Times-Picayune,* September 16, 1970. Judge Bagert's wife owned the building first rented to the NCCF near St. Thomas. The legality of their eviction from that location was being questioned by NCCF's New Orleans legal aid (NOLAC) attorney before the events on Piety.
10. Roy Reed, "Panthers 'Tried' 2 Police Agents," *The New York Times,* September 19, 1970, and Paul Delaney, "Blacks in New Orleans Say They Are Sheltering Panther Leader Wounded in Police Raid," *The New York Times,* September 20, 1970.

11. Simon, Introduction to *Race and Rumors of Race*, vii.
12. Simon, Introduction, ix.
13. Kolb, "Exceptional Incidents," 5, 8, 10.
14. Martin Arnold, "Police and Panthers: Urban Conflict in Mutual Fear," *New York Times*, October 26, 1970.
15. "Police, Hold It," *New Orleans Times-Picayune*.
16. "Went Into Area to Help Restore Calm—Beaten Pair," *New Orleans Times-Picayune*, September 24, 1970.
17. Arnold, "Police and Panthers."
18. "Black Community Is Victim In Reign Of Terror," *The Louisiana Weekly*, September 19, 1970, and ""11 Are Shot; 16 Arrested," *New Orleans Times-Picayune*, September 16 and 20, 1970.
19. "Take Issue With Mayor, Media, Chief," *The Louisiana Weekly*, September 26, 1970.
20. Hilliard, Introduction to *The Huey P. Newton Reader*, 11–2, 14–5.
21. Umoja, "Repression Breeds Resistance: The Black Liberation Army and the Radical Legacy of the Black panther Party," in *Liberation, Imagination of the Black Panther Party*, 5.
22. Umoja, "Repression Breeds Resistance," 14.
23. Ward Churchill, "'To Disrupt, Discredit and Destroy': The FBI's Secret War against the Black Panther Party," in *Liberation, Imagination of the Black Panther Party*, eds. Kathleen Cleaver and George Katsiaficas (New York: Routledge, 2001): 102.
24. Churchill, "'To Disrupt, Discredit and Destroy,'" 102.
25. Umoja defends Cleaver's position, 3; Hilliard speaks for Newton's, 11–13.
26. Hilliard, Introduction, 18; Umoja, "Repression Breeds Resistance," 3–4.
27. Foner, Introduction to *The Black Panthers Speak*, xxviii.
28. Foner, Introduction, xvi and xvi, note 4.
29. Foner, Introduction, 2–4; "Panthers, Other Radicals Down to Specific Issues," *New Orleans Times-Picayune*, September 7, 1970.
30. "Panthers, Other Radicals."
31. Lee Linder, "To Rap, Not to Be Busted," *New Orleans Times-Picayune*, September 8, 1970.
32. "Panthers, Other Radicals." "Black Panther Confab Ends on Peaceful Note," *The Louisiana Weekly*, September 12, 1970, reports that when the full delegation, calling for a "new socialism of black-white coalition," heard proposals from individual workshops, the biggest cheer was for the gay liberation front which told those assembled, "You can't win this revolution without us. An army of lovers can't lose."
33. Foner, Introduction, 183. and Paul Delaney, "Police Officials Endorse Senate Bills Aimed at Curbing Urban Guerilla Warfare," *The New York Times*, October 7, 1970. Congress made it a crime to provide explosives, membership, or aid to terrorist organizations, all defined as acts of violence against the United States. Murder of police or firefighters; attempts to harm police or firefighters; crossing state lines to hurt or abet hurting police were also all defined as a national assault. The bills also prohibited periodicals advocating violence against lawmen and overthrow of the government, e.g., the *Black Panther* newspaper and *NOLA Express*, New Orleans radical, alternative press at the time.
34. Arnold, "Police and Panthers."
35. Arend, *Showdown in Desire*, 50.

36. "Racial Violence Is Termed Culmination of Events," *New Orleans Times-Picayune*, September 17, 1970.

37. Arend, *Showdown in Desire*, 58.

38. Arend, *Showdown in Desire*, 58.

39. Arend, *Showdown in Desire*, 14–5.

40. "Giarrusso Praises Work of 2 Agents," *The Louisiana Weekly*, September 26, 1970; and "2 Badly Beaten Spies Recall Horrors of Panther 'Justice,'" *New Orleans Times-Picayune*, September 19, 1970.

41. "Chief Cates Charge Police," *The Louisiana Weekly*, September 26, 1970.

42. Barnett, "Mob Rule in New Orleans."

43. Hair, *Carnival of Fury*.

44. Consistent with their own liberal, nonviolent position, the *Louisiana Weekly* placed an article about a "New African School" opening in the city between the two (September 26, 1970).

45. "Testimony Begins in Trial of 12 Black Panthers" beside "Citizens' Committee Says Parish Prison Deplorable," *The Louisiana Weekly*, August 7, 1971.

46. Arend, *Showdown in Desire*, 49.

47. "Brothers of Slain Youth Await Judge's Decision," *The Louisiana Weekly*, November 14, 1970.

48. "Let's Get Our Thing Together—Together," *The Louisiana Weekly*, October 17, 1970.

49. Blassingame, *Black New Orleans, 1860–1880*, 1, 28. Note not only that New Orleans was exempted from the Emancipation Proclamation the next year but also that Blassingame chose New Orleans as his subject population because of the greater intimacy between the races and the diversity and size of Negro-owned businesses and residences (xvi). Conditions and events at the Desire Housing Development in 1970 were a product of Panther presence, police culture, and 1950s federal housing policy, and also of the built environment and folkways of its locality.

50. Senator John Sparkman of Alabama cited in Mel Scott, *American City Planning Since 1890* (Berkeley: University of California Press, 1969), 622.

51. Scott, Mel, American City Planning, 623.

52. Scott claims that planners and poor residents were ill-prepared for this negotiation and that certain professional attitudes endangered city/citizen partnership (629); he further asserts that these two acts shifted the role of the planner from technician and adviser on physical development to quasi-political strategist of social change (631).

53. "10 Model Cities Contracts OK'd," *New Orleans Times-Picayune*, November 13, 1970.

54. "11 HANO Proposals Get City Planning Unit Okay," *New Orleans Times-Picayune*, September 2, 1970. The Florida Housing Development across the canal was white and full of university students (Arend, *Showdown in Desire*, 47).

55. Furnell Chatman, "Behind the Headlines," *The Louisiana Weekly*, October 31, 1970.

56. Foundational facts about Desire were found at www.hano.org/desire.htm, October 27, 2003. For the dispassionate comment on US public housing, see Alexander von Hoffman, "High Ambitions: The Past and Future of American Low Income Housing Policy," *Housing Policy Debate* 2 (1996): 423–46; for the passionate comments see Arend, *Showdown in Desire*, 58, and Barbara Harlow cited in Singh, "The Black Panthers and the 'Undeveloped Country' of the Left, 79.

57. "11 Are Shot; 16 Arrested" *The Times Picayune* Sept. 16, 1970.
58. "11 Are Shot; 16 Arrested," *New Orleans Times-Picayune*, September 16, 1970. "Hold It; Don't Do It," reports on Borden September 17. *The Louisiana Weekly* headline for September 19, 1970, reads "Black Community Is Victim In Reign Of Terror; 1 Life Lost." Borden's death was reported more fully in "Parents of Slain Youth Told Slaying A Mistake," *The Louisiana Weekly*, September 26, 1970, and the trial of his brothers was subsequently covered as well.
59. "Outlook Brightens For Improved Conditions In Desire Project," *The Louisiana Weekly*, December 19, 1970.
60. Quoted in Kolb, "Exceptional Incidents," 30.
61. Arend, *Showdown in Desire*, 39, 55.
62. See, for example, Lacan, *The Ethics of Psychoanalysis, 1959–1960*.
63. See, for example, the *Chicago Area Transportation Study* (CATS), 1955.
64. Arnold, "Police and Panthers." Arend reports that in 1970 Desire had 10,594 residents, 8,312 of them younger than 21. "11 Are Shot; 16 Arrested" claims there were 14,000 residents of Desire in 1970.
65. "League Battle to Be Marked," *New Orleans Times-Picayune*, September 13, 1970.
66. Arnold, "Police and Panthers."
67. Arend, *Showdown in Desire*, 55, and Singh, "The Black Panthers and the 'Undeveloped Country' of the Left," 83. The courtroom was an extension of that stage. One woman on trial in New Orleans was charged with contempt for having written "political prisoner" on her prison uniform. Other spectacle came at the behest of BPP defense attorneys who convinced the judge to allow a display of police weapons to be entered in evidence alongside the display of NCCF weapons from the Piety headquarters. The jury was left to draw the conclusions about the striking imbalance in fire power ("Defense Rests Its Case in Trial of Panthers," *New Orleans Times-Picayune*, August 6, 1971).
68. Dora Apel reviews a number of recent exhibits of lynching photographs in "On Looking: Lynching Photographs and Legacies of Lynching after 9/11," *American Quarterly* 55 (September 2003): 457–78. Wright's "Big Boy Leaves Home" in *Uncle Tom's Children* is equally vivid on this point.
69. The Hoover reference is in Hilliard, *The Huey P. Newton Reader*, 14. The quotation about the black intellectuals is in Arnold, "Police and Panthers."
70. Ishmael Reed, Introduction, *19 Necromancers from Now* (Garden City, NY: Doubleday, 1970): n.p. In the 1970s, in fact, Reed incurred heavy criticism from some African American reviewers for his satiric treatment of black militancy (and black women) in, for example, *The Last Days of Louisiana Red*. He distrusted the left-wing impulse to describe some black prisoners as "political prisoners." "Field nigger romanticism" he called it in "Self-Interview" in *Shrovetide in Old New Orleans* (New York: Atheneum, 1978): 137, 143. In contrast, one tenet of the BPP 10-point program was to release all black prisoners because they did not receive fair trials (Foner, *The Black Panthers Speak*, 2–4).
71. John O'Brien, Interview with Ishmael Reed in *Conversations with Ishmael Reed*, edited by Bruce Dick and Amnitjit Singh (Jackson, MS: University Press of Mississippi, 1995): 18.
72. Reed, *Shrovetide*, 25.
73. Simmons, *Deep Surface: Mass Culture and History in Postmodern American Fiction*, 85.

74. Reed, "Neo-HooDoo Manifesto," in *Conjure* (Amherst, MA: University of Massachusetts Press, 1972): 20–25.
75. Reed, *Necromancers*, 19, n.p.
76. O'Brien, Interview with Ishmael Reed, 17–8. Henry Louis Gates explicitly credits Reed: "It is fair to say that *The Signifying Monkey*, as a theory of criticism and as the shape it has assumed in this book, at the very least began with (and at most was shaped by) my explication of Reed's difficult novel. If anything, Reed's text is the text-specific element from which my theory arose, from his characterization of *Esu-Elegbara* as Papa La Bas to his explicit splitting of the narrative voices of showing (mimesis) and telling (diegesis)." Quoted from *The Signifying Monkey* (New York: Oxford University Press, 1988): 217–18.
77. Reed, *Shrovetide*, 72.
78. Ishmael Reed, *Conjure*, 46. Reed criticizes Laveau in his review of Henderson, but honored her grave when I was with him in New Orleans in the 1980s and does so in *Shrovetide*.
79. Hilliard, *The Huey P. Newton Reader*, 16–8, and Foner, *The Black Panthers Speak*, 183.
80. Reed, "Shrovetide in Old New Orleans," in *Shrovetide in Old New Orleans*, 32–33.
81. Reed, *The Last Days of Louisiana Red*, 174.
82. Kolb, "Exceptional Incidents," 6, 8.
83. Arend, *Showdown in Desire*, 38, 56, 67.
84. Reed, *Mumbo Jumbo*, 4–5, 7.
85. Quoted in Fox, "Blacking the Zero: Towards a Semiotics of Neo-Hoodoo," in *The Critical Response to Ishmael Reed*, 54.
86. Reed, *Mumbo Jumbo*, 7, and Gates, *The Signifying Monkey*, 221.
87. Reed, "Neo-HooDoo Manifesto" in *Conjure*, 20.
88. All the forces opposing Jes Grew—the Atonists; Heirophant 1, their leader; the Wallflower Order; the Knights Templar, Hinckle Von Vampton; and private police power Buff Musclewhite—are active, secret agents engaged in the production of hegemony. At their headquarters they use the new invention, the television, to track and map the outbreaks of Jes Grew between New Orleans and Chicago as it travels via music on the radio and the attractions of dance (63–5). And they marshal the forces of press and radio in their cause, knowing Jes Grew has no control over who speaks for it (69). They launch their own magazine and, with the help of radio, plan the Depression that forces Jew Grew underground once more. "It will be a controlled panic. It will be our Panic" (155). But technology is not only the purview of the Atonists. The Haitians have a yellow back radio loa that they feed with the stories of innovative artists threatened by the Atonists (151). From fellow American houngan Black Herman, LaBas learns how essential new forms and new technologies can be to the transmission of the Work. The Haitians tell their American friends that these new forms are their special talent; they put the HooDoo in Voodoo (152).
89. Reed, *Mumbo Jumbo*, 18.
90. Reed, *Mumbo Jumbo*, 53, then 50.
91. Reed, *Mumbo Jumbo*, 206 and 214–15.
92. Reed, *Mumbo Jumbo*, 214–15. Papal infallibility was declared in July 1870, and Nast produced this cartoon for the cover of *Harper's Weekly*, October 1, 1870.
93. LeRoi Jones's blurb is on the back of David Henderson's *The Low East*.

94. Reed, *Mumbo Jumbo*, 5, 4, and 93.
95. Reed, *Mumbo Jumbo*, 48. In "Was 9/11 the First Terrorist Attqck on American Soil?," *Another Day at the Front: Dispatches from the Race War* (New York: Basic Books, 2003), Reed observes that the United States has always been a site of terrorism for blacks, 157-160 (160).
96. Reed, *Mumbo Jumbo*, 65.
97. Reed, *Shrovetide in Old New Orleans*, 7.
98. Reed interviewed by Shamoon Zamir, *Callaloo* 17 (Fall 1994): 1131–56. Also, Reed, *Shrovetide in New Orleans*, 133.
99. Ishmael Reed, "Eldridge Cleaver" in *The Reed Reader* (New York: Basic Books, 2000).
100. Lawson and Kramer, Introduction, *Conversations*, xvi.
101. Reed, in interview with O'Brien, 9.
102. Simmons, *Deep Surfaces*, 94.
103. Thomas, "Two Crowns of Thoth: A Study of Ishmael Reed's *The Last Days of Louisiana Red*," in *Critical Response*, 38–41.
104. McGee, *Ishmael Reed and the Ends of Race*, 128–29.
105. John Pecoul's opinion cited in Kolb, "Exceptional Incidents," 30.
106. Harold Bethune, "Widely Different Views Voiced On NCCF And Its Impact On N.O.," *The Louisiana Weekly*, December 5, 1970.
107. "NCCF Refuses to Leave Desire," *New Orleans Times-Picayune*.
108. Clarence Doucet, "Desire Housing Project Panthers Ready 'To Die,'" *New Orleans Times-Picayune*, November 22, 1970.
109. "Giarrusso Airs Tactics," *New Orleans Times-Picayune*, November 27, 1970; Kolb, "Exceptional Incidents," 22.
110. Orissa Arend in *The Louisiana Weekly*, October 27–November 2, 2003.
111. Arend, *Showdown in Desire*, 13.
112. Arend, *Showdown in Desire*, 66. The federal government's theory of repatriating Japanese Americans after internment lends corroboration to Jones's conviction. The post-War repatriation government document *People in Motion* explicitly announces the goal of channeling Nisei men into nuclear families and away from any reestablished communal Issei leadership. In the absence of such families, former internees would then be directed to central government agencies for aid.
113. Doucet, *New Orleans Times-Picayune*, November 22, 1970.
114. "29 Still Held," *New Orleans Times-Picayune*, November 27, 1970.
115. Bethune, "Widely," *The Louisiana Weekly*, December 5, 1970.
116. Arend, *Showdown in Desire*, 27; Kolb, "Exceptional Incidents," 22–3.
117. Arend, *Showdown in Desire*, 56–7. Faggen remarks that he had never seen anything like the physical and psychological brutality at Angola. The story of the Panthers at Angola is told by Rahim in Arend and by Scott Fleming, the attorney of the Angola 3, in "Lockdown at Angola," *Liberation, Imagination and the Black Panther Party*.
118. "A Desire to Heal," *The Louisiana Weekly*, September 22–28, 2003 and "A Day to Remember," *New Orleans Times-Picayune*, September 18, 2003.
119. Harvey, *Spaces of Hope*, 17.
120. Arend, *Showdown in Desire*, 13.
121. See caption of photograph, *The Louisiana Weekly*, December 5, 1970, and "Young, agile, pragmatic, Rumsfeld supports…," *The New York Times*, November 30, 1970.
122. Quoted in Kolb, "Exceptional Incidents," 24.
123. Quoted in Kolb, "Exceptional Incidents," 31.

124. Paul Keegan, "Thinnest Blue Line," *The New York Times Sunday Magazine*, March 31, 1996.
125. It is not only in fiction that Reed's words fight their way out of despair. In an essay as close to realist urban analysis as Reed comes, when he wants to rail against the "drug fascists" and distant city leadership ruining his neighborhood in Oakland, he presents himself in the second person throughout. Although the essay says he sees no—finds no—solution to the "crackers," it also enacts a narration in defiance of the physical distance that makes boosters' ideas for economic development irrelevant to the devastation in his neighborhood. You, reader, will be me. "My Oakland, There is a There There," *Writin is Fightin*, 25–42.
126. See "New Orleans Crafts Guild Fundraiser" in the September 2004 addition of the Urban Conservancy newsletter archived at http://emm.securesites.net/mailman/private.uc

Chapter 6

1. Ishmael Reed, "Neo-HooDoo Manifesto," in *Conjure* (Amherst, MA: University of Massachusetts Press, 1972): 20, 22.
2. Kaplan, "Violent Belonging and the Question of Empire Today—Presidential Address to the American Studies Association, October 17, 2003," *American Quarterly*, 1–18; and her book, *The Anarchy of Empire In the Making of U.S. Culture*. Regarding Jefferson's idea of empire, see especially, Martin Bruckner, "The Critical Place of Empire in Early American Studies," *American Literary History* 15 (Winter 2003): 809–21.
3. Emphasizing the interface of race, slavery and African American gothicism, Teresa Goddu argues that the gothic needs to be read in relation to race and identifies three topics for initiating that investigation: (1) certain bodies are manufactured as monstrous, (2) the gothic is a "locale" for intervening in racial discourse, and (3) African American gothic insists that American gothic be read in conjunction with other African and Caribbean traditions. "Vampire Gothic," *American Literary History*, 125–41.
4. Goddu, "Vampire Gothic," 138. See, for example, John T. Matthews's argument about open Caribbean secrets in Faulkner's *Absalom, Absalom!* in "Recalling the West Indies: From Yoknapatawpha to Haiti and Back," *American Literary History* 16 (Summer 2004): 238–62.
5. George Haggerty. "Anne Rice and the Queering of Culture," 5–18; also James R. Keller *Anne Rice and Sexual Politics*; and Doane and Hodges, "Undoing Feminism: From the Preoedipal to Postfeminism in Anne Rice's Vampire Chronicles," *American Literary History*, 422–42.
6. Auerbach, *Our Vampires, Ourselves*.
7. Latham, *Consuming Youth: Vampires, Cyborgs and the Culture of Consumption*.
8. Gruesz, *Ambassadors of Culture: The Transamerican Origins of Latino Writing*, 108.
9. See Benjamin's *Arcades Project* on the ambiguity of this promise for him; see also David Harvey, *Paris, the Capital of Modernity*.
10. Dickinson, *Haunted City: An Unauthorized Guide to the Magical, Magnificent New Orleans of Anne Rice*, 1–4.
11. http://www.Annerice.com. In 1976, when Rice published her first vampire tale, St. Elizabeth's was still a home for troubled girls run by the Catholic

church in accordance with contemporary social science paradigms. *Clarion Herald*, May 13, 1976. Rice's doll museum only delayed its fate as the luxury condominiums, proposed then by others and what it is now.

12. Jana Marcus records the event in 1996 with photographs and interviews *In the Shadow of the Vampire: Reflections from the World of Anne Rice*, xii.
13. http://www.Annerice.com.
14. Rice, *Interview with the Vampire*, 144.
15. Anne Reifenberg, "Nobody Said Boo When Anne Rice Came to New Orleans." *The Wall Street Journal*. Eastern edition (August 8, 1996).
16. Reifenberg, "Nobody Said Boo."
17. Reifenberg, "Nobody Said Boo."
18. Reifenberg, "Nobody Said Boo." The clash of Kith and Kin LLC with the city over exclusive rights to "Inside the World of Anne Rice Walking Tour" was reported at http://www.AnneRice.com in November 2000. After the death of her husband in 2002 and departure of her son for California, Rice moved to a gated community in the suburbs, selling the Garden District properties. Andrew Jacobs, "Dark Days in New Orleans as Anne Rice Goes Suburban," *The New York Times* (May 17, 2004).
19. Rice, *Interview*, 41.
20. Dickinson, *Haunted City*, xiii.
21. See the world maps of the Vampire Chronicles in Katherine Ramsland, *The Vampire Companion: The Official Guide to Anne Rice's The Vampire Chronicles*, 542–552. See also the categories of fans Marcus identifies from a book signing in Northern California: "There were tour groups, internet groups, reading groups, role-playing game groups. Just pick your fantasy."
22. Telephone interview with Robert McNulty, former assistant director of the NEA and current director of Partners for Livable Communities, formerly Partners for Livable Places (August 4, 2004). McNulty asserted that through regime changes in Washington from Johnson to Nixon to Carter, the NEA enjoyed robust support.
23. April 25, 1973, press release in file: "City Edges Financial History" and file: "Draft Report of the City Edges Project," December 1973 in VCC Records Box 1, in City Archives, New Orleans Public Library (NOPL).
24. "Coast" (Cote des Allemands) was used geohistorically to describe the upriver German farming settlement rather than a downriver French plantation settlement. German immigrants in New Orleans have typically been displaced in city discourse just as their names were frequently Francocized.
25. Rice, *Interview*, 6.
26. Rice, *Interview*, 7.
27. Rice, *Interview*, 7–8.
28. Rice, *Interview*, 11.
29. Rice, *Interview*, 12. The Jordan/Rice 1994 film converts the initial tragedy from death of a brother to death of a wife and thus alters the political unconscious driving the vampire fantasy. From the outset, the film establishes Louis as a human rooted in a more conventional heterosexual family.
30. Franklin and Moss, *From Slavery to Freedom: A History of Negro Americans*, 83.
31. Chesnutt, *Paul Marchand, F.M.C.*, and Bell, *Revolution, Romanticism, and the Afro-Creole Protest Tradition in Louisiana 1718–1868*.
32. Anne Rice, *Feast of All Saints*, 515–27.
33. Baker, *Turning South Again: Re-thinking Modernism, Re-reading Booker T*, 80–84.

34. Rice, *Interview*, 49–50.
35. Rice, *Interview*, 49.
36. Rice, *Interview*, 42.
37. Rice, *Interview*, 51.
38. Rice, *Interview*, 57.
39. Haraway, "Universal Donors in a Vampire Culture: It's All in the Family: Biological Kinship Categories in the Twentieth-Century United States." *Uncommon Ground: Rethinking the Human Place in Nature*, 321–366.
40. Rice, *Interview*, 42.
41. Rice, *Interview*, 45
42. Rice, *Interview*, 58, 60.
43. Rice, *Interview*, 65.
44. Haraway, 366.
45. Rice, *Interview*, 40, 98, 170.
46. Keller, 15–9; Haggerty, "Anne Rice and the Queering of Culture, " 5-18.,
47. Rice, *Interview*, 104.
48. Rice, *Interview*, 130.
49. Rice, *Interview*, 84.
50. Rice, *Interview*, 122.
51. Jordan, director, *Interview with the Vampire*. Rice, *Interview*, 161.
52. Aldon Nielsen, *Writing Between the Lines: Race and Intertextuality*, 101.
53. Rice, *Interview*, 162.
54. Olaudah Equiano quoted in Nielsen, *Writing Between the Lines,* 110.
55. Rice, *Interview*, 180.
56. Hurston, *Tell My Horse: Voodoo and Life in Haiti and Jamaica*, 179–98.
57. Rice, *Interview*, 200.
58. King, Introduction to *New Orleans: The Place and The People*.
59. Wright, *The Politics of Design in French Colonial Urbanism*.
60. Partners for Livable Places arose in 1977 from the NEA as a consortium concerned with livability and the built environment. "Initially focused on design and culture as resources for livability," according to their Web site, in 1979 it launched a program to document "the economic value of design and cultural amenities," and by the 1990s they added a "human dimension" focusing on social equity and human potential. At that time they changed their name to Partners for Livable Communities. http://www.livable.com/about/history.htm
61. Phone interview with McNulty, August 4, 2004.
62. File: Latin Architectural Heritage: NEA Correspondence, April 19, 1978, in Box 1 Files: Latin Roots in the Built Environment in City Archives of the NOPL.
63. The conference boasts being the first large public forum for Andres Duany and Elizabeth Plater-Zyberk of subsequent New Urbanist fame. A different sort of invitee was the Archbishop of Santa Fe, Roberto Fortune Sanchez, a supporter of compesinos and their local clerical support in Central America, but he was unable to attend. Letter to Lynda Friedmann from Sanchez, January 10, 1978, in File: "Latin Roots—Speaker Correspondence" and conference program in Box 1 VCC Records, 1952–1979, City Archives, NOPL.
64. Memo from Lois Fishman to Lynda Friedman received February 13, 1978, in File: "Latin Architectural Heritage—Speakers/Topics" in Box 1 VCC Records, City Archives, NOPL.
65. Letter from Gloria Powers to Braniff International Airlines regarding the Bogotá exhibit in File: "Latin Architectural Heritage Exhibits," File: "Latin Roots in the Built Environment: VC Walking Tour," and File: "Latin Roots in

the Built Environment/Latin Neighborhood Tour," Box 1 VCC Records, City Archives, NOPL.

66. "General Somoza to Visit Sate," *New Orleans Times-Picayune* (June 28, 1975).

67. "Somoza and the Shah," *New Orleans Times-Picayune* (September 14, 1978).

68. For Catholic coverage of Central American disasters, see *The Clarion Herald*, (August 1974–1976). For coverage of the sisters' redefinition see especially (December 12, 1974; August 21, 1975; September 18, 1975; September 25, 1975).

69. "Nicaragua—Past, Present...," *New Orleans Times-Picayune* (December 12, 1979).

70. *New Orleans Times-Picayune* (February 2 and 11, April 1, 1973; January 2, 1975; September 10 and 12, 1978; July 18, 1979; May 8, 1980) and *Clarion Herald* (March 4, 1976).

71. "A spirit of New Orleans?" *New Orleans Times-Picayune* (April 27, 1976).

72. Harvey, *Paris*, 321.

73. Harvey, *Paris*, 321.

74. *La lanterne* journal cover, figure 118, in Harvey, *Paris*, 339.

75. Rice's ellipsis, *Interview*, 335, 336, 338.

76. Telephone interview with former Vieux Carré Commission director, Lynda Friedmann, August 31, 2004.

Chapter 7

1. In 1994, there were 425 murders in New Orleans, the highest number ever (NOPD 1994 Statistical Report).

2. Asbury, *The French Quarter: An Informal History of the New Orleans Underworld*, 270–76.

3. Robert Tallant, *Voodoo in New Orleans*, 68–73.

4. Asbury, *The French Quarter*, 270–76; and Tallant, *Voodoo in New Orleans*, 72.

5. Both Asbury and Tallant repeat stories of her prayers with the condemned and the altars they built together in the jail cells. Tallant adds that Laveau provided coffins for the bodies of the indigent, executed men. In reading Zora Neale Hurston's work on the legacy of Laveau in New Orleans hoodoo, David Estes particularly notes Laveau's emphasis on improvisational voodoo altars that appear in domestic spaces, not in "white commercial, judicial, and religious edifices" ("The Neo-African Vatican: Zora Neale Hurston's New Orleans," in *Literary New Orleans in the Modern World*, edited by Richard S. Kennedy [Baton Rouge: Louisiana State University Press, 1998]: 66–82, 77). Hurston cites hoodoo doctor Luke Turner's story in which Laveau commanded him, "Go to your own house and build an altar. Power will come" (*Mules and Men*, reprinted from 1935 [New York: Harper and Row, Publishers, 1990]: 185; quoted in Estes, 76). The jail cells in which Laveau built purportedly Catholic altars with her advisees were a kind of domestic place but within a judicial edifice, an appropriately liminal space for the building of syncretic altars and the practice of improvised rituals conducted by a woman of color in the politically volatile world of 1850s, 1860s, and 1870s New Orleans. For a nineteenth-century version of this story about Laveau's construction of altars see "The Condemned," *Daily Picayune* (May 10, 1871), cited in the Robert Tallant Papers, reel #7, mss. folder 5B1 *Voodoo in New Orleans* (1946), City Archives, New Orleans Public Library (NOPL).

6. *Daily Picayune* (June 17, 1881), cited in the Robert Tallant papers, reel #7, mss. folder 5B1 *Voodoo in New Orleans* (1946), City Archives, NOPL.

7. Tallant, *Voodoo in New Orleans*, 72.

8. *New Orleans Democrat* (June 17, 1881), cited in the Robert Tallant papers, reel # 7, mss. Folder 5B1 *Voodoo in New Orleans* (1946).

9. Prejean, *Dead Man Walking: An Eyewitness Account of the Death Penalty in the United States*, subsequently *DMW*, 8.

10. Jacobs and Kaslow, *The Spiritual Churches of New Orleans: Origins, Beliefs, and Rituals of an African-American Religion*, 92.

11. In *Revolution, Romanticism, and the Afro-Creole Protest Tradition in Louisiana 1718–1868*, Bell identifies a much earlier spiritualist movement, one influenced by French and French Caribbean revolutionary upheaval and European mesmerists. Denying the centrality of voodoo in New Orleans nineteenth-century politics but corroborating the significance of Catholicism, Bell focuses attention on the black Creoles of New Orleans. "Rooted in the egalitarianism of the age of democratic revolution, a Catholic universalist ethic, and Romantic philosophy, their republican idealism produced the postwar South's most progressive vision of the future," 2–3.

12. Jacobs and Kaslow, *The Spiritual Churches*, 30–1.

13. Jacobs and Kaslow, *The Spiritual Churches*, 91.

14. Logsdon and Bell, "The Americanization of Black New Orleans, 1850–1900," in *Creole New Orleans; Race and Americanization*, 201–61.

15. Laveau retired from public life in 1875, says Tallant, the year after the Battle of Liberty Place, one such white rebellion in Reconstruction New Orleans, and two years before the decimation of Reconstruction and the New Orleans police reforms. She apparently weathered the brutal post–Civil War white police regime of 1866–67. See Rousey, *Policing the Southern City: New Orleans, 1805–1889*, 102, 107.

16. Baudier, *The Catholic Church in Louisiana*, 209–310, especially 259.

17. Baudier, *The Catholic Church in Louisiana*, 258.

18. Nolan, *A History of the Archdiocese of New Orleans*, 8.

19. Dominguez, *White by Definition: Social Classification in Creole Louisiana*, 95.

20. Baudier, *The Catholic Church in Louisiana*, 179.

21. Baudier, *The Catholic Church in Louisiana*, 211.

22. Hirsch and Logsdon, Introduction to Part II, "The American Challenge," in *Creole New Orleans*, 91–100.

23. Logsdon and Bell, "The Americanization," 234.

24. Boyer, *The City of Collective Memory: Its Historical Imagery and Architectural Entertainments*.

25. New Orleans City Archives TX420 1852–1862, NOPL, indicates New Orleans Parish Prison was probably supervised by the Sheriff and governed by state law rather than municipal ordinance.

26. Asbury, *The French Quarter*, 257.

27. Both academic historian Mark T. Carleton and the public historians of the Angola Museum cite the squalid conditions in New Orleans's jail as the reason for building the state institution in Baton Rouge. Carleton cites Tocqueville as the source. Tocqueville may well have seen swine housed with prisoners in New Orleans in January 1832, but he was not looking at Parish Prison, a massive structure erected virtually simultaneous to the similar structure in Baton Rouge. See not only Alexis de Tocqueville, *Journey to America*, translated by George Lawrence, edited by J.P. Mayer, revised with

A.P. Kerr (Westport: Greenwood Press, 1981), but also Gustave de Beaumont, *On The Penitentiary System and its Application in France* (Philadelphia: Carey, Lea and Blanchard, 1833); and George W. Pierson's classic, *Tocqueville and Beaumont in America* (New York: Oxford University Press, 1938). It would appear that in the 1830s Louisiana committed itself to prison reform at both locations. This said, records from the 1850s and 1860s, including an 1861 account by a visiting English journalist, again indicate vile conditions in New Orleans jails, including Parish Prison (Rousey 101, note 65).

28. Carleton, *Politics and Punishment: The History of the Louisiana State Penal System*, 20.
29. Carleton, *Politics and Punishment*, 194.
30. "Prior to 1952 the [Louisiana State Penal] system was essentially a business enterprise, administered either by politicians or by [private] lessees, with both forms of management seeking to extract as much money as possible from the labor of thousands of semi-skilled 'state slaves.'. . . Even by 1968 the transition noted above had not been completely effected." See Carleton, 192. In 1998 there were 1800 workers at "the farm" and wages ranged from 4 cents to 20 cents per hour. See *The Farm: Life Inside Angola*, documentary film, directed by Jonathan Stack and Liz Garbus with Wilbert Rideau. Carleton argues that modern rehabilitation requires a diversification of operations away from farming (197).
31. Angola Museum. http://angolamuseum.org/story/htm
32. The latter three circumstances have all been recorded in successful films. Those films are the two documentaries *The Wildest Show in the South: The Angola Prison Rodeo*, directed by Simeon Soffer; *The Farm*; and the feature film *Dead Man Walking*, directed by Tim Robbins. Arguably, Angola is equally infamous as the home of the Angola 3—now 2—Black Panthers some still believe were framed for a murder in the 1970s, and as the prison entrapping renowned and reformed *Angolite* editor Wilbert Rideau. It is equally famous as the place where John Lomax first recorded Huddie Ledbetter singing "Irene" in 1933. Lomax had Ledbetter's pardon plea recorded on the flip side of "Irene" thus winning Lead Belly's release from the governor in 1934.
33. The legislature reinstated the death penalty as a possible punishment in 1977. Prejean, *DMW*, 18, 36, and 43.
34. Prejean, *DMW*, 23.
35. Odum and Moore, *American Regionalism: A Cultural-Historical Approach to National Integration*.
36. Stuart Hall et al. popularized Stan Cohen's definition of moral panic in their 1978 book on the British media and public response to mugging, *Policing the Crisis*. See Stan Cohen, *Folk Devils and Moral Panics: The Creation of the Mods and Rockers* (London: MacGibbon and Kee, 1972), and Stuart Hall, Chas Critcher, Tony Jefferson, John Clarke, and Brian Roberts, *Policing the Crisis: Mugging, the State, and Law and Order*.
37. Foucault, *Discipline and Punish: The Birth of the Prison*,.
38. Plumwood, "Inequality, Ecojustice, and Ecological Rationality," *Debating the Earth: the Environmental Politics Reader*.
39. Plumwood, "Inequality," 566.
40. Prejean, *DMW*, 35. We can see the practice drill in *The Farm*.
41. Both *The Farm* and Tim Robbins's film *Dead Man Walking* make clear that death by lethal injection occurs in two phases. The first numbs the muscles making them unable to respond. After that first injection, witnesses see a body

completely at rest, but inside that body is suffocating. The second injection stops the heart. John Wesley Brown, a man awaiting execution interviewed in *The Farm,* observes that it is the sequence of this process that frightens him. Why not just stop the heart, he wonders.

42. Prejean, *DMW,* 23–4.
43. Prejean, *DMW,* 24. In *The Farm,* first the narrative voiceover and later warden Burl Cain announce that 85 percent of Angola inmates will die there.
44. Jason Berry recounts with Catholic pride, "With a 30,000-copy first edition, book and author have been profiled in *The New York Times Magazine, Vogue* and in several television news programs. Jason Epstein, her editor, sent copies to all the Supreme Court justices" (Rev. of Prejean's *Dead Man Walking, National Catholic Reporter,* 9). Garry Wills reviewed the book for the *New York Review of Books* (Rev. of Prejean's *Dead Man Walking, New York Review of Books,* 3–4). Raymond Schroth predicted in *America,* a Jesuit publication, that "*Dead Man Walking* may become another *Silent Spring*" (Rev. of Prejean's *Dead Man Walking, America,* 20). In *The New Yorker,* Terrence Rafferty described the book as "both the most moving memoir of relationships with condemned men since Truman Capote's 'In Cold Blood' and the most persuasive argument against capital punishment since Camus's savage, irrefutable essay 'Reflections on the Guillotine,'" ("Amazing Grace," Rev. of Robbins's *Dead Man Walking, The New Yorker,* 68). So successful was Sister Helen's book that Lucy Silvio, C.S.J., president of the Sisters of St. Joseph of Medaille, felt the need to explain how much money the order is making and what they are doing with it ("Raking in the Money?" *America* [8 March 1996]: 10–11).
45. Silvio, "Raking in the Money?" 11.
46. Helen Prejean, C.S.J, "Report from the Front," http://www.prejean.org
47. Schattschneider, *The Semisovereign People: A Realist's View of Democracy in America.*
48. Schattschneider, *The Semisovereign People,* emphasis his, 17–8.
49. Heggie, *Dead Man Walking,* an opera in two acts; and Schaller, director, *And Then One Night: The Making of* Dead Man Walking, film.
50. Wood and Fels, *The Power of Maps,* 184.
51. Dodge, "Living by Life: Some Bioregional Theory and Practice," reprinted from 1981, in *Home! A Bioregional Reader,* 8. Although dubious about pinning down a single means of defining a bioregion, Dodge surveys six proposals. One is to measure the biotic shift, the percentage of species differentiation, and vaguely draw a permeable territory inside which this shift is gradual. A second proposal is to map a bioregion by a watershed, but Dodge notes that the drainage areas of many rivers are too large for this to be practical. A third is land formation, which is often related to water shed. The short-grass prairie or a specific river basin is a reasonably distinct land formation. The fourth proposed definition echoes Odum's concept of folkways in suggesting a cultural or phenomenological mapping: your turf is what you think it is. The fifth is a spirit place, a territory defined by "psyche-tuning, power-presences" such as Mount Shasta or the Pacific Ocean, a "predominate psychophysical influence where you live." And the last proposal is definition of territorial boundaries of sorts through land elevation.
52. Daniel Kemmis, Foreword in *Bioregionalism,* edited by Michael McGinnis (New York: Routledge, 1999): xvi.
53. Kemmis, Foreword, xvi.

54. Peter Calthorpe and William Fulton, *The Regional City* (Washington, DC: Island Press, 2001): 282.

55. Frug, *City Making: Building Communities without Building Walls*.

56. Scott, *Seeing Like a State: How Certain Schemes to Improve the Human Condition Have Failed*).

57. Wood and Fels, *The Power of Maps*, emphasis and ellipses are his, 182–83.

58. Wood and Fels, *The Power of Maps*, 32. Some geographers claim that "ideas such as 'cultural space' and 'knowledge maps' apply a complex and nonlinear transformation to the physical space, and [thus] the two are ultimately 'unmappable'" (C.J. Keylock quoted in Nadine Schuurman, *Critical GIS: Theorizing an Emerging Science*, Monograph 53, *Cartographica* 36 [Winter 1999]: 23). My notion of emergent spirit regions are surely prey to this criticism as well. But, as Nadine Schuurman counters in her analysis of the philosophy of Geographic Information Science (GIS)—that ascendant, computerized mapping system so ubiquitous a force in our present lives—as much as scientists insist on precise categories, even GIS is dependent upon a language, and no language is without ambiguity. If amateurs engage in map-making, they cannot solve the problems about reality and representation that plague GIS as they do all codes of communication, but those amateurs can share in the expression and influence of "visual intuition" that makes GIS products so seductive. In map-making, spatial thinking, which is to say metaphorical thinking, finds another means of expression. Summarizing the impact of George Lakoff's 1987 book (*Women, Fire, and Dangerous Things: What Categories Reveal about the Mind*) on geographers' understanding of the relation between cognition and space, Helen Couclelis puts it this way: "His thesis was/is that (a) all thinking is to some degree metaphorical, (b) all metaphorical thinking is grounded in complex but not further decomposable elements that are inherently spatial (the image schemata), therefore (c) all thinking is to some degree spatial" (personal communication to Nadine Schuurman, 78).

59. Mathur and da Cunha. *Mississippi Floods: Designing a Shifting Landscape*.

60. Odum and Moore, *American Regionalism*, 277.

61. I take inspiration for this atlas from two sources. One is a 1969 effort in Detroit to change that city's urban geography by engaging diverse citizens in map-making accompanied by essays and photographs and journals so as to create an urban "Atlas of Love and Hate" (Wood, 239, note 14). This effort was never published but stands nonetheless as a model for a New Orleans and environs atlas in which *Dead Man Walking* participates. The other inspiration is Barbara Allen's more recent use of informal maps to collect information from Alsen, Louisiana, residents about the health effects of living in the Mississippi River petrochemical corridor ("The Popular Geography of Illness in the Industrial Corridor," *Transforming New Orleans and Environs: Centuries of Change*, 182–83).

62. Harvey, *Justice, Nature, and the Geographies of Difference*, 4–5.

63. Soja, *Postmetropolis: Critical Studies of Cities and Regions*.

64. Bill Quigley more recently acted as legal support for the movement to receive state approval of a higher minimum wage in the city of New Orleans. New Orleanians voted to accept the higher minimum wage February 2, 2002. See "New Orleans Votes Higher Wage" in the *Iowa City Press-Citizen* (February 4, 2002).

65. More specifically, the additional sites of Catholic presence are Loyola University in Uptown New Orleans, where the loved ones of crime victims from St. Thomas and other poor New Orleans communities meet; Prejean's

mother's home in Baton Rouge; the office of Catholic Governor Edwin Edwards in Baton Rouge; the office of Catholic Pardon Board President Howard Marsellus in Baton Rouge; the office of Catholic head of Corrections in Louisiana C. Paul Phelps in Baton Rouge; the Catholic homes of the LeBlancs and Bourques in St. Martinville and the Harveys' Christian home in Covington, families of the teenagers murdered by Sonnier and Willie, respectively; the Catholic home of the Sonniers in St. Martinville; the work stations within Death Row of Catholic and other Christian prison workers, including the warden; and the chapel outside St. Martinville where Prejean is invited to join Lloyd LeBlanc in his predawn vigil to pray for his murdered son and for the living. *The Farm* emphasizes the spiritual frame of reference at Angola, where life and death, forgiveness and revenge, are a palpable daily presence. Warden Burl Cain wishes that victims were more forgiving of inmates who deserve it but acknowledges that it is hard. "We see this struggle [here] more than anyone else. That's the battle between the spiritual and the worldly."

66. Although the region Prejean maps is not commensurate with any existing state or church territory, it may be helpful to know that in 1977, before the Archdiocese of New Orleans lost territory to the new diocese of Houma and Thibodaux to its southeast, 48.4 percent of the population was Catholic according to the Catholic Church in North America (http://www.rc.net/org/ccita/diocese/dnewo.html) consuited in 2001. This territory did not include Baton Rouge or Lafayette near St. Martinville, already separate dioceses in heavily Catholic parishes. see http://www.catholic-hierarchy.org/diocese/dnewo.html.

67. Prejean, *DMW*, 1.

68. Prejean, *DMW*, 3. Robbins's film begins with a different image of St. Thomas, one where children play, adults study, and the residents council can forcefully request Sister Helen's attendance at their meeting.

69. Prejean, *DMW*, 5–6.

70. Prejean, *DMW*, 7.

71. Prejean may have learned this lesson about systems from the St. Thomas Residents Council (STRC) trained in institutional racism by the People's Institute for Survival and Beyond. Determined to exercise control over the systems that defined their lives, in 1989, STRC demanded that all service providers working in St. Thomas—including religious-based organizations—sign a statement committing them to power-sharing with and accountability to residents. See Reichl, "Learning from St. Thomas: Community, Capital, and the Redevelopment of Public Housing in New Orleans," *Journal of Urban Affairs*, 169–87; and Young and Christos-Rodgers, "Resisting Racially Gendered Space: The Women of the St. Thomas Resident Council, New Orleans" in *Marginal Spaces: Comparative Urban and Community Research*, 95–112.

72. Prejean, *DMW*, 9.

73. City of New Orleans Housing Authority Annual Reports. 1979 and 1980, City Archives, New Orleans Public Library.

74. Jones, "The Bottom-Up Approach to Collaboration for Social Change: A Case Study of the St. Thomas/Irish Channel Consortium," cited in Young and Christos-Rodgers, 101.

75. Housing Authority of New Orleans (HANO), http://www.hano.org; Urban Land Institute, 1993; and NOPD Annual Reports, City Archives, New Orleans Public Library. Also see Reichl, "Leaning from St. Thomas," 174 and177.

76. David Rusk, "St. Thomas Needs a Mixed-Income Population," *New Orleans Times-Picayune* (October 10, 2001).

77. See "Public Housing: HUD's Takeover of the Housing Authority of New Orleans: Testimony Before the Subcommittee on Housing Opportunity and Community Development; Committee on Banking, Housing and Urban Affairs; House of Rep Hearing in House of Representatives HUD Report." *GAO Report* (8 July 1996): GAI.5/2T-RCED: 96-212, 4 and "HUD Hearing in House of Representatives: Re Take-Over of Hano," *HUD Report* (8 July 1996): Y4B221: 104-64, 34-35, 58-59.

78. Take 1978 as indicative of murder statistics during the period of Prejean's narrative: 127 black men were murdered in New Orleans compared with 16 white men, 14 black women, and 3 white women (New Orleans Police Department 1978–1997 Annual Statistical Reports, City Archives, New Orleans Public Library).

79. Prejean, *DMW*, 9. The Neville Brothers' song "Angola Bound" ironically conveys the familiarity of Angola to many New Orleanians of poorer neighborhoods (Aaron and Charles Neville, "Angola Bound"). "Angola Bound" is now the name of an annual symposium on prison music held at Angola (www.angolamuseum.org).

80. Prejean, *DMW*, 16–7.

81. Prejean, *DMW*, 12.

82. Prejean, *DMW*, 10.

83. Lynne Jensen, "Hope House Not Giving Up on St. Thomas," *New Orleans Times-Picayune* (July 16, 2001).

84. In 1981, Prejean began a Bridges program that invited participants to share this experience of St. Thomas. For $75 they could stay in an adjacent dormitory (*New York Times* [September 16, 1985]).

85. Prejean, *DMW*, 31.

86. Prejean, *DMW*, 54–5.

87. Prejean, *DMW*, 57.

88. Prejean, *DMW*, 56. After this controversy in 1984, Edwards appeared at the Alexandria Press Club sporting mock stigmata. A photograph of him at this event appears in *New Orleans Magazine* (May 1991): 48.

89. Prejean, *DMW*, 56.

90. Prejean, *DMW*, 57.

91. Prejean, *DMW*, 57.

92. Prejean, *DMW*, 61–3. To observe the work of two Louisiana Pardon Boards, see the documentary film, *The Farm*.

93. Prejean, *DMW*, 65.

94. By his choice, Howard Marsellus did witness the execution of Tim Baldwin on September 10, 1984. He later admitted that he believed Baldwin was innocent (*DMW*, 170).

95. Wood, *The Power of Maps*, 183.

96. Prejean, *DMW*, 99.

97. Prejean, *DMW*, 108–09.

98. Prejean, *DMW*, 120.

99. Prejean, *DMW*, 91.

100. Prejean, *DMW*, 38. M. Dwayne Smith's 1987 study of race bias in Louisiana death penalty sentencing from 1976 to 1982, the years when Sonnier and Willie were sentenced, confirms findings about other states' sentencing practices: the race of the victims not the race of the perpetrator was the prejudicial factor in juries' decisions. "Those charged with murdering whites were twice

as likely to receive a death sentence as were those who killed blacks." Smith also found that those who killed women in Louisiana were more likely to receive a death sentence. He admits that studies such as his have overlooked important, determining factors, primarily social class. Smith, "Patterns of Discrimination in Assessment of the Death Penalty: The Case of Louisiana," *Journal of Criminal Justice*, 279–86.

101. Prejean, *DMW*, 111.
102. Prejean, *DMW*, 116.
103. Young and Rogers, "Resisting Racially Gendered Space," 102.
104. Prejean, *DMW*, 129.
105. deCerteau, *The Practice of Everyday Life.*
106. Jacoby, *Wild Justice: The Evolution of Revenge*, 10; quoted in Prejean, *DMW*, 142.
107. Bakhtin, "Forms of Time and Chronotope in the Novel," 252.
108. Prejean, *DMW*, 133.
109. Prejean, *DMW*, 229, 230–31, 236, 237–38.
110. Prejean, *DMW*, 11–2.
111. Prejean, *DMW*, 150. See Hartman, *Scenes of Subjection: Terror, Slavery, and Self-Making in Nineteenth-Century America* for a much fuller explanation of the construction of black people as abject and whites as active. The St. Thomas Residents Council has vehemently resisted this lingering stereotype through proactive engagement with HANO, the social service providers in their neighborhood, and real estate developers who proposed to change it. See Young and Christos-Rodgers and Reichl, "Learning from St. Thomas."
112. John 10:17–8; quoted in Prejean, *DMW*, 193.
113. Prejean, *DMW*, 169–74; Berry, Review of Prejean's *Dead Man Walking*, 9.
114. Edwards's 1985–1986 and 2000 trials were visible everywhere on national media: *The New York Times, Time, Newsweek, The New Republic.* But see especially, Erroll Laborde, "Thrice a Governor: The Life and Times of Edwin Edwards" *New Orleans Magazine* 25 (May 1991): 38–45+. See also Allan Katz, "Anecdotes and Prognostications," *New Orleans Magazine* 25.9 (May 1991): 46–48+. And Prejean, *DMW*, 42.
115. Bridges, *Bad Bet on the Bayou: The Rise of Gambling in Louisiana and the Fall of Governor Edwin Edwards*, 356, 374.
116. Prejean, *DMW*, 212, 215.
117. Prejean, *DMW*, 197.
118. Her subsequent strategy was to testify in international fora, such as the Russian Dumas. (http://www.prejean/org provides a December 2001 description of her experiences there.)
119. Wood, *The Power of Maps*, 28.
120. Prejean, *DMW*, 213.
121. Prejean, *DMW*, 242.
122. Reichl, "Learning from St. Thomas," 176.
123. Young and Christos-Rodgers, "Resisting Racially Gendered Space," 103.
124. Reichl, "Learning From St. Thomas," 177.
125. Cook and Lauria, "Urban Regeneration and Public Housing in New Orleans," *Urban Affairs Review*, 538–57.
126. Interview with Barbara Major, May 1993, quoted in Young and Christos-Rodgers, "Resisting Racially Gendered Space," 106.
127. Young and Christos-Rodgers, "Resisting Racially Gendered Space," 106 and 103.
128. Leslie Williams, "St. Thomas 'Guide' to Oversee Facelift," *New Orleans Times-Picayune* (January 4, 1996).

129. Interview with Fannie McKnight, May 23, 1994, quoted in Young and Christos-Rodgers, "Resisting Racially Gendered Space," 107.
130. Calthorpe and Fulton, *The Regional City*, 244.
131. Housing Authority of New Orleans (HANO), http://www.hano.org.
132. The *New Orleans Times-Picayune* tells one hopeful story of relocation, that of Mrs. Evelyn Melancon, the first black resident in her building in the 1960s. Thirty-five years later, she, a model tenant, has been spared relocation to another public housing development by the intervention of a nun who works in a local social service agency. Mrs. Melancon will move to a shotgun house in the neighborhood. Her neighbor, Mrs. Lillie Petite, also a grandmother with dependents, will instead be moved first to the Florida housing development and then to the high-rise Guste public housing development. See Lynn Jensen, "Sweet Sorrow: New Homes Give New Lease on Life," *New Orleans Times-Picayune* (June 11, 2001).
133. HRI has provided details on the site as it existed when they were awarded the contract in 1998, details of the redevelopment plan, and information in support of their view that Wal-Mart is a necessary, beneficial, and compatible neighbor for St. Thomas, one that will bring sales taxes from the Wal-Marts in Jefferson and St. Bernard Parishes back to Orleans Parish. http://www.hrihci.com.
134. Schuurman, *Critical GIS*, 82, 91.
135. Rhonda Bell, "A Complex Undertaking," *New Orleans Times-Picayune* (October 26, 2001). Other evidence of STRC's disappointment came in the form of a protest at the September 7, 2001, "Justice for All," annual ball where HRI CEO Pres Kabacoff was presiding as honorary chair. The protest participants charged that "his image of the great liberal-minded developer is unwarranted as long as he destroys housing opportunities for poor people" (e-mail from the St. Thomas Community Law Center provided in Alexander Riechl's correspondence with the author).
136. http://www.hano.org
137. http://www.hrihci.com
138. HRI notes that when they signed on to the project, the average family in St. Thomas consisted of a single mother and three children with an average income of less than $5,000 per year. Between 1992 and 1995, there were eighteen murders in the neighborhood. The site generated no property or sales tax, and the contiguous, "blighted" warehouse district paid less than $25,000 in sales taxes per year. I infer their definition of community from this proffered data. http://www.hrihci.com
139. Project Top 10 by 2010. Dateline: New Orleans and the River Region. http://www.metrovision.org/dateline.html
140. Greg Thomas and Robert Scott, "Wal-Mart May Build Supercenter Uptown," *New Orleans Times-Picayune* (July 21, 2001).
141. Calthorpe and Fulton, *The Regional City*, 3–4.
142. Young and Christos-Rogers, "Resisting Racially Gendered Space," 110.
143. Jensen, "Hope House Not Giving Up on St. Thomas."
144. Eric Elie Lolis, "The Lost Residents of St. Thomas," *New Orleans Times Picayune* (January 2, 2002).

Epilogue

1. Codrescu, *Hail Babylon: In Search of the American City at the End of the Millennium*, xx.
2. Heard, *French Quarter Manual: An Architectural Guide to New Orleans' Vieux Carré*, 151.
3. See the arguments about Disneyland in Francaviglia's *Mainstreet Revisited: Time, Space and Image—Building in Small Town America*.
4. Vella, *Intimate Enemies: The Two Worlds of the Baroness de Pontalba*, 273–74.
5. Nolan, *A History of the Archdiocese of New Orleans*, 97.
6. Nolan, *A History of the Archdiocese of New Orleans*, 97.
7. Nolan, *A History of the Archdiocese of New Orleans*, 122.

Bibliography

Newspapers

Clarion Herald (New Orleans)
Daily Picayune (New Orleans)
Des Moines Register
Gambit (New Orleans)
Iowa City Press-Citizen
New Orleans Democrat
New Orleans Item
New Orleans States
New Orleans States-Item
New Orleans Times-Picayune
New York Times
Wall Street Journal
Washington Post

Archives

The Historic New Orleans Collection
US Housing and Urban Development
The Louisiana Collection, Tulane University
Louisiana Division, City Archives and Special Collections, New Orleans Public
    Library
The Louisiana State Museum
NAACP Papers, Manuscripts Division, Library of Congress
The New York Historical Society
The US Securities and Exchange Commission
Books, Articles, Films and Websites.
Adorno, Theodor W. *Negative Dialectics*. Translated by E.B. Ashton. New York:
    Basic Books, 1968.
Algren, Nelson. *The Last Carousel*. New York: Putnam, 1973.

————. *Nelson Algren's Own Book of Lonesome Monsters.* New York: Bernard Geis Associates, 1963. Distributed by Random House.

————. *Never Come Morning.* New York: Harper and Brothers, 1942.

————. *Nonconformity: Writing on Writing.* New York: Seven Stories Press, 1996.

————. *Notes From a Sea Diary: Hemingway All the Way.* New York; Putnam, 1965.

————. *Somebody in Boots.* New York: Vanguard; London: Constable, 1935.

————. *A Walk on the Wild Side.* New York: Noonday, 1956.

————. *Who Lost an American?* New York: Macmillan Co., 1963.

Allen, Barbara. "The Popular Geography of Illness in the Industrial Corridor." In *Transforming New Orleans and Environs: Centuries of Change,* edited by Craig E. Colten, Pittsburgh: University of Pittsburgh Press, 2000.

AMG. "Music guide," http://www.allmusic.com

Angola Museum. http://angolamuseum.org

Apel, Dora. "On Looking: Lynching Photographs and Legacies of Lynching After 9/11." *American Quarterly* 55 (September 2003): 457–78.

Arend, Orissa. *Showdown in Desire.* New Orleans, 2003.

Arnold, E., and S. Stamberg. "Streetcar Anniversary: Part II," *Weekly Edition,* National Public Radio, December 6, 1997.

Asbury, Herbert. *The French Quarter: An Informal History of the New Orleans Underworld.* New York: Knopf, 1936.

Atkinson, B. "*Streetcar* Tragedy: Mr. Williams's Report on Life in New Orleans." Reprinted from *New York Times,* December 14, 1947. In *The Critical Response to Tennessee Williams,* edited by George W. Crandell. Westport, CT: Greenwood, 1996.

Auerbach, Nina. *Our Vampires, Ourselves.* Chicago: University of Chicago, 1995.

Baker, Houston. *Turning South Again: Re-thinking Modernism, Re-reading Booker T.* Durham, NC: Duke University Press, 2001.

————. "Workings of the Spirit: Conjure and the Space of Black Women's Creativity." *Workings of the Spirit: The Poetics of Afro-American Women's Writing.* Chicago: University of Chicago Press, 1991.

Bakhtin, M.M. "Forms of Time and of the Chronotope in the Novel." Translated by Caryl Emerson and Michael Holquist. In *The Dialogic Imagination: Four Essays,* edited by M. Holquist. Austin: University of Texas Press, 1981.

Barnett, Ida Wells. "Mob Rule in New Orleans." In *On Lynchings.* New York: Arno Press, 1969 .

Barry, John. *Rising Tide: The Great Mississippi Flood of 1927 and How it Changed America.* New York: Simon and Schuster, 1997.

Baudelaire, Charles. "Allegory." *Les Fleurs du Mal.* Translated by Richard Howard. Boston: Godine, 1982.

Baudier, Roger. *The Catholic Church in Louisiana.* New Orleans: Louisiana Library Association, 1972. Reprinted 1939.

Baumbauch, Richard O., Jr., and William E. Borah. *The Second Battle of New Orleans: A History of the Vieux Carré Riverfront Expressway Controversy.* Tuscaloosa: University of Alabama Press, 1981.

Beaumont, Gustave de. *Marie, or, Slavery in the United States: A Novel of Jacksonian America.* Translated by Barbara Chapman. Palo Alto, CA: Stanford University Press, 1958.

Beauregard, Robert A. *Voices of Decline: the Postwar Fate of U.S. Cities,* revised ed. New York: Routledge, 2003.

Bell, Caryn Crosse. *Revolution, Romanticism, and the Afro-Creole Protest Tradition in Louisiana 1718–1868*. Baton Rouge: Louisiana State University Press, 1997.

Bell, Caryn Crosse, and Joseph Logsdon. "The Americanization of Black New Orleans, 1850–1900." In *Creole New Orleans: Race and Americanization*, edited by A.R. Hirsch and J. Logsdon. Baton Rouge: Louisiana State University Press, 1992.

Bell, Shannon. *Reading, Writing, and Rewriting the Prostitute Body*. Bloomington, IN: Indiana University Press, 1994.

Benjamin, Walter. *The Arcades Project*. Translated by Howard Eiland and Kevin McLaughlin. Cambridge: Harvard University Press, 1999.

———. "Central Park," *New German Critique* 34 (1985):32–58.

Bernhard, John H., Letters to the Editor, The New Republic (Sept. 15, 1947): 39.

Berry, Jason. Review of Prejean's *Dead Man Walking*. *National Catholic Reporter* (2 July 1993): 9.

Blassingame, John. *Black New Orleans, 1860–1880*. Chicago: University of Chicago Press, 1973.

Bottles, Scott. *Los Angeles and the Automobile: The Making of the Modern City*. Berkeley: University of California Press, 1987.

Boutang, Pierre-Andre. *L'Abecedaire de Gilles Deleuze*. Documentary film with Claire Parnet, 1996.

Boyer, M. Christine. *The City of Collective Memory: Its Historical Imagery and Architectural Entertainments*. Cambridge, MA: MIT Press, 1994.

Brady, Patricia. "Forward." In *Literary New Orleans*, edited by Judy Long. Athens, GA: Hill Street Press, 1999 .

Branch, Taylor. *Parting the Waters: America in the King Years, 1954–63*. New York: Simon and Schuster, 1988.

Bridges, Tyler. *Bad Bet on the Bayou: The Rise of Gambling in Louisiana and the Fall of Governor Edwin Edwards*. New York: Farrar, Straus and Giroux, 2001.

Brownell, Blaine. "A Symbol of Modernity: Attitudes Toward the Automobile in Three Southern Cities during the 1920s." *American Quarterly* 24 (1972).

Bryan, Violet. *The Myth of New Orleans in Literature: Dialogues of Race and Gender*. Knoxville: University of Tennessee Press, 1993.

Buell, Lawrence. *Writing for an Endangered World: Literature, Culture and Environment in the U.S. and Beyond*. Cambridge, MA: Harvard University Press, 2001.

Calthorpe, Peter, and William Fulton. *The Regional City*. Washington, DC: Island Press, 2001.

Campbell, Scott. "Green Cities, Growing Cities, Just Cities? Urban Planning and the Contradictions of Sustainable Development." *Journal of the American Planning Association* 62 (1996): 296–312.

Capote, Truman. "New Orleans (1946)." In *Literary New Orleans*, edited by Judy Long. *Literary New Orleans*. Athens, GA: Hill Street Press, 1999.

Carleton, Mark T. *Politics and Punishment: The History of the Louisiana State Penal System*. Baton Rouge: Louisiana State University Press, 1971.

Carson, Robert. *What Ever Happened to the Trolley? A Micro Historical and Economic Study of the Rise and Decline of Street Railroads in Syracuse, New York, 1860–1941*. Washington, DC: University Press of America, 1978.

Carter, Hodding. "An Introduction with Love." *The Past as Prelude: New Orleans 1718–1968*. New Orleans: Tulane University Press, 1968.

Chase, John. *Frenchmen, Desire, Good Children*. New York: Collier, 1979.

Chesnutt, Charles. *Paul Marchand, F.M.C.* Princeton, NJ: Princeton University Press, 1999.

Chicago Area Transportation Study (CATS), 1955.

Chicago Historical Society, "A Century of Progress," http://www.chicagohs.org/history/century.html

Ciment, Michel, editor. *Elia Kazan: An American Odyssey.* London: Bloomsbury Publishing Ltd., 1988.

Cleaver, Kathleen, and George Katsiaficas, editors. *Liberation, Imagination and the Black Panther Party.* New York: Routledge, 2001.

Codrescu, Andrei. *Hail Babylon: In Search of the American City at the End of the Millennium.* New York: St. Martin's Press, 1998.

———. "The Muse Is Always Half-Dressed in New Orleans." In *The Muse Is Always Half-Dressed in New Orleans and Other Essays.* New York: St. Martin's Press, 1993.

Cohen, Stan. *Folk Devils and Moral Panics: The Creation of the Mods and Rockers.* London: MacGibbon and Kee, 1972.

Coles, Robert. *Walker Percy: An American Search.* Boston: Little, Brown and Co., 1978.

Colten, Craig, editor. *Transforming New Orleans and its Environs: Centuries of Change.* Pittsburgh: University of Pittsburgh Press, 2000.

Connerton, Paul. *How Societies Remember.* New York: Cambridge University Press, 1989.

Conroy, Marianne. "Acting Out: Method Acting, the National Culture, and the Middlebrow Disposition in Cold War America." *Criticism* 35 (1993): 239–63.

Cook, Christine C., and Mickey Lauria. "Urban Regeneration and Public Housing in New Orleans." *Urban Affairs Review* 30 (1995): 538–57.

Crandel, George W., editor. *The Critical Response to Tennessee Williams.* Westport, CT: Greenwood Press, 1996.

Creecy, James R. "A Duel in New Orleans, in 1829." *Scenes in the South and Other Miscellaneous Pieces.* Washington, DC, 1860.

Creecy, Mrs. James R. "Introduction." In *Scenes in the South and Other Miscellaneous Pieces.* Washington, DC, 1860.

Cronon, William. "The Trouble with Wilderness" In *Uncommon Ground: Rethinking the Human Place in Nature,* edited by W. Cronon. New York: W.W. Norton, 1995.

Danks, Adrian. "In the Waterfront," http://www.rottentomatoes.com.

David, Nanette J. *Prostitution: An International Handbook on Trends, Problems, and Policies.* Westport, CT: Greenwood Press, 1993.

De Beauvoir, Simone. *A Transatlantic Love Affair: Letters to Nelson Algren.* New York: The New Press, 1998.

DeCerteau Michel. *The Practice of Everyday Life,* translated by Steven Rendall. Berkeley: University of California Press, 1984.

DeLombard, Jeannine. "'Eye-Witness to the Cruelty:' Southern Violence and Northern Testimony in Frederick Douglass's 1845 *Narrative.*" *American Literature* 73 (2001): 245–75.

Denning, Michael. *The Cultural Front: the Laboring of American Culture in the 20th Century.* New York: Verso, 1996.

Dick, Bruce, and Amnitjit Singh, editors. *Conversations with Ishmael Reed.* Jackson, Mississippi: University Press of Mississippi, 1995.

Dickinson, Joy. *Haunted City: An Unauthorized Guide to the Magical, Magnificent New Orleans of Anne Rice.* New York: Citadel Press, 1998.

Diocese of Baton Rouge. http:\\www.catholic-hierarchy.org/diocese

Dmytryk, Edward, director. *Walk on the Wild Side*, motion picture. Columbia Pictures, 1962.

Doane, Janice, and Devon Hodges. "Undoing Feminism: From the Preoedipal to Postfeminism in Anne Rice's Vampire Chronicles." *American Literary History* 2 (1990): 422–42.

Dodge, Jim. "Living by Life; Some Bioregional Theory and Practice." Rpt. 1981. In *Home! A Bioregional Reader,* edited by Van Andrus, Christopher Plant, Judith Plant, and Eleanor Wright. Philadelphia: New Society Publishers, 1990.

Dominguez, Virginia. *White by Definition: Social Classification in Creole Louisiana.* New Brunswick, NJ: Rutgers University Press, 1986.

Donohue, H.E.F. *Conversations with Nelson Algren.* New York: Hill and Wang, 1964.

Douglas, Ann. *Terrible Honesty: Mongrel Manhattan in the 1920s.* New York: Farrar, Straus and Giroux, 1995.

Drew, Bettina. *Nelson Algren: A Life on the Wild Side.* New York: G.P. Putnam's Sons, 1989.

———. *Texas Stories of Nelson Algren.* Austin: University of Texas Press, 1995.

Drucker, Peter. *Concept of the Corporation.* New York: John Day, 1946.

Dupont, Robert L. "New Orleans: The Case for Urban Exceptionalism." *Journal of Urban History* 30 (2004): 881–93.

Dyer, Richard. *Heavenly Bodies: Film Stars and Society.* London: British Film Institute, 1986.

Estes, David C. "The Neo-African Vatican: Zora Neale Hurston's New Orleans." In *Literary New Orleans in the Modern World*, edited by Richard S. Kennedy. Baton Rouge: Louisiana State University Press, 1998 .

Fabre, Michel. *The Unfinished Quest of Richard Wright,* 2nd ed. Translated by Isabel Barzun. Urbana: University of Illinois Press, 1993.

Ferguson, Otis. "On the Bum," Review of Nelson Algren's *Somebody in Boots* and Edward Anderson's *Hungry Men, The New Republic* (July 17, 1935): 286–287

Finnegan, Ruth. *Tales of the City: A Study of Narrative and Urban Life.* Cambridge, UK: Cambridge University Press, 1998.

Flaherty, Robert, director. *The Louisiana Story*, motion picture. 1948.

Flink, James J. *The Car Culture.* Cambridge, MA: MIT Press, 1975.

Foner, Philip S., editor. *The Black Panthers Speak.* New York: J. B. Lippincott Co., 1970.

Foucault, Michel. *Discipline and Punish: The Birth of the Prison.* Translated by Alan Sheridan. New York: Vintage Books, 1979.

Fox, Robert Elliot. "Blacking the Zero: Towards a Semiotics of Neo-Hoodoo." In *The Critical Response to Ishmael Reed.* Edited by Bruce Allen Dick. Westport, CT: Greenwood Press, 1999.

Francaviglia, Richard. *Mainstreet Revisited: Time, Space and Image-building in Small Town America.* Iowa City: University of Iowa Press, 1996.

Franklin, John Hope, and Alfred A. Moss, Jr. *From Slavery to Freedom: A History of Negro Americans.* New York: McGraw-Hill, 1988.

Friedman, John, and Clyde Weaver. *Territory and Function: the Evolution of Regional Planning.* Berkeley: University of California Press, 1979.

Frug, Gerald. *City Making. Building Communities without Building Walls.* Princeton, NJ: Princeton University Press, 1999.

Gates, Henry Louis. *The Signifying Monkey.* New York: Oxford University Press, 1988.

Gelfand, Blanche. *The American City Novel*. Norman: University of Oklahoma Press, 1954.

Gerber, David. "Heroes and Misfits: The Troubled Social Reintegration of Disabled Veterans in *The Best Years of Our Lives*." *American Quarterly* 46 (1994): 545–74.

Gibb, George Sweet, and Evelyn H. Knowlton. *History of Standard Oil Co. (New Jersey): The Resurgent Years 1911–1927*. New York: Harper and Brothers, 1956.

Giles, James R. *Confronting the Horror: The Novels of Nelson Algren*. Kent, OH: Kent State University Press, 1989.

Goddu, Teresa. "Vampire Gothic." *American Literary History* 11 (1999): 125–41.

Gotham, Kevin Fox. "Marketing Mardis Gras: Commodification, Spectacle, and the Political Economy of Tourism in New Orleans." *Urban Studies* 39 (2002): 1735–56.

Gronbeck-Tedesco, John. "Ambiguity in the Plays of Tennessee Williams." *Mississippi Quarterly* 48 (1995): 735–49.

Gruesz, Kirsten Silva. *Ambassadors of Culture: The Transamerican Origins of Latino Writing*. Princeton, NJ: Princeton University Press, 2002.

Guilbeau, James. *The St. Charles Street Car or The History of the New Orleans and Carrollton Railroad*. 3rd ed. New Orleans: Louisiana Landmarks Society, 1992.

Haas, Edward F. *DeLessups S. Morrison and the Image of Reform: New Orleans Politics, 1946–1961*. Baton Rouge: Louisiana State University Press, 1974.

Habermas, Jürgen. *The Structural Transformation of the Public Sphere: An Inquiry into a Category of Bourgeois Society*. Translated by Thomas Burger. Cambridge, MA: MIT Press, 1991.

Haggerty, George. "Anne Rice and the Queering of Culture." *Novel* 32 (1998): 5–18.

Hair, William Ivy. *Carnival of Fury: Robert Charles and the New Orleans Race Riot of 1900*. Baton Rouge: Louisiana State University Press, 1976.

Halberstam, David. *The Fifties*. New York: Villard, 1993.

Hale, Allean. "Two on a Streetcar." *Tennessee Williams Literary Journal* (Spring 1989): 31–43.

Hall, Gwendolyn Midlo. "The Formation of Afro-Creole Culture." In *Creole New Orleans: Race and Americanization*, edited by A.R. Hirsch and J. Logsdon. Baton Rouge: Louisiana State University Press, 1992.

Hall, Stuart, Chas Critcher, Tony Jefferson, John Clarke, and Brian Roberts. *Policing the Crisis: Mugging, the State, and Law and Order*. New York: Holmes and Meier Publishers, Inc., 1978.

Haraway, Donna. "Universal Donors in a Vampire Culture: It's All in the Family: Biological Kinship Categories in the Twentieth-Century United States." In *Uncommon Ground: Rethinking the Human Place in Nature*, edited by William Cronon. New York: W.W. Norton and Company, 1996.

Hartman, Saidiya. *Scenes of Subjection: Terror, Slavery, and Self-Making in Nineteenth-Century America*. New York: Oxford University Press, 1997.

Harvey, David. *Paris: The Capital of Modernity*. New York: Routledge, 2003.

———. *Justice, Nature, and the Geography of Difference*. Oxford: Blackwell Publishers, 1996.

———. *Spaces of Hope*. Berkeley: University of California Press, 2000.

Hayden, Dolores. *The Power of Place: Urban Landscapes as Public History*. Cambridge, MA: MIT Press, 1995.

Hayman, Ronald. *Tennessee Williams: Everyone Else Is an Audience.* New Haven, CT: Yale University Press, 1993.

Heard, Malcolm. *French Quarter Manual: An Architectural Guide to New Orleans' Vieux Carré.* New Orleans: Tulane School of Architecture, 1997.

Hearn, Lafcadio. "The Last of the Voudoos." In *The World from Jackson Square: A New Orleans Reader,* edited by Etolia S. Basso. New York: Farrar, Straus and Company, 1948.

Heggie, Jake. *Dead Man Walking.* An opera in two acts. Libretto by Terrence McNally. Premiered San Francisco, 2001.

Helfand, Judith, and Daniel B. Gold, directors. *Blue Vinyl,* documentary film. Toxicomedy Pictures, 2002.

Henderson, David. *The Low East.* Richmond, CA: North Atlantic Books, 1980.

———. *De Mayor of Harlem: the Poetry of David Henderson.* New York: E. P. Dutton, 1970.

Hennick, Lewis C., and E. Harper Charlton. *The Streetcars of New Orleans, 1831–1965.* Gretna, LA: Pelican, 1965.

Heyl, Barbara Sherman. *The Madam as Entrepreneur: Career Management in House Prostitution.* New Brunswick, NJ: Transaction Publishers, 1979.

Hidy, Ralph W., and Muriel E. Hidy. *History of Standard Oil Co. (New Jersey): Pioneering in Big Business 1882–1911.* New York: Harper and Brothers, 1955.

Hilliard, David, and Donald Weise, editors. *The Huey P. Newton Reader.* New York: Seven Stories Press, 2002.

Hirsch, Arnold R. *Making the Second Ghetto: Race and Housing in Chicago, 1940–1960.* New York: Cambridge University Press, 1983.

———. "Simply a Matter of Black and White: The Transformation of Race and Politics in Twentieth-Century New Orleans," In *Creole New Orleans: Race and Americanization,* edited by Arnold R. Hirsch and Joseph Logsdon. Baton Rouge: Louisiana State University Press, 1992.

Hirsch, Arnold, and Joseph Logsdon. "The American Challenge." In *Creole New Orleans: Race and Americanization* edited by A. R. Hirsch and J. Logsdon. Baton Rouge: Louisiana State University Press, 1992.

———. "Franco-Africans and African-Americans," In *Creole New Orleans: Race and Americanization,* edited by A.R. Hirsch and J. Logsdon. Baton Rouge: Louisiana State University Press, 1992.

Historic Restorations, Inc. http://www.hrihci.com

Hobson, Barbara Meil. *Uneasy Virtue: the Politics of Prostitution and the American Reform Tradition.* New York: Basic Books, 1987.

Hollandsworth, James G. *An Absolute Massacre: The New Orleans Race Riot of July 30, 1866.* Baton Rouge: Louisiana State University Press, 2001.

Horn, Robert. "Walk on the Wild Side" [regarding biography of *Bangkok Post*'s night owl columnist Bernard Trink], *Time* (Asia) (October 16, 2000).

Housing Authority of New Orleans. http://www.hano.org

Hurston, Zora Neale. *Mules and Men.* New York: Harper and Row, 1990.

———. Review of Robert Tallant's *Voodoo in New Orleans. The Journal of American Folklore* 60(1947): 436–438.

———. *Tell My Horse: Voodoo and Life in Haiti and Jamaica.* New York: Harper and Row, Publishers, 1990.

Jacobs, Claude F., and Andrew J. Kaslow. *The Spiritual Churches of New Orleans: Origins, Beliefs, and Rituals of an African-American Religion.* Knoxville: University of Tennessee Press, 1991.

Jacobs, Jane. *The Death and Life of Great American Cities.* New York: Random House, Inc., 1961.

Jacoby, Susan. *Wild Justice: The Evolution of Revenge.* New York: Harper and Row, 1983.

Jones, Crystal Handy. "The Bottom-Up Approach to Collaboration for Social Change: A Case Study of the St. Thomas/Irish Channel Consortium." MA thesis, University of New Orleans, 1993.

Jordan, Neil, director. *Interview with the Vampire,* motion picture. Warner Studios, 1994.

Kammen, Michael. *Mystic Chords of Memory: The Transformation of Tradition in American Culture.* New York: Knopf, 1991.

Kane, Harnett T. "Land of Louisiana Sugar Kings." *National Geographic Magazine* 113 (1958): 531–67.

———. *Queen New Orleans: City by the River.* New York: William Morrow and Company, 1949.

Kaplan, Amy. *The Anarchy of Empire In the Making of U.S. Culture.* Cambridge, MA: Harvard University Press, 2002.

———. "Violent Belonging and the Question of Empire Today—Presidential Address to the American Studies Association, October 17, 2003." *American Quarterly* 56 (2004): 1–18.

Kaplan, Carla, editor. *Every Tongue Got to Confess: Negro Folktales from the Gulf States.* New York: HarperCollins Publishers, 2001.

Katz, Allan. "Anecdotes and Prognostications," *New Orleans Magazine* 25(1991): 46–48.

Kazan, Elia. *Elia Kazan: A Life.* New York: Alfred A. Knopf, 1988.

———. "Notebooks for a *Streetcar Named Desire.*" In *Directors on Directing: A Source Book of the Modern Theater,* edited by Toby Cole and Helen Krich Chinoy. New York: Bobbs-Merrill, 1963.

———, director. *Panic in the Streets,* motion picture. Fox Studios, 1950.

———, director. *A Streetcar Named Desire,* motion picture. 1993. (Censored scenes reinserted from Warner Brothers, 1951.)

Keller, James R. *Anne Rice and Sexual Politics.* Jefferson, NC: McFarland and Company, Inc., Publishers, 2000.

Kelly, Lionel. "The White Goddess." In *Confronting Tennessee Williams's* Streetcar: *Essays in Critical Pluralism,* edited by Philip Kolin. Westport, CT: Greenwood Press, 1993.

Kelman, Ari. *A River and Its City: The Nature of Landscape in New Orleans.* Berkeley: University of California Press, 2003.

Kemmis, Daniel. "Foreword." In *Bioregionalism,* edited by Michael McGinnis. New York: Routledge, 1999.

King, Grace. *New Orleans: The Place and the People.* New York: Macmillan Company, 1913.

Klein, Jim, director. *Taken for a Ride,* documentary film. New Day Films, 1996.

Kolb, Carolyn. "Exceptional Incidents: The Black Panthers in New Orleans 1970–71." Division of Urban Research and Policy Study Working Paper Number 57. New Orleans: College of Urban and Public Affairs, 1999.

Kolin, Philip. "Reflection on/of *A Streetcar Named Desire.*" In *Confronting Tennessee Williams's* A Streetcar Named Desire: *Essays in Critical Pluralism,* edited by Philip Kolin. Westport, CT: Greenwood Press, 1993.

———. *Williams:* A Streetcar Named Desire. Plays in Production. New York: Cambridge University Press, 2000.

Kuprin, Alexander. *Yama, or the Pit.* Translated by Bernard Guilbert Guerney. New York: Modern Library, 1932.

Kwitny, Jonathan. "The Great Transportation Conspiracy: A Juggernaut Named Desire," *Harper's* (February 1982): 14–21.

Lacan, Jacques. *The Ethics of Psychoanalysis, 1959–1960,* edited by Jacques-Alain Miller. Translated by Dennis Porter. New York: W.W. Norton and Co., 1997.

Lakoff, George. *Women, Fire, and Dangerous Things: What Categories Reveal about the Mind.* Chicago: University of Chicago, 1987.

Latham, Robert. *Consuming Youth: Vampires, Cyborgs and the Culture of Consumption.* Chicago: University of Chicago Press, 2002.

Lawson, Lewis A., and Victor A. Kramer, editors. *More Conversations with Walker Percy.* Jackson: University Press of Mississippi, 1993.

Leavitt, Mel. *A Short History of New Orleans.* San Francisco: Lexikos, 1982.

Levinson, Sanford. *Written in Stone: Public Monuments in Changing Societies.* Durham, NC: Duke University Press, 1998.

Lewis, Pierce F. *New Orleans: The Making of an Urban Landscape.* Cambridge, MA: Ballinger, 1976.

Leverich, Lyle. *Tom: The Unknown Tennessee Williams.* New York: Crown Publishers, 1995.

Lipsitz, George. *Rainbow at Midnight: Labor and Culture in the 1940s.* Urbana: University of Illinois Press, 1994.

Livable Communities. "History," http://www.livable.com/about/history.htm

Logsdon, Joseph, and Caryn Crosse Bell. "The Americanization of Black New Orleans, 1850–1900," In *Creole New Orleans: Race and Americanization,* edited by A.R. Hirsch and J. Logsdon. Baton Rouge: Louisiana State University Press, 1992.

Lomax, Alan. *The Folk Songs of North America.* Garden City, NY: Doubleday and Co., 1960.

Long, Alecia P. *The Great Southern Babylon: Sex, Race and Respectability in New Orleans, 1865–1920.* Baton Rouge: Louisiana State University Press, 2004.

Lott, Eric. *Love and Theft: Blackface Minstrelsy and the American Working Class.* New York: Oxford University Press, 1993.

Lowenthal, David. "Identity, Heritage, and History." In *Commemorations: The Politics of National Identity,* edited by John R. Gillis. Princeton, NJ: Princeton University Press, 1994.

Marcus, Jana. *In the Shadow of the Vampire: Reflections from the World of Anne Rice.* New York: Thunder's Mouth Press, 1997.

Markowitz, Gerald, and David Rosner. *Deceit and Denial: The Deadly Politics of Industrial Pollution.* Berkeley: University of California Press, 2002.

Martin, Ralph G. "New Orleans Has Its Face Lifted," *The New Republic* (June 2, 1947): 16–19.

Mathur, Anuradha, and Dilip da Cunha. *Mississippi Floods: Designing Shifting Landscape.* New Haven, CT: Yale University Press, 2001.

Matthews, John T. "Recalling the West Indies: From Yoknapatawpha to Haiti and Back." *American Literary History* 16 (2004): 238–62.

McCann, Graham. *Rebel Males: Clift, Brando and Dean.* London: Hamish Hamilton, 1991.

McGee, Patrick. *Ishmael Reed and the Ends of Race.* New York: St. Martin's, 1997.

McHale, Brian. *Postmodernist Fiction.* New York: Methuen, 1987.

Melosi, Martin V. *The Sanitary City: Urban Infrastructure in America from Colonial Times to the Present.* Baltimore: Johns Hopkins University Press, 2000.

"Middle South Utilities." In *Moody's Public Utility Manual* (1954): 257.

Mitchell, Reid. *All on a Mardi Gras Day*. Cambridge, MA: Harvard University Press, 1995.

Mizell-Nelson, Michael, writer and producer. *Streetcar Stories*, documentary film. Berkeley: University of California, 1995.

Montello, Martha. "From Eye to Ear in Percy's Fiction: Changing the Paradigm for Clinical Medicine." In *The Last Physician: Walker Percy and the Moral Life of Medicine*, edited by Carl Elliott and John Lantos. Durham, NC: Duke University Press, 1999.

Morris, Christopher. "Impenetrable but Easy: The French Transformation of the Lower Mississippi Valley and the Founding of New Orleans." In *Transforming New Orleans*, edited by C. Colten. Pittsburgh: University of Pittsburgh Press, 2000.

Moses, Robert, director. *Arterial Plan for New Orleans*. Andrews and Clark, Consulting Engineers, 1946.

Mulvey, Laura. "Visual Pleasure and Narrative Cinema." In *Contemporary Literary and Cultural Studies*, edited by Robert Con Davis and Ronald Schleifer. New York: Longman Publishing Group, 1994.

Mumford, Lewis. "The Highway and the City." In *The Highway and the City*. New York: Harcourt, Brace & World, 1963.

Murphy, Brenda. *American Realism and American Drama, 1880–1940*. New York: Cambridge University Press, 1987.

———. *Tennessee Williams and Elia Kazan: A Collaboration in Theatre*. New York: Cambridge University Press, 1992.

"Nelson Algren Talks with NOR's Editor-at-Large," *New Orleans Review* (1969): 130–132.

Neville, Aaron, and Charles Neville. "Angola Bound." On *Warm Your Heart*, compact disc. A&M Records, 1991.

Nielsen, Aldon. *Writing Between the Lines: Race and Intertextuality*. Athens: University of Georgia Press, 1994.

Nolan, Charles E. *A History of the Archdiocese of New Orleans*. Strasbourg, France: Editions du Signe, 2000.

Odum, Howard, and Harry Estill Moore. *American Regionalism: A Cultural-Historical Approach to National Integration*. New York: Henry Holt and Co., 1938.

Odum, Howard, and Katherine Jocher. *In Search of the Regional Balance of America*. Westport, CT: Greenwood Press, 1945.

Odum, Howard. *Race and Rumours of Race*. Introduction by Bryant Simon. Baltimore: Johns Hopkins University Press, 1997.

Okada, John. *No-No Boy*. Seattle: University of Washington Press, 1957.

"Old Girl's New Boy," *Time* (November 24, 1947): 26–29.

Paglia, Camille. *Sex, Art, and American Culture*. New York: Vintage, 1992.

Peddie, Ian. "Poles Apart? Ethnicity, Race, Class and Nelson Algren." *Modern Fiction Studies* 47 (Spring 2001): 118–45.

Pelongo, Bob. Interview with Nelson Algren. *Arizona Quarterly* 45 (Spring 1989): 101–6.

Percy, Walker. *The Message in the Bottle*. New York: Farrar, Straus and Giroux, 1954.

———. *The Moviegoer*. New York: Avon, in arrangement with Knopf, 1961.

———. "Naming and Being." *The Personalist: An International Review of Philosophy, Religion, and Literature*. (1960): 148–57.

————. *Signposts in a Strange Land,* edited by Patrick Samway. New York: Farrar, Straus and Giroux, 1991.

Percy, William Alexander. *Lanterns on the Levee: Recollections of a Planter's Son.* New York: Alfred A. Knopf, 1941.

Perez, August. *The Last Line: A Streetcar Named St. Charles.* Gretna, LA: Pelican, 1973.

Pickrell, Don H. "A Desire Named Streetcar: Fantasy and Fact in Rail Transit Planning," *Journal of the American Planning Association* 58 (1992): 158–76.

Pierson, George, W. *Tocqueville and Beaumont in America.* New York: Oxford University Press, 1938.

Pindell, Richard. "Basking in the Eye of the Storm: The Esthetics of Loss in Walker Percy's *The Moviegoer.*" *Boundary* 2, 4 (1975): 219–30.

Plan and Program for the Preservation of the Vieux Carré. Historic Demonstration Study, conducted by the Bureau of Governmental Research, for the City of New Orleans (December 1968).

Plumwood, Val. "Inequality, Ecojustice, and Ecological Rationality." *Debating the Earth: the Environmental Politics Reader,* edited by John S. Dryzek and David Schlosberg. New York: Oxford University Press, 1998.

Popple, Charles Sterling. *Standard Oil Company (New Jersey) in World War II.* New York: Standard Oil Company (New Jersey), 1952.

Portelli, Alessandro. *The Death of Luigi Trastulli and Other Stories: Form and Meaning in Oral History.* Albany, NY: SUNY Press, 1991.

Prejean, Helen, C.S.J. *Dead Man Walking: An Eyewitness Account of the Death Penalty in the United States.* New York: Vintage Books, 1993.

————. "Report from the Front," http://www.prejean.org

Project Top 10 by 2010. "Dateline: New Orleans and the River Region," http://www.metrovision.org/dateline.html

Prose, Francine. *Marie Laveau.* New York: Berkley Publishing/Putnam, 1977.

Rafferty, Terrence. "Amazing Grace." Review of Tim Robbins's *Dead Man Walking. The New Yorker* 71 (January 8, 1996): 68–71.

Rampersad, Arnold. "Foreword." In *Mules and Men,* edited by Zora Neale Hurston. New York: Harper and Row, 1990.

Ramsland, Katherine. *The Vampire Companion: The Official Guide to Anne Rice's The Vampire Chronicles.* New York: Ballantine Books, 1995.

Reed, Ishmael, editor. *19 Necromancers from Now.* Garden City, NY: Doubleday, 1970.

Reed Ishmael. *Another Day at the Front: Dispatches from the Race War.* New York: Basic Books, 2003.

Reed, Ishmael. *Conjure.* Amherst, MA: University of Massachusetts Press, 1972.

————. *The Last Days of Louisiana Red.* New York: Atheneum, 1989, reprinted from 1974.

————. *Mumbo Jumbo.* New York: Atheneum, 1972.

————. *The Reed Reader.* New York: Basic Books, 2000.

————. *Shrovetide in Old New Orleans.* New York: Atheneum, 1989, reprinted from 1978.

————. *Writin' Is Fightin'.* New York: Atheneum, 1988.

Reichl, Alexander J. "Historic Preservation and Progrowth Politics in U.S. Cities." *Urban Affairs Review* 42 (March 1997): 513–35.

————. "Learning from St. Thomas: Community, Capital, and the Redevelopment of Public Housing in New Orleans." *Journal of Urban Affairs* 21 (April 1999): 169–87.

Reitzes, Dave. "Who Speaks for Clay Shaw?" http://mcadams.pose.mu.edu/shaw1.htm

Rice, Anne. http://www.Annerice.com

———. *Feast of All Saints*. New York: Ballantine Books, 1979.

———. *Interview with the Vampire*. New York: Ballantine Books, 1976.

Riesman, David. "Abundance for What?" In *Abundance for What?* New York: Doubleday and Co., Inc., 1964.

Roach, Joseph. *Cities of the Dead: Circum-Atlantic Performance*. New York: Columbia University Press, 1996.

Robbins, Tim, director. *Dead Man Walking*, motion picture. Polygram Filmed Entertainment: Working Title/Havoc Production, 1995.

Rose, Mark H. *Interstate: Express Highway Politics, 1939–1989*. Knoxville: University of Tennessee Press, 1990.

Rotella, Carlo. *October Cities: The Redevelopment of Urban Literature*. Berkeley: University of California Press, 1998.

Rousey, Dennis C. *Policing the Southern City: New Orleans, 1805–1889*. Baton Rouge: Louisiana State University Press, 1996.

Rowly, Hazel. *Richard Wright: The Life and Times*. New York: Henry Holt & Co., 2001.

Rumble, John W. *Country and Western Classics: Roy Acuff*, liner notes. Time-Life Records, 1983.

Samway, Patrick S.J. *Walker Percy: A Life*. New York: Farrar, Straus and Giroux, 1997.

Saxon, Lyle. *Fabulous New Orleans*. New York: Century, 1928 and 1939.

St. Clair, David J. *The Motorization of American Cities*. New York: Praeger, 1986.

Schaller, Linda, director. *And Then One Night: The Making of* Dead Man Walking, documentary. KQED, 2001.

Schattschneider, E.E. *The Semisovereign People: A Realist's View of Democracy in America*. New York: Holt, Rinehart and Winston, 1960.

Schnickel, Richard. *Brando: A Life in Our Time*. New York: Atheneum, 1991.

Schram, Ross. "Queer Case of Quinby," *Mass Transportation* 42 (1946): 62–5.

Schroth, Raymond A. Review of Prejean's *Dead Man Walking*. *America* (September 18, 1993): 20.

Schuurman, Nadine. *Critical GIS: Theorizing an Emerging Science*. Monograph 53. *Cartographica* 36 (1999).

Scott, Allen J. *Regions and the World Economy: The Coming Shape of Global Production, Competition, and Political Order*. New York: Oxford University Press, 1998.

Scott, James C. *Seeing Like a State: How Certain Schemes to Improve the Human Condition Have Failed*. New Haven, CT: Yale University Press, 1998.

Scott, Mel. *American City Planning Since 1890*. Berkeley: University of California Press, 1969.

Searight, Sarah. *New Orleans*. New York: Stein and Day, 1973.

Sejour, Victor. "The Mulatto." In *The Norton Anthology of African American Literature*, edited by Henry Louis Gates, Jr., and Nelly Y. McKay. New York: W.W. Norton and Company, 1997.

Sieburth, Richard. "Benjamin the Scrivener." In *Benjamin: Philosophy, History, Aesthetics*, edited by Gary Smith. Chicago: University of Chicago Press, 1989.

Sieburth, Richard. "Benjamin the Scrivener." *Assemblage* 6 (1988).

Silvio, Lucy. "Raking in the Money?" *America* (March 8, 1996): 10–1.

Simmons, Philip E. *Deep Surfaces: Mass Culture and History in Postmodern American Fiction*. Athens, GA: University of Georgia Press, 1997.

Simon, Bryant. "Introduction." In *Race and Rumors of Race: The American South in the Early 40s,* by Howard Odum. Baltimore: Johns Hopkins University Press, 1997.

Simpson, Lewis P. "Home by Way of California: The Southerner as the Last European." In *Southern Literature in Transition: Heritage and Promise,* edited by Phillip Castille and William Osborne. Memphis: Memphis State University Press, 1983.

Singh, Nikhil Pal. "The Black Panthers and the 'Undeveloped Country' of the Left." In *The Black Panther Party Reconsidered,* edited by Charles E. Jones. Baltimore: Black Classic Press, 1998.

Sloan, Alfred P. *My Years with General Motors.* New York: Doubleday/Currency, 1990, reprinted from 1964.

Smerk, George M. "The Streetcar: Shaper of American Cities." *Traffic Quarterly* 21 (1967): 569–84.

Smith, M. Dwayne. "Patterns of Discrimination in Assessment of the Death Penalty: The Case of Louisiana." *Journal of Criminal Justice* 15 (1987): 279–86.

Soffer, Simeon, director. *The Wildest Show in the South: The Angola Prison Rodeo,* documentary film. Gabriel Films, 2000.

Soja, Edward. *Postmetropolis: Critical Studies of Cities and Regions.* Oxford: Blackwell, 2000.

Spoto, Donald. *The Kindness of Strangers: The Life of Tennessee Williams.* Boston: Little, Brown, 1985.

Stack, Jonathan, and Liz Garbus, with Wilbert Rideau, directors. *The Farm: Life Inside Angola,* documentary film. Gabriel Films, 1998.

Sugrue, Thomas. *The Origins of the Urban Crisis: Race and Inequality in Postwar Detroit.* Princeton, NJ: Princeton University Press, 1996.

Szondi, Peter. "Walter Benjamin's City Portraits," In *On Walter Benjamin: Critical Essays and Recollections,* edited by Gary Smith. Cambridge, MA: MIT Press, 1988.

Tallant, Robert. *Gumbo Ya-Ya.* Boston: Houghton Mifflin Co., 1945.

———. *The Romantic New Orleanians.* New York: E.P. Dutton and Co., Inc., 1950.

———. *Voodoo in New Orleans.* New York: The Macmillan Company, 1946.

———. *The Voodoo Queen.* New York: Putnam, 1956.

Tocqueville, Alexis de. *Journey to America.* Translated by George Lawrence, edited by J.P. Mayer, revised with A.P. Kerr. Westport, CT: Greenwood Press, 1981.

———. *The United States Penitentiary System and Its Application in France,* 1833.

Tolson, Jay. *Pilgrim in the Ruins: A Life of Walker Percy.* New York: Simon and Schuster, 1992.

Tregle, Joseph G., Jr. "Creoles and Americans." In *Creole New Orleans: Race and Americanization,* edited by Arnold R. Hirsch and Joseph Logsdon. Baton Rouge: Louisiana State University Press, 1992.

Tuan, Yi-Fu. *Topophilia: A Study of Environmental Perception, Attitudes, and Values.* New York: Columbia University Press, 1974.

Umoja, Akinyele Omowale. "Repression Breeds Resistance: The Black Liberation Army and the Radical Legacy of the Black Panther Party." In *Liberation, Imagination and the Black Panther Party,* edited by Kathleen Cleaver and George Katsiaficas. New York: Routledge, 2001.

Vella, Christina. *Intimate Enemies: The Two Worlds of the Baroness de Pontalba.* Baton Rouge: Louisiana State University Press, 1997.

Vesey, Catherine, and Frédéric Dimanche. "From Storyville to Bourbon Street: Vice, Nostalgia and Tourism." *The Journal of Tourism and Cultural Change* 1 (2003): 54–70.

von Hoffman, Alexander. "High Ambitions: The Past and Future of American Low Income Housing Policy." *Housing Policy Debate* 2 (1996): 423–46.

Ward, Robert. "From the Vagrant to the Fugitive: Institutional Models in Nelson Algren's *Somebody in Boots.*" *49th Parallel* 2 (Spring 1999). http:// artsweb.bham.ac.uk/49thparallel

Weinstein, Richard S. "The First American City." In *The City: Los Angeles and Urban Theory at the End of the Century,* edited by Edward W. Soja and Allen J. Scott. Berkeley: University of California Press, 1996.

Wheeler, Stephen M., and Timothy Beatley. "Introduction." In *The Sustainable Urban Development Reader,* edited by S. Wheeler and T. Beatley. New York: Routledge, 2004.

White, Lawrence. *The Automobile Industry Since 1945.* Cambridge, MA: Harvard University Press, 1971.

Williams, Raymond. "Between Country and City." In *Second Nature,* edited by Richard Mabey with Susan Clifford and Angela King for Common Ground. London: Jonathan Cape, 1984.

Williams, Tennessee. *A Streetcar Named Desire.* New York: New Directions, 1947.

Wills, Gary. Review of Prejean's *Dead Man Walking. New York Review of Books* 40 (September 23, 1993): 3–4.

Wilson, Elizabeth. *The Sphinx in the City: Urban Life, the Control of Disorder, and Women.* Berkeley: University of California Press, 1991.

Wiltz, Christine. *The Last Madam: A Life in the New Orleans Underworld.* New York: Faber and Faber, Inc., 2000.

Wimick, Charles, and Paul M. Kinsie. *The Lively Commerce: Prostitution in the United States.* Chicago: Quadrangle Books, 1971.

Windham, Donald, editor. *Tennessee Williams' Letters to Donald Windham, 1940–1965.* New York: Holt, 1977.

Wood, Denis, with John Fels. *The Power of Maps.* New York: The Guilford Press, 1992.

Wright, Gwendolyn. *The Politics of Design in French Colonial Urbanism.* Chicago: University of Chicago Press, 1991.

Wright, Richard. Introduction to Nelson Algren's *Never Come Morning.* New York: Harper and Brothers, 1942.

———. *Uncle Tom's Children.* New York: Harper and Brothers, 1940.

Yergin, Daniel. *The Prize: The Epic Quest for Oil, Money, and Power.* New York: Simon and Schuster, 1991.

Young, Alma H., and Jyaphia Christos-Rodgers. "Resisting Racially Gendered Space: The Women of the St. Thomas Resident Council, New Orleans." In *Marginal Spaces: Comparative Urban and Community Research,* edited by Michael Peter Smith. New Brunswick, NJ: Transaction Publishers, 1995.

Young, Dean, and Denis Lebrun. "Blondie," cartoon. May 21, 1999.

Young, Jeff. *Kazan: The Master Director Discusses His Films: Interviews with Elia Kazan.* New York: Newmarket Press, 1999.

Zamir, Shamoon. Interview with Ishmael Reed. *Callaloo* 17 (1994): 1131–56.

Index